Practicing Civil Discovery

Practicing Civil Discovery

William M. Janssen
PROFESSOR OF LAW
CHARLESTON SCHOOL OF LAW

Steven Baicker-McKee
JOSEPH A. KATARINCIC CHAIR OF
LEGAL PROCESS AND CIVIL PROCEDURE AND
ASSOCIATE PROFESSOR OF LAW
DUQUESNE UNIVERSITY SCHOOL OF LAW

CAROLINA ACADEMIC PRESS
Durham, North Carolina

Library of Congress Cataloging-in-Publication Data

Names: Janssen, William M., author. | Baicker-McKee, Steven, author.
Title: Practicing civil discovery / William M. Janssen, Steven Baicker-McKee.
Description: Durham : Carolina Academic Press, 2019.
Identifiers: LCCN 2019036949 | ISBN 9781531006198 (paperback) |
ISBN 9781531006204 (ebook)
Subjects: LCSH: Discovery (Law)—United States. | Civil procedure—
United States.
Classification: LCC KF8900.J36 2019 | DDC 347.73/72—dc23
LC record available at https://lccn.loc.gov/2019036949

Carolina Academic Press
700 Kent Street
Durham, North Carolina 27701
Telephone (919) 489-7486
Fax (919) 493-5668
www.cap-press.com

Printed in the United States of America

Acknowledgments

This is a book by two colleagues, who began a friendship as law clerks that has continued and enriched our lives for more than thirty years.

Professor Janssen thanks his co-author for our many enjoyable adventures through federal civil procedure together, as well as Christopher T. Lewis and Jessica L. Carroll for their tremendous assistance in research and editing. He dedicates his work on this book to two former civil procedure students, Alex Bush (class of 2012) and K.J. Williams (class of 2018), who passed from this life before having the opportunity to leave what would have been immeasurable handprints on our profession and the lives of their clients.

Professor Baicker-McKee is grateful for the assistance of his research assistants, Nicoline van de Haterd and Ashley Puchalski, his many students who beta tested this book over the last several semesters, and his wife Carol. Oh, and for the wisdom, humor, and support of his dear friend, Professor William "Did I Mention I'm an Eagles Fan" Janssen.

Preface

As two trial attorneys who have collectively spent more than forty years engaged in complex litigation across the country, we came to academia with a sense of personal appreciation for the importance of discovery in civil litigation. Developments over recent years have only intensified our view of the importance of robust discovery coverage in law school curricula. Trials occur infrequently, so the discovery stage is where the vast majority of cases are won or lost (plus where the majority of the legal work occurs and the majority of legal fees are incurred). Additionally, the increased emphasis on producing graduates who are able to "hit the ground running" dictates that recently-graduated lawyers, upon whom much of the discovery burden often falls, be trained in this area.

Additionally, we believe that discovery is ideally suited for simulation classes or other experiential learning environments. While students can learn procedural topics like jurisdiction, pleading standards, and dispositive motion theory by reading cases and attending class, they have a difficult time getting a sense of the real dynamics of discovery without a hands-on struggle through discovery tasks. Sometimes, first-year casebooks contribute to this comprehension gap by de-emphasizing civil discovery with a hope that the missing coverage will be remedied later in some upper-level skills class.

With those considerations in mind, we set out to draft a text to be used both as a companion to a favorite 1L casebook and in a variety of upper-level litigation-oriented classes, whether specifically dedicated to discovery or that include significant discovery content. We spent a few years working on this project, using our classes as captive focus groups, refining our approach to address the input from our students. The final result is this text, which students have praised with comments like "I wish every law school book were like *Practicing Civil Discovery*." We also vetted the manuscript with other professors and incorporated many of their generous suggestions.

We've structured *Practicing Civil Discovery* to give instructors and students maximum flexibility. We have included one recurring fact pattern that can be used throughout the semester for discovery assignments. The fact pattern involves an amusement park accident with some light, whimsical aspects to engage the classroom and provide some opportunities for creativity and fun.

But we have been careful to not allow the fact pattern to dominate the text. The book's structure allows different fact patterns to be substituted at the instructor's discretion, should particular teaching objectives counsel such a path. Throughout the chapters, we also use a variety of different fact patterns to illustrate the workings of the individual discovery topics to make the book more interesting and lessen the chance of fact-pattern fatigue.

Within each chapter, and throughout the text, we strive to deliver the book's content with a consistent cadence—we try to set the stage for each topic with an introduction that places the topic in context with an explanation aimed at a typical law student's level of understanding and familiarity with discovery. We then explain the workings of the discovery device, using embedded hypotheticals, with answers, so that students can test and refine their understanding. We include practical tips about how the discovery device works in the real world, then end each chapter with unanswered hypotheticals that make for productive class discussion. Finally, we conclude each chapter with exemplars of documents related to the chapter topic.

We hope that you find *Practicing Civil Discovery* both effective and enjoyable. We have collaborated on a number of other projects, and we always ask for feedback from our readers. Please tell us what you liked, what you didn't like, and any errors you've found. We greatly value your opinions and observations, and we will strive to incorporate your ideas in future editions.

WILLIAM M. JANSSEN
(843) 377-2442
wjanssen@charlestonlaw.edu

STEVEN BAICKER-MCKEE
(412) 398-0696
baickermckees@duq.edu

About the Authors

WILLIAM M. JANSSEN is a Professor of Law at the Charleston School of Law in Charleston, South Carolina. He teaches Civil Procedure, Products Liability, Mass Torts, and a constitutional seminar course, and has been voted Professor of the Year by the students of his law school on several occasions. He is co-author of *A Student's Guide to the Federal Rules of Civil Procedure, Mastering Multiple Choice—Federal Civil Procedure*, the *Federal Civil Rules Handbook*, Volume 12B of *Federal Practice and Procedure*, as well as numerous book chapters and articles. He is also the sole author of *Federal Civil Procedure Logic Maps*, and a contributing author of *Attorney-Client Privilege in the United States*.

Prior to joining the Charleston law faculty, Professor Janssen was a litigation partner at Saul Ewing LLP in Philadelphia for many years, serving as chair of the firm's interdisciplinary Life Sciences practice group and as a member of the firm's governing Executive Committee. He is a member of the Food and Drug Law Institute and an emeritus member of the International Association of Defense Counsel.

Professor Janssen received his B.A. from Saint Joseph's University, and then his J.D. from the American University Washington College of Law, where he was Executive Editor of the *American University Law Review* and a member of the Moot Court Board. He clerked for the Honorable James McGirr Kelly on the United States District Court for the Eastern District of Pennsylvania and for the Honorable Joseph F. Weis, Jr. on the United States Court of Appeals for the Third Circuit.

Professor Janssen resides in Charleston, South Carolina, with his wife Mary Kay, to whom he dedicates his work on this book.

STEVEN BAICKER-MCKEE is the Joseph A. Katarinck Endowed Chair in Legal Process and Procedure and an Associate Professor of Law at the Duquesne University School of Law. He teaches upper-level litigation skills simulation courses, Civil Procedure, and Environmental Law, and was voted Professor of the Year by the students. He is co-author of *A Student's Guide to the Federal Rules of Civil Procedure*, *Learning Civil Procedure*, *Mastering Multiple Choice—Federal Civil Procedure*, the *Federal Civil Rules Handbook*, and the *Federal Litigator*, as well as numerous book chapters and articles.

Prior to joining Duquesne University, Professor Baicker-McKee was a litigator at Babst Calland in Pittsburgh for more than 20 years, serving on the firm's Operating Committee and Board of Directors. He has been recognized as one of the Outstanding Lawyers of America and elected to the Academy of Trial Lawyers.

Professor Baicker-McKee received his B.A. from Yale University, then spent the next several years building fine furniture and custom cabinets before attending law school. He received his J.D. from Marshall-Wythe School of Law, College of William and Mary, where he was on the Board of Editors of the *William and Mary Law Review*. He then clerked for the Honorable Glenn E. Mencer on the United States District Court for the Western District of Pennsylvania.

Professor Baicker-McKee resides in Pittsburgh, Pennsylvania with his wife Carol. Professor Baicker-McKee is grateful for her love and support (and editing skills).

Contents

Conventions Used in This Book · xix

I | **What Is "Discovery"?** · **3**

    Getting the View · 3

    A. A Definition of "Discovery" · 3

    B. Trying a Civil Lawsuit Without Discovery · · · · · · · · · · · · · · · · 4

    C. The Long History of Trial-Day Surprises · · · · · · · · · · · · · · · · 6

    D. The American Experience · 8

    E. American Discovery—Alone in the World · · · · · · · · · · · · · · · 11

    F. Why Discovery Matters in America Today · · · · · · · · · · · · · · · 12

    G. Learning to Embrace Civil Discovery · 15

    H. Your Canvas · 17

II | **How Discovery Begins** · **21**

    Getting the View · 21

    How This Discovery Concept Works · 22

    A. Discovery Planning Conference · 22

    B. Discovery Plan · 24

    C. What the Court Does After Receiving the
        Parties' Discovery Plan · 24

    D. "Disclosures": Mandatory Discovery · 25

        1. Initial Disclosures · 25

        2. Expert Disclosures (and Expert Discovery) · · · · · · · · · 31

        3. Pretrial Disclosures · 31

From Classroom to Practice   32

A. Discovery Planning Conference   32

B. Discovery Plan   33

C. "Disclosures": Mandatory Discovery   34

    1. Initial Disclosures   35

    2. Expert Disclosures   36

    3. Pretrial Disclosures   36

Practice Samples   38

III | Scope of Discovery   49

Getting the View   49

How This Discovery Concept Works   50

A. "Relevance"   50

    1. Admissibility vs. Discoverability   55

    2. Limitations on the Scope of Discovery in Rule 26(b)(1)   57

B. "Proportionality"   57

C. "Nonprivileged"   61

    1. Attorney-Client Privilege   62

    2. Nonprivileged But Still Shielded: Trial Preparation Material   64

    3. Comparing Work Production Protection with
       Attorney-Client Privilege   72

    4. Facts and Evidence Not Privileged   72

    5. Asserting Privilege / Protection Claims   74

    6. Inadvertent Production   76

    7. Trial Preparation Materials Protection for Statements   76

    8. Additional Constraints on the Scope of Discovery   77

    9. Altering the Scope of Discovery   77

From Classroom to Practice   80

Practice Samples   82

IV | The Discovery Tools   89

PART 1. INTRODUCTION   89

Getting the View   89

From Classroom to Practice   91

PART 2. INTERROGATORIES—RULE 33   92

Getting the View   92

How This Discovery Tool Works   92

A. Asking Interrogatory Questions   92

1. What Can Be Asked   93
2. Numbers and "Subparts"   93
B. Answering Interrogatory Questions   95
1. Basic Requirements   95
2. Business Records Option   95
3. Objecting to Interrogatories   97
C. The Uses of Interrogatory Answers   102
From Classroom to Practice   103
A. Form   103
B. "Instructions" and "Definitions"   103
C. Drafting "Defensively"   105
D. The Challenge of "Lawyered" Answers   106
Practice Samples   108

PART 3. PRODUCTION REQUESTS—RULE 34   **115**
Getting the View   115
How This Discovery Tool Works   116
A. No Numerical Limit   116
B. Early Service   116
C. "Possession, Custody, or Control"   117
D. Objections   122
E. Producing Responsive Documents   123
1. Collecting Responsive Documents   123
2. Conducting the Privilege Review   124
3. Providing the Responsive, Nonprivileged Documents   124
F. No Duty to Create Documents   125
G. Cost of Responding   126
H. Electronically Stored Information   126
1. ESI Is Fully Discoverable from Many Sources   127
2. ESI Tools   128
3. Form of ESI Production   129
4. Metadata   130
5. Preservation   131
From Classroom to Practice   132
A. E-Discovery Planning   132
Practice Samples   135

PART 4. REQUESTS FOR ADMISSION—RULE 36   **142**
Getting the View   142
How This Discovery Tool Works   143

A. The Types of Admissions That Can Be Sought   143
  1. Admit a Fact   143
  2. Admit a Document's Genuineness   143
  3. Admit the Application of Law to Fact, or Opinions   144
  4. Procedures for Requests   146
B. The Burdens Imposed on Responders   147
C. The Uses of Admissions   152
From Classroom to Practice   153
A. Form   153
B. The Ominous Danger of the "Forgotten" Discovery Tool   153
Practice Samples   155

PART 5. PHYSICAL AND MENTAL EXAMINATIONS—
    RULE 35   **167**
Getting the View   167
How This Discovery Tool Works   168
A. Prerequisites   168
B. Examination Details   171
C. Additional Considerations   172
D. Reports   176
From Classroom to Practice   176
Practice Samples   179

PART 6. DEPOSITIONS—
    RULE 30 [ALSO RULES 27, 28, 31 & 32]   **188**
Getting the View   188
How This Discovery Tool Works   190
A. When a Deposition Is Permitted   191
B. Setting Up a Deposition   192
  1. Authorized Officer   192
  2. Place of the Deposition   192
  3. "Notice" of the Deposition   193
C. Conducting a Deposition   194
  1. "Discovery Deps" Versus "Trial Deps"   194
  2. Preliminaries   194
  3. Questions and Answers   194
  4. Objections   197
    i. Objections to "Form"   197
    ii. Objections to Substance   198

iii. The Manner of Making Objections   199

iv. Other Deposition Objections   201

5. Instructions Not to Answer a Question   201

6. Post-Deposition Procedures   201

D. Special Types of Depositions   204

1. Entity Depositions   204

i. Deposing—and Binding—an Entity   205

ii. Procedure for Rule 30(b)(6) Depositions   205

iii. Non-Rule 30(b)(6) Entity Depositions   207

2. Before-the-Lawsuit Depositions   207

3. After-the-Lawsuit Depositions   208

4. Deposition by Written Questions   208

E. Using Deposition Testimony   209

F. Using Depositions of Treating Physicians   210

G. Sanctions for Deposition Misconduct   210

From Classroom to Practice   211

A. Taking a Good Deposition   211

B. Defending a Deposition Well   214

Practice Samples   217

V | **Discovery of Experts**   **229**

Getting the View   229

How Expert Discovery Works   236

A. Expert Disclosures—Rule 26(a)(2)   236

1. Categories of Experts   236

2. Form and Content of Expert Disclosures   237

i. Retained Experts   237

ii. Non-Retained Experts   238

iii. Consulting Experts   239

3. Rebuttal Testimony   239

4. Time and Sequence for Disclosures   239

5. Failure to Disclose/Inadequate Disclosure   240

B. Expert Depositions   241

C. Expert Trial Preparation Materials   242

From Classroom to Practice   243

A. Selecting Experts   243

B. Initial Engagement   244

C. Expert Depositions   245

Practice Samples   247

VI | **Discovery of Nonparties: Subpoenas; Informal Discovery**
Rule 45   **261**

Getting the View   261
How Subpoenas Work   262
A. Overview of Rule 45   262
B. Subpoena Procedures   262
   1. Contents of a Subpoena   262
   2. Issuance of a Subpoena   263
   3. Service of a Subpoena   263
   4. Nonparties Only   264
C. Protections for the Recipient   268
   1. Place of Performance   268
   2. Undue Burden or Expense   268
D. Challenges to and Enforcement of Subpoenas   269
E. Performance of Subpoenas   270
From Classroom to Practice   271
How Informal Discovery Works   272
From Classroom to Practice   274
Practice Samples   276

VII | **Supplementing Discovery Responses**
Rule 26(e)   **283**

Getting the View   283
How This Supplementation Duty Works   284
A. What Triggers the Duty to Supplement   284
B. What Must Be Supplemented   291
C. When Must It Be Supplemented   291
D. Consequences of a Failure to Supplement   292
From Classroom to Practice   292
Practice Samples   294

VIII | **Policing Discovery**   **297**

Getting the View   297
How These Discovery Devices Work   298
A. Problems at the Outset—Discovery Planning   298
B. Problems with Mandatory Disclosures   299
   1. Sanctions   299
   2. Motions to Compel   301

C. Problems with Responses to Interrogatories and
    Production Requests   304
D. Special Problems with Production Requests: Electronically
    Stored Information   305
E. Problems with Responses to Requests for Admission   308
F. Problems with Depositions   310
G. Problems with Physical/Mental Exams   312
H. Problems with Disobedience to a Court's Discovery Orders   312
From Classroom to Practice   312
Practice Samples   319

IX | **Discovery Planning and Strategy**   **325**
Getting the View   325
A. Be Thoughtful and Case-Specific   325
B. Work Backwards from Your Endpoint   326
How Discovery Planning and Strategy Works   328
From Classroom to Practice   330
Practice Samples   332

X | **Appealing Discovery Rulings**   **335**
Getting the View   335
How This Discovery Concept Works   336
From Classroom to Practice   338

Index of Primary Authorities   339
Index of Secondary Authorities   345

Conventions Used in This Book

References to "Rules" in this book are to the Federal Rules of Civil Procedure, unless otherwise expressly noted. The reason for this book's heavy use of the Federal Rules of Civil Procedure is explained in Chapter 1, Section G. Because those Rules are so dynamic, with amendments made nearly every year, this book does not reprint the Rules in order to avoid mispresenting Rule language as current when, in fact, it may have become superseded.

This book contains only a modest number of case decisions; all are excerpts. Omissions preceding the start of the excerpt occur in nearly all instances and are not noted as such. The same is true with omissions following the end of the excerpt. Omissions within the excerpt are indicated with stars (* * *) unless they appear within a sentence or paragraph in which case they are indicated with ellipses (. . .). Deletions from the excerpts of parallel citations, parentheticals following citations, references to cited or quoted sources, and internal footnotes are not noted unless they are germane to this book's objectives.

Sprinkled throughout many of the chapters are hypotheticals followed by answers. These hypotheticals are intended to teach new concepts through the use of fact-based illustrations. The best approach for these hypotheticals is to read the hypothetical, analyze it, settle on your answer, and only then read the supplied answer. Many of the chapters also include additional hypotheticals at the end, this time without a printed answer. These chapter-ending hypotheticals are intended to trigger thoughtful analysis and discussion during class. Read and analyze these before class and come prepared to explain your reasoning.

Practicing Civil Discovery

I
—

What Is "Discovery"?

A. A Definition of "Discovery"

In the law, "discovery" is a term of art, and one that is easily defined. Discovery is a pretrial process used by litigants for exchanging information as they prepare a civil lawsuit. That's the definition. Unpacking the nuances behind that definition requires a bit more effort:

- Discovery is a *pretrial* process: it usually occurs before (and often long before) the trial begins.

- Discovery is *non-exclusive*: information can be acquired for use in civil lawsuits through other means, separate from the formal discovery process. For example, an attorney may gather information informally by performing Internet searches, interviewing a willing eyewitness, or visiting a roadway accident scene. Such informal information gathering is often less expensive than formal discovery, and conducting it may often be performed without notice to opposing parties.

- Discovery is *obligatory*: using all, some, or none of the tools of discovery generally lies within the discretion of the parties, but once discovery is formally invoked, it imposes duties both on the party requesting the information and on the party receiving the information. If ignored, those duties can trigger potentially devastating consequences.

- Discovery is a **collection of procedures**: the rules governing discovery establish various procedures for requesting and delivering information of many different types—including answers to questions posed in writing or orally, review of documents and electronically stored data, inspection of physical objects, examination of a person's physical or mental condition, entry onto land, and previews of the opinions and analyses of testifying expert witnesses.

- Discovery is used by **parties**: the procedures of discovery are (typically) restricted to persons and entities who are named as parties in a civil lawsuit. But, although only parties can *invoke* discovery, discovery can sometimes be *directed* to *non-parties*. So, for example, eyewitnesses to an event may be compelled by the parties to provide information about what those witnesses saw, heard, smelled, felt, or tasted.

- Discovery is, finally, a process of information exchange in **preparation for civil lawsuits**. With very few exceptions, unless a lawsuit is already filed and unless the requested information is being sought to explore issues in that pending lawsuit, the discovery process cannot be used. Also, information exchanges in other contexts (in criminal cases or administrative proceedings, for example) could be quite different.

So, that's how the definition of "discovery" unpacks. Now, why should you care?

B. Trying a Civil Lawsuit Without Discovery

Suppose there is a chef who works at a busy restaurant.

Night after night, the chef finds that he is suffering from persistent, worsening headaches. The chef purchases over-the-counter pain relief medications, but none seems to work for him. Finally, the chef stops in for a visit with his regular family doctor. The doctor performs a few in-office exams, draws blood for a blood test, and has his staff conduct diagnostic imaging of the chef's head. A few days later, the doctor phones the chef and tells him that he is suffering from migraine headaches. The doctor writes the chef a prescription for a powerful anti-migraine medicine, to be taken daily in conjunction with an improved diet, an exercise regimen, and a reduction in work stress. The chef begins taking his medicine. Six weeks later, the chef suffers a massive heart attack and dies. The medicine contained no warning that its use could increase the risk of heart attacks.

The chef's spouse contacts a lawyer, inquiring whether the migraine medicine caused the chef's death. After consulting with an expert cardiologist, the lawyer decides to file a lawsuit against the migraine medicine's manufacturer seeking compensation for the chef's allegedly wrongful death. To win at trial, the lawyer will likely need to prove that the medicine (or its warning) was defective and that this defectiveness caused, or meaningfully contributed to causing, the chef's death.

After receiving service of the lawsuit, the medicine manufacturer will file its answer, likely denying responsibility for the chef's death. For the manufacturer to win at trial, it will need to defend against the claim that its medicine or warning was defective, and probably also try to show why the medicine did not cause or contribute to causing the chef's death. Assume that those two pleadings—the complaint by the chef's spouse and the answer by the manufacturer—are the only two pleadings that will be filed in the case.

What if the next event in this lawsuit were the trial?

What wouldn't the parties know as that trial began? The chef's lawyer may have researched the migraine medicine and been briefed by the expert cardiologist. But the chef's lawyer is unlikely to know how the medicine manufacturer developed the drug, how the drug was tested, whether those tests were scientifically sound, and what the test results showed. The chef's lawyer is unlikely to know if the medicine manufacturer ever checked whether its new drug could pose heart risks and, if it checked, what it discovered. The chef's lawyer is also unlikely to know if the manufacturer received word that other patients who took the medicine developed heart-related (or other) complications, and whether such reports revealed any patterns. Nor is the chef's lawyer likely to know if the manufacturer ever considered adding a warning about heart attacks and, if so, why it chose not to give that warning.

On the other side of the trial aisle, what wouldn't the manufacturer's lawyer know as the trial opens? Was the chef's doctor a good one or a careless one? What did the doctor's in-office testing reveal (the physical exam, blood test, and medical imaging)? Did the chef have other medical conditions that could explain his death, or that show that a prescription for the migraine medicine was unwise for the chef? Why did the doctor order the chef to improve his diet, exercise more, and reduce his work stress? Did the doctor suspect diet, inactivity, and stress might be causing the migraines, and could those same sources also cause heart problems? Did the chef obey his doctor's instructions and eat better, get active, and reduce his stress? Did the chef actually take the migraine medicine? Did he take it as directed, or did he miss days (or over-use the medicine)? Was the chef a smoker? Did he drink alcohol or use other drugs? Was he taking other medications at the same time that might have interacted dangerously with the migraine medicine? Did the chef have a family history of, or genetic predisposition toward, heart troubles? Was there an autopsy, and, if so, what did it reveal? Is there an expert cardiologist who thinks the chef's death is attributable to the migraine medicine? If yes, why does that expert think so, what are that expert's qualifications to form such an opinion, and on what data and reasoning was that opinion based?

That's a lot not to know.

Without pretrial discovery, trying a civil lawsuit would be a blind walk into a dark room. Worse, because the other side is also highly motivated to persuade the factfinder, that blind walk will be buffeted by unknown information and adversaries jumping from the shadows at unpredictable moments throughout the trial. It would be trial by surprise (or, more accurately, by ambush). Trial outcomes would be less about the merits of a case or defense, and more about each side's lawyering skill in surprising the other side and in dealing with surprises launched from the other side. Lawyers would be unprepared to respond to their adversary's evidence because they, along with the courtroom spectators, would be seeing and hearing most of it for the first time at trial. Evenings would be spent in a mad scramble to assemble opposing evidence to meet the day's surprises. Clients would be unready for their day in court. Settlement entrées would be either baldly uninformed guesses (before trial) or, once trial begins, frenetic efforts to mitigate the fallout from unexpected trial-day developments.

All in all, that sure would be one nerve-wracking way to run a justice system. And it's the way, for centuries, civil justice was often administered.

C. The Long History of Trial-Day Surprises

The robust pretrial exchange of information among the parties to a civil lawsuit is a relatively new tradition. This sort of information-sharing in advance of the start of trial just did not use to happen. Consider what we know about civil pretrial information sharing in ancient Greece. There, such exchanges were reserved principally for those circumstances where the information might otherwise be lost (and not to enable the adversary to better prepare for trial). For example, the evidence of those too ill to attend court or who were going to be away during the time of trial could be preserved in a pretrial writing (the distant forebear of today's "deposition"), if done so in the presence of witnesses. Contract inspection was a bit more liberally permitted, but only as to the contracting parties. Thus, written contracts that were deposited into someone's care for safekeeping could be compelled to be presented, at a given time and place, for inspection by both contracting parties. Beyond these narrow windows of pretrial information sharing, "[d]ocumentary evidence in the hands of an opponent could not be secured except by his consent." ROBERT J. BONNER, EVIDENCE IN ATHENIAN COURTS 25–27, 64–65 (1905).

The law in ancient Rome seems to have been only modestly more permissive. It did not permit defendants to pose any pretrial questions to a plaintiff, but it did allow plaintiffs to ask questions of a defendant in order to verify certain, narrowly prescribed types of threshold facts, such as requesting that the defendant confirm that he was a true heir of a deceased debtor, the true owner of a tort-causing animal, or the true possessor of a shaky structure that might collapse. Like in Greece, Roman law's tolerance for pretrial information exchange was not to help litigants prepare for their trial day, but simply "to prevent dishonest defendants from turning the trial process into a game of three-card monte." Joseph E. Fortenberry, *A Note on the Purpose of Roman Discovery*, 9 J. LEGAL HIST. 214, 218 (1988). *See generally* Robert Wyness Millar, *The Mechanism of Fact-Discovery: A Study in Comparative Civil Procedure*, 32 ILL. L. REV. 261, 264 (1937–38) ("So far . . . as any general system of discovery is concerned, none appears in the classical Roman law.").

The same seems true during the ensuing Byzantine age. *See id.* at 266 (this period, "like the classical, was without any general system of discovery").

The Middle Ages saw the arrival of a few procedures that expanded pretrial information exchanges, though, again, only modestly. Italian courts in this era, for instance, permitted "interrogations," questions that a plaintiff could ask the judge to pose to a defendant and, once posed, if admitted by a defendant, resulted in a judicial confession. This procedure was later replaced by "positiones," affirmative statements (not questions) that a party submitted to the judge, which the judge would then pose to both parties for admission. If "positiones" were denied, the requesting party would be left to prove that fact at trial; if "positiones" were admitted, the fact would be considered proved. These procedures, however, seemed restricted to only "ultimate" facts, not evidentiary ones, and could not be relied upon to offer much trial preparation help. *See id.* at 266–76.

Medieval English law depended originally on the exchange of highly technical, inflexible, and lengthy written pleadings, which would inform adversaries and the court of the general nature of a litigant's trial objectives. But, especially in more complex disputes, trial details remained largely an unfolding mystery, with surprise witnesses, testimony, and evidence the routine order of the day. Indeed, pretrial information exchanges made little sense in the justice system of this age, where "the litigation process was looked at not as a rational quest for truth, but rather a method by which society could determine which side God took to be truthful or just." Stephen N. Subrin, *Fishing Expeditions Allowed: The Historical Background of the 1938 Federal Discovery Rules*, 39 B.C. L. REV. 691, 694–95 (1998) (footnote omitted).

On the equity side of the English justice system, a different approach was developing. By the fifteenth century, the English equity tribunals had moved to a more revealing process of factual disclosures, later enhanced by the eighteenth century with a formalized practice of interrogatories to a defendant and limited access to an opponent's documents (but only if a judge could first be persuaded to order it). Nonetheless, so useful did these equity procedures become in aiding trial preparation that litigants in the law courts often hurried over to the equity tribunals, filing a "bill of discovery" there in pursuit of even these modest—but, arguably, still revolutionary—pathways for pretrial information exchange. A discovery doorway had opened, but the path remained cramped and unreliable. Recounting this English experience led one scholarly review to conclude: "Pretrial discovery as an integral part of a lawsuit was nonexistent prior to the nineteenth century." Harvard Law Review Ass'n, *Developments in the Law—Discovery*, 74 HARV. L. REV. 940, 946

(1961). *See also* JOSEPH STORY, COMMENTARIES ON EQUITY JURISPRUDENCE § 1484 (3d Eng. ed. 1920) (noting lack of discovery among the "defects" of the English law courts and the availability of limited discovery as a strength of the English equity courts).

D. The American Experience

The modern civil justice system of the United States has its roots in English legal tradition—unsurprisingly, given that the United States began as British colonies. Here, as in England, broadening access to civil discovery clashed with a cultural identity that was steeped in notions of rugged self-sufficiency and independence. Accordingly, a litigant's integrity and resourcefulness, along with the skills and ingenuity of that litigant's chosen lawyer, ought to suffice for trial. To this age, the notion that court procedures might be commandeered to aid adversaries in finding the evidence to defeat one another was viewed as "distasteful." *See* Subrin, *Fishing Expeditions Allowed*, 39 B.C. L. REV. at 694–95.

America's first major advance in widening civil pretrial information exchange was the one pioneered by New York's David Dudley Field in the mid-nineteenth century. New York's "Field Code" innovated by replacing the equity court "bill of discovery" with a series of new information exchange procedures, which, progressive as they were for the time, remained still quite limited. A party could request the right to inspect a document in an adversary's possession, but the adversary could refuse (with little consequence). A party could demand that the opponent respond to requests for admissions, but those were restricted only to conceding the genuineness of documents. A party could depose a witness, but only if the witness was an opposing party, only if the deposition was in place of live trial testimony, and only if the questioning was conducted before a judge. *See* Stephen N. Subrin, *David Dudley Field and the Field Code: A Historical Analysis of an Earlier Procedural Vision*, 6 LAW & HIST. REV. 311, 332–33 (1988). The New York "Field Code" was an advance, to be sure, and one reproduced in many sister states, but the greatest innovation would have to wait until three-quarters of a century later. In the meantime, pretrial procedures and innovations varied markedly from state to state, causing a cluttered patchwork of rules that the U.S. Congress muddled further with its Conformity Act of 1872, which obligated federal courts to use procedures that would "conform as near as may be" to those procedures employed by the states in which those federal courts were located. *See generally Nudd v. Burrows*, 91 U.S. 426, 441–42 (1875) (discussing the Act of June 1, 1872, ch. 225, § 5, 17 Stat. 196, 197).

In early summer 1935, the U.S. Supreme Court appointed a committee to undertake the task of drafting a set of procedural rules for the federal courts that would, the Court hoped, "secure one form of civil action and procedure" for both actions at law and cases in equity, "while maintaining inviolate the right of trial by jury in accordance with the Seventh Amendment of the United States Constitution and without altering substantive rights." 295 U.S. 774 (1934). As the Committee began its work, Professor Edson Sunderland of the University of Michigan assumed the laboring oar in preparing a draft set of new discovery rules. His view of the critical importance of civil discovery would permeate the new federal discovery rules that took effect three years later: "Discovery procedure serves much the same function in the field of law as the X-ray in the field of medicine and surgery; and if its use can be sufficiently extended and its methods simplified, litigation will largely cease to be a game of chance." *See* Subrin, *Fishing Expeditions Allowed*, 39 B.C. L. Rev. at 717 (quoting Edson N. Sunderland, *Improving the Administration of Civil Justice*, in 167 Annals of the American Academy of Political & Social Science 75–76 (1933)).

What emerged was truly groundbreaking. The new federal discovery rules borrowed liberally from discovery experiments then in use in various states but, in sum, pressed further than any one state had ever gone. The result was arguably the most robust litigation-related information exchange system the world had ever seen. *See id.* at 719. All federal courts would now follow a nationally uniform set of discovery procedures. Obtaining prior permission from a judge was no longer a prerequisite for most federal discovery tools, nor was the requirement that a judge be present to preside during every use of those tools. Oral depositions, interrogatories, requests for admissions, requests to inspect documents and things or to enter onto someone else's land, and even requests to probe the body (and mind) of an adversary were all expressly authorized for federal civil litigation. Importantly, the scope of allowable federal discovery was made broad and generous, and courts were given the means to discipline those who behaved mischievously during discovery.

When they took effect on Friday, September 16, 1938, the new federal discovery rules carried with them many aspirations. This bold, new approach to discovery would, it was hoped, eliminate trial by surprise and minimize the effect of trial tricks. Trials would witness an increase in the volume of relevant evidence. Trial durations would shrink as irrelevant evidence, unnecessary witnesses, and uncontroverted issues were eliminated. Even the number of trials would be reduced as the prospect of the discovery to come would disincentivize the filing of baseless claims and defenses, summary judgments would cull lawsuits that the fruits of discovery could not support, and settlements would end disputes on terms that the parties—informed by the discovery process—could more readily accept. *See* William A. Glaser, Pretrial Discovery and the Adversary System 11–12 (1968).

If all these heady objectives came to pass, surely American discovery would ensure a quality of justice humankind had never before encountered. A leading scholar of the age, Professor Charles Alan Wright of Texas, wrote of the new innovations, "The 'sporting theory of justice' was rejected. Victory was intended to go to the party entitled to it, on all the facts, rather than to the side that best uses it wits." The proponents of the new federal rules, he lauded, had prevailed in a pursuit where "surprise, dearly cherished by an earlier generation of trial lawyers, would be minimized or ended altogether." CHARLES ALAN WRIGHT, THE LAW OF FEDERAL COURTS § 81, at 540 (4th ed. 1983) (footnotes omitted).

But harsh opposition confronted these efforts to widen the path of pretrial information exchange. The broadened federal discovery, opined one judge, "goes a long way towards asking a lawyer to prepare his adversary's case." A different judge worried that liberalized discovery would "increase so-called speculative litigation or litigation based on suspicion rather than facts, with the hope that such fishing may reveal a good cause of action as alleged or otherwise." Another critic complained that discovery would "whittle down the right of trial by jury" as pretrial information exchanges functionally deprived litigants of their day in court. *See* Subrin, *Fishing Expeditions Allowed*, 39 B.C. L. REV. at 727–34.

The spirited debate over the benefits and costs of robust civil discovery, begun in this setting with the adoption of the federal discovery rules, has never really resolved. For decades, the siren of "discovery abuse" has marked this controversy. At one pole, advocates of robust discovery claim it as the surest guarantee that civil justice cannot be evaded by a lack of access to dispositive facts and evidence, or by obfuscation or concealment. At the other pole, opponents insist that the notion of robust discovery, pure of heart in theory, has become distorted into a gruesome, unfair practice that pursues litigation victory by inflicting unjustifiable costs, disruptions, and pain on an adversary, along with delays (and even fundamental inequities) in the administration of justice. This latter view has found a sympathetic ear at the highest levels of American justice. *See Bell Atl. Corp. v. Twombly*, 550 U.S. 544, 559 (2007) ("the threat of discovery expense will push cost-conscious defendants to settle even anemic cases before reaching those proceedings").

Suffice it to say that from the moment they were drafted in 1935 through today, there has developed no firm consensus on whether the halcyon goals of 1938 have been realized. Perhaps no consensus was ever possible. There have been, after all, millennia of experiences in resolving civil disputes. So many different perspectives and voices contribute to this debate, often animated by their own experiences and personally felt senses of justice and injustice. Over the years, the federal discovery rules have been amended numerous times to fix a perceived weakness here or there, or to enhance an identified opportunity, yet the refinements have never quieted the debate. The controversy over the benefits and costs of robust discovery rages on.

This much, however, is true. The civil discovery process as it exists today in the federal courts is stable, robust, reasonably uniform, and easy to invoke. The information-sharing door in America, controversial as it might be to some, is open wide.

E. American Discovery—Alone in the World

America has led the world in experimenting with broad civil discovery. But, alas, most of the world has not followed. Civil discovery available in other countries is almost always less—and sometimes far less, even nonexistent—compared to what is permitted here. *See, e.g., Intel Corp. v. Advanced Micro Devices, Inc.*, 542 U.S. 241, 262 n.12 (2004) ("Most civil-law systems lack procedures analogous to the pretrial discovery regime operative under the Federal Rules of Civil Procedure."); *Heraeus Kulzer, GmbH v. Biomet, Inc.*, 633 F.3d 591, 594 (7th Cir. 2011) ("Discovery in the federal court system is far broader than in most (maybe all) foreign countries. . ."); Stephen N. Subrin, *Discovery in Global Perspective: Are We Nuts?*, 52 DePaul L. Rev. 299, 300 (2002) ("From a comparative law perspective, we really are different in our approach to discovery."); *id.* at 306–07 ("It would be a mistake to conclude that pretrial discovery in the United States is totally different from other countries. . . . Nonetheless, the number of discovery mechanisms available to the American lawyer as a matter of right, the degree of party control over discovery, the extent to which liberal discovery in the United States has become what almost looks like a constitutional right, and the massive use of discovery of all kinds in a substantial number of cases surely sets us apart.") (footnote omitted).

So committed has the United States been to encouraging other nations to embrace our style of robust pretrial information exchanges that Congress enacted a statute to permit "any interested person" to come to the United States and seek discovery from anyone residing or found here with the intent of using the fruits of that discovery in a foreign tribunal's proceeding. *See* 28 U.S.C. § 1782. *See also Intel Corp.*, 542 U.S. at 247–49 (explaining statute's history). One federal appeals court explained the motivation behind this curious federal law: "[I]t may seem odd that Congress would have wanted foreign litigants to be able to take advantage of our generous discovery provisions. The stated reason was by setting an example to encourage foreign countries to enlarge discovery rights in their own legal systems[, t]hat might benefit U.S. litigants in those countries." *Heraeus Kulzer, GmbH*, 633 F.3d at 594 (citations omitted).

American efforts to prod the world toward robust pretrial discovery have not enjoyed great success to date. *See, e.g., Heraeus Kulzer, GmbH*, 633 F.3d at 596 ("A party to a German lawsuit cannot demand categories of documents from his opponent. All he can demand are documents that he is able to identify specifically—individually, not by category."); David J. Karl, *Islamic Law in Saudi Arabia: What Foreign Attorneys Should Know*, 25 Geo. Wash. J. Int'l L. & Econ. 131 (1991) ("Saudi law does not have any procedures for pretrial discovery."); Toshiro M. Mochizuki, *Baby Step or Giant Leap? Parties' Expanded Access to Documentary Evidence Under the New Japanese Code of Civil Procedure*, 40 Harv. Int'l L.J. 285, 286 (1999) (noting that, at least prior to 1998, "the Japanese Code of Civil Procedure had made all information presumptively non-discoverable").

Indeed, not only have the nations of the world largely resisted America's lead, they have, on occasion, reacted with alarm at the very prospect of our style of discovery. *See* JOEL WM. FRIEDMAN & MICHAEL G. COLLINS, THE LAW OF CIVIL PROCEDURE: CASES AND MATERIALS (3d ed. 2010) ("The discovery system in the United States is considered extreme by many other commercial nations; not surprisingly, foreign parties often are aghast and offended by the nature of discovery when they become involved in litigation in our courts."). Sometimes, nations have responded with laws intended to shield their citizens from American-style discovery, even when the lawsuits involving those citizens are pending in the United States. *See, e.g.,* Ela Barda & Thomas Rouhette, *The French Blocking Statute and Cross-Border Discovery,* 84 DEF. COUN. J. 1 (2017) (describing the operation of France's discovery-blocking statute). Those attempts have not met with much success in American courts, however. *See, e.g., Societe Nationale Industrielle Aerospatiale v. U.S. Dist. Court for S. Dist. of Iowa,* 482 U.S. 522, 544 n.29 (1987) ("It is well settled that such statutes do not deprive an American court of the power to order a party subject to its jurisdiction to produce evidence even though the act of production may violate that statute.").

F. Why Discovery Matters in America Today

Discovery matters. It is difficult to imagine a scholarly study that could quantify, in any comprehensive sense, the true impact of discovery on civil lawsuits in the United States. But it is undeniable that discovery is impactful—both positively and negatively.

Discovery is about *more information* in civil lawsuits. More information about the parties and their claims. More information about the details and context of the dispute itself. More information about what is known by others. Our migraine-suffering chef's death (discussed in Section B of this chapter) makes the point well. To try a civil lawsuit without discovery would leave a potentially cavernous amount of highly relevant, case-influencing, even case-dispositive information unknown and undeveloped. Nevertheless, as highlighted in Section D of this chapter, the case-enlightening benefits of discovery come at a cost.

Discovery matters in a positive sense because it supplies a wide array of tools designed to allow litigants to learn the information they need to press, or defend against, a civil claim. That learning is impactful in numerous ways. It permits a broader appreciation for the nuances of an opponent's legal positions. It reveals insights into the strengths and vulnerabilities of those positions. It allows litigants, after learning facts from one discovery request, to tailor new, subsequent discovery requests to follow up on those new leads. It permits the court, on motion, to assess more accurately whether a genuine clash of competing evidence truly exists or whether no trial is needed at all. It enables the litigants to anticipate their opponent's theories and trial moves, and thus better prepare for the courtroom. It enhances the ability of litigants to reliably value their case (mindful of its factual strengths and vulnerabilities), which in turn positions the dispute for a possible out-of-court settlement. And, because it enables the parties to seek out and obtain a fulsome understanding of the information germane to the dispute, discovery increases the likelihood that the party who ought to prevail, under the law, will actually do so. That, unquestionably, serves the goals of our system of civil justice.

Discovery matters in a negative sense because discovery is intrusive, often costly (sometimes numbingly so), and delaying. Discovery forces litigants to open their lives, private thoughts, and businesses to invasive inspections. This can be quite disconcerting and disruptive, especially for those who have little prior exposure to the civil litigation process. Discovery can also prove quite costly, depending on the amount of information that is "discoverable" (that is, relevant to the dispute and permitted by the discovery rules), the difficulty in gathering that information, the enormity of the task of reviewing that information once gathered, and the nature and ferocity of disagreements over access. Discovery is also, by its very nature, delaying. The discovery tools permit a request to be made, grant time for preparing a response, and then tolerate judicially umpired fights that could involve lengthy written briefing and oral argument. Even under the smoothest of circumstances, discovery takes time. And when a discovery dispute reaches a judge, the task confronting the court is often exasperating. The parties often use discovery tools in a focused hunt, without ever really being able to accurately predict what information that hunt may unearth. Judges, for the same reason, are often quite vexed in trying to accurately balance the costs of a discovery request against its benefits: the true benefits of a discovery request are usually not learned until what is sought is finally delivered. At that point, obviously, the costs have been incurred. And the parties, as partisans, are motivated to stake out positions that lie at diametrically polar positions on the discovery spectrum: the requesting party wants the most fulsome exchange of information possible, while the responding party wants to limit the intrusion and its costs, disruption, and exposure. The expectation that a court can strike some accurate, thoughtful balance in such a circumstance is, in the words of one judge, "hollow": "We cannot prevent what we cannot detect; we cannot detect what we cannot define; we cannot define 'abusive' discovery except in theory, because in practice we lack essential information." Frank H. Easterbrook, *Discovery as Abuse*, 69 B.U. L. Rev. 635, 638–39 (1989) (footnote omitted) (quoted in *Bell Atl. Corp. v. Twombly*, 550 U.S. 544, 560 (2007)).

Discovery matters in a numbing sense because we now live in the cyber age. Technological progress has complicated this stage of litigation enormously. In a pre-computer age, metal filing cabinets, wooden shelves, and desk drawers held most of the discoverable information sought in routine civil lawsuits. No longer. The realities of technology are just plain startling: 2.5 quintillion bytes of data are created each day (and that number is rising); of all the data in world, 90% of it was generated in the last two years; and *each minute* it is estimated we send 16 million text messages and 156 million emails. *See* Bernard Marr, *How Much Data Do We Create*

Every Day? The Mind-Blowing Stats Everyone Should Read, Forbes (May 21, 2018) (available at https://www.forbes.com/sites/bernardmarr/2018/05/21/how-much -data-do-we-create-every-day-the-mind-blowing-stats-everyone-should-read /#7d66e41460ba). Consider this growth just on an individual level: each person produces nearly 800 megabytes of new information each year, or the equivalent of 30 feet of books per person per year. *See* Shira A. Scheindlin, Daniel J. Capra, & The Sedona Conference, Electronic Discovery and Digital Evidence: Cases and Materials 39–42 (2009).

Every email is a new kernel of information. Each time that email is forwarded, that's another new kernel of information. Each new document is a new kernel of information. Each change to a document is a new kernel of information. Each unit of data entry is a new kernel of information. Each voicemail, text, web search, social media post, and shared photo is a new kernel of information. This list could go on and on. The point of the matter is that, today, the challenges of managing discovery have grown along with the exponential growth in information itself. The stakes are often far higher than they ever were. For even a small company with just a handful of employees, the chore of identifying, collecting, reviewing, assembling, and producing discoverable information can be withering.

So, of course, discovery matters. In good ways, in bad ways, and in breath-taking ways, but it matters.

Ask any experienced practicing litigator. Almost without fail, they can share stories of countless times when something learned in discovery redirected their litigation, changed their approach or trial themes, inspired a motion battle that ended in a pretrial victory (or loss), or coaxed out a settlement that was considered unthinkable earlier in the lawsuit. Discovery matters. Most experienced litigators will confirm that it is the rare civil case that isn't won or lost during discovery. In contemporary civil litigation, case-resolving victories occur far more often in discovery than they do in trials. One very well-regarded practitioner journal expressed the notion eminently well:

> Most cases settle, and victory is not in the scathing cross[-examination], but in the tedious review of documents. Success is in the details, the expertly drafted interrogatories or request for records, and in the ingenious strategy to obtain the statement allegedly protected by privilege. For it is discovery which we do. The motions, the papers, the depositions. This is the [sometimes] numbing, ditch digging work that determines the winner . . . .

Discovery, 1997 A.B.A. Sec. Litig. 23. To learn discovery is to learn how to litigate successfully.

And that's why you should care.

G. Learning to Embrace Civil Discovery

This book isn't just about theory (at least not mostly so). It will, of course, supply you with enough core theory to help you understand the various stages, tools, and processes of civil discovery. But this book is primarily designed for practical, hands-on learning. The goal is to have you actually work with the tools and processes of civil discovery. Section H of this chapter, which follows next, contains a fact-pattern template that your professor may have you rely upon in practicing the techniques described here.

Why practice? You now know that discovery matters, and why it does. It matters to every case. Often, it matters profoundly. But practicing discovery can also matter in ways that might seem unexpected. Discovery is also an aspect of civil litigation where newly minted attorneys can set themselves apart.

Imagine a senior attorney coming to your office, asking you to help out on a case that is about to enter the discovery phase. The case is very important to the firm, the attorney cautions you, and you are told there are already 200 boxes of documents and 20 gigabytes of information that now need to be reviewed. You're also told that discovery directed toward other parties needs to be drafted and properly issued. What's your response? Are you ready? Do you understand what you are being asked to do and how to do it properly?

Now consider the senior attorney's reaction to your response. Does a look of lost disorientation wash across your face? Do you ask elementary questions, revealing a lack of understanding of the discovery process and how to execute it well? Do you roll your eyes, make a joke about putting you out of your misery, and then begin your review of the materials begrudgingly? Or do you acknowledge the assignment with confidence, your mind spinning with tools and strategies, and eagerly embrace the task ahead? Do you appreciate the case-impacting (and career-propelling) opportunity the assignment represents, and put your newly acquired discovery expertise to work in search of information useful to your client's case?

Those are quite different responses. Which reactions do you think will inspire the senior attorney to seek you out for the next big case?

Why does this text focus on the Federal Discovery Rules? This book will use the federal discovery rules as the tools for its discussions and exercises. There are a few reasons why. First, the federal discovery rules mark the historical sea change in robust pretrial information exchange; this is the set of procedures that was revolutionary in its creativity back in 1938 and which has been amended often in the many decades since. It represents the most comprehensively, exhaustively considered and debated set of discovery procedures in the country. Second, the federal discovery rules apply in every federal court throughout the United States, its territories and possessions, and the District of Columbia. Third, many States have modeled their discovery procedures on those contained in the federal rules. All in all, the federal discovery rules offer the ideal place to learn American discovery.

How is this text organized? This book is grouped into ten chapters, designed to move progressively through the discovery process—with one notable caveat. You may wonder why the chapter on discovery strategy is near the end of the book. Should lawyers propound written discovery, conduct depositions, disclose their expert testimony, and only later develop their discovery strategy? Of course not; strategic discovery planning in a case should begin as early as possible. From a learning perspective, though, it is cumbersome to engage in thoughtful discovery planning without a deep understanding of the operation of all the discovery techniques. For example, when thinking about the best way to fill a hole in the evidence, it is important to take into account the advantages and disadvantages of the various discovery tools, so that the lawyer appropriately chooses between, for example, an interrogatory, a deposition, or a request for admission directed at the sought-after information. Accordingly, while discovery planning should be the first step in practice, this book situates it near the end so that students will have a better understanding of the menu of discovery tools before they delve into discovery planning.

With that caveat in mind, here is a preview of the book's organization:

- **What Is Discovery** has just oriented you to the history and context of discovery, and why mastering this discipline is so important in civil litigation.

- **How Discovery Begins** sets out the opening stages of discovery management and describes the obligatory disclosures that must occur in most civil litigations.

- **The Scope of Discovery** introduces the reach of federal discovery and describes the criteria and analysis performed to test whether information is "discoverable."

- **The Discovery Tools** details the various tools adopted for use in civil litigation (interrogatories, production requests, admission requests, physical and mental exams, and depositions), and explains how each of those tools function in practice.

- **Discovery of Experts** provides an overview of the role expert witnesses play in civil litigation, and how their credentials, backgrounds, opinions, and explanations are discovered.

- **Discovery from Non-Parties** introduces the methods for acquiring information from persons and entities who are not formal parties to a civil litigation yet still may have valuable knowledge to impart.

- **Supplementation** explains the requirements for updating discovery responses after they are supplied.

- **Policing Discovery** details the obligations imposed on all participants in discovery, and how mischief in discovery is addressed.
- **Discovery Strategy** outlines the approaches lawyers use to devise and implement discovery to optimize their trial objectives.
- **Appealing Discovery Rulings** offers a glimpse into the procedures for obtaining appellate review of a trial court's discovery rulings.

H. Your Canvas

As promised, your *Practicing Civil Discovery* canvas is set out in the paragraphs below. This is a fictional factual scenario that your professor may use to have you practice the various discovery events and tools you will be encountering in the chapters to come:

Sara Marceau and Sidney Lemieux wanted an unconventional wedding—traditional weddings, they felt, are boring and stuffy. "Destination weddings"—where everyone flies to a tropical island and the wedding ceremony is barefoot on the beach—are delightful in theory, but Sara and Sid did not want to impose that financial burden on their wedding party and guests. They settled on what they thought was the perfect solution. They would get married at Bunnywood, the local amusement park. It fit their vision and their budget, and they were sure it would make for a memorable wedding.

They were right; the event was indeed memorable. Just not in the way they expected. In many traditional weddings, the wedding party walks down the aisle to the area where the couple exchanges their vows. But, for their Bunnywood wedding, Sara and Sid planned to substitute a ride on the Killer Rabbit, one of Bunnywood's old wooden-track roller coasters, for the traditional walk down the aisle.

The Killer Rabbit was constructed in 1920 and is one of the oldest continuously operating roller coasters in the world. It was the first roller coaster to use a wheel underneath the track, allowing the designers to create "airtime" spots where the riders fly up out of their seats. It features a drop of 70 feet—enormous at the time of the ride's creation—followed by a "double dip" that made the ride famous. It has a top speed of 45 miles per hour. Although the Killer Rabbit does not contain loops, rolls, or inversions, coasters like the Killer Rabbit instill fear in their riders by virtue of the uncertainty about whether the rickety wooden track will hold together for one more ride.[1]

At the appointed time, Sara, Sid, and the rest of the wedding party were escorted

---

1. This Point of View (POV) video of a similar ride will give you the sense of the Killer Rabbit: https://www.youtube.com/watch?v=tWh9ofIm-B8

to the front of the line and allowed to occupy all four of the Killer Rabbit's cars. To mirror the manner in which the bride is the last one to walk down the aisle (and because the Killer Rabbit was designed so that the last seats provided the strongest airtime during the famous double dip section of the ride), Sara and Sid took the last seats on the Killer Rabbit.

The ride got off to a normal start, but on one of the turns, the long-rusted, long-screeching bolt connecting the last car to the car in front of it sheared off. Because this roller coaster was powered only by gravity after the first ascent, the last car continued to roll along with the three connected cars in front of it, but differences in weight and friction eventually caused some separation between the connected cars and the single last car. As an older roller coaster, the Killer Rabbit did not have an automated magnetic braking system, and instead had a manually operated braking system. When the ride attendant pulled the brake lever, the brakes slowed the first three cars, causing the car Sara and Sid were riding in to slam into the slowing third car in front of them.

None of the wedding guests in the first two cars had been aware of the last car's separation. Towards the end of the ride, some of the guests in the third car noticed the last car's separation and, though somewhat concerned, thought that the separating car was a clever stunt that Sara and Sid had arranged for their "roll" down the aisle. When Sara and Sid's car slammed into the car ahead of them, the force of the impact startled the passengers in the three still-linked cars but, beyond that momentary, fleeting startle, none of those passengers was injured. Sara and Sid were not so lucky. At the moment of impact, Sara was standing up and leaning forward with her arms braced against the seat back in front of her, hoping to dull the impact with her arms and hands, and Sid was leaning out the car to his left, trying to grab hold of a rope that he hoped might help him slow the decoupled, speeding car. The force of that impact wrenched Sid to his side and propelled Sara violently into the metal back of the seat in front of her. Instead of proceeding to the pavilion where the ceremony was to occur, Sara and Sid were transported by ambulance to the nearby hospital. The wedding ceremony did not occur. And Sara and Sid did not take their honeymoon, which they had booked in Hawaii.

The consequences of this accident extended beyond the cancellation of the wedding ceremony and honeymoon. Sara was a professional mime. She had landed a part in *Speechless,* the first mime musical, scheduled to debut on Broadway a few months after the wedding. The show had received rave reviews as "revolutionary" and "dumbfounding" in early workshop performances, was trending strongly on social media, and was already being touted as likely to sweep the Tony awards. In fact, Sara and Sid timed the wedding and honeymoon so that Sara would be back in time to start rehearsals for the show. Unfortunately, Sara's broken wrists and ankle prevented her from performing—Sara could not effectively portray being trapped in a box, pulling herself along by grasping a rope, or walking into a stiff wind, all of which were incorporated into the mime dance numbers—and Sara was forced to withdraw from the production. Sid was an accountant by trade and, although his dislocated shoulder was healing, a new and persisting deep-ache and instability affected his left knee (which had been a problem for him since he injured it in a hockey accident three years earlier) and left him unable to continue as the first-line starting center in his Sunday night men's league.

Sara and Sid engaged Steve Goodman to represent them. During the course of Goodman's pre-complaint investigation, Goodman learned that Bunnywood had engaged Amusement Rides of Scranton LLC to conduct periodic safety inspections of its rides on a rotating basis, so that each ride was inspected once per week. An inspector from that company had examined the Killer Rabbit the morning of the accident. The inspection report he gave to Bunnywood that same morning showed a check mark in the box on the inspection report next to the phrase "safe to operate."

Goodman also learned that Scranton Amusement Rides, Inc. ("SCARI") had manufactured the Killer Rabbit in 1927. From an old, yellowing newspaper article, Goodman learned that, in the 1940s and 1950s, other amusement rides manufactured by SCARI were reported to have had a flurry of malfunctions, several apparently involving bolt fatigue and failure, and resulting in apparent injuries. The same article noted that the local district attorney had launched an investigation of SCARI in September 1956.

Finally, Goodman learned that the manual braking feature of the Killer Rabbit allowed the ride attendant to more gradually slow the cars in the event of an incident like the one occurring at Sara and Sid's wedding. The attendant on the day of the accident was Frank "Ferris Wheel" Bueller. Unfortunately, Bueller was watching a YouTube video on his smart phone when the bolt sheared, and he did not realize that the car Sara and Sidney were riding in had separated from the other cars. If Bueller had been paying closer attention and had activated the emergency braking system, Sara and Sid likely would have avoided injury.

· · · · · · ·

That is your canvas. Now, let's learn the "nuts and bolts" (and core strategies) for practicing civil discovery.

II

How Discovery Begins

GETTING THE VIEW

In general, civil litigants have broad discretion in choosing what information to seek from their fellow parties and nonparties. But that discretion is not without limits. There are constraints. Three of those constraints, along with four functional caveats, is where our discussion of the process of discovery will begin.

First, before initiating any discovery, the parties are obligated to confer with one another in a **discovery planning conference**. It is here where the parties will develop their joint **discovery plan** and talk through any issues they anticipate may arise during the discovery process.

Second, there are three categories of information that ordinarily must be exchanged by the parties to a civil lawsuit: "**initial disclosures**," governed by Rule 26(a)(1) of the Federal Rules of Civil Procedure; "**expert disclosures**," governed by Rule 26(a)(2); and "**pretrial disclosures**," governed by Rule 26(a)(3). These three categories of information are mandatory and must always be exchanged (unless some exception applies, or a court order or party stipulation provides otherwise). A handy hint: the Rules (and this book) use the term "disclosures" to refer to these categories of mandatory information exchanges.

Third, once discovery is underway, the parties are bound by the limits on the **scope** of allowable discovery set out in Rules 26(b) and 26(c). In other words, the parties cannot use the discovery process to request information that is categorically off-limits (*e.g.,* information that is not relevant, that is privileged, that is not proportional to the needs of the case, or that a court order has otherwise foreclosed). The scope of allowable discovery will be discussed in detail in the Scope of Discovery chapter.

Finally, four functional caveats must be remembered about discovery mechanics:

1. ***Ethical Discovery:*** An ethical obligation applies to every mandatory disclosure, discovery request, discovery response, and discovery objection. All those documents must be signed, with the act of signing constituting the signer's certification that the document abides by the Rules governing ethical discovery. *See* Fed. R. Civ. P. 26(g).

2. ***Changing the Rules:*** Nearly all the requirements and procedures we are about to learn can be altered, either by the court or by agreement of the parties. Rule 29 makes this point expressly—the parties can modify the discovery Rules by stipulation among themselves, *provided* that they will need court approval to do so if their modification would interfere with a deadline set by the court for closing discovery, for a hearing on a motion, or for trial. *See* Fed. R. Civ. P. 29.

3. ***Sequence of Discovery:*** Provided the parties have already convened their discovery planning conference, the discovery tools created by the Rules can be used in any sequence a party prefers (absent a contrary court order or stipulation of the parties). *See* Fed. R. Civ. P. 26(d)(1) & (d)(3).

4. ***Filing Discovery with the Court:*** The volume of pages of material involved in discovery (*e.g.*, disclosures, requests, responses, objections, deposition notices, deposition transcripts, etc.) can be mountainous. Consequently, to conserve physical and digital space in the office of the court clerk, discovery papers like these are *not* filed with the clerk unless (a) the court so orders or (b) the papers are used in the proceedings. *See* Fed. R. Civ. P. 5(d)(1)(A).

HOW THIS DISCOVERY CONCEPT WORKS

The discovery process begins with the **discovery planning conference** and the parties' joint **discovery plan**. All civil litigation (with a few exceptions) will also trigger mandatory **disclosures**. Each is discussed in turn.

A. Discovery Planning Conference

The discovery planning conference is mandatory, as is its agenda. The parties to a lawsuit are required to meet with one another "as soon as practicable," but not later than 21 days before the date of the scheduling conference with the court (or no later than 21 days before the time set for the court to issue its official scheduling order, if no scheduling conference is to occur). *See* Fed. R. Civ. P. 26(f)(1). Unless and until the parties complete their conference, the door to discovery remains shuttered to them; no discovery happens until the parties have conferred (with one minor exception for production requests, discussed in the *Production Requests* subchapter). *See* Rule 26(d)(1). The parties can attend the conference telephonically or through other means, but the court always retains the authority to order the parties or their attorneys to meet in person. *See* Rule 26(f)(2).

During the conference, the parties are obligated to confer on a number of different topics (*e.g.*, discussing claims, defenses, and the possibility of an early settlement), but the topic of discovery is an integral agenda item. Specifically, the Rule obligates the parties to complete three discovery-related tasks during their discussions: (1) make (or arrange for making) their respective initial disclosures; (2) discuss any issues concerning the preservation of discoverable information; and (3) develop a discovery plan. *See* Rule 26(f)(2). (Local Rules often require discussion of additional discovery topics, such as procedures for handling electronic discovery.) The Rule imposes on the parties the joint responsibility for arranging the conference and for attempting, in good faith, to agree on a proposed discovery plan. *See id.*

Hypothetical

Q: Suppose Natalie was seriously injured when a poorly maintained section of roof fell on her as she watched a movie with friends in Creaky Theater. Natalie's lawyer filed a lawsuit against Creaky Theater, and then met with Creaky Theater's attorney for their Rule 26(f) discovery planning conference. The two attorneys agreed on many things, but could not agree on whether Natalie should be forbidden from removing any of her social media posts (as the Theater's attorney insisted) or whether the Theater should be required to disable an auto-archive feature on all its computers (as Natalie's attorney insisted). Although the lawyers conferred in good faith, they just could not agree on these items. Is there any way the attorneys can still comply with their Rule 26(f) obligations?

A: The aspirational goal of the Rule 26(f) conference requirement is full agreement: complete assent by all parties, following a mature, collaborative discussion, on all aspects of the discovery process that is about to unfold. In this way, the presiding judge—whose duty it is to oversee the discovery process—can benefit from their views and thoughts as he or she formalizes the case's discovery plan. *See* Fed. R. Civ. P. 26(f) advisory committee note (1993). Sometimes, however, notwithstanding their good faith, the parties cannot come to an agreement on all components of the discovery path forward. In that event, the parties are required to supply to the court their competing proposals on areas of disagreement as well as a report on those items on which they agree. *See id.*

B. Discovery Plan

Within 14 days after their conference, the parties must submit to the court a written discovery plan. *See* Fed. R. Civ. P. 26(f)(2). Its required contents, fixed by the Rule, are designed to smoke out the parties' objectives and concerns regarding the discovery process that is about to begin. *See* Rule 26(f)(3). The discovery plan must supply the court with the parties' views on, and proposals for, the following discovery items:

A. *Mandatory Disclosures:* Any changes the parties propose to the timing, form, or requirement of mandatory disclosures generally, and a status report on the initial disclosures specifically.

B. *Anticipated Discovery Logistics:* The subjects of anticipated discovery, when discovery should be finished, and whether discovery ought to be conducted in "phases."

C. *ESI:* Any anticipated issues involving the disclosure, discovery, or preservation of electronically stored information (ESI).

D. *Privilege and Work Product:* Any anticipated issues (or agreements) concerning claims of privilege or work product, including whether a court order is requested pursuant to Federal Rule of Evidence 502 (relating to waiver and inadvertent disclosures).

E. *Limitations:* Any proposed limitations (or modification of Rule-imposed limitations) on discovery.

F. *Protective Orders:* Any proposed protective order or pretrial order the court is requested to issue, including proposed terms for the court's scheduling order.

C. What the Court Does After Receiving the Parties' Discovery Plan

The Rules direct the presiding judge to issue a "Scheduling Order," also known as a "Case Management Order" (CMO), for every lawsuit. The court must issue the Order once the judge has received the parties' written report from their planning conference (which will include the parties' discovery plan) or after the judge convenes a special conference with the parties to discuss these matters. *See* Fed. R. Civ. P. 16(b)(1). Whether to convene a conference or not is a matter left to the judge's discretion, and often is influenced by the judge's personal preferences (*e.g.,* some judges like to meet with the attorneys at the outset of a trial to get to know them), the burden of an in-person conference (*e.g.,* whether some attorneys are from distant cities, requiring costly travel), and the circumstances of the lawsuit (*e.g.,* whether intricate complexities or logistical complications exist or are likely to arise).

In the Scheduling Order, the judge will set parameters for the discovery phase of the lawsuit. The Order will fix a deadline for the completion of all discovery. The Order may also adjust discovery requirements ordinarily governed by the Rules (for example, by adjusting the dates for initial disclosures, modifying the extent of discovery, setting special procedures for discovery of electronically stored information, memorializing any agreement the parties had reached concerning privileged material or work product, and mandating that no formal motions regarding discovery disputes be filed until the parties first request a conference with the judge). *See* Rule 16(b)(3)(A)–(3)(B).

D. "Disclosures": Mandatory Discovery

Mandatory disclosures are not optional or discretionary. As this label confirms, mandatory disclosures *must* be exchanged by the litigants, unless some exception, court order, or party stipulation allows otherwise. There are three types of mandatory disclosures:

1. Initial Disclosures

Typically, the very first information that is exchanged among the parties (after the pleadings) are initial disclosures. The duty to exchange initial disclosures was added to the Federal Rules of Civil Procedure in 1993, and the inclusion was controversial. Some objected that imposing a mandatory initial disclosure obligation on litigants offended the adversarial structure of the American system of civil litigation: if an adversary was too careless, too inattentive, or too irresponsible to request discovery from an opponent, why should the Rules help that party out? Others argued that the information encompassed by initial disclosures was so frequently sought, and so core to the lawsuit, that it was simply more efficient to require its automatic exchange rather than waste time and resources drafting and responding to discovery requests. The original controversy has quieted, but not entirely. Nonetheless, today, initial disclosures are a settled staple of civil litigation under the Federal Rules.

There are four categories of information that must be exchanged during initial disclosures:

1. ***Witnesses:*** Parties must identify those persons who are "likely to have discoverable information" that the disclosing party "may use to support

its claims or defenses" (unless that use would be limited to impeachment), by identifying those persons' names, addresses, phone numbers, and subjects-known.

2. *Evidence:* Parties must also provide a copy (or description by category) of all documents, electronically stored information, and tangible things in their possession, custody, or control that they "may use to support its claims or defenses" (unless that use would be limited to impeachment).

3. *Damages:* Parties claiming damages must provide a computation of each category of damages they are claiming (including access to non-privileged documents or other material on which the computation is based).

4. *Insurance:* Parties must also allow the inspection and copying of any insurance agreement that may pay all or part of any judgment in the lawsuit (or to reimburse payments made to satisfy the judgment).

The first two of these four categories require the disclosure of only those witnesses and evidence that the disclosing party "may use" to support its claims or defenses. The term "may use" has a reach that some consider surprising, as the following case illustrates:

ARCELORMITTAL INDIANA HARBOR LLC
v.
AMEX NOOTER, LLC

320 F.R.D. 455 (N.D. Ind. 2017)

CHERRY, United States Magistrate Judge

[Owner (ArcelorMittal) operated a harbor facility in Indiana. ArcelorMittal sued one of its vendors (Amex Nooter), alleging that the vendor took certain actions that caused a fire that damaged that facility. In its investigation of the fire, ArcelorMittal hired a "consulting expert" (Dr. Hoffman) to help it determine the fire's cause. To aid in that consultation, ArcelorMittal provided Dr. Hoffman with 41 pages of documents for his consideration. Later, after learning Dr. Hoffman's conclusions, ArcelorMittal decided to call him to testify as an expert witness at trial. When Dr. Hoffman released his expert report, he acknowledged his review of the 41 pages of materials. Those 41 pages, however, had not been identified in ArcelorMittal's initial disclosures.]

Amex Nooter contends that ArcelorMittal should have produced the [41 pages of] documents as part of its initial disclosures pursuant to Rule 26(a)

(1)(A)(ii), arguing that ArcelorMittal knew and now knows that these documents "may be used in support of its claims or defenses" because Arcelor-Mittal gave the documents to its testifying expert for consideration. . . . During the parties' informal attempts to resolve this dispute, ArcelorMittal represented, "We do not intend to use any of the information listed below to support our claims." Similarly, in its response brief, ArcelorMittal reasserts that it "has not intended to use the documents at issue to support its claims at any time following the filing of its Complaint." ArcelorMittal further states that it is willing to stipulate that it will not use any of these documents to support its claims or defenses in this litigation. Amex Nooter argues that this statement is patently false because ArcelorMittal has affirmatively "used" the information to support its claims by providing the information to its testifying expert as a basis for his opinions.

Rule 26(a)(1) requires a party to provide "information . . . that the disclosing party has in its possession, custody, or control and *may use to support its claims or defenses,* unless the use would be solely for impeachment. . . ." Fed. R. Civ. P. 26(a)(1)(A)(ii) (emphasis added). In the year 2000, Rule 26(a)(1) was revised to this current language, and the advisory committee's notes explain that the purpose of the amendment was to establish a nationally uniform practice with regard to initial disclosures and that the "scope of the disclosure obligation is narrowed to cover only information that the disclosing party may use to support its position." Fed. R. Civ. P. 26(a) advisory committee's notes to 2000 amendment. The notes further explain that the word "use" in this rule "includes any use at a pretrial conference, to support a motion, or at trial." *Id.* "The disclosure obligation is also triggered by intended use in discovery, apart from use to respond to a discovery request; use of a document to question a witness during a deposition is a common example." *Id.*

* * *

At the time ArcelorMittal made its initial disclosures . . . , it did not intend to directly use the 41 pages of documents to support its claims and defenses, and it still does not. At some point, ArcelorMittal decided to designate Dr. Hoffman as a testifying expert and subsequently disclosed him as an expert and served his expert report. . . . In his report, Dr. Hoffman identified the "facts or data" he considered, including the 41 pages of documents, as required by Rule 26(a)(2)(B)(ii). ArcelorMittal produced the documents to Amex Nooter, who requested them the same day that the expert report was served.

* * *

The facts surrounding the 41 pages of documents in this case appear to present an unusual set of circumstances involving a party who provides to its *consulting* expert, two years before initiating litigation, documents that the party has never itself intended to directly use to support its claims but that remain in the possession of that consulting expert and then are listed, in the expert report, as having been considered by the consulting expert in his subsequent capacity as a retained expert. Generally, the documents a party gives to a retained expert for consideration are documents the party may otherwise use directly to support its claims and will have already been disclosed through initial disclosures under Rule 26(a)(1)(A)(ii). Or, if the documents a party gives to its retained expert are not documents the party itself intends to use, if the documents are relevant, it is likely . . . that the documents are responsive to a request for production from the opposing party and will have already been disclosed through discovery responses.

Parties are unlikely to purposefully "hide" documents or information by only disclosing them through a retained expert's report because the failure to produce the information through initial disclosures (or their supplementation) would likely lead to the exclusion of the documents under Rule 37(c)(1) if the party tried to use the information to support its claims in the litigation; and . . . the failure to earlier disclose information that the party itself intends to use may result in the exclusion of the expert's report as well.

Whether or not the 41 pages in this unique situation should have been produced before the service of Dr. Hoffman's expert report . . . is not dispositive of the instant motion because there is no harm to Amex Nooter. First, the Court considers whether Amex Nooter has suffered unfair surprise or prejudice and finds that it has not. Although Amex Nooter argues generally that it was prejudiced because it would have pursued written discovery and depositions of ArcelorMittal employees and third parties differently if the documents had been produced earlier, Amex Nooter identifies no information in the 41 pages of documents that would have changed how it conducted fact discovery. Amex Nooter does not explain what questions it would have asked differently during the depositions it already took or why it would depose any additional individuals based on the documents. Amex Nooter argues generally that "the trajectory of the cross examination of ArcelorMittal's employees . . . about the pre-fire events and post-fire investigation would have been different." But Amex Nooter gives no examples of how the documents would have changed the cross examinations. Amex Nooter reasons that, "had [certain of the documents] . . . been identified and produced, the calculus of whom it wished to depose would have been different." Amex Nooter does not explain *how* that calculus would have been different. . . . Thus, Amex Nooter has shown no prejudice.

Moreover, . . . Amex Nooter's expert disclosure deadline has not yet passed. Therefore, Amex Nooter's expert will have the benefit, if any, of the 41 pages of documents in preparing a report. . . . Because there is no prejudice, there is no need for ArcelorMittal to provide a cure. However, the Court notes that Amex Nooter asks to be given an opportunity to identify the authors of the newly produced documents. Because the author of some of these documents is not identified, the Court **ORDERS** ArcelorMittal to identify for Amex Nooter . . . , in writing, with reference to each document by bates number, the author of each document in the 41 pages at issue on this motion. [Finally, as regards] . . . the likelihood of trial disruption, and the Court finds that there is none. Although the Court is resetting certain deadlines, the trial setting will not be affected. . . . Although Amex Nooter argues that ArcelorMittal breached its duties under Rule 26, Amex Nooter does not contend that ArcelorMittal acted in bad faith. Nor is there evidence of bad faith, especially in light of ArcelorMittal's stipulation that it will not use these documents at trial.

Accordingly, the Court finds that there is no harm to Amex Nooter in the timing of ArcelorMittal's disclosure of the 41 pages of documents. As a result, the Motion for Sanctions is denied.

Hypothetical

Q: Creaky Theater's attorney is in the process of preparing initial disclosures on behalf of his client in defending against Natalie's personal injury claim. While flipping through documents, the attorney comes upon a roofer's bill, paid by the Theater a year ago after the roofer finished re-sealing the roof. The bill contained a troubling handwritten note from the roofer, reading: "While re-sealing your roof, I noticed some weakness in spots. You really should get this checked. You don't want your roof falling in on your movie-goers!" Does the Theater's attorney, in initial disclosures, have to supply Natalie's lawyer with a copy of this bill? Must the roofer's name be listed in the initial disclosure witness list?

A: Litigants are required in their initial disclosures to supply a copy of (or de-scribe, by category and location) only those documents that the disclosing party may use "to *support* its claims or defenses." Fed. R. Civ. P. 26(a)(1)(A)(ii) (emphasis added). Likewise, litigants are required only to identify those witnesses having discoverable information that the disclosing party may use "to *support* its claims or defenses." Rule 26(a)(1)(A)(i) (emphasis added). Accordingly, litigants are not required by this Rule to identify unfavorable documents or unfavorable witnesses, unless for some reason the disclosing party "may use" those documents or witnesses. *See Comm. for Immigrant Rights of Sonoma Cty. v. County of Sonoma*, 2009 WL 1833988, at *3 (N.D. Cal. June 23, 2009) ("There is no obligation . . . under Rule 26 to do the adversary's work and disclose witnesses harmful to the disclosing party's case."). Thus, Creaky Theater's attorney need not provide a copy of (or describe) the roofer's bill or identify the roofer in the Theater's initial disclosures. But this omission will come with a consequence. The Theater will not later be able to "use" the bill or the roofer's testimony in any motion, hearing, or at trial unless the Theater is able to show that failing to disclose the bill or roofer was "substantially justified" or that the use was "solely for impeachment." *See id.*

Along with the obligations to disclose "may use" witnesses and evidence are the final two initial disclosure categories: damages computation and insurance information. Both are helpful to the parties in making early, tentative assessments of both the magnitude of the lawsuit and the availability of insurance monies to pay some or part of any possible resulting judgment. The damages computation is a disclosure required of anyone asserting a claim for damages (*e.g.*, the plaintiff through the complaint, the defendant through a counterclaim or crossclaim, etc.). The insurance information, conversely, is a disclosure required of anyone from whom damages are being sought.

Hypothetical

Q: Unlike plaintiffs who may have had many months to think through strategy, witnesses, and documentary evidence before filing the lawsuit, defending parties are often at a time disadvantage. They and their lawyers may be learning about a dispute (or the theory chosen to litigate that dispute) for the first time as they read the newly served complaint. In such cases, they may not yet have a firm understanding of what witnesses and evidence they "may use" to support their defenses. Plaintiffs, too, can suffer from this same sort of incomplete knowledge; they may be thinking through a defense for the first time as they encounter it while reading the defendant's answer or pre-answer motion. How can a party make its pretrial disclosures under such circumstances? If a plaintiff believes its adversary's initial disclosures are deficient in some way, does that excuse the plaintiff from having to prepare and serve initial disclosures of its own?

A: Parties must make their initial disclosures on the basis of "information then reasonably available to it." *See* Fed. R. Civ. P. 26(a)(1)(E). As we'll see in Chapter 7, parties then have a duty to "timely" supplement their initial disclosures if those disclosures are later found to be incomplete or incorrect in some material respect.

See Rule 26(e). Parties, thus, are not excused from making their initial disclosures merely because their pretrial investigation work is still underway. *See* Rule 26(a)(1)(E). Nor is a party excused from making initial disclosures because an adversary has failed to make its initial disclosures or has made them deficiently. *See id.* If, without a substantial justification, a party fails to make a required initial disclosure and that failure is not harmless, the delinquent party may not use the undisclosed information in any motion, hearing, or at trial. *See* Rule 37(c)(1).

2. Expert Disclosures (and Expert Discovery)

The second category of mandatory disclosures concerns experts. *See* Fed. R. Civ. P. 26(a)(2). Expert witnesses often play a pivotal role in civil litigation. For example, they can help the jury understand a client's medical condition and prognosis for recovery; appreciate complex financial concepts in an accounting malpractice case; or reconstruct the forces, angles of impact, and likely causes of a vehicular collision. In these and countless other ways, expert witnesses will have an often formidable, perhaps even dispositive impact on how a civil litigation unfolds. Consequently, learning the conclusions of expert witnesses, the assumptions that support those conclusions, and how those conclusions were reached are critical objectives in discovery. Because of the importance of disclosures and discovery from expert witnesses, this topic will be explored separately in the Discovery of Experts chapter later in this book.

3. Pretrial Disclosures

The final category of mandatory disclosures occurs late in the life of the lawsuit, as the trial date nears. *See* Fed. R. Civ. P. 26(a)(3). No later than 30 days before trial, the parties must provide to the court (by filing) and to one another the following (unless the evidence will be used only for impeachment):

1. ***Testifying Witnesses:*** The names, addresses, and phone numbers of those witnesses that party expects to call at trial, as well as any other witnesses that party may call if the need arises.

2. ***Witnesses by Deposition:*** The identity of those witnesses whose testimony will be presented by deposition (and not by live testimony), and access to a transcript of the pertinent parts of the deposition.

3. ***Documents and Other Evidence:*** The identity of every document or other exhibit that party expects to offer into evidence at trial, as well as any other evidence that party may offer if the need arises.

Note the "may call"/"will call" distinction in the first two of these pretrial disclosures. The distinction has a very precise objective: to require the disclosing party to reveal to its opponent those witnesses and evidence it actually intends to use at trial (separate from those witnesses and evidence that, though at-the-ready, the disclosing party only intends to call "if the need arises"). The goal here is to ferret out trial-planning details, so that the adversary can more meaningfully prepare to meet that presentation and the court can understand the likely length and complexity of the trial.

To optimize the benefit of this exchange of pretrial disclosures as the trial approaches, the Rules establish a formal procedure for objecting to an adversary's now-disclosed trial evidence. After receiving an adversary's pretrial disclosures, parties are allotted 14 days to serve and file objections to the admissibility of the proposed evidence (including objections based on allowable use of deposition testimony under Rule 32(a)). *See* Fed. R. Civ. P. 26(a)(3)(B). Any objections not made during this 14-day period are waived, unless the court, for good cause, excuses the failure or the objections are grounded in the evidence's lack of relevance or adequate probative value. *See id.*

FROM CLASSROOM TO PRACTICE

These discovery tools—the planning conference, discovery plan, and mandatory disclosures—provide what might be called the "starting gun" for civil discovery. These procedures get the discovery process started, and endeavor to ensure that the process begins sensibly and productively.

A. Discovery Planning Conference

The founding goal of the Federal Rules of Civil Procedure was to achieve a "just, speedy, and inexpensive determination" of every civil lawsuit. *See Brown Shoe Co. v. United States*, 370 U.S. 294, 306 (1962) ("the touchstones of federal procedure"). The discovery planning conference is a quintessential example of how the Rules pursue those goals.

Consider the setting. Left to their own preferences, the parties and their counsel are often unlikely to want to meet and discuss anything with one another at the outset of litigation. Posturing is, more typically, the preferred behavior. Meeting with an adversary—particularly in the very early days of a lawsuit—can seem like a sort of surrender, as if one were summoned to appear, meekly and weakly, before a combatant to beg for terms to resolve the conflict.

The discovery planning conference aims to neutralize those inclinations by making an early meeting among the litigants a mandatory part of every civil litigation. Under the Rules, litigants now have no choice. They are *required* to meet with one another, and early. *See* Fed. R. Civ. P. 26(f)(1). That mandate is enforced in a very practical way—until the conference has been held, all discovery is on hold. That is an unwelcome stall in the litigation march, and provides strong motivation to do precisely what the Rules prefer: to confer "as soon as practicable." *See id.* So, the parties will confer, sometimes in person and other times by phone, to talk through the discovery process. In doing so, their obligation to generate a written discovery plan to be submitted to the judge usually helps to focus their discussions.

Well-founded, reasoned disagreement can occur in litigation, and there is no penalty for a good faith failure during the planning conference to agree on all agenda items. Obstruction is something else entirely, however. Obstructionist behavior at the conference is discouraged in several, very practical ways. First, the Rules make the parties *jointly responsible* for arranging their conference. They are also *jointly responsible* for attempting, *in good faith*, to agree on a proposed discovery plan. And they are *jointly responsible* for submitting their plan to the court. *See* Rule 26(f)(2). Thus, the duty of a successful conference is made a shared one. Second, the Rules impose consequences for failing to collaborate in good faith, as we will see in the Policing Discovery chapter. Obstructionist behavior risks an award of counsel fees and expenses. *See* Rule 37(f). Third, the sanctioning of misconduct at the conference sets an ominous tone that badly colors the court's impression of the litigation. If the very first involvement by the presiding judge is the chore of sorting through poor behavior at the planning conference, the court's patience with the attorneys and their clients is undermined. Very little good comes from this sort of obstruction, and lawyers who engage in it are unlikely to be serving their clients well.

B. Discovery Plan

Directing the parties to collaborate on a proposed plan for the discovery of the lawsuit has an obvious purpose. By compelling the parties to meet and discuss discovery early in the life of the lawsuit (and by directing them to produce jointly a written submission for the court's reference), the Rules force each of the parties to think through discovery, substantively and critically, *before* launching into it. What does each party want to explore through discovery? How will that discovery be pursued? What discovery methods are to be invoked? Are there likely to be controversial discovery requests—seeking information that an adversary believes to be off-topic, too extraneous or inconsequential, or too disruptive or costly to perform? How will electronically stored information be pursued, and can the parties agree on how to collect it effectively and efficiently? Are there information preservation issues to address, like the retention of documents and communications stored on an electronic platform? Will there likely be disputes concerning the reach of the attorney-client privilege (or some other privilege), or over what falls within the scope of the work product protection? Can the parties agree, in advance, on a procedure for dealing with claims of waiver and inadvertent disclosure?

In forcing each of the parties to think carefully through their respective discovery hopes and worries, the Rules endeavor to anticipate—and work collaboratively through—roadblocks and disagreements before they metastasize into unproductive, disruptive, and costly discovery battles. It is an aspirational goal, to be sure. It will not always be achieved. But in pursuing it, the Rules are designed to lessen the pain of discovery, to increase constructive and collaborative information exchange, and to mitigate costs.

There is one last, very tangible, immediate, and practical effect of the parties' discovery plan. Recall that, after receiving and reviewing the parties' discovery plan, the judge is tasked to issue the Scheduling Order for the lawsuit. So, the discovery plan—and, especially, those portions of the plan that are agreed upon by the parties—will likely influence the judge in establishing some core attributes of the lawsuit's discovery process. How much time will the lawyers have to conduct their discovery? Will any of the ordinary discovery requirements set by the Rules be adjusted? Which ones, and in what ways? How will privilege and work product issues (along with the unnerving questions of waiver and inadvertent disclosures) be treated during the lawsuit?

By supplying the judge with their thinking (and, hopefully, their areas of broad agreement) on the path of discovery, the parties enjoy an important opportunity to persuade the judge through their submission to set the discovery process to best meet their perceived discovery needs. While the judge is not obligated to follow the parties' recommendations (and might not, in all cases), the parties' thoughts and agreements on discovery will undoubtedly be borne in mind as the judge crafts the lawsuit's Scheduling Order.

The opposite is, of course, also true. As mentioned earlier, if the parties' discovery planning conference does not occur at all, or if it does not proceed in good faith, the judge's first exposure to the lawsuit will be refereeing a fight. That sets off the lawsuit on an obviously unproductive footing, and likely foretells a difficult future path ahead, with every issue devolving into a belligerent battle that will drive up litigation costs for both sides (and for their clients!). This path is also a terrible lost opportunity—without a cooperative, collaborative result to report to the judge, the parties will have surrendered an ability to exercise some measure of control over scheduling by having no agreed-upon discovery plan to present to the judge.

C. "Disclosures": Mandatory Discovery

Each of the mandatory disclosure requirements has a common objective—to ensure that the parties exchange certain categories of information that the Rules consider critical in cabining in the sprawl of discovery while still allowing the parties to prepare adequately for trial.

1. Initial Disclosures

The four categories of initial disclosures supply the litigants with a bit of a head start into discovery. They ensure the disclosure of core, preliminary source information that any adversary is likely to want to know as the discovery process begins. They are also to be early targets for discovery follow up. By reading through an adversary's initial disclosures, a party can quickly identify those witnesses and other evidence that the adversary is considering using to support its litigating positions. Taking the depositions of those listed witnesses, or serving focused written discovery to obtain those witnesses' documents and electronically stored information, may become an early strategic priority. Similarly, learning the itemized components of a claimant's damages expectation (and what evidence the claimant has to prove those items of damages) can help direct useful follow-up written discovery of the claimant as well as valuable discovery of others, including non-parties such as hospitals, physicians, employers, vendors, and the like. Lastly, acquiring an early appreciation of whether insurance money might be available to pay any resulting judgment may dramatically impact the lawyer's valuation of the case itself and the lawyer's view of acceptable settlement ranges.

One nuance, related to the second initial disclosure obligation (evidence that the disclosing party "may use"), offers an often unhighlighted practical benefit to disclosing parties. They can satisfy their initial disclosures obligation by identifying such evidence "by category and location." Doing so permits the disclosing party to divulge the existence of materials that are encompassed in the "may use" definition without having to list them item by item. This allows more time for gathering, organizing, and reviewing those materials. Almost certainly, the materials will be requested later in the discovery process (as we will discuss in the Discovery Tools chapter), but at least the task of assembling them will be a bit less frenetic.

Hypothetical

Q: Natalie's attorney, on reviewing Creaky Theater's initial disclosures, will not learn about the roofing bill's cautionary handwritten note to have the "weaknesses" in the Theater's roof "checked" to avoid the roof "falling in on your moviegoers." The attorney will also not know the identity of the roofer who made those ominous observations. That information, however, could prove very useful to Natalie, and even potentially prove dispositive on the question of Creaky Theater's breach of a duty owed to her. Yet, neither of those pieces of information will be divulged in initial disclosures. Isn't that the very sort of unshared information that the broad American discovery rules were drafted to avoid?

A: Initial disclosures are the beginning, not the end, of pretrial information exchanges. They identify witnesses and evidence that may be used *offensively* against an adversary, and this offers a very helpful beginning to discovery. But *unfavorable* witnesses and evidence known by a party are not immune from later discovery. They just need to be pursued through other discovery devices. While initial disclosures will not reveal the roofer's note or the roofer's name, an interrogatory ("Have you, over the course of the past three years, ever had the roof of the Theater inspected for any purpose?") or a request for production ("Produce any documents in your possession, custody, or control that discuss the condition of the Theater's roof or contain any recommendation relating to the Theater's roof.") will hit the target. *See Gomas v. City of New York*, 2009 WL 962701, at *2 (E.D.N.Y. Apr. 8, 2009) ("[T]he issue before the Court is not whether the information in question was discoverable . . . had plaintiff made a timely demand for it; rather, the issue is whether defendants were obligated to disclose that information without such a demand. As previously discussed, they were not.").

No doubt, the parties will want to explore discovery beyond what they learn in the initial disclosures. But the initial disclosures will almost certainly guide the parties in deciding what more discovery to seek, in what form, and from whom. The initial disclosures can also help the parties in tailoring their requests to try to avoid costly, useless discovery dead-ends.

2. Expert Disclosures

Practical advice on expert disclosures and discovery will be discussed in the Disclosure of Experts chapter later in this book.

3. Pretrial Disclosures

These disclosures, made toward the end of the pretrial stage, ensure that every party is aware of the witnesses and other evidence the adversaries may use during the coming trial. They provide a final checklist, of sorts, to allow the parties to better anticipate how the trial will unfold. This is not to say there are never surprises at trial. There sometimes are. A known witness may offer unexpected information, an obscure reference in some document may be revealed to have an unexpected significance, or a blistering cross-examination could present an unexpected vulnerability. These sorts of surprises, however, are usually explained by a party's inadequate case preparation. What pretrial disclosures are intended to avoid are surprises over who will testify and what evidence will be offered. After the pretrial disclosures are exchanged, that mystery should be largely gone.

Hypotheticals: Mastering the Nuances

Incomplete Knowledge: In her lawsuit with Creaky Theater, Natalie learns that the defendant intends to argue that Natalie had chosen to sit in a portion of the Theater that was cordoned off with a bright yellow sign reading "Section Closed." The falling roof section landed only in this cordoned-off area of the Theater. Natalie believes she sat in this cordoned-off area for a reason, but does not remember the details (was it because the Theater sold her seats, and none but the cordoned-off ones were available?). She has been trying to locate friends who attended the movie with her that night, but cannot reach them to check their recollections. How can Natalie and her attorney make proper and safe initial disclosures of her "may use" witnesses?

Well, They Did It First: Natalie's initial disclosure worries may be gone. Creaky Theater just served Natalie's attorney with a set of initial disclosures that read, "Our list of disclosable witnesses and evidence will be served at a later time, once we have completed our investigation of this claim." Does Creaky Theater's initial disclosures help Natalie's inability to fully complete her own initial disclosures?

Hiding Witnesses and Evidence: Rule 11 does not apply to discovery. *See* Rule 11(d). But a special, Rule 11-like ethical obligation does apply, imposing similar sorts of duties on litigants during discovery. *See* Rule 26(g). A misbehaving party can be sanctioned for violating those ethical mandates. But what if a party is willing to take those risks for some tactical reason? Does anything prevent a party, after weighing the risks of sanctions, from deliberately choosing not to identify a crucial witness or document in initial disclosures or pretrial disclosures, with the goal of springing that witness or document on the adversary as a surprise at trial? The risk of after-the-fact sanctions may not be enough of a deterrence against this sort of mischief. Does anything restrain that type of misbehavior?

The Recalcitrant, Pouting Adversary: Why should attorneys endeavor to cooperate at all with each other in their discovery planning meeting or in crafting their discovery plan? Because the other side are true adversaries in the lawsuit, won't any cooperation require compromise? Isn't that a type of strategic surrender? Why would an attorney ever want to compromise in discovery this early, and without knowing more of how the other side intends to behave during the discovery process?

PRACTICE SAMPLES

Sample 2-1: DISCOVERY PLAN

IN THE UNITED STATES DISTRICT COURT
DISTRICT OF WEST CAROLINA

Pat and Vickie Traggler, *individually and on behalf of* *Max Traggler, a minor,*))))) Plaintiffs,)) v.))) USafe Swim Co.,)) Defendant.)	Civil Action No. 00-CV-98765

Written Report of Parties' Rule 26(f) Conference and Discovery Plan

The parties to this lawsuit, through their counsel signing below, convened a video conference to confer and develop their discovery plan. This written report outlines the results of the conference and the parties' discovery plan.

1. **Nature and Basis of the Claims and Defenses:**

   (A) The Plaintiffs (the "Tragglers") are the parents of a minor child who suffered serious and permanently disabling personal injuries as a result of falling into an above-ground swimming pool designed, manufactured, and distributed by USafe Swim Co. ("USafe"). The Tragglers claim that USafe's design, manufacture, and supplied warnings were defective, unreasonably dangerous, and negligent. The Tragglers claim damages individually and on behalf of their minor child.

   (B) USafe designs, manufactures, and distributes above-ground swimming pools. USafe denies that any of its pools are defective, unreasonably dangerous, or negligent, and that if the minor child sustained any injuries in or by one of its swimming pools, causes other than the pool's design, manufacture, or distribution were responsible.

2. Possibility for Prompt Settlement or Resolution:

The parties have discussed settlement, but their valuations of the case at this time remain far apart. The parties intend to revisit this topic with one another after a period of discovery.

3. Initial Disclosures:

The parties agree that they will exchange their initial disclosures within 7 days of the submission of this written report.

4. Discovery Plan:

(A) <u>Changes to Rule 26(a) Disclosures</u>: The parties have agreed to no changes to the disclosure requirements set by Rule 26(a), beyond the exchange date listed above.

(B) <u>Subjects for Discovery</u>:

1) <u>The Tragglers</u>: The circumstances, history, and user experience of USafe's swimming pools, including their design, manufacture, warning, and distribution.

2) <u>USafe</u>: The identity, assembly, installation, and use of the swimming pool at issue, including all events on the day of, and before, the incident.

(C) <u>Discovery Cut-Off</u>: The parties propose a period of 9 months for discovery.

(D) <u>Discovery Phasing</u>: The parties propose that non-expert discovery begin promptly, and expert discovery begin 6 months thereafter. The parties have agreed to exchange all expert disclosures required by Rule 26(a)(2) no later than 45 days prior to the start of expert discovery.

(E) <u>Electronically Stored Information (ESI)</u>: The parties anticipate disagreement concerning the scope and breadth of the discovery of ESI, but pledge to attempt to resolve those issues before involving the court. Discussions in this regard have begun. At this time, the parties anticipate no issues concerning preservation of ESI. Both parties have issued "discovery hold" requests to those persons and entities those parties believe most likely to possess discoverable information.

(F) <u>Privilege and Protection</u>: In the event of the inadvertent disclosure of any information shielded by a privilege or work product protection, the parties have agreed:

1) to abide by the terms of the proposed Federal Rule of Evidence 502(d) order accompanying this written report as Exhibit A, which order they respectfully request the court now enter; and

2) to the following terms of a clawback procedure:

    i. If any disclosing party learns that it has inadvertently produced privileged or protected information, that party shall so notify all parties, in writing, as soon as practicable upon learning of the production, describing the inadvertently produced information, why it is subject to a privilege or protection, and the circumstances of the inadvertence; and

    ii. Upon receiving such written notice, all receiving parties shall return, destroy, or sequester the identified inadvertently produced information, and, if distributed to others, reasonably undertake to retrieve it; and

    iii. Certify, in writing, to disclosing counsel within 5 days of receipt of such written notice that all such information has been returned, destroyed, or sequestered; and

    iv. Within 5 days of its written certification, any receiving party may contest the claim of privilege or protection, and the parties agree to meet and confer, in good faith, in an attempt to resolve that contest; and

    v. If the contest is not resolved by the parties themselves, they may request a conference with the court (with any filings made under seal) to resolve the dispute; and

    vi. The disclosing party shall bear the burden of proving the claim of privilege or protection; and

    vii. The inadvertent disclosure shall not constitute a waiver or forfeiture of any privilege or protection that may be claimed for that information; and

    viii. In ruling on the contest, the circumstances of the inadvertent production shall themselves not be grounds for denying any claim of privilege or protection.

(G) Changes to Discovery Limits: The parties have agreed to the following changes to the discovery limits set by the Federal Rules of Civil Procedure:

1) Interrogatories: The number of permissible interrogatories shall be increased to 50 per side, including subparts; and

2) _Depositions:_ The number of permissible depositions shall be increased to 20 per side.

Respectfully submitted,

ETTORE & DONNELLY, LLC   BENJARVUS, GREEN-ELLIS, LLC

By: _____/s/_____   By: _____/s/_____
Attorney for Plaintiffs   _Attorney for Defendant_
Pat and Vickie Traggler   _USafe Swim Co._

Dated: August 1, 20____

[CERTIFICATE OF SERVICE]

EXHIBIT A
IN THE UNITED STATES DISTRICT COURT
DISTRICT OF WEST CAROLINA

Pat and Vickie Traggler,	)
individually and on behalf of	)
Max Traggler, a minor,	)
	)
Plaintiffs,	)
	)
v.	) Civil Action No. 00-CV-98765
	)
USafe Swim Co.,	)
	)
Defendant.	)

Stipulated Agreement and Order
Regarding Fed. R. Evid. 502

And now, this _____ day of _____, 20____, at the joint request of the parties to this lawsuit, whose stipulation is memorialized by the signatures of their counsel below, and after finding good cause to do so, it is hereby ORDERED:

1. Notwithstanding the provisions of Rule 502(b) of the Federal Rules of Evidence, the inadvertent disclosure of any document or information

by any party to this lawsuit shall not, for the purposes of this or any other proceedings, constitute a waiver or forfeiture by the disclosing party of any privilege or other protection that might otherwise attach to the disclosed document or information.

2. The terms of paragraph 1 shall apply regardless of whether the disclosing party undertook reasonable actions to either prevent or cure the inadvertent disclosure.

3. Any party receiving inadvertently produced documents or information shall return, destroy, or sequester such documents or information within 5 days of receiving notice from the disclosing party of the inadvertent disclosure, and shall make no use of, nor distribute to any other person or entity, such documents or information absent a court order or specific written stipulation by the parties otherwise.

4. A receiving party may contest a claim of privilege or protection over any inadvertently disclosed document or information by following the procedures the parties have established in written discovery plan to this Court, dated _____.

5. The Court shall retain jurisdiction over any dispute concerning the interpretation, effect, or implementation of this Order

So stipulated, this 1st day of August, 20_____:

ETTORE & DONNELLY, LLC   BENJARVUS, GREEN-ELLIS, LLC

By: ____/s/_____   By: ____/s/_____
Attorney for Plaintiffs   *Attorney for Defendant*
Pat and Vickie Traggler   *USafe Swim Co.*

BY THE COURT:

_____
J.

So ordered, this ____ day of _____, 20____

Sample 2-2: INITIAL DISCLOSURES

IN THE UNITED STATES DISTRICT COURT
DISTRICT OF WEST CAROLINA

Pat and Vickie Traggler,	)	
individually and on behalf of	)	
Max Traggler, a minor,	)	
	)	
Plaintiffs,	)	
	)	
v.	)	Civil Action No. 00-CV-98765
	)	
USafe Swim Co.,	)	
	)	
Defendant.	)	

Initial Disclosures by
Defendant USafe Swim Co.

In accordance with Rule 26(a)(1) of the Federal Rules of Civil Procedure, Defendant USafe Swim Co. ("USafe") makes the following initial disclosures for purposes of this litigation:

1. **Individuals with Discoverable Information That USafe May Use to Support Its Claims or Defenses, Unless the Use Would Be Solely for Impeachment:**

    a. Dr. Amanda Nilsson, USafe Swim Co, 123 Main Street, Anytown, 98765—(491) 555-1212—directed development of above-ground pool line; *Subjects of Information:* history, circumstances, and logistics of the development of above-ground pool line.

    b. Karl Walker, USafe Swim Co., 123 Main Street, Anytown, 98765—(491) 555-1212—design director for Pool Model AEF-137; *Subjects of Information:* design objectives and strategy of AEF-137; design development; design implementation.

    c. Carmen Flores, USafe Swim Co., 123 Main Street, Anytown, 98765—(491) 555-1212—director of customer relations for above-ground pool line; *Subjects of Information:* customer outreach for above-ground pool line; customer solicitation and marketing for that pool line; customer comment policy, procedures, and data on above-ground pool line.

d. Matt Ward, USafe Swim Co., 123 Main Street, Anytown, 98765—(491) 555-1212—regulatory affairs manager for above-ground pool line; *Subjects of Information:* policies and procedures for ensuring that above-ground pool line met or exceeded applicable regulatory standards.

e. Vincent Sullivan, USafe Swim Co., 123 Main Street, Anytown, 98765—(491) 555-1212—director of manufacturing plant for above-ground pools; *Subjects of Information:* policies and procedures for manufacturing above-ground pools, including factory rules and operations, quality-assurance, packaging, and preparation for delivery.

f. Officer Betty Vasquez, West Carolina State Police Barracks, 388 Walnut Lane, Anytown, 98765—(491) 345-9999—chief investigator of minor's accident; *Subjects of Information:* history, procedures, and results of investigation.

2. **Documents, Electronically Stored Information, and Tangible Things in USafe's Possession, Custody, or Control That USafe May Use to Support Its Claims or Defenses, Unless the Use Would Be Solely for Impeachment:**

a. Design file for Pool Model No. AEF-137 (retained at USafe Swim Co. headquarters, 123 Main Street, Anytown, 98765)

b. Manufacturing file for Pool Model No. AEF-137 (retained at USafe Swim Co. headquarters, 123 Main Street, Anytown, 98765)

c. Customer comment file for Pool Model No. AEF-137 (retained at USafe Swim Co. headquarters, 123 Main Street, Anytown, 98765)

d. Regulatory approvals for Pool Model No. AEF-137 (retained at USafe Swim Co. headquarters, 123 Main Street, Anytown, 98765)

e. Investigative Summary prepared by Officer Betty Vasquez (retained at USafe Swim Co. headquarters, 123 Main Street, Anytown, 98765)

3. **Computation of Damages Claimed by USafe, Along with Access to Unprivileged/Unprotected Documents or Other Evidentiary Material on Which Computation Is Based:**

a. At this time, USafe is making no claim for damages against the Tragglers.

4. **Access to Any Insurance Agreement Under Which an Insurance Business May Be Liable to Satisfy All or Part of a Possible Judgment in the Action:**

a. Always Safe Professional Insurance Company, General Liability Coverage Policy No. 567-TB-44910P-G20198X3. A copy of the policy is attached to these initial disclosures.

Dated: August 6, 20_____

BENJARVUS, GREEN-ELLIS, LLC

By: _____/s/_____
Attorney for Defendant
USafe Swim Co.

[CERTIFICATE OF SERVICE]

Sample 2-3: PRETRIAL DISCLOSURES

IN THE UNITED STATES DISTRICT COURT
DISTRICT OF WEST CAROLINA

Pat and Vickie Traggler,	)	
individually and on behalf of	)	
Max Traggler, a minor,	)	
	)	
Plaintiffs,	)	
	)	
v.	)	Civil Action No. 00-CV-98765
	)	
USafe Swim Co.,	)	
	)	
Defendant.	)	

Pretrial Disclosures by
Plaintiffs Pat and Vickie Traggler

In accordance with Rule 26(a)(3) of the Federal Rules of Civil Procedure, Plaintiffs Pat and Vickie Traggler (the "Tragglers"), individually and on behalf of Max Traggler, a minor, make the following pretrial disclosures for purpose of this litigation:

1. Witnesses Whom the Tragglers Expect to Present:

a. Pat Traggler

b. Vickie Traggler

c. Donovan Traggler

d. Patrick J. Traggler, Sr.

e. Constance Traggler

f. Phillip J. Clanterman, M.D.

g. Rochelle A. Whitberg, M.D.

h. Jayson Kleig, R.N.

i. Paramedic Nancy Heil

j. Paramedic Noelle Herschneider

k. Office Betty Vasquez

l. Patrolman Kenny Cartmenter

m. Patrolwoman Shondra Williams

n. Lawrence V. Quickley, Ph.D., M.B.A.

o. Dr. Amanda Nilsson

2. **Witnesses Whom the Tragglers May Call If the Need Arises:**

a. Karl Walker

b. Carmen Flores

c. Matt Ward

d. Vincent Sullivan

e. Rolf Svetberg, M.D.

f. Orville Huntington, R.N.

g. Officer John McGuire

h. Custodians of records, if needed to authenticate any documents

i. Impeachment and/or rebuttal witnesses, as needed as the testimony develops

3. **Designation of Witnesses the Tragglers Expect to Present by Deposition**

a. Phillip J. Clanterman, M.D.—who will appear by videotape deposition (the Tragglers intend to play Dr. Clanterman's entire video deposition as recorded during the evening of November 8, 2020)

b. The Tragglers reserve the right to supplement this designation list should a witness, from whom live testimony is anticipated, becomes unexpectedly unavailable.

4. Documents and Other Exhibits that the Tragglers Expect to Present:

    a. Exhibit Nos. 1–392, as listed in the inventory attached here as Exhibit A

5. Documents and Other Exhibits That the Tragglers May Offer if the Need Arises:

    a. Exhibit Nos. 393–601, as listed in the inventory attached here as Exhibit B

Dated: July 3, 20____

ETTORE & DONNELLY, LLC

By: _____ /s/ _____
Attorney for Plaintiffs
Pat and Vickie Traggler

[CERTIFICATE OF SERVICE]

III

Scope of Discovery
Rule 26

GETTING THE VIEW

As the chapters to follow will show, the Rules establish a series of incredibly power-ful discovery tools to facilitate the development of the facts and the evidence that will be used to support or oppose those facts. In those chapters, you will learn that a party can, for example, command another party to scour all of its files in search of documents, electronically stored information, and tangible things relevant to the dispute, and to produce the documents—even the damaging, "smoking gun" ones. Or to appear in a conference room and be orally interrogated for hours under oath about the strengths and weaknesses of the party's claims or defenses. Or to admit facts that, while true, may also be genuinely devastating to that party's legal position. Or even to submit to a physical or mental examination by a doctor selected by an opposing party.

Of course, this unmistakable discovery power is susceptible to great mischief and misuse, not just to constructive application. A lawyer might try to pry into an oppo-nent's tax history or marital infidelity, not because those matters are related in any way to a claim or defense in the case but rather to create unfair settlement leverage by embarrassing, humiliating, annoying, or otherwise burdening the opponent. Similarly, but less blatantly, a lawyer may conduct extensive discovery that may mar-ginally qualify as relevant to the claims in the case but with the true, primary pur-pose of driving up an opponent's costs and frustration, again to try to coerce a more favorable settlement.

Even when the parties' motives are pure, the adversarial nature of the U.S. civil litigation system leads to disparate objectives. Fundamentally, the parties have the same litigating goals, which are, at the same time, identical to and polar-opposite from those of their adversaries. When *seeking* discovery, each party will want broad, all-encompassing discovery that endeavors to leave no stone unturned in the search of helpful evidence (and "smoking guns"). When *responding* to discovery, each party will want narrow, tightly constrained discovery that imposes the least burden, cost, and disruption.

Rule 26 of the Federal Rules of Civil Procedure provides the mechanisms for striking the critical balance between these competing concerns. The Rule sets the broad scope of discovery fundamental to a just result but then imposes limits and procedures designed to curb excess and abuse. In this way, Rule 26 establishes the overarching ground rules that govern all of the individual discovery activities permitted in civil discovery (and discussed in the chapters that follow). Maybe the most important provision in Rule 26 is Rule 26(b)(1), which defines the general scope of discovery as "any *nonprivileged* matter that is *relevant to any party's claim or defense* and *proportional to the needs of the case*" Fed. R. Civ. P. 26(b)(1) (emphasis added).

Consider all the concepts that are packed into that short phrase. First, the Rule confirms that privileged matters—like attorney-client communications—are exempt from discovery. Second, it deems as discoverable any matter relevant to a claim or defense already in the case (and, correspondingly, deems as non-discoverable any matter not so relevant). Finally, it requires a balancing of the benefits and burdens of discovery to ensure that the sweep of discovery is "proportional." Let's examine each of those three "scope" concepts in turn.

HOW THIS DISCOVERY CONCEPT WORKS

A. "Relevance"

Discovery has long been described in federal court as "broad" or "liberal," and the basis for that perception is the definition of the scope of discovery we just unpacked from Rule 26(b)(1). Although the Rules impose some limitations and protections on discovery as discussed below, the breadth of discovery in federal court derives from the second phrase in that definition—"relevant to any party's claim or defense."

The Rules do not define "relevant." While the term is used extensively in the evidence realm, the courts have provided a separate (though similar) definition of "relevant" for discovery purposes. The Supreme Court described "relevant" as broadly encompassing "any matter that bears on, or that reasonably could lead to other matter that could bear on" a claim or defense in the case. *Oppenheimer Fund, Inc. v. Sanders*, 437 U.S. 340, 351 (1978). Other sources define "relevant" to mean "germane," *West Penn Power Co. v. NLRB*, 394 F.3d 233, 242 (4th Cir. 2005), or as requiring merely a "rudimentary showing" of "a cogent nexus between a claim or defense and the piece of information sought," Christopher C. Frost, Note, *The Sound and the Fury or the Sound of Silence?: Evaluating the Pre-Amendment Predictions and Post-Amendment Effects of the Discovery Scope-Narrowing Language in the 2000 Amendments to Federal Rule of Civil Procedure 26(b)(1)*, 37 Ga. L. Rev. 1039, 1067 (2003) (quoted approvingly in *United Oil Co. v. Parts Assocs.*, 227 F.R.D. 404, 409 (D. Md. 2005)).

A logical related question is, "relevant to what?" Rule 26 used to extend discovery to any matter relevant to the "subject matter" of the action but was amended in 2000 to narrow the scope to matters relevant to "any party's claim or defense." Thus, discovery is tied to the matters set forth in the pleadings—a plaintiff may not conduct discovery designed to develop a new claim, even if the new claim is closely related to the claims already pleaded in the complaint, nor may a defendant conduct discovery to support a defense not asserted in the answer. How this "relevance" standard applies is often one of the major contests in discovery "scope" fights.

INLINE PACKAGING, LLC.

v.

GRAPHIC PACKAGING INT'L, INC.

2016 WL 7042117 (D. Minn. July 25, 2016)

BRISBOIS, United States Magistrate Judge

[Inline Packaging, LLC and Graphic Packaging International, Inc. were both in the business of making microwave packaging that browns and crisps food in a microwave. Graphic is the "big player" in the market, with annual revenues of over $3 billion, and Inline brought this action alleging that Graphic was engaging in anticompetitive conduct in violation of federal law. During discovery, Graphic objected to certain discovery as not relevant, and Inline filed a motion seeking to compel Graphic to provide substantive responses.]

B. Analysis

The threshold inquiry with regard to discovery issues is whether the moving party seeks *discoverable* material. *Prokosch v. Catalina Lighting, Inc.*, 193 F.R.D. 633, 635 (D. Minn. 2000). Pursuant to Federal Rule of Civil Procedure 26(b)(1), the scope of discoverable material is limited to that which is relevant to the parties' claims or defenses.... [T]here are two aspects of relevance on which the parties disagree that, alone or together, apply to twenty-one of the twenty-five discovery requests that remain at issue, namely the subject matter scope of relevance and the temporal scope of relevance in the present case. Accordingly, the Court will first address the disputed aspects of the scope of relevance in the present case.

1. *Subject Matter Scope of Relevance*

* * * In the present case, the gravamen of the parties' dispute concerning the subject matter scope of relevance is whether Inline is entitled to discovery concerning products, patents, entities, and instances of conduct for which Inline has not already provided specific allegations in its Complaint indicating that the product, patent, entity, or instance of conduct is related to Inline's alleged claims. Inline takes the position that it is not required to identify specific products, patents, entities, or instances of conduct without the benefit of taking discovery because it needs discovery to determine which products, patents, entities, and instances of conduct relate to its claims.

Historically, courts were reluctant to impose strict pleading requirements on antitrust plaintiffs and favored broad discovery in antitrust cases. See, *e.g.*, *Jack Loeks Enterprises, Inc. v. W.S. Butterfield Theatres, Inc.*, 13 F.R.D. 5, 8 (E.D. Mich. 1952) ("It is not necessary in an antitrust action to set out in detail the acts complained of nor the circumstances from which plaintiff draws his conclusion that violations of acts of Congress have occurred and that plaintiff had been damaged."). * * * In recent years, however, the requirements for pleading have been raised. In 2007, the United States Supreme Court issued its opinion in *Bell Atl. Corp. v. Twombly*, 550 U.S. 544 (2007), which itself involved allegations of antitrust conspiracy that, under the previous pleading standards, would not have required the pleading of specific factual allegations. . . . Citing a need to cabin the trend towards expensive and burdensome antitrust discovery, the Supreme Court in *Twombly* rejected previous caselaw, which it characterized as allowing wholly conclusory statements of claims to survive motions to dismiss if there was a possibility that a plaintiff could later prove some set of as yet undisclosed facts to support their claim. *Twombly*, 550 U.S. at 558–63. In abrogating the previous pleading standard, the *Twombly* court held that a plaintiff would be required to allege sufficient specific facts in its complaint to raise its claim beyond a speculative level. *Id.* at 555. * * *

While *Twombly* itself involved only the requirements for pleading necessary to survive a Rule 12(b)(6) motion to dismiss, in the wake of *Twombly* courts have limited the subject matter scope of discovery to evidence concerning only specific products and entities that a plaintiff identifies in its complaint. See, *e.g., In re Skelaxin (Metaxalone) Antitrust Litig.*, 292 F.R.D.

544, 551, 555 (E.D. Tenn. 2013) (denying motion to compel discovery to the extent the motion sought evidence concerning products other than those specifically identified in the complaint and to the extent that the motion sought evidence of other antitrust suits involving the defendants that were not mentioned in the complaint) . . . .

In addition, the recent amendments to Federal Rule of Civil Procedure 26(b)(1) clarify that the scope of discovery is limited to evidence that is relevant to claims or defenses already existing in the case.

Based on all of the foregoing, the Court concludes that the subject matter scope of discovery in the present case is limited to the patents, products, entities, and instances of anti-competitive conduct specifically alleged in support of the claims or defenses identified in the pleadings.

2. *Temporal Scope of Relevance*

* * * In its memorandum in support of the motion to compel, Inline argues that discovery back to January 1, 2000, is relevant to its claim under section 2 of the Sherman Act, that Graphic used anti-competitive conduct to achieve or maintain a monopoly position in the microwave susceptor food packaging product market, and is also relevant to the issue of damages.

As a general principle, courts tend to allow discovery for a reasonable temporal period antedating the filing of a complaint and the beginning of the pertinent statute of limitations. *See, e.g., Bell v. Lockheed Martin Corp.,* 270 F.R.D. 186, 193 (D.N.J. 2010), *aff'd,* No. CIV. 08–6292, 2010 WL 3724271 (D.N.J. Sept. 15, 2010); *Paul v. Winco Holdings, Inc.,* 249 F.R.D. 643, 649 (D. Idaho 2008).

With regard to monopolization claims under section 2 of the Sherman Act, the caselaw indicates that what constitutes "a reasonable temporal period" of discovery is generally significantly greater than in cases involving other types of claims. See, *e.g., Baush Mach. Tool Co. v. Aluminum Co. of Am.,* 72 F.2d 236, 239 (2d Cir. 1934) (holding that district court erred by excluding information of the defendant's anticompetitive conduct "even though the transactions occurred long before the injury complained of"). The Court's review of the caselaw indicates that courts have been more inclined to establish the temporal scope of discovery as beginning significantly earlier than the filing of the complaint or the extent of the statute of limitations period where there are specific factual allegations or other specific indications in the record indicating that the anti-competitive conduct occurred further in the past. *See, e.g., Pappas v. Loew's, Inc.,* 13 F.R.D. 471, 472 (M.D. Pa. 1953) (allowing discovery for eighteen-year period preceding the filing of antitrust monopoly claim, which coincided with a defendant's admission that it had contracts with others that were the basis of the anticompetitive conspiracy charge during that time period). However, the fact that a plaintiff has not made specific allegations indicating that anti-competitive conduct was occurring at a point in time beyond the statute of limitations period has not prevented courts from establishing the temporal scope of discovery as extending for a reasonable beyond the statute of limitations. *See, e.g., Hillside Amusement Co. v. Warner Bros. Pictures,* 7 F.R.D. 260, 261 (S.D.N.Y. 1944) (allowing discovery back to 1919 even though there were no specific allegations indicating the date on which the anti-competitive conduct commenced, where the court found it apparent that "many years are embraced within [the complaint's] narrative").

In the present case, the specific instances of anti-competitive conduct identified in the Complaint are alleged to have occurred in 2013 and 2014. Nevertheless, as in *Hillside Amusement,* it is apparent to the Court that Inline's specific allegations indicating that Graphic currently possesses a monopoly in the microwave susceptor food packaging market embrace within their narrative many years. In addition, Inline has specifically alleged that it has been injured by Graphic's alleged anti-competitive conduct. Accordingly, the Court concludes that the temporal scope of relevance includes within it the time period in which Inline has participated in the microwave susceptor food packing market and has allegedly been damaged by Graphic's anti-competitive conduct. However, as Inline has not specifically alleged that Graphic's alleged anti-competitive conduct commenced prior to Inline's entry into the market and because Inline has not identified any other specific market participant who was allegedly harmed by Graphic's alleged anti-competitive conduct, the Court concludes that Inline has failed to establish the relevance of any information pertaining to Graphic's conduct that occurred before Inline entered the microwave susceptor market in 2002.

Based on all of the foregoing, the Court concludes that the temporal scope of relevance in the present case is defined by the period beginning on January 1, 2002, to the present.

In *Inline Packaging,* the court addressed two of the common arguments in discovery scope disputes. First, Inline sought to conduct discovery pertaining to some of Graphic's products that Inline had not identified in the complaint. Even though the same antitrust principles would likely have applied to both the products that Inline named in the complaint and the other products that were the subject of Inline's discovery and motion, the court decided not to compel Graphic to respond to the discovery on the grounds that it was not relevant to a claim in the case.

Second, Inline sought all responsive information dating back to the year 2000. Because Inline did not even enter the market until 2002, however, the court concluded that any potentially anticompetitive conduct before 2002 could not have harmed Inline and excluded such information from discovery. Setting time constraints on discovery is a frequent topic of dispute between parties, and courts are often called on to exercise their discretion and set a good compromise timeframe.

1. Admissibility vs. Discoverability

"Discoverability" and "admissibility" are two different legal attributes that should never be confused with one another. "Discoverability" refers to a party's ability, during the pretrial stages of a litigation, to *see and examine* information held by an opponent or third-party. Rule 26(b) addresses when information is "discoverable." Conversely, "admissibility" refers to a party's ability to later *use* information at trial. The Federal Rules of Evidence principally address that latter question. Whether information will ultimately prove to be admissible at trial is a determination that is often impossible (and always impractical) to make during the discovery stage.

It is quite possible that information might be "discoverable" but not "admissible." Consider, for example, hearsay evidence. During discovery, a personal injury plaintiff may be obligated to divulge what a nurse told him that a doctor had said a fellow doctor had advised. The hearsay rules are likely to prevent that plaintiff from telling the jury at trial the same information. But allowing the *discoverability* of this information is still very important. Once that information is learned during discovery, the parties can then choose to seek discovery from the nurse, the first doctor, and/or the second doctor to learn, first-hand, what was said. Later, at trial, a party could call the second doctor to the witness stand where, under oath, her testimony regarding her advice would no longer be hearsay. In this way, broad discoverability helps to unearth sources of important new information that might otherwise never be found. Rule 26 codifies this point unambiguously: "Information within this scope of discovery need not be admissible in evidence to be discoverable." *See* Rule 26(b)(1). Accordingly, a party from whom discovery is sought cannot resist that discovery unilaterally on the grounds that the information is unlikely to be admissible later at trial.

If the documents or information will not be admissible at trial, you may be asking yourself, why do opposing parties want it? After all, if the evidence is inadmissible, won't the requesting party be unable to use it? There are several reasons.

First, admissibility can be difficult to assess outside the full context of the trial. Whether an out-of-court statement is hearsay, for example, depends on a whole host of considerations, such as the purpose for which the statement is offered and whether the statement qualifies for any of the exceptions to the hearsay rule.[1] Allowing the

---

1. If you haven't taken an evidence course yet, think of hearsay as an out-of-court statement offered to prove the truth of the matter asserted. For example, suppose a party wanted to testify that, while attending a movie, the party heard someone stand up and shout, "The theater is on fire." If the party was trying to prove that the theater was, in fact, on fire at that time, the statement might be hearsay. Conversely, if the party is trying to explain why the party fled the theater, the statement might not be

responding party to make a unilateral decision that the requesting party would offer the evidence in a manner that would render it inadmissible hearsay and to withhold it on that basis would create problems. First, the responding party might honestly, but incorrectly, assess the admissibility issue. Second, attorneys might be tempted to deem problematic evidence to be inadmissible simply to justify withholding it.

Second, inadmissible evidence can lead to admissible evidence. Sticking with our hearsay example, inadmissible hearsay statements can often be converted into proper, admissible testimony by calling the person making the statement to the witness stand and having the person repeat the statement. Thus, a party must provide documents and information within the scope of discovery and responsive to a discovery request, without regard to the party's assessment of ultimate admissibility.

Hypothetical

Q: Suppose Nailed-It, the manufacturer of an electric nail gun, is sued by DIY Danny, a customer who, while trying to nail two small pieces of wood together, instead nailed his fingers together. Nailed-It realizes that a guard would prevent similar injuries in the future, and immediately begins manufacturing the nail gun with the guard. During discovery, DIY Danny requests copies of all design modifications to the nail gun's design over the past ten years. Nailed-It's counsel is familiar with Rule 407 of the Federal Rules of Evidence, which provides that, when a party improves its product's design after an accident (behavior the law calls "subsequent remedial measures"), evidence of those improvements is not admissible to prove negligence, culpable conduct, a defect in the product or its design, or a need for warnings or instructions. The purpose of this evidentiary exclusion is to promote parties taking these protective measures—society does not want companies to forgo remedial measures out of fear that those measures will then be used against the party. Must Nailed-It produce documents related to the new guard if it receives a document request properly seeking such documents?

A: Rule 407 speaks to the ***admissibility*** of evidence, not its ***discoverability***. While evidence of Nailed-It's decision to add a guard to its nail guns may be inadmissible, it is discoverable. *See Parshall v. Menard, Inc.*, 2017 WL 980501, *3 (E.D. Mo. Mar. 14, 2017). Similarly, Rule 408 of the Federal Rules of Evidence shields certain settlement communications from admission into evidence but does not

---

hearsay—the statement in the second context is being offered to explain the recipient's conduct, which does not depend on whether the theater was or was not actually on fire. *See Anderson v. United States*, 417 U.S. 211, 219 (1974).

render them undiscoverable. *See ArcelorMittal Indiana Harbor LLC v. Amex Nooter, LLC*, 2016 WL 614144, *3–4 (N.D. Ind. Feb. 16, 2016).

2. Limitations on the Scope of Discovery in Rule 26(b)(1)

While the starting point for discovery is the broad scope of relevance, Rule 26 attempts to balance the competing concerns and burdens of discovery by imposing additional limitations on the process. Two of these limitations are found right in the definition of the scope of discovery in Rule 26(b)(1): the concepts of proportionality and privilege.

B. "Proportionality"

Rule 26(b)(1) declares that certain discovery is foreclosed—that is, outside the scope authorized by the Rules, *even* if relevant to a claim or defense in the case—if it is not "proportional to the needs of the case." Rule 26(b)(1) contains a list of factors for the court to consider in evaluating proportionality:

- the importance of the issues at stake in the action;
- the amount in controversy;
- the parties' relative access to relevant information;
- the parties' resources;
- the importance of the discovery in resolving the issues; and
- whether the burden or expense of the proposed discovery outweighs its likely benefit.

The proportionality limitation represents one of the efforts in the Rules to provide some balance between the needs of the parties for access to relevant information and the burdens that discovery imposes. Thus, if to answer an opponent's discovery request a party will have to spend $1 million in a copious search through its enormous volume of electronic records and the case involves a breach of contract claim seeking $500,000 in damages, the discovery may be disallowed as not proportional to the needs of the case (the amount in controversy is not determinative of proportionality—a civil rights case seeking nominal monetary damages but advancing important rights might warrant expensive discovery dwarfing the amount in controversy—but it is an important consideration). Remember, however, that parties must stake their positions regarding discovery before it occurs—which obviously creates quite a conundrum. Neither party is likely to know the percentage chance of finding a relevant document, or the importance of that as-yet-unfound document to the issues in the case. Neither party may know precisely the full cost of the search, although that component is easier to estimate. Thus, proportionality necessarily involves educated speculation.

As the court described in *Curtis v. Metro. Life Ins. Co.*, the party seeking to resist discovery on this basis has the initial burden of demonstrating that the discovery is not proportional, but the party seeking the discovery may have to respond with its own evidence in rebuttal.

CURTIS

v.

METRO. LIFE INS. CO.

2016 WL 687164 (N.D. Tex. Feb. 19, 2016)

HORAN, United States Magistrate Judge

Plaintiff Dewayne Curtis ("Plaintiff") has filed a Motion to Compel Discovery from Metropolitan Life Insurance Company (the "Motion to Compel"), seeking to compel the production of certain documents and interrogatory answers from Defendant Metropolitan Life Insurance Company ("Defendant" or "MetLife").

* * *

[U]nder Rules 26(b)(1) and 26(b)(2)(C)(iii), a court can—and must—limit proposed discovery that it determines is not proportional to the needs of the case, . . . and the court must do so even in the absence of a motion. *See Crosby v. La. Health Serv. & Indem. Co.*, 647 F.3d 258, 264 (5th Cir. 2011).

But a party seeking to resist discovery on these grounds still bears the burden of making a specific objection and showing that the discovery fails the proportionality calculation mandated by Rule 26(b) by coming forward with specific information to address – insofar as that information is available to it—the importance of the issues at stake in the action, the amount in controversy, the parties' relative access to relevant information, the parties' resources, the importance of the discovery in resolving the issues, and whether the burden or expense of the proposed discovery outweighs its likely benefit.

The party seeking discovery, to prevail on a motion to compel or resist a motion for protective order, may well need to make its own showing of many or all of the proportionality factors, including the importance of the issues at stake in the action, the amount in controversy, the parties' relative access to relevant information, the parties' resources, and the importance of the discovery in resolving the issues, in opposition to the resisting party's showing.

Note that the *Curtis* opinion states that the court has an independent obligation to evaluate proportionality even if the parties do not object to the discovery on that basis. A number of courts have recognized this duty.

The evaluation of the proportionality factors is not formulaic. Rather, the court has broad discretion to consider and weigh the factors under the totality of the circumstances. Some courts conduct the proportionality analysis in a holistic fashion. *See Small v. Amgen, Inc.*, 2016 WL 7228863, at *7 (M.D. Fla. Sept. 28, 2016) ("Specifically, the Court finds that requiring Defendants to produce all discovery sought irrespective of the underlying indication would potentially impose an undue and unacceptable burden on the Defendants. Moreover, the Court finds that the nature of the potential burden outweighs and eclipses the other proportionality factors."). Other courts apply each factor individually.

BOYINGTON
v.
PERCHERON FIELD SERVICES, LLC

2016 WL 6068813 (W.D. Pa. Oct. 14, 2016)

GIBSON, United States district judge

[Eric Boyington brought a Fair Labor Standards Act (FLSA) claim, contending that his employer, Percheron Field Services, improperly classified him and other co-workers as exempt employees. Boyington sought production of all email communications sent by or received from any of the plaintiffs from or through a Percheron email account. The plaintiffs contended that such emails would show the hours worked by the plaintiffs and the specific tasks they performed—issues relevant to their employment status. The court carefully considered each factor before ruling the discovery proportional.]

First, the issues at stake, namely Plaintiffs' wrongful-classification claims, are of importance to Plaintiffs, who—as Defendant concedes—were improperly classified and not properly paid overtime compensation. Second, the amount in controversy, although unknown at this time, is alleged to be "in excess of several million dollars", and there is no indication this estimate is inaccurate. This factor thus also weighs in favor of Plaintiffs. And, as Defendant concedes, Defendant has greater resources and relatively greater access to the underlying information. Thus, the third and fourth factor also tilt in favor of Plaintiffs.

The Court acknowledges Defendant's argument that "the [R]ule must not be used to 'justify unlimited discovery requests addressed to a wealthy party', and should instead be employed to 'prevent use of discovery to wage a war of attrition or as a device to coerce a party, whether financially weak or affluent.'" But there is no indication that Plaintiffs are seeking production of their emails as an improper litigation strategy. On the contrary, it appears that Plaintiffs are pursuing production of their emails as a legitimate avenue of discovery on the issue of damages. Defendant's argument against production of the Plaintiffs' emails focuses primarily on the fifth and sixth factors—the importance of the discovery in resolving the issues and whether the burden or expense of the proposed discovery outweighs its likely benefit. Defendant argues that the Plaintiffs' emails are of minimal relevance and that production would be exorbitantly expensive.

* * *

Notwithstanding Defendant's argument that the Plaintiffs' emails are only of slight relevance to resolving the damages issue, the Court finds that they would likely be sufficiently probative—and that the issue of damages is important enough—to satisfy Rule 26(b)(1)'s fifth factor. And the Court finds that Defendant's cost estimate satisfies Rule 26(b)(1)'s sixth and final factor.

With respect to Rule 26(b)(1)'s sixth factor, Defendant estimates that, using keyword searches to limit the review, reviewing the combined emails "would likely cost $735,000–$798,964 and take a team of 20 attorneys 12 weeks to complete." The Court recognizes this would be a significant expenditure. But given the Court's denial of Plaintiffs' request to compel production of the emails of Defendant's executives, project managers, and ROW supervisors—discussed below—the cost of review and production will be significantly less. . . . Thus, the Court finds both that the Plaintiffs' emails are relevant and that their production does not run afoul of Rule 26(b)(1)'s proportionality requirement.

Hypothetical

Q: In *DIY Danny v. Nailed-It*, DIY Danny sought all documents related to the original design and manufacture of the nail gun. Nailed-It has been manufacturing the nail gun since 1968 and some, but not all, of the current model's design features trace back to the original model. A search through Nailed-It's manufacturing facility uncovers a box of old computer tapes, with a label reading "design documents." Nailed-It sends a photograph of one of the tapes to a computer consultant, who responds that the tape was of a type used in the late 1960s through the late 1970s, and that reading the contents of the tapes today would necessitate a complex conversion process that would cost $48,000. Nailed-It objects that the discovery is not proportional to the needs of the case, and DIY Danny responds with a motion to compel Nailed-It to search the tapes and to provide accessible copies of any design document pertaining to the nail gun. How will the court likely analyze this issue, and how should the parties support their arguments?

A: Rule 26(b)(1) contains a list of the six factors that the court will likely consider in order to determine the proportionality of DIY Danny's production request. To support their positions, each party should submit evidence relating to these factors. Thus, for example, Nailed-It would submit a written estimate from the computer consultant about the costs to convert and read the tapes. It might also submit affidavits from employees about the likelihood of finding design documents for the nail gun on the tapes. Both parties might submit evidence and argument about the issues and amounts at stake in the litigation, other sources of design information, and the significance of the design documents to the litigation.

C. "Nonprivileged"

The definition of the scope of discovery also includes the term "nonprivileged." The Rule's intent, then, is to shield from discoverability material that is protected by a privilege. So, what is considered "privileged" for purposes of federal court litigation? The answer depends on the nature of the privilege claim (and a detailed exploration of the contours of each possible privilege is outside the scope of this book). Broadly understood, a privilege shields material from discovery (here) and, later, from use at trial. It exists when the law says it does. A privilege represents the law's considered conclusion that the value of the information to the lawsuit is outweighed by a different value that the law ranks higher and more important.

Consider, for example, the attorney-client privilege. A client may have confided in her attorney that she is deeply worried about her case, that the litigation is proving stressful and expensive, and that she is considering abandoning her lawsuit. The opposing party might love to know this information; it could impact settlement posture, litigation strategy, tactics, and discovery plans. But the law will shield this confidentially disclosed worry from discovery because the law specially values the opportunity for clients to speak with their attorneys frankly, privately, and without risk, a value the law safeguards and incentivizes through the attorney-client privilege. *See generally* 1 Paul R. Rice, Attorney-Client Privilege in the United States § 2:3 (2018–2019) ("The rationale is that, by protecting client communications designed to obtain legal advice or assistance, the client will be more candid and will disclose all relevant information to his attorney, even potentially damaging and embarrassing facts. Complete client disclosure helps to ensure quality legal advice and assistance, and makes it possible for the client to better understand his obligations and responsibilities under the law.") (footnotes omitted).

Federal law governs whether a federal privilege applies. *See* Fed. R. Evid. 501. For state law claims that are in federal court under, for example, the court's diversity or supplemental jurisdiction, the federal court applies the privilege law of the state whose substantive law applies. *See id.* Thus, if a federal court is adjudicating a tort claim as to which Pennsylvania law applies, the federal court will also apply Pennsylvania law regarding privileges. Conversely, for a claim in federal court under a federal statute, the federal court will apply federal common law regarding privileges.

Therefore, for any given case, it is necessary to consult the applicable body of law to determine if a privilege applies and, if so, what the elements of that privilege are. Because the most common and consistently applicable privilege is the attorney-client privilege, it is discussed in greater detail below. But the federal and state courts have recognized other privileges as well, including:

- the Fifth Amendment privilege against self-incrimination (which protects individuals from being forced to incriminate themselves);

- the national security privilege (which allows the government to resist disclosures that might endanger foreign policy objectives and especially citizens or soldiers);

- the clergy-penitent privilege (which applies to confessions made to religious authority figures);

- the marital testimonial privilege (which prevents disclosure of communications between spouses);

- the doctor-patient privilege (which shields certain communications between a doctor and patient);

- the critical self-examination privilege (where entities are assessing what went wrong following an incident or conducting a critical examination of potential problems in their processes); and

- the deliberative process privilege (which protects the internal deliberative process of governments and governmental agencies).

1. Attorney-Client Privilege

Although the precise contours of the attorney-client privilege vary from state to state, the following are typically recognized as elements of this privilege:

1. A communication

2. between an attorney and client

3. designed to facilitate legal representation and

4. made in confidence.

Each of these elements contains important limitations on the attorney-client privilege. The first two requirements—that the allegedly privileged material be in the form of a communication between a lawyer and client—reflect the underlying purpose of the privilege to promote candid and uninhibited communication between a lawyer and client. (Even here, differences exist among the states: some states follow the classical view of the privilege which protects, broadly, communications made by a client to an attorney for the purpose of seeking legal advice but, far more narrowly, communications by an attorney to a client only when the attorney's communications would divulge the content of the client's prior protected communications. *See generally* 1 Paul R. Rice, Attorney-Client Privilege in the United States § 5:2 (2018–2019).) Both clients and lawyers should feel free to use whatever words they prefer when discussing legal matters without fear that their words will be later used against them. Note, though, that it is only the words they choose for their communications that enjoy the privilege; the facts and evidence relating to the events that are the subject of the legal advice are not shielded, just the communications between attorney and client about the events.

But who is the "client" whose communications are protected? The answer is readily apparent when the client is an individual person, but not as obvious when the client is a company or other organization. A leading attorney-client privilege case in the federal courts is *Upjohn Co. v. United States*, 449 U.S. 383 (1981), in which the Supreme Court addressed who was considered the "client" for purposes of the second element when the client was a corporation (*i.e.*, a fictional entity that cannot communicate). In *Upjohn*, the Court deemed privileged communications between a company's lawyer and its employees, even if those employees were not executives who were part of the company's "control group" (so long as the other elements of the privilege are satisfied).

The third element—that the communication be designed to facilitate legal representation—can also be complex when the party is a corporation. "In-house" lawyers—those who are employees of the corporation, rather than working "outside" in a law firm—may be included in many internal meetings and committees, and their involvement in a communication will not, by itself, render the communication privileged. Thus, for example, creating a memorandum for business purposes, and then sending a copy to in-house counsel, does not cloak the memorandum with privilege. *See Phillips v. C.R. Bard, Inc.*, 290 F.R.D. 615, 643 (D. Nev. 2013) ("Here, it does not appear that these meeting minutes were sent to Ms. Edwards for the purpose of rendering legal advice. . . . [T]here is nothing in these meeting minutes that indicates the provision of legal advice. Rather, this appears, at best, to have been a ministerial task of forwarding notes that were taken of the meeting.").

Finally, the circumstances in which the attorney and client first make the communication and subsequently handle it affect its eligibility for the privilege. A discussion between a lawyer and client in the lawyer's office is more likely to be deemed privileged than one occurring in a crowded restaurant where the conversation is readily overheard by others. Similarly, a memorandum from an attorney that the client stores in a locked file cabinet is more likely to be deemed privileged than one that the client posts on the break room bulletin board. In short, if the parties to the communication do not act as if they intend for the communication to be confidential, the courts are unlikely to treat it as privileged.

2. Nonprivileged But Still Shielded: Trial Preparation Material

In addition to the privileges described above, certain other material that is related to litigation but not squarely encompassed within the attorney-client privilege may also be immunized from discovery. The United States Supreme Court formally recognized this separate category of protected information in 1947 in the landmark case *Hickman v. Taylor*.

HICKMAN v. TAYLOR

329 U.S. 495 (1947)

MURPHY, Associate Justice

[In February 1943, the tugboat "John M. Taylor" sank while helping another tug (the "Philadelphia") tow a car-float across a river. Five of the sunk tugboat's nine crew members drowned. Three days after the sinking, the sunk tugboat's owners and insurers hired attorney Samuel B. Fortenbaugh, Esq. to represent them in lawsuits anticipated from the families of the decedents.]

* * *

[Attorney] Fortenbaugh privately interviewed the survivors and took statements from them with an eye toward the anticipated litigation; the survivors signed these statements on March 29. Fortenbaugh also interviewed other persons believed to have some information relating to the accident and in some cases he made memoranda of what they told him. At the time when Fortenbaugh secured the statements of the survivors, representatives of two of the deceased crew members had been in communication with him. Ultimately claims were presented by representatives of all five of the deceased; four of the claims, however, were settled without litigation. The fifth claimant, petitioner herein, brought suit in a federal court . . ., naming as defendants the two tug owners, individually and as partners, and the railroad.

One year later, petitioner filed 39 interrogatories directed to the tug owners. The 38th interrogatory read:

State whether any statements of the members of the crews of the Tugs 'J. M. Taylor' and 'Philadelphia' or of any other vessel were

taken in connection with the towing of the car float and the sinking of the Tug 'John M. Taylor'. Attach hereto exact copies of all
such statements if in writing, and if oral, set forth in detail the
exact provisions of any such oral statements or reports.

Supplemental interrogatories asked whether any oral or written statements, records, reports or other memoranda had been made concerning any
matter relative to the towing operation, the sinking of the tug, the salvaging
and repair of the tug, and the death of the deceased. If the answer was in the
affirmative, the tug owners were then requested to set forth the nature of all
such records, reports, statements or other memoranda.

The tug owners, through Fortenbaugh, answered all of the interrogatories
except No. 38 and the supplemental ones just described. While admitting
that statements of the survivors had been taken, they declined to summarize
or set forth the contents. They did so on the ground that such requests called
'for privileged matter obtained in preparation for litigation' and constituted
'an attempt to obtain indirectly counsel's private files.' It was claimed that
answering these requests 'would involve practically turning over not only the
complete files, but also the telephone records and, almost, the thoughts of
counsel.'

In connection with the hearing on these objections, Fortenbaugh made a
written statement and gave an informal oral deposition explaining the circumstances under which he had taken the statements. But he was not expressly asked in the deposition to produce the statements. The District Court
. . . held that the requested matters were not privileged. . . . The court then
decreed that the tug owners and Fortenbaugh, as counsel and agent for the
tug owners, forthwith 'Answer Plaintiff's 38th interrogatory and supplemental interrogatories; produce all written statements of witnesses obtained by
Mr. Fortenbaugh, as counsel and agent for Defendants; state in substance any
fact concerning this case which Defendants learned through oral statements
made by witnesses to Mr. Fortenbaugh whether or not included in his private
memoranda and produce Mr. Fortenbaugh's memoranda containing statements of fact by witnesses or to submit these memoranda to the Court for
determination of those portions which should be revealed to Plaintiff.' Upon
their refusal, the court adjudged them in contempt and ordered them impris-
oned until they complied.

The Third Circuit Court of Appeals [reversed.] . . . It held that the information here sought was part of the 'work product of the lawyer' and hence
privileged from discovery under the Federal Rules of Civil Procedure. The
importance of the problem, which has engendered a great divergence of
views among district courts, led us to grant certiorari.

The pre-trial deposition-discovery mechanism established by Rules 26 to 37 is one of the most significant innovations of the Federal Rules of Civil Procedure. Under the prior federal practice, the pre-trial functions of notice-giving issue-formulation and fact-revelation were performed primarily and inadequately by the pleadings. Inquiry into the issues and the facts before trial was narrowly confined and was often cumbersome in method. The new rules, however, restrict the pleadings to the task of general notice-giving and invest the deposition-discovery process with a vital role in the preparation for trial. The various instruments of discovery now serve (1) as a device, along with the pre-trial hearing under Rule 16, to narrow and clarify the basic issues between the parties, and (2) as a device for ascertaining the facts, or information as to the existence or whereabouts of facts, relative to those issues. Thus civil trials in the federal courts no longer need be carried on in the dark. The way is now clear, consistent with recognized privileges, for the parties to obtain the fullest possible knowledge of the issues and facts before trial.

In urging that he has a right to inquire into the materials secured and prepared by Fortenbaugh, petitioner emphasizes that the deposition-discovery portions of the Federal Rules of Civil Procedure are designed to enable the parties to discover the true facts and to compel their disclosure wherever they may be found. It is said that inquiry may be made under these rules, epitomized by Rule 26, as to any relevant matter which is not privileged; and since the discovery provisions are to be applied as broadly and liberally as possible, the privilege limitation must be restricted to its narrowest bounds. On the premise that the attorney-client privilege is the one involved in this case, petitioner argues that it must be strictly confined to confidential communications made by a client to his attorney. And since the materials here in issue were secured by Fortenbaugh from third persons rather than from his clients, the tug owners, the conclusion is reached that these materials are proper subjects for discovery under Rule 26.

As additional support for this result, petitioner claims that to prohibit discovery under these circumstances would give a corporate defendant a tremendous advantage in a suit by an individual plaintiff. Thus in a suit by an injured employee against a railroad or in a suit by an insured person against an insurance company the corporate defendant could pull a dark veil of secrecy over all the pertinent facts it can collect after the claim arises merely on the assertion that such facts were gathered by its large staff of attorneys and claim agents. At the same time, the individual plaintiff, who often has direct knowledge of the matter in issue and has no counsel until some time after his claim arises could be compelled to disclose all the intimate details of his case. By endowing with immunity from disclosure all that a lawyer discovers in the course of his duties, it is said, the rights of individual litigants in such cases are drained of vitality and the lawsuit becomes more of a battle of deception than a search for truth.

* * *

We agree, of course, that the deposition-discovery rules are to be accorded a broad and liberal treatment. No longer can the time-honored cry of 'fishing expedition' serve to preclude a party from inquiring into the facts underlying his opponent's case. Mutual knowledge of all the relevant facts gathered by both parties is essential to proper litigation. To that end, either party may compel the other to disgorge whatever facts he has in his possession. The deposition-discovery procedure simply advances the stage at which the disclosure can be compelled from the time of trial to the period preceding it, thus reducing the possibility of surprise. But discovery, like all matters of procedure, has ultimate and necessary boundaries.

* * *

We also agree that the memoranda, statements and mental impressions in issue in this case fall outside the scope of the attorney-client privilege and hence are not protected from discovery on that basis [because the communications were between an attorney and witnesses, not a client]. * * * But the impropriety of invoking that privilege does not provide an answer to the problem before us. Petitioner has made more than an ordinary request for relevant, non-privileged facts in the possession of his adversaries or their counsel. He has sought discovery as of right of oral and written statements of witnesses whose identity is well known and whose availability to petitioner appears unimpaired. He has sought production of these matters after making the most searching inquiries of his opponents as to the circumstances surrounding the fatal accident, which inquiries were sworn to have been answered to the best of their information and belief. Interrogatories were directed toward all the events prior to, during and subsequent to the sinking of the tug. Full and honest answers to such broad inquiries would necessarily have included all pertinent information gleaned by Fortenbaugh through his interviews with the witnesses. Petitioner makes no suggestion, and we cannot assume, that the tug owners or Fortenbaugh were incomplete or dishonest in the framing of their answers. In addition, petitioner was free to examine the public testimony of the witnesses taken before the United States Steamboat Inspectors. We are thus dealing with an attempt to secure the production of written statements and mental impressions contained in the files and the mind of the attorney Fortenbaugh without any showing of necessity or any indication or claim that denial of such production would unduly prejudice the preparation of petitioner's case or cause him any hardship or injustice. For aught that appears, the essence of what petitioner seeks either has been revealed to him already through the interrogatories or is readily available to him direct from the witnesses for the asking.

* * *

In our opinion, neither Rule 26 nor any other rule dealing with discovery contemplates production under such circumstances. That is not because the subject matter is privileged or irrelevant, as those concepts are used in these rules. Here is simply an attempt, without purported necessity or justification, to secure written statements, private memoranda and personal recollections prepared or formed by an adverse party's counsel in the course of his legal duties. As such, it falls outside the arena of discovery and contravenes the public policy underlying the orderly prosecution and defense of legal claims. Not even the most liberal of discovery theories can justify unwarranted inquiries into the files and the mental impressions of an attorney.

Historically, a lawyer is an officer of the court, and is bound to work for the advancement of justice while faithfully protecting the rightful interests of his clients. In performing his various duties, however, it is essential that a lawyer work with a certain degree of privacy, free from unnecessary intrusion by opposing parties and their counsel.

Proper preparation of a client's case demands that he assemble information, sift what he considers to be the relevant from the irrelevant facts, prepare his legal theories, and plan his strategy without undue and needless interference. That is the historical and the necessary way in which lawyers act within the framework of our system of jurisprudence to promote justice and to protect their clients' interests. This work is reflected, of course, in interviews, statements, memoranda, correspondence, briefs, mental impressions, personal beliefs, and countless other tangible and intangible ways—aptly though roughly termed by the Circuit Court of Appeals in this case as the "work product of the lawyer." Were such materials open to opposing counsel on mere demand, much of what is now put down in writing would remain unwritten. An attorney's thoughts, heretofore inviolate, would not be his own. Inefficiency, unfairness, and sharp practices would inevitably develop in the giving of legal advice and in the preparation of cases for trial. The effect on the legal profession would be demoralizing. And the interests of the clients and the cause of justice would be poorly served.

* * *

We do not mean to say that all written materials obtained or prepared by an adversary's counsel with an eye toward litigation are necessarily free from discovery in all cases. Where relevant and non-privileged facts remain hidden in an attorney's file and where production of those facts is essential to the preparation of one's case, discovery may properly be had. Such written statements and documents might, under certain circumstances, be admissible in evidence or give clues as to the existence or location of relevant facts. Or they might be useful for purposes of impeachment or corroboration. And production might be justified where the witnesses are no longer available or can be reached only with difficulty. Were production of written statements and documents to be precluded under such circumstances, the liberal ideals of the deposition-discovery portions of the Federal Rules of Civil Procedure would be stripped of much of their meaning. But the general policy against invading the privacy of an attorney's course of preparation is so well recognized and so essential to an orderly working of our system of legal procedure that a burden rests on the one who would invade that privacy to establish adequate reasons to justify production through a subpoena or court order. That burden, we believe, is necessarily implicit in the rules as now constituted.

* * *

Under ordinary conditions, forcing an attorney to repeat or write out all that witnesses have told him and to deliver the account to his adversary gives rise to grave dangers of inaccuracy and untrustworthiness. No legitimate purpose is served by such production. The practice forces the attorney to testify as to what he remembers or what he saw fit to write down regarding witnesses' remarks. Such testimony could not qualify as evidence; and to use it for impeachment or corroborative purposes would make the attorney much less an officer of the court and much more an ordinary witness. The standards of the profession would thereby suffer.

Denial of production of this nature does not mean that any material, non-privileged facts can be hidden from the petitioner in this case. He need not be unduly hindered in the preparation of his case, in the discovery of facts or in his anticipation of his opponents' position. Searching interrogatories directed to Fortenbaugh and the tug owners, production of written documents and statements upon a proper showing and direct interviews with the witnesses themselves all serve to reveal the facts in Fortenbaugh's possession to the fullest possible extent consistent with public policy. Petitioner's counsel frankly admits that he wants the oral statements only to help prepare himself to examine witnesses and to make sure that he has overlooked nothing. That is insufficient under the circumstances to permit him an exception to the policy underlying the privacy of Fortenbaugh's professional activities. If there should be a rare situation justifying production of these matters, petitioner's case is not of that type.

* * *

We therefore affirm the judgment of the Circuit Court of Appeals.

In 1970, the Federal Rules of Civil Procedure partially codified the common law work product doctrine that *Hickman v. Taylor* created with a new provision expressly protecting "trial preparation materials." The protection for trial preparation materials/work product exists for very pragmatic purposes. Like the attorney-client privilege, which is designed to foster open and full communication between client and lawyer, the trial preparation materials doctrine is designed to facilitate preparations for litigation. In the absence of the protection, parties and their lawyers would be reluctant to memorialize their work in any form that could later be discovered. To avoid creating discoverable documents, they might only communicate orally about the litigation. Preserving information about litigation matters in writing can be important, though, so the protections for trial preparation materials allows the parties and their lawyers to prepare for litigation efficiently and effectively without worrying that anything they memorialize will be handed over to the opposing party.

This protection for trial preparation materials (or "attorney work product") operates like a privilege, but technically is not a privilege (and thus rules like Fed. R. Evid. 501, which applies to privileges, do not apply). In contrast to the attorney-client privilege, the trial preparation materials doctrine applies equally and consistently to claims arising under federal law and claims arising under state law, and has the following elements:

1. A document or tangible thing

2. prepared in anticipation of litigation

3. by or for a party or its representative.

The critical element in most circumstances is the requirement that the trial preparation material have been prepared "in anticipation of litigation." Most courts apply the protection to materials prepared when litigation is expected but has not yet commenced, such as when a party has received a letter threatening litigation. Conversely, even if litigation is ongoing, a document will not be protected if it was prepared in the normal course of business. The focus is on the purpose of the document's preparation. *See In re Professionals Direct Ins. Co.*, 578 F.3d 432, 439 (6th Cir. 2009) (the party must demonstrate that litigation was the "driving force" behind the preparation of the document).

The protection for trial preparation materials is not absolute, however. Documents that otherwise qualify as trial preparation materials are discoverable (assuming they are relevant, not privileged, and proportional to the needs of the case) if the party seeking the documents shows that it has a "substantial need" for the documents and cannot, without "undue hardship," obtain their "substantial equivalent" by other means. *See* Fed. R. Civ. P. 26(b)(3)(A).

Q&A

Hypothetical

Q: In *DIY Danny v. Nailed-It*, one of DIY Danny's early thoughts after nailing his fingers together was dollar signs. DIY Danny immediately decided he would sue Nailed-It and asked his wife to take photographs of his hand and the positioning of the wood pieces for use in the litigation, and he dictated a memo describing precisely what happened. After his release from the emergency room, he contacted a lawyer and handed over both the photographs and his dictated memo. In discovery, Nailed-It requested all photographs of DIY Danny's injuries and any notes he had regarding the incident. DIY Danny's lawyer refused to produce the photographs and memo, asserting that they were protected either as privileged materials or as trial preparation materials. At DIY Danny's deposition, he testified that he no longer had the two pieces of wood he had been trying to nail together. He also testified that he couldn't remember some of the details of the incident. Nailed-It then moved to compel production of the photographs and memo, contending that it was entitled to them based on its substantial need and lack of ability to obtain their substantial equivalent. How will the court likely rule on Nailed-It's motion?

A: As a starting point, the attorney-client privilege is unlikely to apply to the photographs but could apply to the memo (the privilege protects only communications, not underlying facts, so the photographs and DIY Danny's recollections of what happened that day are freely discoverable, although his memo may qualify as a privileged communication provided DIY Danny prepared the memo for the purpose of sharing those thoughts with his attorney). Additionally, both the photographs and the memo will qualify as trial preparation materials, even though DIY Danny had not yet hired a lawyer. They are documents or tangible things prepared in anticipation of litigation by a party. However, this is the classic situation where a party might be able to obtain materials that otherwise qualify as trial preparation materials. Nailed-It can argue that understanding precisely what happened when DIY Danny nailed his fingers together is critical to its defense. Thus, it has a substantial need for the documents. DIY Danny's failure to save the pieces of wood and his seemingly fading memory about the details of the incident, however, deprive Nailed-It of any way to obtain substantially equivalent information. Thus, a court would likely order DIY Danny to produce the documents. *See Thai Le v. Diligence, Inc.*, 312 F.R.D. 245, 247–48 (D. Mass. 2015).

Remember the Court's description in *Hickman* of an attorney's thoughts as "inviolate." The trial preparation materials protection preserves that concept; Rule

26(b)(3)(A) provides that in the event that a court orders protection of trial preparation material based on the substantial need exception, the producing party may redact (delete) the attorney's mental impressions, which get "near absolute" protection. Thus, in the hypo above, if DIY Danny's attorney had made notes about strategy on the back of the photographs or on the memo (for example, notes as to how the attorney might use the photographs or memo during discovery, in settlement discussions, or at trial), those notes could be redacted before production.

3. Comparing Work Production Protection with Attorney-Client Privilege

Sometimes, a document can be *both* privileged under the attorney-client privilege and protected by the work product protection, as the above example illustrates. Thus, the two doctrines can, on occasion, overlap. It is important to remember, however, that there are important differences between the two. First, the attorney-client privilege can apply to oral or written communications, whereas the trial preparation material protection only applies to a "document or tangible thing" (although some courts will apply the related work product doctrine to protect an attorney's mental impressions even if not captured in a document—*see, e.g., Bear Republic Brewing Co. v. Central City Brewing Co.*, 275 F.R.D. 43, 45 (D. Mass. 2011)). Second, the attorney-client privilege only applies to communications with lawyers (or their agents), whereas the trial preparation material doctrine can apply to documents prepared by the "party or its representative." Thus, a document created by a low-level employee with no attorney involvement can be deemed trial preparation materials if the employee prepared the document in anticipation of litigation. Third, trial preparation materials protection is limited to documents pertaining to *litigation*, whereas the attorney-client privilege applies to all sorts of *legal advice*, whether or not litigation-oriented. Finally, how the nondiscoverability protection is lost or forfeited ("waiver") operates differently for the two doctrines; the attorney-client privilege is waived if the communication is not treated confidentially (for example, the communication is disclosed to *any third party* outside the scope of the privilege), whereas the trial preparation materials protection is only waived by disclosure to *the opposing party*.

4. Facts and Evidence Not Privileged

It is important to remember that the attorney-client privilege and the trial preparation materials/work product protection cannot be used to shield the *facts* or *evidence*. In other words, if a party is asked in discovery to state the color of the traffic light at the time of an accident, the party cannot avoid responding by claiming that the party has told his attorney what color the light was, and, for that reason, that the color of the traffic light has now become privileged information. The fact—the traffic light's color—does not become privileged by describing it to an attorney, even though the words the client chose when speaking to the attorney are privileged. Likewise, if the party received a traffic citation from a police officer, the party cannot shield the citation from discovery by "confidentially" providing it to his attorney.

Hypothetical

Q: In *DIY Danny v. Nailed-It*, when DIY Danny met with his lawyer, he divulged that, at the time he was using the nail gun, he was also using his cell phone to video-record how he nailed to the beat of his favorite rapper whose music was playing at an ear-numbing volume in the workshop, and that he was planning to upload the video onto his YouTube channel. Worried that the recording will make him look inattentive or careless while nailing, DIY Danny sought to shield the recording by placing the phone into the possession of his lawyer, telling the lawyer that he was providing this information and cell phone in confidence. During discovery, Nailed-It served a production request seeking any video recordings of the incident, and DIY Danny's lawyer asserted that the cell phone video was covered by the attorney-client privilege and the trial preparation materials protection and refused to produce it. Must DIY Danny produce the nail gun?

A: Yes. A party cannot cloak a piece of evidence like the cell phone video by handing it to a lawyer. The attorney-client privilege protects *communications* between a lawyer and client, not the underlying evidence. *See generally* 1 Paul R. Rice, Attorney-Client Privilege in the United States § 5:1 (2018–2019). Likewise, the trial preparation materials doctrine protects documents and tangible things prepared in anticipation of litigation, whereas DIY Danny prepared the video recording for YouTube, not for purposes of anticipated litigation.

Hypothetical

Q: Nailed-It also asks during discovery whether DIY Danny was distracted by talk radio, music, or any other activities at the time of the accident. DIY Danny says to his lawyer, "our conversation was privileged, right, you don't have to disclose that I was making a rap video at the time of the accident, do you?" Must DIY Danny disclose this information that he had provided to his attorney?

A: Yes. DIY Danny's discussion with his lawyer about the video—the words he chose when speaking with his lawyer—is privileged, but the underlying fact that he was making a rap video at the time of the accident is not. The *fact* that he was making a video is not a communication between a client and a lawyer for the purpose of obtaining legal advice and is therefore not shielded by the attorney-client privilege. Likewise, the *fact* that he was making a video is not a document prepared in anticipation of litigation and is therefore not trial preparation materials/work product.

Hypothetical

Q: Right after the accident, DIY Danny prepared a memo he titled "6 Ways I'm Gonna Get Rich Off This." When Nailed-It asked during discovery for any memoranda related to the accident, DIY Danny listed his memo as protected trial preparation materials and withheld it from production. During oral questioning of DIY Danny later in discovery (as explained in the section on depositions below), Nailed-It asked Danny about the circumstances surrounding the creation of the memo, such as when he created it, why he created it, and to whom he has shown it. DIY Danny's lawyer objected to each of these questions as seeking protected trial preparation material. Was DIY Danny's lawyer correct?

A: No. While the contents of the memo may or may not be protected trial preparation materials, the circumstances of the memo's creation are not. Parties are entitled to explore the basis of a privilege assertion so that they can evaluate the validity of the privilege assertion and, if appropriate, present a challenge of the assertion to the court. Details like the purpose of the creation of the memo, the timing of the memo's creation, and any disclosure of the memo can be critical to assessing the validity of the assertion and are not shielded.

5. Asserting Privilege/Protection Claims

A party who wishes to invoke a privilege or the work product protection to shield (or "withhold") material from disclosure during discovery must follow an intricate procedure designed to ensure that all invocations of a privilege or protection are proper. Rule 26(b)(5) describes that procedure. It requires that the party expressly assert the privilege or protection (identifying which privilege or protection is being claimed) and then describe the nature of the documents or information withheld on the basis of the privilege or protection in sufficient detail that other parties can assess whether the material was appropriately withheld. Privileged communications are typically listed in a "privilege log"—a chart that lists the document being withheld, the nature of the privilege asserted, all of the participants in the communication, the date of the document's creation, and enough of a description of the document to support the privilege without actually disclosing the communication's content. Such a foundation is essential to allowing the opponent, and perhaps the court, to evaluate whether the privilege or protection assertion is proper and decide whether to challenge the assertion.

The Rules do not specify the timing for providing an opposing party with a privilege log, and the courts have taken different approaches. Some courts require delivery of the log at the same time the response to the document request is due—within 30 days of the request. *See, e.g., SEC v. Yorkville Advisors, LLC*, 300 F.R.D. 152, 157 (S.D.N.Y. 2014). Other courts allow a "reasonable time" for delivery of the privilege log. *See Segar v. Holder,* 277 F.R.D. 9, 17 (D.D.C. 2011). Regardless, however, courts consistently hold that failure to timely deliver an adequate privilege log results in waiver of the privileges and protections.

Identifying and logging privileged documents can be an extremely difficult and time-consuming process. The legal team is often presented a virtual mountain of documents, including: paper letters, memoranda, invoices, contracts, reports, and other "hard-copy" documents; emails; documents saved as images (sometimes searchable and sometimes not); spreadsheets; electronic calendars; electronically transcribed voice messages; text messages; etc. Some documents are easily identified as potentially privileged—those on the letterhead of outside counsel, for example. But these are typically only the tip of the privileged iceberg.

The exponential growth in electronically stored information has exacerbated the privilege logging process. On the one hand, computers can greatly aid in finding privileged documents because electronically stored information is often also electronically searchable. Thus, the legal team typically searches for the name of each attorney likely to be involved along with other tell-tale search terms like "attorney," "privileged," "legal," "law," "advice," etc., into whatever computer technology the team is using to electronically find the obvious candidates for further privilege analysis.

Even for these obvious candidates, however, the process does not end with their identification. Take, for example, an email that is addressed to one recipient, with copies sent to three additional "cc" recipients, one of whom is an attorney. The litigation team for this client—senior lawyers, junior lawyers, paralegals, etc.—must assess the content of the message to see if it appears on its face to qualify for protection, and may need to follow up with the participants to explore the nature of the communication. The litigation team must also evaluate the nature of the non-lawyer recipients to evaluate waiver (remember that the attorney-client privilege is waived by failing to treat the communication as confidential, so sharing the communication with employees who do not have a "need to know" might result in waiver of the privilege). Furthermore, the litigation team must determine if the email was forwarded to other recipients, who may have forwarded it further, and so on, with waiver a risk at each step.

The process is even more time-consuming and difficult for privileged documents that are not captured by the computer search—such as paper documents, electronic documents that are not searchable, and searchable electronic documents that are privileged but do not contain the tell-tale search terms or language that flag them for the computer as privileged. Finding these documents typically involves a laborious, manual screening process. For the paper documents and the non-searchable electronic documents, that typically means a member of the litigation team personally reviewing the document. In cases involving a lot of documents, such reviews can be extremely expensive, and are far from perfect.

Not surprisingly, despite the litigation team's good faith and diligent efforts, privileged and protected documents sometimes slip through the screening process and are produced to the opponent inadvertently. This is deeply concerning for several reasons. First, it could result in a waiver (or loss) of an otherwise applicable privilege or protection. (Remember, as explained above, sharing a confidential document with an unauthorized reader can forfeit the nondiscoverability protection.) Second, it unintentionally gives opponents access to information they would otherwise have no right to see (and, depending on the nature of the information, that access could reveal litigation strategy, trial themes, witness goals, cross-examination plans, or settlement objectives—any of which could profoundly damage the case or defense). Third, it creates understandable friction between attorneys and their clients, who now will come to learn about a professional failure that the clients might consider careless, negligent, or even incompetent.

6. Inadvertent Production

In the spirit of professional courtesy, and mindful that even the best, most conscientious legal team may, from time to time, overlook a privileged or protected document and allow it to be inadvertently produced during discovery, many lawyers will offer to return a document they identify as inadvertently produced. Sometimes, though, circumstances lead the parties to disagree about the handling of inadvertently produced documents, and the Rules contain a procedure for such situations.

Rule 26(b)(5) codifies a process sometimes referred to as "clawback," which allows a party to seek the return of (ergo, to seek to "clawback") inadvertently produced documents. Under this procedure, a party who becomes aware of an inadvertently produced document notifies the opposing party. The opposing party retains the right to challenge the clawback demand, but must, in the first instance, either return, sequester, or destroy the document, and may not use the document unless the court so orders. Alternatively, the parties can craft their own alternative process for addressing inadvertently disclosed documents—frequently the result of the parties' Rule 26(f) discovery planning conference.

7. Trial Preparation Materials Protection for Statements

If a party or its representative obtains a statement from a witness in anticipation of litigation, the statement might qualify as trial preparation materials. (Remember the witness statements Attorney Fortenbaugh obtained from eyewitnesses to the tugboat sinking in *Hickman v. Taylor*? Those are classic—and quite common—examples.) Rule 26(b)(3), however, contains a limited exception pertaining to the discovery of witness statements. It provides that any person—party or nonparty—may obtain a copy of his or her own statement. Fed. R. Civ. P. 26(b)(3)(C). Thus, if a party gave a statement, that party may obtain a copy of the statement if in the possession of an opponent. A party does not have a general right, however, to obtain a copy of a witness's statement from an opponent.

8. Additional Constraints on the Scope of Discovery

In addition to the protections for privileged matter and trial preparation materials/work product discussed above, Rule 26 imposes a number of other limitations on discovery. Two of these—the protections for electronically stored information and for communications with experts—are discussed below in sections specific to those areas. Rule 26(b)(2)(C) contains three other general limitations on the scope of discovery. These limitations are mandatory—the introductory language instructs that the court "must" limit—"on motion or on its own"—any discovery:

1. that is unreasonably cumulative or duplicative;

2. that can be obtained from some other source more conveniently, less burdensomely, or less expensively; or

3. if the party seeking the discovery has already had ample opportunity to obtain the information by discovery in the action.

Although "mandatory," each of these three limitations contains wiggle room for the court to exercise discretion—*e.g.*, the discovery must be "unreasonably" cumulative or "more conveniently" obtained, or the other side must have had "ample" opportunity to obtain the information. In light of the broad discretion accorded to the courts under the proportionality analysis and the location of that limitation within the scope of discovery definition in Rule 26(b)(1), challenges to discovery as cumulative or burdensome are more likely to be framed in terms of proportionality rather than in these Rule 26(b)(2)(C) limitations.

9. Altering the Scope of Discovery

The discovery system in federal court has been described as "trans-substantive." *See* Robert M. Cover, *For James Wm. Moore: Some Reflections on a Reading of the Rules,* 84 Yale L.J. 718, 718 (1975). Used in this sense, the word "trans-substantive" means that the discovery rules are "one-size fits all." With a few limited exceptions, the rules apply to all sizes and complexities of cases in all substantive areas of the law. In order to accommodate the differing needs of the vast variety of cases that come before the courts, therefore, some tailoring often needs to occur on a case-by-case basis. The Rules provide the mechanisms for fitting the general process to the particulars of each specific case.

As discussed in the How Discovery Begins chapter, one of the first events in the discovery process is a meeting between the parties to plan for discovery and to memorialize their discussions in a written report to the court. During that planning process, the parties might agree to modify any of the discovery procedures and then to present that agreement to the court in their written report. Alternatively, if the parties cannot agree on such a modification, one party might propose the modification as part of its portion of the written report. In either event, the court ultimately will decide whether to follow the proposed modifications by including them in the court's Rule 16 Case Management Order.

Another mechanism is found in Rule 29 of the Federal Rules of Civil Procedure, which authorizes the parties to stipulate to alter the normal, default discovery procedures. Such stipulations might address the scope of discovery, the manner for handling privilege assertions or inadvertent production, the time allowed for responding to discovery requests, or the limits on the discovery devices (e.g., raising or lowering the allowed number of interrogatories). Rule 29 places one important limitation on the parties' ability to stipulate to alternative discovery procedures, however: the parties may not stipulate to extend a discovery date if the extension would interfere with the court's schedule for the end of discovery, for hearing a motion, or for conducting the trial. Thus, the parties are free to give each other extensions or otherwise vary intermediate dates, but they need court permission to change the dates the court sets for discovery or trial.

For problems that the Case Management Order does not address or that arise after the entry of the order, and as to which the parties cannot reach agreement among themselves, Rule 26(c) provides another mechanism for altering the discovery terrain. Rule 26(c) allows the court to enter a special ruling that forecloses or limits certain discovery (called a "protective order") for a variety of purposes. Thus, a party can ask the court to rule that a topic, while technically within the scope of discovery, is nonetheless off limits for the case. Thus, for example, in a case where one party's tax returns are technically relevant, but just barely so, and the court is persuaded that the intrusion of producing the tax returns outweighs their importance in the case, the court might prohibit discovery related to the tax returns.

Rule 26(c) provides that protective orders are obtained by filing a motion and authorizes entry of a court-issued limitation on discovery if the moving party demonstrates "good cause" for the relief it seeks. ("Good cause" is one of the burdens of persuasion for motions—it is not precisely defined but is a somewhat heightened burden. *See Hobley v. Chicago Police Commander Burge,* 225 F.R.D. 221, 224 (N.D. Ill. 2004) ("Good cause is difficult to define in absolute terms, but generally signifies a sound basis or legitimate need to take judicial action.").) Rule 26(c) also contains a list of the types of relief that the court may grant in a protective order. The list includes things like forbidding particular categories of discovery, changing the limits or conditions for discovery (or who bears the cost of the discovery), deeming certain facts established, or staying the case until a party participates properly in discovery. Like many discovery motions, as explained in the Policing Discovery chapter, a party must meet and confer with opposing counsel before filing a motion for protective order, and the prevailing party ordinarily is awarded its attorney's fees in connection with the motion. *See* Rule 26(c)(1)(A)–(H).

Hypothetical

Q: DIY Danny asks during discovery for all the design documents for the nail gun in Nailed-It's possession, custody, or control. Nailed-It has the past ten years of design documents scanned and archived on its current computer system, but drawings prior to that are stored on an old legacy computer system. Nailed-It obtains an estimate from a consultant to search for, locate, translate, and produce older drawings, and learns that it would be extremely expensive to obtain the older drawings. It objects, and DIY Danny files a motion seeking to require Nailed-It to produce the drawings (see the Policing Discovery chapter for a discussion of such motions). In its response, can Nailed-It seek to require DIY Danny to pay the consultant's costs to obtain the older drawings?

A: Yes. Rule 26(c)(1)(B) authorizes protective orders "specifying the terms, including the time and place or the allocation of expenses, for the disclosure or discovery." Thus, Nailed-It might file a motion for a protective order shifting the costs of producing the requested discovery.

One particularly common form of protective order occurs in connection with confidential or proprietary information. Such information—if relevant and proportional—is discoverable; the protections for *privileged* matter do not shield confidential or proprietary matter. Broad disclosure or misuse of such information, however, could be harmful to the responding party. For example, in our Nailed-It hypothetical, Nailed-It might not want the design drawings for its nail gun to fall into the hands of its competitors. Thus, it would want to limit the use of the drawings to purposes related to the litigation, and to prohibit disclosure of the drawings outside the litigation. The parties would typically enter into a stipulated protective order describing how DIY Danny could use or share the documents and specifying what happens to the documents at the end of the litigation. The parties would then present the stipulated protective order to the court for signature. Once signed, it becomes a formal order of the court, enforceable through the court's contempt powers. (But don't be too sanguine about the guarantees of confidentiality from such orders—if confidential information, once shared, is disclosed on the Internet, the fact that the Internet disclosure was unauthorized or contrary to a court order may offer only cold comfort; efforts to claw the information back are likely to prove unsuccessful, even using the full force of a court order. *See* William G. Childs, *When the Bell Can't Be Unrung: Document Leaks and Protective Orders in Mass Tort Litigation,* 27 Rev. Litig. 565 (2008).)

FROM CLASSROOM TO PRACTICE

We now know that discovery is broad but not unbounded. It is limited to: (1) non-privileged matter that is (2) relevant to any party's claim or defense and (3) proportional to the needs of the case.

But who makes that determination? Ultimately, of course, the court may be called on to decide, but in the first instance, the parties make their own determinations. The requesting party makes judgments as to what is and is not within this scope, and then poses its requests to the other side accordingly. The responding party makes judgments as to what is and is not within this scope and called for by a discovery request, and then responds (or objects) accordingly. Remember, though, that the United States' civil litigation system is an adversarial one—meaning each lawyer's primary duty is to his or her client (within the bounds of the rules and legal ethics). The responding party is incentivized to construe the scope of discovery and the discovery requests narrowly, deeming marginal or burdensome content outside the scope, whereas the requesting party would usually prefer to get over-inclusive responses. But it is only the responding party—the one whose knowledge, documents, electronically stored information, and tangible things is being sought—who knows what information exists and which to produce.

Accordingly, the discovery system depends to a large measure on the responding party's good faith participation in the process (as reflected in the Rule 26(g) signature certifications and the sanctions for violating that rule, as discussed below in the Policing Discovery chapter). Litigators are, as a group, motivated to win their cases. Most litigators will likely face many situations where they are tempted to withhold a harmful document based on a tortured or "carefully parsed" reading of a discovery request and the applicable rules. As the Policing Discovery chapter explains, there can be severe consequences for lack of good faith if the lack of good faith becomes known. But even if a lawyer thinks he or she can bend the rules without being detected, the system depends on good faith conduct by the lawyers participating in it. A good rule of thumb is to picture yourself explaining your reasoning to a judge. If your argument makes you blush or squirm, you are probably better off not making it, even if you think the other side won't find out.

Hypotheticals: Mastering the Nuances

Preliminaries: In DIY Danny's nail gun lawsuit, Nailed-It immediately served discovery requests related to DIY Danny's domicile. Nailed-It also asked for DIY Danny's Facebook username and password. DIY Danny objected to that discovery as outside the scope of discovery because it did not pertain to the merits of his claim or Nailed-It's defense to his claim. What would Nailed-It's lawyer likely argue in response? If the issue is presented to the court in a motion seeking to compel DIY Danny to provide the information, how do you think a court would be likely to rule and why?

The Other Gun: DIY Danny served discovery requests on Nailed-It asking for design information about other models of nail guns that Nailed-It manufactures and about any reports of injuries from users of those other models of nail guns. Nailed-It does not want to produce any documents or information about other models. What is Nailed-It's best objection to or argument against such discovery? What is DIY Danny's best argument that he is entitled to the information? If the issue is presented to the court in a motion to compel, how do you think a court would be likely to decide? Why?

The Investigation: Nailed-It's lawyer hired Philip Barlowe, an investigator, to assist her in defending DIY Danny's lawsuit. Barlowe conducted an interview with DIY Danny's neighbor, who had heard DIY Danny cry out in pain after the accident and had come over to help. Barlowe kept a notebook in which he transcribed the interview and captured his own thoughts about the cause of the accident. DIY Danny sought Barlowe's notebook in discovery. Is he entitled to the notebook? If so, to all of the notebook or only portions? If he is entitled, how can DIY Danny ensure that he has received all the pertinent portions? Can Nailed-It argue that the transcribed interview statements are hearsay? What other arguments might Nailed-It advance in opposition to DIY Danny's request?

PRACTICE SAMPLES

Sample 3-1: PRIVILEGE LOG

PRIVILEGE LOG – NAILED IT
C.A. No. 2:19-cv-1498

Doc. No.	Date	Author	Recipient	CC:	Subject	Privilege Basis
4505	02/10/16	Maxwell Hammer; Mildred Screwdriver		Agatha Chisel, Esq.	Memo recording decisions reached during meeting about nail gun safety features	Attorney-Client
4507	01/30/16	Mildred Screwdriver	Maxwell Hammer	Agatha Chisel, Esq.	Letter procedures for responding to demand letters for nail gun accidents	Attorney-Client
4594	00/00/00	Mildred Screwdriver			Undated handwritten note ("4/24") regarding the DIY Danny claim	Work Product
4599	10/31/80	Stanley Wrench	Maxwell Hammer	Agatha Chisel, Esq.	Memo discussing safety labels for nail gun products	Attorney-Client
4607	11/12/16	Maxwell Hammer	Agatha Chisel, Esq.		Memo providing comments on safety labels	Attorney-Client/ Work Product
4641	12/22/16	Agatha Chisel, Esq.	Maxwell Hammer		Memo regarding OSHA regs	Attorney-Client
4642	08/15/16	Agatha Chisel, Esq.	Maxwell Hammer		Memo regarding developments in product liability laws	Attorney-Client
4645	11/17/16	Maxwell Hammer	Mildred Screwdriver	Agatha Chisel, Esq.	Internal memorandum re safety instruction labels	Attorney-Client
4647	00/00/00	Maxwell Hammer			Undated handwritten notes regarding the DIY Danny claim	Work Product

4590	10/28/10	Maxwell Hammer	Mildred Screwdriver	Agatha Chisel, Esq.	Memo summarizing presentation at the annual safety meeting	Attorney-Client
4711	10/09/11	Maxwell Hammer	Mildred Screwdriver	Agatha Chisel, Esq.	Memo summarizing presentation at the annual safety meeting	Attorney-Client
4921	00/00/00	Mildred Screwdriver			Undated handwritten note ("3/24") regarding claims discussions at safety committee meeting	Work Product

Sample 3-2: CONFIDENTIALITY ORDER

IN THE UNITED STATES DISTRICT COURT
DISTRICT OF WEST CAROLINA

DIY Danny,	)
	)
Plaintiff,	)
	)
v.	) Civil Action No. 00-CV-98765
	)
Nailed-It,	)
	)
Defendant.	)

Protective Order Governing
Production of Documents and Information

IT IS HEREBY ORDERED this _____ day of _____, 20__, that the following confidentiality procedures shall govern production of documents and information in this matter:

1. The Parties agree that discovery and the pretrial phases of the above-captioned case (hereinafter, the "Litigation") may require production of documents and disclosure of other information that warrants protection against unrestricted disclosure and use (the "Confidential Material"). This

Protective Order Governing Production of Documents and Information ("Protective Order") shall govern the discovery and pretrial phases of this case, but shall not govern proceedings during trial nor does it prohibit any Party from seeking a protective order or other appropriate relief from the Court to govern proceedings during trial.

2. Any party from whom discovery is sought (the "Designating Party") shall have the right to designate as confidential documents and information, including but not limited to any transcript that contains Confidential Material, by marking or otherwise designating such documents and information as "CONFIDENTIAL." Documents and information so designated are referred to as "Designated Material." Each Designating Party agrees to exercise such right in good faith. Information obtained from sources of public records may not be treated as Confidential Material even if a party produces a copy of such information from its files and designates it as Confidential Material.

3. The fact that any Designated Material is disclosed in this Litigation pursuant to the terms of this Protective Order shall not be construed in any other context or proceeding before the Court, or any other government agency, or tribunal, as a waiver or admission that such information is or is not confidential or proprietary.

4. Designated Material produced by, received from (directly or indirectly), or concerning any Party to this matter shall be treated as confidential by all other Parties and shall be used only for purposes of this Litigation. Except as expressly permitted in this Protective Order, or as otherwise provided by order of the Court or by other applicable rules, no Party shall disclose such Designated Material to any person other than the following persons and only to the extent necessary for any such person to perform his, her, or their work associated with this Litigation or as necessary to facilitate the prosecution or defense of this Litigation:

    a. attorneys for the Parties, including in-house counsel who are participating or assisting in the conduct of the Litigation or employees of any such Party's attorneys who are working under such attorneys' supervision;

    b. any person who otherwise would be entitled to review Designated Material as a result of (i) financial or regulatory audit obligations or (ii) local, state, federal or other laws;

    c. any current director, officer, employee, representative, or insurer of a Party;

    d. outside experts and consultants working with counsel to assist in the conduct of the Litigation, and for no other purposes, but

> only if such outside experts and consultants have been made aware of the existence of this Protective Order and agree to its terms in writing;
>
> e. the Court, Court personnel, court reporters, or any of their personnel involved in this Litigation; or
>
> f. witnesses in the Litigation whose testimony relates to, or who otherwise must review, Confidential Material, but only if such witnesses have been made aware of the existence of this Protective Order and have agreed to its terms in writing or on the transcribed record during deposition proceedings.

5. If the Parties or their representatives wish to disclose any Designated Material to persons other than those referred to in paragraph 4 above, then counsel may do so only with prior written consent (including consent given via email) of the Party that produced the Designated Material under terms and conditions agreed to by the Parties, or upon Order of the Court following a motion with notice to opposing counsel. In the event any person or Party receives a subpoena or other process seeking Confidential Material, that person or Party shall promptly provide a copy of such subpoena or process to all Parties and shall provide reasonable cooperation with respect to any procedure to protect such information or matter as may be sought by the Party whose interests may be affected. To enable a Designating Party(ies) to take legal action to protect Confidential Material that may be subject to disclosure in response to a subpoena or other legal process, the subpoenaed Party shall not disclose Confidential Material *designated by any other Party* except in compliance with: (i) a final and non-appealable order of a forum having jurisdiction over such subpoena; (ii) a written agreement signed by the Parties; (iii) a failure by the Designating Party(ies) to confirm, in writing, within five business days of receipt of a full, complete copy of the subpoena or other legal process, that such Party(ies) intends to resist, limit or otherwise contest the subpoena or such legal process; or (iv) even assuming the five-business-days written notice is provided, a failure by one or more of the Designating Parties to file timely papers in the appropriate court, tribunal, or other proceeding, resisting, seeking to limit, or otherwise contesting the subpoena or legal process through which Confidential Material is sought. The timeliness of the papers referenced in subparagraph 5(iv) shall be determined by application of the rules of the appropriate court, tribunal, or other proceeding.

6. The information and/or documents covered by this Protective Order may not be used, copied, or disclosed by any person to whom such information and/or documents have been furnished or otherwise disclosed, for any

purpose other than in connection with this Litigation. Otherwise, the information and documents covered by this Protective Order may not be used for any other purposes whatsoever, including the prosecution of claims in any other action.

7. As to documents obtained during discovery, it shall be the duty of the Party claiming confidentiality of such information to designate in writing to the other Parties, at or prior to the time of disclosure of any such materials, which of such materials are considered to be confidential and proprietary and, therefore, covered by this Protective Order. The Designating Party shall stamp or mark "CONFIDENTIAL" or the equivalent on all materials that are considered to be confidential and proprietary on or before the time of the delivery to the opposing Party(ies), and such stamp or mark shall constitute a designation in writing sufficient to satisfy the requirements of this Protective Order. A Party may designate information disclosed at deposition as "CONFIDENTIAL" by requesting the court reporter to so designate the transcript at the time of the deposition, or by designation in writing to the other Parties prior to the deponent's deadline under Rule 30 of the Federal Rules of Civil Procedure to return the original and any changes to the deposition.

8. In the event any Party discovers it has inadvertently or previously produced Confidential Material that has not been designated "CONFIDENTIAL," it may, at any time, designate the documents or information as "CONFIDENTIAL" by subsequent notice in writing specifically identifying the documents or information and furnishing the correct designation, in which event the Parties shall henceforth treat such information as provided in this Protective Order. No person or Party shall incur any liability hereunder with respect to any disclosure which occurred prior to receipt of such written notice.

9. Any Party may object to the confidentiality designation of any Designated Material by serving written notice of objection on all other Parties specifying with reasonable particularity the materials to which objection was made. Within twenty days after the service of such notice, the Designating Party shall respond in writing specifying the basis for the designation objected to, or otherwise withdrawing the designation. If the Designating Party does not withdraw the designation, the objecting Party may, within twenty days after service of the written response, file a motion for a determination by the Court as to the validity of the objection. In the event such a motion is filed, confidentiality of the material in issue shall be preserved pending resolution of the issue by the Court and for a period of thirty days thereafter to allow the Designating Party an opportunity to seek review of such order. If such review is sought within that period, the Designated Material in question shall continue to be subject to the restriction of this Order until the final conclusion of all such review.

10. This Order shall be without prejudice to the right of any Party to oppose disclosure of any documents or information for any reason other than confidentiality. The terms of this Protective Order may be changed only by written agreement of the Parties or order of the Court, and is without prejudice to the rights of any party to move for relief from any of its provisions, or to seek or agree to different or additional protection for any particular document or information.

11. A Party seeking to file a document comprising or containing Designated Material, or purporting to reproduce or paraphrase Designated Material, shall first request leave from the Court to file that document under seal and comply with Court rules for filing any such document. The sealed envelopes or sealed containers containing Designated Material shall be marked with information required by Court rules, identify each document and thing within, and bear a statement substantially in the following form:

CONFIDENTIAL

Pursuant to Court Order dated _____, 20__, this envelope or container containing the above-identified papers filed by [name of Party] is not to be opened nor the contents thereof displayed or revealed, except by order of the Court.

12. If authorized by the Court, courtesy copies of documents containing Designated Material may be sent to the Court in full with the particular pages containing Designated Material stamped "CONFIDENTIAL" and the cover page marked "THIS COPY NOT TO BE FILED."

13. This Protective Order does not affect the right of any Party to claim any applicable privilege or work product protection of any information and/or any Party's right, subject to the provisions of Federal Rules of Civil Procedure and applicable law, to seek the return or oppose the return of any privileged information or work product that has been disclosed.

14. With the exception of the exclusion addressed in paragraph 1 of this Protective Order, the restrictions in this Order shall remain in effect for the duration of this Litigation unless terminated by stipulation executed by counsel of record for the Parties or by order of the Court. The provisions of this Protective Order, insofar as they restrict the communication, treatment, and use of Designated Material, shall continue to be binding after the termination of this Litigation unless the Court orders otherwise.

15. All notices made under this Protective Order shall be made in writing to the Parties through their undersigned counsel.

UNITED STATES DISTRICT JUDGE

IV

The Discovery Tools

PART 1.
INTRODUCTION

GETTING THE VIEW

Once the parties have conducted their discovery conference, the court has issued its Case Management Order, and the parties have made their initial Rule 26(a) disclosures, the parties may begin to use the tools of discovery. These tools are not mandatory. There is no obligation, for example, for one party to take a witness's deposition, to propound written questions or admission requests, or to insist on the right to examine and copy documents, computer data, and tangible things. Rather, doing so is a matter of voluntary choice (in contrast to the three mandatory disclosures, discussed in the How Discovery Begins chapter, that are triggered automatically at the junctures specified in Rule 26(a)). When, which, how, and in what order to use the tools of discovery are decisions that lie almost exclusively within each party's discretion. Strategy and litigation tactics generally drive that decision-making. In most complex cases, using the tools of discovery well is often where cases are won and lost, and where the lion's share of the legal fees and time are spent.

Although the decision whether, and how, to *invoke* the tools of discovery is a discretionary one, the obligation to *respond* to discovery requests is not. Once a discovery tool is invoked to seek information from a party or nonparty, a proper response is required. Failing to respond timely and properly can have devastating consequences. So, our tour through the tools of discovery will introduce not only how each tool is used but also what responses it compels.

The Federal Rules of Civil Procedure authorize five tools of discovery, each explained separately in the subchapters that follow:

- Interrogatories under Rule 33
- Production requests under Rule 34
- Requests for admission under Rule 36
- Mental or physical examinations under Rule 35
- Depositions under Rules 28–32

With one limited exception (for service of production requests), the parties may not use these tools of discovery until after their Rule 26(f) discovery conference, and they must complete their use by the deadline fixed for the end (or "close") of discovery, as set forth in the court's Case Management Order.

Within those time parameters, each party is free to deploy these discovery tools in any order it chooses, without regard to the sequence other parties choose (unless the court issues a protective order phasing or dictating the sequence of discovery). See Fed. R. Civ. P. 26(d)(3).

As creatures of habit, often guided by their own experience and the advice of colleagues, lawyers tend typically to follow their preferred, individualized approaches to sequencing their use of the discovery tools. Many lawyers like to begin with at least one round of written discovery (e.g., interrogatories, requests for production, and/or requests for admission) to obtain basic information and core, threshold materials, and then move on to more targeted discovery and depositions later, with the benefit of what was learned during the first "round" of discovery. Other times, this typical cycle may be altered for strategic reasons. For example, taking an early deposition of a critical witness, just weeks into the life of a lawsuit, can meaningfully reduce the risk that the witness's testimony will be as influenced by defending counsel as it would be later, after that defending counsel has become more familiar with the case and better able to prepare the witness. But doing so means that what is learned later in discovery cannot be explored with that witness; most witnesses can only be deposed once during a lawsuit.

One final reminder before we embark into the discovery tools: formal discovery is not the only way lawyers obtain evidence. Remember our definition of "discovery" from the What Is "Discovery"? chapter. The discovery tools are non-exclusive pathways to information. Lawyers are usually free to gather facts and evidence informally, without using these tools of discovery. Internet searches, interviews of cooperative witnesses, and visiting an accident or incident scene are all information gathering tools that can prove quite effective and yet do not require the use of the tools we will now learn. Talented lawyers never forget to consider these information paths to evidence.

FROM CLASSROOM TO PRACTICE

The required physical form for the discovery tools is not prescribed in the Federal Rules of Civil Procedure, except in the most general of terms. Every discovery request, response, and objection must be signed by an attorney of record (or, if unrepresented, by the parties themselves). *See* Fed. R. Civ. P. 26(g)(1). Each must begin with a caption, noting the court's name, the case's docket number as assigned by the court, and a title describing the document. *See* Fed. R. Civ. P. 7(b)(2) & 10(a). Each should also contain a Certificate of Service, verifying the date and method of service to all other parties in the lawsuit. *See* Fed. R. Civ. P. 5(a)(1)(C).

Although these national requirements are few, you should always check the local rules of the applicable federal district court and the presiding judge's chambers' rules—they may impose additional formatting requirements for the discovery tools.

PART 2.
INTERROGATORIES—RULE 33

GETTING THE VIEW

Interrogatories are written questions that require a response in writing and under oath. It is, obviously, a very straightforward discovery tool. But it is not without its nuances.

Interrogatories have a limited audience: they may only be sent to parties in the lawsuit. Accordingly, this tool will not be useful for obtaining information from, for example, nonparty bystander eyewitnesses. Interrogatories also have a limited volume: absent consent from the answering party or a court order, only 25 discrete interrogatory questions can be sent to any one party. Interrogatories are usually answered by a party's attorney, rather than by the party himself or herself. Consequently, those answers can be fairly well-"lawyered"—meaning, they are often artfully (and unhelpfully) worded and burdened with qualifications and limitations; they typically lack the forthcoming candor and completeness that a non-attorney author might supply.

Interrogatories, like all other discovery tools, may be used (or not used) at each party's choice. With advantages and limitations, most litigators find that interrogatories serve an important, but limited, role in their discovery arsenal.

HOW THIS DISCOVERY TOOL WORKS

The procedures set by Rule 33 for interrogatories divide easily into three categories: asking interrogatory questions, answering interrogatory questions, and using interrogatory answers.

A. Asking Interrogatory Questions

We start with two preliminary interrogatory attributes. First, as noted above, interrogatory questions can only be posed to parties. Thus, if the source of information is a nonparty, interrogatories are not the tool to use. Second, interrogatories may not be issued until after the parties have convened the Rule 26(f) discovery planning conference we discussed in Chapter 2. *See* Fed. R. Civ. P. 26(d)(1).

1. What Can Be Asked

Interrogatories can be used to seek any sort of information that is properly discoverable. *See* Fed. R. Civ. P. 26(b)(1) (information is discoverable if it is (a) relevant to a party's claim or defense, (b) nonprivileged, and (c) proportional to the needs of the case). This permitted scope of interrogatories—and all other discovery, for that matter—was discussed in Chapter 3. Beyond that threshold scope limitation, the content and manner of framing an interrogatory question lies entirely within the asking party's prerogative.

Interrogatories may be used to ask about facts. But they may also be used to ask about opinions and contentions relating to facts or the application of law to facts. *See* Rule 33(a)(2). Indeed, these sorts of "contention" inquiries can be quite useful. A party may permissibly ask an adversary to explain the basis and factual underpinnings of a claim or defense. Thus, a plaintiff could, for example, ask a defendant to explain its factual basis for contending that a claim is time-barred by the statute of limitations. Or a defendant might ask a plaintiff to describe the factual basis for contending that a back injury will cause permanent loss of earning capacity. *See In re Rail Freight Fuel Surcharge Antitrust Litig.*, 281 F.R.D. 1, 4 (D.D.C. 2011) ("'Contention interrogatories' that ask a party what it contends or to state all the facts upon which it bases a contention are perfectly legitimate."); *Barnes v. D.C.*, 270 F.R.D. 21, 24 (D.D.C. 2010) ("This type of request 'can be most useful in narrowing and sharpening the issues, which is a major purpose of discovery'") (quoting Rule 33's advisory committee's notes). Courts have ruled that the work product doctrine ordinarily does not foreclose such questions. *See In re Rail Freight Fuel Surcharge Antitrust Litig.*, 281 F.R.D. at 4. But the Rule does permit the court, in appropriate circumstances, to postpone the time for responding to questions about opinions and contentions. *See* Rule 33(a)(2).

2. Numbers and "Subparts"

The 25-interrogatory limit was added to Rule 33 in 1993 in an effort to rescue parties from being deluged by the costs and burdens of a tsunami of interrogatories (though the parties can agree to expand this number or the court may expand it on motion.) *See* Fed. R. Civ. P. 33(a)(1). Counting to "25" can sometimes prove to be a challenge. The Rule directs that "all discrete subparts" of an interrogatory question count as *separate* questions. But the Rule doesn't explain how to detect whether "discrete subparts" are present or not. One court, after studying how judges were applying this "discrete subpart" language over the years, settled on this test: subparts of a single interrogatory that are "logically or factually subsumed within and necessarily related to" the primary question asked in an interrogatory should count as one single question only. *See Erfindergemeinschaft UroPep GbR v. Eli Lilly & Co.,* 315 F.R.D. 191, 194-97 (E.D. Tex. 2016). Otherwise, the subparts count as separate questions.

Hypothetical

Q: Suppose Grammar School installed a set of swings in its recess yard. Several children were clowning around one day, with six standing and jumping on the same swing seat. That seat buckled under the weight of the jumping students and collapsed, badly injuring Ricky. The lawyer representing Ricky's parents in a lawsuit against the swing manufacturer asked the following interrogatories:

1. Please provide the names, job titles, and addresses of each person involved in the design of Grammar School's swing.
2. Please provide the names, job titles, and addresses of each person involved in the manufacture, marketing, and installation of Grammar School's swing.

If the "discrete subpart" test used by the Texas federal court in the *Erfinder-gemeinschaft UroPep GbR* case were employed, how many interrogatories would be left for Ricky's parents' lawyer to ask?

A: The likely answer is that 4 of the 25 interrogatories allotted to Ricky's parents have been used, leaving 21 more that could be asked. Here's why: the numbering used by the lawyer ("1.", "2.") does not, alone, answer this question because subparts within an interrogatory can sometimes count as additional interrogatories. Question No. 1 asks three pieces of information – the names, job titles, and addresses of anyone involved in designing the swing. A court is likely to consider those pieces of information as logically subsumed within the broader, central question (namely, who designed the swing?). So, even though Question No. 1 asks for three pieces of information, it is likely to be counted as a single interrogatory. Conversely, Question No. 2 is likely to be counted as three interrogatories. It, too, asks for the same three pieces of information (name, job title, and address), but it asks for that information concerning three separate, independent events: who manufactured the swing, who marketed the swing, and who sold the swing. Because those events will likely not be considered factually subsumed within a single inquiry, but instead fairly constitute three separate inquiries, Question No. 2 will probably use up three of the 25 interrogatories available to Ricky's parents.

B. Answering Interrogatory Questions

1. Basic Requirements

The party to whom an interrogatory is directed must answer it fully, separately, in writing, sworn under oath, and within 30 days of the date it was served. *See* Fed. R. Civ. P. 33(b). This deadline can be—and often is—extended by agreement of the parties or by court order. If the answering party is an entity (such as a corporation, partnership, association, or governmental agency), the answer must capture all information known by the entity, and not just information known personally by the person typing up the entity's response. In other words, there is a duty to conduct a search of the entity and its personnel to ensure that its answers are institutionally complete. *See In re Auction Houses Antitrust Litig.*, 196 F.R.D. 444, 445 (S.D.N.Y. 2000) (duty to provide information in answering party's possession, within its control, or otherwise obtainable by it).

2. Business Records Option

Some interrogatory questions require an extraction of information from documentary sources. Consider the lawsuit Ricky's parents filed against the manufacturer of the Grammar School swing. The parents might ask an interrogatory seeking to learn about every occasion, over the years, on which the design of the swing was altered by the manufacturer, including the date of each re-design, the purpose for each re-design, the personnel involved in each re-design, the reason for each re-design, and any new materials used in each re-design. The swing manufacturer may retain design files for each of these re-designs and the task of paging through those files to extract the particular items of information sought by Ricky's parents might prove quite labor-intensive. In such a circumstance, the pool manufacturer can choose to give the parents' attorney access to its various re-design files and permit that attorney to cull through those materials and extract the requested information herself. This document-inspection type of interrogatory response—permitted by Rule 33(d) of the Federal Rules of Civil Procedure—can only be employed, however, when certain prerequisites have been met:

UNITED STATES EX REL. LANDIS
v.
TAILWIND SPORTS CORP.

317 F.R.D. 592 (D.D.C. 2016)

COOPER, United States District Judge

[A federal False Claims Act action was filed against the former lead rider of a professional cycling team, Lance Armstrong. The complaint alleged that Mr.

Armstrong made false statements in connection with sponsorship agreements he signed with the U.S. Postal Service. At issue were four interrogatories served by the U.S. Government on Mr. Armstrong (Nos. 16-19) that asked him to identify the value he contended that the Postal Service received from those sponsorship arrangements.]

[In responding to the four interrogatories,] Armstrong pointed the government to specified page ranges of the report of one of his experts . . . . For each of the four interrogatories, Armstrong then assured the government that "the answer to this interrogatory may be determined by examining . . . [the expert reports] and all documents cited and referenced therein." He closed his response to each interrogatory as follows: "Information responsive to this request may also be located in previously-produced documents, including as set forth in Attachment A, and the burden of deriving or ascertaining the answer will be substantially the same for the government as it is for Armstrong." Attachment A contains identifying information for over two hundred deposition transcripts and for hundreds of other documents produced by the government in discovery.

* * *

[The court finds that Armstrong's responses] vastly exceed what Rule 33(d) allows. . . .

[P]erhaps most glaringly, Armstrong has not described the relevant documents "in sufficient detail to enable [the government] to locate and identify them as readily as [he] could." *Id.* 33(d)(1). When employing Rule 33(d), a responding party must "specifically identify the documents that contain the answers." . . . "[M]aking only a general reference to a mass of documents or records" is an abuse of Rule 33(d). . . . This is precisely what Armstrong has done. He asserts, for each interrogatory, that responsive information may be found in "previously-produced documents, including"—but not limited to—those listed in the exhibit labeled "Attachment A." Yet this sprawling spreadsheet does nothing to "specif[y]" which documents support Armstrong's valuation contentions. Nor is the government's requested specification "make-work"—it is an elementary requirement of Rule 33(d). When deploying that rule's time-saving features, a responding party must "precisely specif[y] for *each* interrogatory. . . the actual documents where information will be found." . . .

[R]elatedly, Armstrong may not waste the government's time by stating that responsive information "may" be found in certain locations. When a Rule 33(d) response is contested, the responding party "must show that a review of the documents will actually reveal answers to the interrogatories." . . . It is not enough to claim that "[t]o the extent Armstrong has information respon-sive" to the government's interrogatories, it will be found in certain locations. The Court has been given no basis for assessing whether "the documents, in fact, contain all of the information sought by the interrogatories.". . .

Rule 33(d) cannot be used for documents other than "business records." Whatever that term's precise scope in this context, it does not encompass deposition transcripts or discovery materials generally. . . . Armstrong's At-tachment A nonetheless identifies 222 deposition transcripts. It goes on to list hundreds of other documents by Bates number only. The Court has no way of knowing whether these faceless materials are business records eligible for Rule 33(d) treatment.

Thus, the option of giving a requesting party access to documents rather than providing a written, textual answer is available only when: (1) a review of the party's business records will actually provide the answer requested; (2) the relevant records can be specifically identified; and (3) the burden of extracting the answers would be substantially the same for the answering party as it would be for the requesting party. *See* Fed. R. Civ. P. 33(d).

3. Objecting to Interrogatories

Interrogatory questions can be objectionable for many reasons. The questions may seek discovery that is not proper (*e.g.*, not relevant, not proportional, or privi-leged or work product protected). The questions may be vague or unclear. The ques-tions might be unfairly far-reaching, or otherwise would impose too great of a bur-den. The questions could simply be oppressive. Answering parties are permitted to object to an interrogatory on these, or other, grounds, and such an objection excus-es that party from supplying a substantive answer. But this prerogative is condi-tioned. First, all objections must be asserted timely or they are waived (absent a court order excusing the delay). *See* Fed. R. Civ. P. 33(b)(4). Second, all objections must be stated with specificity and signed by the party's attorney. *See id.* Third, all objections must also be well-grounded and asserted ethically. *See* Rule 26(g)(1)(B). Fourth, all objections are subject to review by the court which may, on motion by the asking party, sustain them or overrule them and compel a substantive response. *See* Rule 37(a)(3)(B)(iii).

LYNN

v.

MONARCH RECOVERY MANAGEMENT, INC.

285 F.R.D. 350 (D. Md. 2012)

GRIMM, United States Magistrate Judge

[Plaintiff filed this action against the defendant for repeatedly phoning him in a manner that violated federal and state telephone consumer protection laws. Plaintiff served defendant with various interrogatories, to some of which defendant objected. Plaintiff then requested the court to compel defendant to respond.]

Interrogatory # 15

Plaintiff's Interrogatory #15 states: "Describe fully your involvement in and knowledge of the calls alleged in this suit, including but not limited to the creation, initiation, delivery, arrangement or coordination of the necessary phone lines, provision of numbers, provision of any script or prerecorded message, or any other product or service in any way related to the alleged calls." Defendant objected to this interrogatory "as vague and ambiguous," noting that Defendant "does not understand this interrogatory." Plaintiff argues that responses to this interrogatory should be compelled because Defendant has failed to answer, giving only "a frivolous objection that [Defendant] could not understand this perfectly straightforward question to describe [Defendant's] involvement with the collection calls at issue." In its response, Defendant notes that subsequent conversations with Plaintiff's counsel have indicated that, through Interrogatory #15, counsel may be "seeking the identity of the person(s) responsible for [Defendant] dialer campaigns." To that end, Defendant supplements its response by referring Plaintiff to its response to Interrogatory #1, "identifying Anthony Mazzacano, as Chief Strategy Officer/Owner who manages [Defendant's] dialer and telephone resources and has knowledge and information regarding the dialer and dialer technology, and Brian Holmes as the person who builds and manages [Defendant's] dialer campaigns." In his reply, Plaintiff states that his interrogatory "does not seek the identity of employees," as Defendant appears to believe. Rather, "[i]t seeks a full description of [Defendant's] involvement in and knowledge of the calls alleged in the suit."

Generally, the "party objecting to discovery as vague or ambiguous has the burden of showing such vagueness or ambiguity." . . . [*See Hall v. Sullivan*, 231 F.R.D. 468, 470 (D. Md. 2005)] (explaining that objections to interrogatories must be specific and non-boilerplate). Defendant's original answer to Plaintiff's Interrogatory # 15 is non-specific and boilerplate, as it asserts only that the interrogatory is "vague and ambiguous," and that Defendant does not understand it. Defendant elaborates on its objection in its response to Plaintiff's motion, explaining that "[i]t is not clear to [Defendant] what a 'product or service in any way related to the alleged calls' means in context with other aspects of the request which seeks information regarding voice scripts that may have been used in connection with any calls, the hardware used to place the calls, and the 'creation, initiation, delivery, arrangement or coordination' of phone lines and/or phone numbers."

While a responding party "'should exercise reason and common sense to attribute ordinary definitions to terms and phrases utilized in interrogatories,'" . . ., there are limits to how accommodating the responding party must be in trying to understand and respond to a poorly worded, compound, and ambiguous interrogatory. I agree that Interrogatory #15 is unnecessarily compound, confusing, and ambiguous. It is equally clear, however, that the central aim of the interrogatory is to obtain facts relating to the telephone calls that are at issue in this case, which surely is discoverable. Counsel are DIRECTED to confer to clarify the nature of Plaintiff's request . . .

Interrogatories # 16 and # 17

Plaintiff's Interrogatory #16 states: "Identify any and all persons who made or assisted you in making calls for you to Plaintiff or 301-620-2250." Plaintiff's Interrogatory #17 states: "Identify fully all persons who approved the making of the calls [sic] on your behalf." Defendant answered both interrogatories by stating that it objected to the questions "as overbroad and unlimited in time." Subject to that objection, Defendant directed Plaintiff to "see the individuals identified in [Defendant's] Response to Interrogatory No. 1, above." In his motion, Plaintiff states that counsel "agreed to limit the question[s] to the [three] accounts involved, and limit the scope to 2010 to 2011." In Plaintiff's view, an answer to Interrogatory #16 "should include [a list of] persons involved in creating any prerecorded voice message that was delivered, as well as live collectors." Plaintiff contends that referral to the persons listed in the answer to Interrogatory #1 is insufficient because it requires Plaintiff to guess, among those persons listed, who "really approved the making of the calls." Defendant responds that its answer to Interrogatory #1 identifies the collectors who called Plaintiff's number," and identifies the individuals who build and manage Defendant's dialer and telephone resources and campaigns. In his reply, Plaintiff states that the persons identified in Defendant's answer to Interrogatory #1 are "managers, supervisors, collectors, technology persons, etc., but not . . . the person(s) who made the calls." "Some person or persons," Plaintiff states, "made the calls," and "Plaintiff wants to know who." Additionally, according to Plaintiff, Defendant's answer to Interrogatory #1 does not make clear "who authorized the making of the calls." As a result, Plaintiff argues that Defendant's responses are deficient and complete answers should be compelled.

Merely stating that an interrogatory is "overbroad" does "not suffice to state a proper objection." . . . Instead, the "objecting party must specify which part of a request is overbroad, and why." Defendant's objection to Plaintiff's Interrogatories # 16 and # 17 failed to do so. However, Plaintiff's counsel later agreed to limit the scope of the question to a one year period, from 2010 to 2011. With this limitation in place, I do not find that Interrogatories # 16 and # 17 are overbroad, and I further find that Defendant's responses are incomplete and evasive, which is tantamount to a failure to answer. *See* Fed. R. Civ. P. 37(a)(4). A party answering interrogatories must provide to the requesting party all "information that is available to it and that can be given without undue labor and expense." . . . To the extent that Defendant knows which employees made the calls, as well as who created the prerecorded voice message delivered to Plaintiff, which employees served as live collectors, and which employees authorized the making of the calls, or is able to obtain such information without undue labor and expense, Defendant must provide that information to Plaintiff.

The court in *Lynn* condemned what it described as "boilerplate" objections to interrogatories, and its condemnation is shared widely among judges. But what are "boilerplate" objections, and why are they disfavored? A federal judge in Michigan explained:

WESLEY CORP.

v.

ZOOM T.V. PRODUCTS, LLC

2018 WL 372700 (E.D. Mich. Jan. 11, 2018)

CLELAND, United States District Judge

i. The Problem of Boilerplate

Defendants' "objections" to these discovery requests are the typical boilerplate objections known and detested by courts and commentators—and receiving parties—around the nation. A "boilerplate" objection is one that is invariably general; it includes, by definition, "[r]eady-made or all-purpose language that will fit in a variety of documents." *Boilerplate*, BLACK'S LAW DICTIONARY (10th ed. 2014). Thus, "[a]n objection to a discovery request is boilerplate when it merely states the legal grounds for the objection without (1) specifying how the discovery request is deficient and (2) specifying how the objecting party would be harmed if it were forced to respond to the request." Jarvey, Matthew L., *Boilerplate Discovery Objections: How They Are Used, Why They Are Wrong, and What We Can Do About Them*, 61 DRAKE L. REV. 913, 914 (2013).

Boilerplate objections to interrogatories and requests for production are not permitted under the Federal Rules of Civil Procedure. Rule 33(b)(4) requires that objections to interrogatories be made "with specificity" and provides that "[a]ny ground not stated in a timely objection is waived unless the court, for good cause, excuses the failure." Rule 34(b)(2)(B) requires that objections to requests for production "state with specificity the grounds for objecting to the request." Rule 34(b)(2)(C) further demands that "[a]n objection must state whether any responsive materials are being withheld on the basis of that objection."

When objections lack specificity, they lack effect: an objection that does not explain its grounds (and the harm that would result from responding) is forfeited. "Boilerplate or generalized objections are tantamount to no objection at all and will not be considered. . .." [citation omitted] Lawyers who purport to "preserve" an objection by including it in a boilerplate statement must be prepared to face the fact that the result of a substance-free objection is generally "the opposite of preservation[,]" i.e., forfeiture. Jarvey, *Boilerplate, supra*, at 925. Similarly, the common "notwithstanding-the-above" designations that frequently follow a boilerplate objection and precede a more substantive response also fail to preserve objections. *Id.* The idea that boilerplate in some talismanic way preserves an objection is fallacy. It has been fairly styled an "urban legend," one that promotes the misuse of the objection process and amounts to nothing less than "a waste of effort and the resources of both the parties and the court." *Id.* [citation omitted].

This court is not the first—nor will it be the last—to condemn the use of boilerplate objections. Indeed, perhaps the only thing more surprising than the pervasive reliance on boilerplate is the practice's continued existence in the face of strong and widespread criticism by federal courts. *See, e.g., Black v. Pension Benefit Guar. Corp.*, 2014 WL 3577949, at *2 (E.D. Mich. July 21, 2014) (Tarnow, J.) ("The Court strongly condemns the practice of asserting boilerplate objections to every discovery request."); *Kristensen v. Credit Payment Servs., Inc.*, 2014 WL 6675748, at *4 (D. Nev. Nov. 25, 2014) (describing a party's "general and additional objections" as "boilerplate objections which are designed to evade, obfuscate, and obstruct discovery"); *Lowe v. Vadlamudi*, 2012 WL 3731781, at *3 (E.D. Mich. Aug. 28, 2010) (Lawson, J.) (noting that a party's boilerplate objections "do not gain in substance through repetition"); *Marti v. Baires*, 2012 WL 2029720, at *11 (E.D. Cal. June 5, 2012) ("The Court will not countenance any party's effort to obstruct discovery through objections or evasive responses which lack any good faith basis."); *Near v. Eli Lilly & Co.*, 2008 WL 11334459, at *1 (S.D. Iowa July 16, 2008) ("[T]he use of boilerplate, unsubstantiated objections is rejected by federal courts."). These cases, in their interpretation of the discovery rules and their denunciation of boilerplate, "are not aspirational, they are the law." *Liguria Foods, Inc. v. Griffith Labs., Inc.*, 320 F.R.D. 168, 191 (N.D. Iowa Mar. 13, 2017).

Hypothetical

Q: In their lawsuit, Ricky's parents served a set of interrogatories on the swing manufacturer that included this question: "We understand your company manufactures garden shovels in addition to recess yard swings. Please provide the names, job titles, and addresses of each person involved in the design of your garden shovels." The manufacturer's attorney is aware that the definition of "discoverability" is broader than "admissibility," and is committed to answering properly under the Rules. Even still, the attorney is unsure whether the requested information must be supplied or whether an objection is permitted. Which would you recommend?

A: The attorney is likely able to object to this question, provided the objection is properly framed and not boilerplate. Although "discoverability" is broad, it is still bounded by Rule 26(b) of the Federal Rules of Civil Procedure as we learned in the Scope of Discovery chapter. So, the following objection is likely both substantively proper and appropriately framed: "The manufacturer objects to this interrogatory as seeking information that is not relevant to any party's claim or defense. Plaintiffs' theory is that the swing seat that injured their son was designed defectively to fail to bear the weight of children; defendant's answer has claimed that the design was not defective. Information relating to an entirely different product line intended for wholly different uses (garden shovels) bears no rational relationship to claims or defenses in this litigation."

C. The Uses of Interrogatory Answers

Rule 33 does not set out a particularized list of approved uses for interrogatory answers. Instead, the Rule directs litigators to the Federal Rules of Evidence for determining how and under what circumstances interrogatory answers may be used in court. *See* Fed. R. Civ. P. 33 (c). Thus, sworn, relevant, probative answers to interrogatories may be offered against the answering party in much the same way as any other testimony might be. *See AMCO Inc. Co. v. Inspired Techs., Inc.*, 648 F.3d 875, 881 (8th Cir. 2011).

Importantly, however, interrogatory answers are not considered binding "judicial admissions"; in this way, Rule 33 interrogatory answers and Rule 36 request for admission answers differ greatly. If doing so would, under the circumstances, not unfairly prejudice an opponent, an answering party may be able to contradict at trial an answer it gave earlier in response to an interrogatory (and the opponent can examine the witness about the nature of the change in testimony). *See Sunshine Heifers, LLC v. Moohaven Dairy, LLC*, 13 F. Supp. 3d 770, 778 (E.D. Mich. 2014).

FROM CLASSROOM TO PRACTICE

A. Form

The styling of interrogatories—the inclusion of prefatory "instructions" and "definitions," the manner of wording questions, the use of separate waves of interrogatory question sets, the ordering of questions, and other formatting features—are all details left to the preferences of each attorney. Attorneys tend to gravitate toward a styling that seems to be working for them in practice (or, more often, one they inherited from a mentor early on in their careers). For example, some (but not all) attorneys like to add an "ANSWER:" space after each interrogatory question where the responding party can type in an answer. Some attorneys supply their opponents with a digital copy of the questions (onto which answers can be typed). Variations abound.

Whatever styling you choose for your interrogatories, bear this overarching principle in mind: you should not blindly incorporate a form or method simply because you (or your mentor) "always does it that way." Think carefully through your interrogatory styling approach. Always ensure it is well adapted to the goal at hand.

B. "Instructions" and "Definitions"

Many attorneys preface their interrogatories with a set of "instructions" and "definitions" to be applied by their opponents when answering the questions. Among commonly used "Instructions" are those directing that: (a) responses be based on all information within the answering party's possession, custody, and control; (b) partial answers include an explanation why complete answers are impossible; and (c) any objection be identified and explained. Likewise, commonly used "Definitions" may define words like "you" and "your" (to refer to the answering party), "identify" (to require a name, address, phone, and email), "product" (to mean the particular product alleged in the complaint to have caused an injury), and "incident" (to be a shorthand reference to a particular accident or event).

These sorts of "Instructions" and "Definitions" are not addressed in either the discovery rules generally or the interrogatory rule specifically. But the practice is widespread among lawyers. Unless a local rule or custom directs otherwise, federal courts tend to allow and enforce a modest set of "Instructions" and "Definitions" that are reasonable and impose no undue burden. *See Ashland Elec. Prod., Inc. v. Bombardier Transportation (Holdings) USA, Inc.*, 2005 WL 8174460, at *2 (D.N.H. Oct. 21, 2005); *Dang v. Cross*, 2002 WL 432197, at *3 (C.D. Cal. Mar. 18, 2002). This is quite sensible. Using the word "you" to avoid re-writing a lengthy party name or "product" to avoid mistyping a complex model number or serial number eases the discovery burden on everyone and allows for shorter, more cleanly written discovery requests. Likewise, a reminder that responses must encompass all information within a party's possession, custody, or control and a request that any objections be reasonably explained could prove useful in a later motion battle before the court challenging the sufficiency of that party's responses.

What becomes less clear are including "Instructions" that more aggressively direct the answering party. For example, one of us authors often included this "Instruction" in interrogatories: "In answering these Interrogatories, your omission of any name, fact, or other item of information from your answer shall be deemed a representation by you that such name, fact, or other item of information was not known to you, your employees, or your representatives at the time you served your answers." The other of us did not include it, and questions whether it would add true litigation value. So, differences in litigation strategy can impact the use of "Instructions" and "Definitions."

What is always unwise is the practice of including lengthy sets of "Instructions" and "Definitions" that are patently objectionable. *See Coleman v. Starbucks*, 2015 WL 2449585, at *5 & n.1 (M.D. Fla. May 22, 2015) (7½ pages of instructions and definitions included some that "appear to have been slapped together haphazardly; number 11 is missing while number 14 appears twice, and there is a part 'D' under definition number 2 but no 'A,' 'B,' or 'C'" and, also, some that "do not make any sense" – "For example, 'data' is defined as 'to state' certain information (e.g., date, author, custodian) about a document or oral communication. … 'Data' is not a verb in common English, and Defendant does not use it like one."). The same is true with using "Instructions" or "Definitions" to evade the limit on the number of interrogatories posed. *See Bottoms v. Liberty Life Assur. Co. of Bos.*, 2011 WL 6181423, at *6 n.1 (D. Colo. Dec. 13, 2011) ("Counsel should not be permitted to violate the intent of [the interrogatory numerical limit] by serving interrogatories in the guise of an instruction or definition.").

In sum, "Instructions" and "Definitions" may be usefully included, but only when they help to streamline the discovery process, not frustrate it. *See Diversified Prod.*

Corp. v. Sports Ctr. Co., 42 F.R.D. 3, 4 (D. Md. 1967) ("the use of unreasonable 'definitions' may render the interrogatories so burdensome to the answering party and to the Court, that objections to the entire series should be sustained with sanctions").

C. Drafting "Defensively"

Although styling may vary among attorneys, seasoned lawyers always draft discovery—and, especially, interrogatories—with their adversary in mind. Ideal questions are drafted in a manner to avoid provoking a well-founded objection from the other side. Discovery fights are costly, both in terms of the client's money and in wasted time (remember, the time for discovery is limited, and if some of it is being squandered battling over an avoidable interrogatory fight and then waiting for the court's ruling, that interrogatory sure hasn't done the questioner much good). A few "rules of thumb" are wise to bear in mind while drafting written discovery—and especially interrogatories:

- ***Ask Simply and Directly:*** Written discovery should be concise and easily understood. An often-invoked basis for an objection is that the request is "vague," "confusing," or "unintelligible." Frame your questions to sidestep that objection; if the question is crisp and clear, an adversary might forebear from objecting simply to avoid being embarrassed before the court.

- ***Ask Narrowly:*** Avoid compound questions and requests; the more cluttered the question, the more likely an objection will succeed.

- ***Proofread to Avoid Typos:*** If the request contains an unintended phrasing or reference gaffe that leaves it muddled or otherwise objectionable, the court is unlikely to rescue the questioner. Pleas of "well, what I meant was. . ." are not going to be well received by a judge.

- ***Define Recurring Terms at the Outset:*** To reduce the risk of typos and confusion, many attorneys define recurring terms in the "definitions" section that precedes their written questions. So, for example, Ricky's parents might define the term "swing" to mean, "The swing seat on Model No. B-284005 Recess Yard Swing Set that Grammar School had installed on its property"; and the term "incident" to mean, "Use of the swing on [DATE] by students at Grammar School during which Ricky fell and sustained the injuries that are the subject of this lawsuit."

- ***Don't Overdo It with Instructions and Definitions:*** A style, for many years, was to clutter written discovery with pages and pages of preliminary "instructions" and "definitions." Be careful with these. A few clear, easily understood, and Rule-consistent "instructions" are fine, accompanied by a small set of "definitions." But as this prefatory part of a discovery request grows in size and complexity, so, too, does the risk that the responding party (and, later, the judge) will ignore it.

- *Avoid Complicated Cross-References (and All Legalese):* Defining recurring terms is fine, but convoluted references are likely to lead to confusion. Thus, avoid "the party of the second part," the "aforementioned fall," the "owner and/or possessor and/or operator," and the like. Think: *clarity.*

- *Avoid Partisan and Condemnatory Phrasing:* An interrogatory asking when the manufacturer first sold its "defectively designed swing seat" is going to yield nothing of value. Instead of supplying the requestor with the date when the "swing" was first sold, the manufacturer will reply, "Never: this company has never sold a defectively designed swing seat." One of the allotted 25 interrogatory questions has now been spent, nothing has been gained, and the answer is probably not improper.

- *Ask Reasonably:* Overshooting is among the most common triggers for a discovery fight. If Ricky's parents ask for all swing set consumer complaints the manufacturer has received since 1933 when it first starting making swing sets, the question will almost certainly provoke an objection, the judge will likely sustain the objection, and the pursuit of important, useful information will be delayed or, perhaps, lost altogether. Frame questions so that a judge, in considering the dispute, is likely to find the scope of the request to be reasonable.

D. The Challenge of "Lawyered" Answers

One important, practical reality associated with using interrogatories guides most experienced litigators in effectively using this discovery tool. Answers to interrogatories are typically prepared by a party's attorney, rather than by the party himself or herself. Consequently, as noted earlier, those answers often come back well "lawyered" with qualifications and limitations.

Consider, again, the lawsuit Ricky's parents filed after their son's fall from the swing. The parents' attorney might send an interrogatory to the manufacturer, asking, "Please explain why the swing was not designed to sustain a greater weight." The manufacturer's answer is likely to be lengthy, qualified, and largely unhelpful:

"Defendant manufacturer objects to this Interrogatory as vague and unanswerable in its present form, as Parents have failed to identify the specific swing at issue, whether it was purchased new or used, whether it was modified in any way or respect by the seller prior to its use, and how it was maintained from the time of purchase. Subject to and without waiving that objection, defendant manufacturer answers that it designs different swing set models to suit the individual preferences of each purchaser. Some purchasers seek to invest in a more economical model, intentionally foregoing design enhancements that might be included in deluxe-grade models. For this reason, and others, defendant manufacturer endeavors to offer a full range of design models, all with differing features, to meet the purchasing parameters of every consumer."

Clearly, this sort of "lawyered" interrogatory answer would not be optimally helpful to the parents in understanding the design question they pose.

Mindful of the likelihood that interrogatory answers will come back "massaged" by the answering lawyer, many experienced attorneys prefer to use interrogatories primarily to pursue "hard" information. Consider, for example, how far less susceptible the following interrogatories are to being "lawyered":

"Please provide the names, job titles, and addresses for each person involved in the design of Model No. B-284005 Recess Yard Swing Set."

"Were the swing seats supplied with the Model No. B-284005 Recess Yard Swing Set ever tested for their maximum weight bearing capacity? If so, please provide the names, job titles, and addresses for each person involved in any way in that testing."

"Please list the case name, court number, and jurisdiction of every lawsuit filed against you alleging a design flaw in Model No. B-284005 Recess Yard Swing Set."

Remember, absent agreement from the opponent or a court order, interrogatories are limited to 25 discrete questions. Using one of those scarce interrogatories only to receive back an unhelpfully "lawyered" answer is an obvious waste of time and energy. To avoid that outcome, attorneys have developed different approaches. Some choose never (as a general rule) to spend one of their interrogatories pursuing information that more easily and directly can be obtained during a deposition or from a request for production of documents. Thus, these attorneys might use interrogatories to ask the court jurisdiction, case name, and docketing numbers of every similar lawsuit filed against the swing manufacturer, but wait for a deposition to ask why a particular swing seat re-design idea was abandoned. Some attorneys like to pose interrogatories in standard "waves," using an early set of questions to pursue witness identification information (like the question, above, seeking the identities of persons who were involved in designing the Model No. B-284005 Recess Yard Swing Set), and later "waves" of interrogatories to pursue added details on new leads that come unearthed during the discovery process. Whatever approach the attorney prefers, being always mindful of the "lawyering" risk of interrogatory responses is likely to serve as a good guide in choosing when to use this discovery tool.

Hypotheticals: Mastering the Nuances

Pushing Up the Volume: In their swing set lawsuit, Ricky's parents' attorney serve on the defendant manufacturer a set of interrogatories that contain 35 separate questions. What are the defendant's options upon receiving this set of interrogatories? Strategically, how should it respond? Can you conjure a reason why the defendant might willingly decide to answer all 35 questions?

Knowledgeable Nonparties: Often, nonparties are critical sources of facts needed for the fair adjudication of a civil dispute. But interrogatories are expressly *not* available for use with nonparties. In the swing set lawsuit, the manufacturer comes to learn that the fellow parents are quite familiar with how the recess yard swing set performed on other occasions, and may have important, eyewitness information vital to the lawsuit. Why should the manufacturer be denied access to these other parents' information simply because they are nonparties?

PRACTICE SAMPLES

Sample 4-1: INTERROGATORIES

IN THE UNITED STATES DISTRICT COURT
DISTRICT OF WEST CAROLINA

Pat and Vickie Traggler, *individually and on behalf of* *Max Traggler, a minor,*	))))	
Plaintiffs,	))	
v.	))	Civil Action No. 00-CV-98765
USafe Swim Co.,	))	
Defendant.	)	

Defendant's First Set of Interrogatories
Directed to Plaintiffs

Defendant USafe Swim Co. ("USafe") requests that plaintiffs Pat and Vickie Traggler, individually and on behalf of the decedent Max Traggler, answer the following interrogatories in writing, under oath, and within thirty days of service.

Instructions

1. These Interrogatories shall be considered continuing in nature. Should you later learn that a response is incomplete or incorrect, you have a duty to timely supplement or correct that response.

2. In answering these Interrogatories, you are to furnish all information in your possession, custody, or control.

3. If you are unable to fully answer any of these Interrogatories, after exercising the diligence the law requires of you to acquire the information, answer the Interrogatory to the fullest extent possible and explain your inability to answer the remainder.

4. If you object to any portion of any Interrogatory on the basis that the information sought is encompassed by a privilege, the work-product protection, or other immunity, state:

    a. The basis for that objection with specificity, and

    b. whether the objection is resulting in your actually withholding of any information, and

    c. the factual foundation for your objection in sufficient detail so as to allow the court to pass on the merits of your objection.

Definitions

1. The term **"Tragglers"** shall mean Pat and Vickie Traggler, jointly or separately, as well as all other persons acting or purporting to act on their behalves.

2. The term **"Max Traggler"** shall mean the minor child, Max Traggler, as well as all other persons acting or purporting to act on his behalf.

3. The terms **"you"**, **"your"**, **"yours"**, **"yourself"**, and **"yourselves"** shall mean to refer to the Tragglers, as defined above.

4. The term **"USafe"** shall mean USafe Swim Co.

5. The term **"Incident"** shall mean Max Traggler's fall into the swimming pool on or about August 17, 2018, which fall gave rise to the filing of the Complaint.

6. The term "**Your Pool**" shall mean the pool into which Max Traggler fell at the time of the Incident.

7. The term "**Complaint**" shall mean the pleading the Tragglers filed to begin the lawsuit against USafe in the United States District Court for the District of West Carolina, and now docketed at No. 00-CV-98765.

8. The term "**Document**" shall mean all forms of written, printed, recorded, or otherwise preserved matter, including (but not limited to) all forms of graphic matter, photographic matter, sound reproductions, video reproductions, and electronically stored information. The term shall specifically encompass letters, correspondence, memoranda, notes, e-mail, texts, instant messaging, social media posts, videotapes, sound or video recordings, faxes, telegrams, cables, pamphlets, records, files, reports, forms, ledgers, medical records, studies, books, papers, diaries, calendars, charts, lists, receipts, invoices, purchase orders, checks, drawings, photographs, worksheets, sketches, graphs, data sheets, tapes, logs, tables, displays, and all other matter written, printed, recorded, transcribed, photographed, or otherwise set down or preserved in any form whatsoever, which is now or formerly was in Plaintiff's possession, custody, or control. Each copy of any Document that varies in any manner from any other copy of any Document shall be deemed to be a separate Document.

FIRST SET OF
INTERROGATORIES DIRECTED TO PLAINTIFFS:

1. Identify Max Traggler, by stating his full legal name, date of birth, social security number, and all addresses at which he resided since birth.

ANSWER:

2. Identify, by name and address, each school and care facility that Max Traggler attended since birth.

ANSWER:

3. Identify each of Max Traggler's treating healthcare professionals, by stating each of their full legal names, occupations, places of business, reasons for treating Max Traggler, and all dates of treatments.

ANSWER:

4. Identify Your Pool, by stating its manufacturer, its model number, its serial number, the date you acquired it, and the manner by which you acquired it (if you purchased it, the business and location from whom you purchased it and the price paid; if you received it through other means, the source and explanation for the acquisition).

   ANSWER:

5. Identify the installation of Your Pool, by stating the date on which you installed it, the reason for the delay (if any) between the date of acquisition and the date of installation, the length of time it took to install it, and the names, addresses, and phone numbers of all persons who assisted you in installing it.

   ANSWER:

6. Identify each of your uses of the owner's manual that accompanied Your Pool, by stating the date on which you first read it; the length of time you spent reading it on that date; and for all other dates on which you read or consulted it, list those dates, the length of time spent reading or consulting, and the reasons for those readings or consultations.

   ANSWER:

7. Identify all times during which Max Traggler used Your Pool, by stating those dates, the approximate length of time of each use, and who (if anyone) was present during each use.

   ANSWER:

8. Identify all of your activities on the day of the Incident, beginning with waking in the morning and concluding with retiring to sleep in the evening.

   ANSWER:

9. Identify your precise physical location and activity five minutes before the Incident occurred.

   ANSWER:

10. At the time of the Incident, identify your precise physical location and activity.

ANSWER:

11. Identify your precise physical location and activity during the two hours following the Incident.

ANSWER:

12. Identify the status of Your Pool's retractable steps at the time of the Incident, by stating if they were in the upper, locked position or in the lowered, accessible position; who placed the steps in that position; for how long they had been in that position; and why they were in that position.

ANSWER:

13. At the time of the Incident, state whether the 2'x2' square red decal reading: "DANGER! Never Leave Pool Steps Down When Children Are Unattended," was still attached to Your Pool adjacent to its retractable steps. If your answer is "no", explain why it was not still attached to Your Pool at that time.

ANSWER:

Respectfully submitted,
Benjarvus, Green-Ellis, llc

By: ___/s/_____
Attorney for Defendant USafe Swim Co.

Dated: September 15, 20____

[CERTIFICATE OF SERVICE]

Sample 4-2: ANSWERS TO INTERROGATORIES

IN THE UNITED STATES DISTRICT COURT
DISTRICT OF WEST CAROLINA

Pat and Vickie Traggler, *individually and on behalf of Max Traggler, a minor,*	))))
Plaintiffs,	))
v.	) Civil Action No. 00-CV-98765)
USafe Swim Co.,	))
Defendant.	)

Answers and Objections by Plaintiffs to Defendant's First Set of Interrogatories Directed to Plaintiffs

Plaintiffs Pat and Vickie Traggler (the "Tragglers"), individually and on behalf of Max Traggler, a minor, answer Defendant USafe Swim Co.'s First Set of Interrogatories Directed to Plaintiff as follows:

OBJECTIONS TO INSTRUCTIONS

1. The Tragglers object to the characterization of Defendant's First Set of Interrogatories as "continuing" to the extent it proposes to impose a duty on the Tragglers beyond what is required under the Federal Rules of Civil Procedure.

2. The Tragglers object to the direction to supply information that is shielded from discovery by the attorney-client privilege, other privileges, and the work product doctrine.

3. The Tragglers object to the direction to supply information concerning the factual content of privileged or otherwise protected information as effectively intruding upon those protections.

OBJECTIONS TO DEFINITIONS

1/2/3. The Tragglers object to these definitions to the extent it would require the Tragglers to conduct an unreasonable inquiry into knowledge known by persons not within their ready access or control.

<u>ANSWERS AND OBJECTIONS TO INTERROGATORIES</u>

1. Maxwell Albus Traggler; February 8, 2013; 123-45-6789; 408 Twin Pines Drive, Harbortown, West Carolina 29999. That was his only address.

2. Schools/daycare: none.

3. See copy of all medical records, attached.

4. USafe Swim Co. is manufacturer; Model No. AEF-137; Serial No. WNX-CV7815268898ZX; August 11, 2018; purchased from Pools R Us, Harbortown, West Carolina; $1,084.17.

5. August 12, 2018; no delay—next day; 3½ hours; two of us and our next-door neighbors (Polly and Mike McWrisson, 410 Twin Pines Drive; phone is unlisted).

6. August 11, 2018; about 1 hour; August 12, 2018; 3½ hours (following instructions during installation).

7. August 12 (several hours; we were); August 15 (several hours; we were); August 17 (several hours; we were).

8. Awoke; breakfast; set-up for birthday party; participate in birthday party; Emergency Room; family visitation; no sleep or bed.

9. Backyard with the party.

10. Backyard with the party.

11. Steps were down; guests were using the pool.

12. Did not notice this sign, and irrelevant to this case. This is a swimming pool marketed to families. It is the obligation of the manufacturer to make a swimming pool that will not threaten the health or safety of its users. This sign has absolutely no bearing on that.

Sincerely,
KAR, PHULCONSUL, & STEADY, LLC

By: ___/s/_____
Attorney for Plaintiffs

Dated: October 3, 20____

[VERIFICATION]
[CERTIFICATE OF SERVICE]

PART 3.
PRODUCTION REQUESTS—RULE 34

GETTING THE VIEW

While interrogatories ask for information through written questions, production requests under Rule 34 seek access to physical materials. The most common form of physical materials sought through production requests is documents (whether in paper or electronic form). In this regard, Rule 34 is extremely powerful—it requires the responding party (typically at its own expense) to conduct a "reasonable investigation" for each and every requested document in the responding party's possession, custody, or control responsive to the request, provided those documents fall within the scope of allowable discovery. The responding party must collect the responsive documents, review them for privilege and protection, log the privileged and protected ones, and potentially organize them to correspond to the request's categories. To invoke this awesome power, the requesting party does not need a court order or even court permission to wield it—all it takes is a simple written request.

So common and predominant is the use of Rule 34 to obtain documents that Rule 34 requests are often referred to as "document requests." This short-hand term may lead some attorneys to forget, however, that Rule 34 also authorizes access to electronically stored documents (not just physical ones) and to other types of physical evidence. Specifically, Rule 34 authorizes access to "tangible things" and to "land." Thus, for example, in a products liability case, the defendant may want its expert to inspect the allegedly defective product itself. A Rule 34 request obligates the plaintiff to provide such an opportunity for inspection. Likewise, in a property boundary dispute, the party not in possession of the property may want a surveyor to come onto the property to survey the metes and bounds. A Rule 34 request obligates the opposing party to allow the surveyor entry onto the land. Nonetheless, although "tangible things" and "land" remain within the reach of Rule 34, documents are most often its target.

Documents often present the most unbiased source of information in a case. Witness testimony is subject to the perceptions, memories, and motivations of those witnesses. When recounted, witness testimony often devolves into a contest of "he said, she said." Documents, on the other hand, are generally fixed, immutable records of some aspect of the dispute. For this reason, parties often make document requests the first step of their discretionary discovery—they want to have all the key documents gathered and inspected as early as possible so they can plan their future discovery.

HOW THIS DISCOVERY TOOL WORKS

Production requests are demanded in a written document prepared and served by one party on another party, without court involvement. Like interrogatories, the scope of production requests is tied to the general scope of discovery in Rule 26(b)(1)—nonprivileged matter relevant to any party's claim or defense and proportional to the needs of the case. And like interrogatories, the recipient must prepare and serve a response, typically within 30 days, responding to the requests and interposing objections, signed by counsel. While many of the procedures under Rule 34 mirror those for interrogatories under Rule 33, there are some important differences and provisions unique to document requests, discussed below.

A. No Numerical Limit

Access to relevant, non-privileged documents is deemed so fundamental to the civil litigation process that the Rules place no numerical limit on the number of document requests a party may serve (unlike interrogatories and depositions). This does not mean, of course, that parties have free rein to inundate opponents with a deluge of document requests designed more to burden the opponent than to obtain relevant documents; the Rules provide protections against such abuses (such as the signature certification/sanction procedures under Rule 26(g) designed to ensure that the requests are being served for a proper purpose and not to harass or drive up the expenses of the opponent, or a motion for an order under Rule 26(c) protecting the recipient from abusive discovery). In practice, though, lawyers are much more likely to use a "belt and suspenders" approach to document requests, erring on the side of over-requesting to avoid missing important documents.

B. Early Service

One aspect of document requests that is not found in any of the other discretionary discovery devices is the authorization of "early service." In the How Discovery Begins chapter, we learned that none of the tools of discretionary discovery can be used until the parties first meet one another for their Rule 26(f) conference and discuss, among other things, a "discovery plan." To ensure that the parties do, in fact, convene that meeting, the Rules shut off the discovery spigot until the meeting has occurred.

But a special exception exists for Rule 34: production requests can be served on parties before their conference convenes. *See* Rule 26(d)(2) (allowing early Rule 34 requests after 21 days have passed since service of the summons and complaint). The objective of this early service option is not to require earlier production of discoverable documents. Rather, the purpose is to identify any problems or issues with document production (and particularly production of electronically stored information) in advance of the court's initial scheduling conference order so that the court can address the problems in its scheduling order. To advance that objective, Rule 34 authorizes a party to serve document requests 21 days after the complaint and summons are served, but does not require the recipient to respond until 30 days after the parties' Rule 26(f) discovery conference (the earliest date they would be due in the absence of this early service). This gives the parties and the court an opportunity to identify, discuss, and address document production issues before the response is due.

C. "Possession, Custody, or Control"

Another important aspect of document requests is the requirement that parties produce all responsive discoverable documents in their *"possession, custody, or control."* *See* Rule 34(a)(1). The term is intended to be all-encompassing, and to prevent parties from deeming documents they do not want to produce as somehow outside their Rule 34 obligations. These three attributes—possession, custody, or control—refer to the party, not the lawyer or the individual with whom the lawyer is interacting for purposes of responding to the discovery. Thus, if a document request asks for all correspondence in a particular category, a corporate party must produce all of the responsive correspondence in the corporation's possession, custody, or control.

Hypothetical

Q: Harry Homeowner was injured while mowing his lawn with a lawnmower manufactured by Lucky Lawnmower, Inc., when the blade struck a rock and a fragment of the blade struck and cut his leg. In his products liability lawsuit against Lucky Lawnmower, Inc., Homeowner served production requests seeking all documents related to or discussing the design for the mower Homeowner was using, the Lucky 2000 model. Lisa Lawyer was representing Lucky Lawnmower, Inc., and she was working with Mark Manager to respond to Homeowner's discovery requests. Manager tells Lawyer that he does not have any documents responsive to Homeowner's request. May Lawyer serve a response indicating that there are no responsive documents?

A: Not based solely on Manager's information. Lawyer and Manager must conduct a reasonable search of Lucky Lawnmower, Inc.'s files and cannot constrain the search to Manager's files.

Hypothetical

Q: Pursuant to Lawyer's instructions, Manager conducts a search of Lucky Lawnmower, Inc.'s files and finds a drawer of design proposals submitted by engineers who were hoping to be selected by Lucky Lawnmower, Inc. to perform the design work on the Lucky 2000. Most of those were proposals by engineering firms the company did not hire. Can Lucky Lawnmower, Inc. decide not to produce the documents because they are not Lucky Lawnmower, Inc.'s documents, but are the engineering firm's documents? Likewise, the engineering firm that Lucky Lawnmower, Inc. did hire has all of the actual design drawings in its files. Must Lucky Lawnmower, Inc. obtain the design drawings from the engineering firm and produce them?

A: The answer to these questions turns on the phrase "possession, custody, or control." While Lucky Lawnmower, Inc. might be able to argue that the rejected design proposals really "belong" to the unselected engineering firms, it cannot dispute having the proposal in its "possession" or "custody." Thus, Lucky Lawnmower, Inc. must produce those documents assuming they are responsive to the request. To determine whether Lucky Lawnmower, Inc. must produce the design drawings prepared by the firm it hired and which reside in that firm's files, Lucky Lawnmower, Inc. might need to analyze its contract with the firm to see what it says about control of the design drawings. As a general matter, however, because Lucky Lawnmower, Inc. engaged the engineering firm, was its client, and paid for the drawings, it very likely "controls" them within the meaning of Rule 34 and would have to produce them.

Whether documents held by another company or person remain in a party's control is a frequently contested issue. For example, in *St. Jude Medical S.C., Inc. v. Janssen-Counotte,* an employer sued a former employee for allegedly stealing the company's trade secrets and related claims. During discovery, the plaintiff sought to compel the employee's new employer, Biotronik, Inc., to search for and produce discoverable documents held by legally distinct, but affiliated, companies in other countries. The court examined whether documents held by such affiliated companies were within the Biotronik's control (although this case involves a subpoena

under Rule 45 rather than a production request under Rule 34, the test for possession, custody, or control is the same under both rules).

ST. JUDE MEDICAL S.C., INC.
v.
JANSSEN-COUNOTTE

305 F.R.D. 630 (D. Or. 2015)

SIMON, United States District Judge

* * *

A. Whether Biotronik, Inc. Must Produce Documents Held by Its European Affiliates

"The Federal Rules of Civil Procedure require a party served with a subpoena
for records to produce those records that are in its 'possession, custody, or
control.'" *In re Citric Acid Litig.*, 191 F.3d 1090, 1107 (9th Cir.1999) (quoting
Fed. R. Civ. P. 45(a)). Because this requirement is in the disjunctive, actual
possession of a document need not be established. Legal ownership of a document also need not be shown. *In re Bankers Trust Co.*, 61 F.3d 465, 469 (6th
Cir. 1995). Control is sufficient. *Citric Acid*, 191 F.3d at 1107.

"Control is defined as the legal right to obtain documents upon demand."
Id. (quotation marks omitted). Thus, a corporate party may be ordered to
produce documents held by a subsidiary that is not a party to the action on
the grounds that such documents are subject to the "effective control" of the
parent. *United States v. Faltico*, 586 F.2d 1267, 1270 (8th Cir. 1978). Even
documents held by a parent company have been held to be within the "control" of a subsidiary when there is a sufficiently "close nature" in the actual
corporate relationship. *Japan Halon Co. v. Great Lakes Chem. Corp.*, 155
F.R.D. 626, 627 (N.D. Ind. 1993). "The control analysis for Rule 34 purposes
does not require the party to have actual managerial power over the foreign
corporation, but rather that there be close coordination between them." *Afros
S.P.A. v. Krauss–Maffei Corp.*, 113 F.R.D. 127, 129 (D. Del. 1986). In addition,
"'[c]ontrol' may be established by the existence of a principal-agent relationship." *Allen v. Woodford*, 2007 WL 309945, at *2 (E.D. Cal. Jan. 30, 2007). In
short,

> "Legal right" is evaluated in the context of the facts of each case. *In
> re Folding Carton Antitrust Litig.*, 76 F.R.D. 420, 423 (D. Ill. 1977).
> The determination of control is often fact specific. Central to each

case is the relationship between the party and the person or entity having actual possession of the document. *Estate of Young v. Holmes*, 134 F.R.D. 291, 294 (D. Nev. 1991).

Id.

The fact-specific question presented here is whether documents and ESI [electronically stored information] held by Biotronik, Inc.'s sister company Biotronik SE, their common parent MS Holding II SE, or another related Biotronik entity are within the effective control of Biotronik, Inc. St. Jude S.C. has presented evidence that Defendant Janssen negotiated with and received her job offer to become Biotronik, Inc.'s President of U.S. operations from Max Schaldach, the beneficial owner of the entire "Biotronik Group," which is defined in paragraph 6 of Janssen's Employment Agreement as "Biotronik and all of its Affiliated Companies." Also participating in the negotiations with Janssen were Christian Bluemel (another high-level executive) and Werner Braun, both of whom are associated with the Biotronik Group's European affiliates. As a result of these negotiations, Janssen was appointed Biotronik, Inc.'s President for U.S. operations, in a new office specifically created for her in New York City, replacing Biotronik, Inc.'s then-President, who was placed in another position with one of the Biotronik Group's European affiliates.

Janssen has admitted that she intentionally deleted all of her copies of her emails and text messages related to her negotiations that led to her becoming President of Biotronik, Inc. When St. Jude demanded copies of those emails, text messages, and related documents from Biotronik, Inc., however, all that was produced was a redacted copy of Janssen's final contract and several pages from her passport and visa application. In addition, Biotronik, Inc. has refused to search the documents or ESI of any of Biotronik, Inc.'s European affiliates, including the files of Messrs. Schaldach, Bluemel, and Braun, with whom Janssen negotiated her move and new employment, on the grounds that the European affiliates are distinct legal entities and that those individuals are not employed by Biotronik, Inc., but only by its European affiliates.

St. Jude S.C. argues that because no documents reflecting any negotiations with Janssen were produced by Biotronik, Inc., a reasonable inference is that the negotiations with Janssen, which she admits took place, were carried out in Europe by Biotronik, Inc.'s European affiliates, including Messrs. Schaldach, Bluemel, and Braun, acting as agents for Biotronik, Inc. Because Biotronik, Inc. is Janssen's actual employer in the United States, St. Jude S.C.'s agency argument is well taken.

A corporation "can only act through its employees, agents, directors, or officers." 9th Cir. Civ. Jury Instruction 4.2 (2007). The negotiations that led to Biotronik, Inc. hiring Janssen in 2014 as its President for U.S. operations presumably were not conducted by any of its own employees, directors, or officers because, if they were, one would reasonably have expected to find some documentary or ESI evidence to that effect. But Biotronik, Inc. says that it conducted a reasonable search and has found none. Biotronik, Inc. also does not argue that any of its employees, directors, or officers handled its side of the employment negotiations with Janssen. Thus, it is reasonable to infer that the persons associated with Biotronik, Inc.'s European affiliates, including Messrs. Schaldach, Bluemel, and Braun, who negotiated Janssen's hiring by Biotronik, Inc., were acting as agents for Biotronik, Inc., Janssen's actual new employer. This is sufficient indicia of effective control to require the European affiliates of Biotronik, Inc., namely the "Biotronik Group" as defined in Janssen's Employment Agreement, to conduct a reasonable and diligent search for documents and ESI responsive to St. Jude S.C.'s Rule 45 subpoena served on Biotronik, Inc.

Thus, documents held by an affiliated corporation may be deemed within the control of a party. Similar reasoning would apply to documents held by a party's accountant or other representative or agent. But what about documents that belong to another entity that the party happens to have in its files?

Hypothetical

Q: When searching for design documents, Manager finds a design document from a competitor that Lucky Lawnmower, Inc. found on the Internet and downloaded. Assuming the design document is responsive to a document request, must Lucky Lawnmower, Inc. produce it, or may it maintain that the design document is not the company's document and that Homeowner could just as easily download the document itself?

A: Lucky Lawnmower, Inc. must produce the design document. Even though Lucky Lawnmower, Inc. did not generate the document, the document is in its possession at a minimum. The fact that Homeowner might be able to locate the document on the Internet himself does not relieve Lucky Lawnmower, Inc. of the obligation to produce it. After all, it might be important for Homeowner to confirm that Lucky Lawnmower, Inc. had a copy of the document, even if Homeowner knew to look for the document and was able to find it.

D. Objections

Rule 34 establishes procedures for objecting to document requests, most of which resemble provisions for objecting to interrogatories but some of which are unique. Like interrogatories, parties must state their objections with "*specificity*." Rule 34(b)(2)(B). Thus, boilerplate objections (*e.g.*, "The plaintiff objects to Document Request No. 1 as overly broad, unduly burdensome, vague, and ambiguous") are often held ineffective. Curiously, while Rule 33 expressly provides that failure to assert a properly specific objection constitutes the waiver of that objection, Rule 34 does not contain a similar provision, and the courts are divided about how to interpret this difference.

A more significant difference in objection procedures is found in Rule 34(b)(2)(C). This provision requires a party interposing an objection to a document request to state whether the party has withheld any documents on the basis of the objection. The purpose of this provision is to enable the requesting party to make a more thoughtful and informed decision about whether to file a motion to compel challenging the objection (a motion type we will discuss in greater detail in the Policing Discovery chapter). If the requesting party knows that the responding party has not withheld any documents on the basis of an objection, the requesting party will be far less likely to incur the costs and to burden the court with a challenge to the objection. The responding party does not need to create a log of each document withheld on the basis of an objection, akin to a privilege log. Rather, a description of the category of documents withheld is sufficient.

Hypothetical

Q: In our Lucky Lawnmower, Inc. lawsuit, suppose a production request seeks all documents reflecting sales of the Lucky 2000 over the previous ten years, and Lucky Lawnmower, Inc. believes only records from the previous five years are relevant and proportional. How should Lucky Lawnmower, Inc. respond?

A: Lucky Lawnmower, Inc. can object that the request is overly broad in terms of time, and state that it is withholding all responsive documents more than five years old. Such an objection would comply with the requirements for objections under Rule 34, and Homeowner is well-equipped to decide whether the older documents are sufficiently important to his case to warrant the expenses and potential delays of filing a motion to compel Lucky Lawnmower, Inc. to produce the older documents.

The objection specificity requirement, added to Rule 34 in the 2015 amendments, has cast some doubt on the long-standing practice of interposing general objections at the beginning of a set of document requests, as described in the section on interrogatories above. Some courts have held that general objections, by their very nature, fail to comply with the specificity requirement. *See, e.g., Auburn Sales, Inc. v. Cypros Trading & Shipping, Inc.,* 2016 WL 3418554, at *3 (E.D. Mich. June 22, 2016) (general objections do not satisfy the requirement that, "for each item or category," the response state objections with specificity; with general objections it is unclear as to which requests the defendants objected and as to which they produced documents). The simultaneous addition in 2015 of the obligation to specify whether the responding party is withholding documents on the basis of each objection further undermines general objections. Assume, for example, in our Lucky Lawnmower, Inc. lawsuit, Homeowner served a set of production requests that included a set of instructions. Lucky Lawnmower, Inc. wants to object to the instructions to the extent they attempt to impose obligations beyond those authorized by the Federal Rules of Civil Procedure, a common objection. Lucky Lawnmower, Inc. may have difficulty determining whether it is withholding any documents on the basis of that objection.

E. Producing Responsive Documents

In addition to providing a written response to the document requests, the responding party must also produce the responsive discoverable documents themselves. *Production* in this context is a legal term of art, and does not necessarily require the producing party to give copies of the documents to the requesting party. Rather, the production process may involve a number of steps, depending on the nature of the party and the volume of documents. The first step is analyzing the requests and determining the nature of the documents that are responsive.

1. Collecting Responsive Documents

Once the responding party has determined which categories of documents it must produce in response to the requests, the responding party must search for and collect those responsive documents. The courts require a good faith, diligent search, not a quick glance in the most likely spot. *See, e.g., Sell v. Country Life Ins. Co.,* 189 F. Supp. 3d 925, 932–33 (D. Ariz. 2015) (sanctioning an insurance company for simply producing a claim file without doing a diligent search of the company's other records). If the party is an individual, that process may be relatively straightforward, but with a corporate client, identifying the appropriate information repositories and record custodians (employees likely to have responsive documents) may require careful thought and consultation with the client. Once the legal team has decided where to look, the team must review all the documents in those locations and identify the responsive ones. For paper documents, this process entails someone physically looking at each document to evaluate responsiveness. The process for electronic documents is described in the section on ESI below.

2. Conducting the Privilege Review

Next, the documents must be reviewed for privilege, as described in the Scope of Discovery chapter. Depending on the nature of the case, the documents may also need to be reviewed for confidentiality. Documents that contain confidential or proprietary information are discoverable, in contrast to privileged documents, but they are often handled differently. Parties typically enter into a confidentiality order that limits disclosure of such documents (as described in more detail in the *Policing Discovery* chapter).

3. Providing the Responsive, Nonprivileged Documents

Finally, parties have a number of options regarding the production process. Rule 34 gives the responding party the choice of making responsive documents available to the requesting party for inspection or of providing a copy of all the responsive documents to the requesting party. Making the documents available for inspection entails allowing the opposing party to review the documents, and then designate and pay for copies of any it selects. The option to make documents available for inspection applies more frequently to paper documents—with electronic documents it is much more common to provide a copy. Even with paper documents, this decision depends on the number of documents being produced. If the documents fit into one or two boxes, it is common for the requesting party to ask to have them all copied (and then to review them, more comfortably, back in the requesting party's offices), whereas if there are hundreds or thousands of boxes, a preliminary, on-site inspection may be more likely.

The responding party also has options for organizing the responsive documents. Rule 34(b)(2)(E)(i) allows the responding party to produce documents "as they are kept in the usual course of business" or to "organize and label them to correspond to the categories in the request." The first of these approaches entails giving an opponent access to all of the party's records in a particular location, rather than segregating the documents relevant to the lawsuit.

Hypothetical

Q: Suppose, in our Lucky Lawnmower, Inc. example, Harry Homeowner requested all of Lucky Lawnmower, Inc.'s purchasing records for any parts used in the Lucky 2000 model over the past 5 years. Lucky Lawnmower, Inc. maintains all of its invoices in one designated file room but does not segregate them by model. Lucky Lawnmower, Inc. is hesitant to incur the expense of having its legal team (or even an employee) spend days looking for invoices related to the Lucky 2000. Does it have any way to avoid those expenses?

A: Lucky Lawnmower, Inc. can allow Homeowner to look through the invoices himself. However, Lucky Lawnmower, Inc. would first have to ensure that there were no privileged documents in the file room or it would risk waiver if it allowed Homeowner access to the files. Furthermore, this approach entails giving Home-owner—Lucky Lawnmower, Inc.'s opponent—unfettered access to the invoices, many of which are not relevant to the lawsuit. Because of these considerations, legal teams are typically uncomfortable providing such unstructured access to their client's documents, and this approach is not frequently used.

More commonly, the responding legal team will organize and label the responsive documents. Under this approach, the responding party attaches a unique designation on each page of each responsive document. The designation (sometimes called a "Bates label") often includes a prefix that identifies which party is producing the documents (perhaps the first few letters of the party's name) and a sequential number. Using this designation system, the responding party then advises the requesting party which documents are being produced in response to each request, complying with the obligation to label and organize the documents.

The labels can be important in subsequent stages of the litigation as well. For example, Rule 37 limits the use of a document that was not properly disclosed during discovery. If a party challenges the use of a piece of evidence on this basis, the absence or presence of a discovery label will help resolve whether the court should allow the document into evidence.

F. No Duty to Create Documents

Production requests differ fundamentally from interrogatories in one very important respect: the responding party's obligation to create content. For interrogatories, the requesting party identifies the information it seeks in an interrogatory. The interrogatory may seek facts or may seek the responding party's contentions regarding an issue in the case. The responding party then must, within the bounds of the Rules, draft language supplying the requested information. In contrast, the Rules generally do not obligate a party responding to production requests to create responsive documents.

Hypothetical

Q: In our Lucky Lawnmower, Inc. example, assume Homeowner served a production request seeking "a list of the sales of the Lucky 2000 over the past five
years." Also assume that Lucky Lawnmower, Inc. has financial records that include
all of the pieces of information necessary to compile the list, but that Lucky Lawnmower, Inc. does not maintain a specific list responsive to the request. How
should Lucky Lawnmower, Inc. respond to the request?

A: Lucky Lawnmower, Inc. will not be required to create the list (although it
would be required, in response to a properly worded production request, to produce the financial records containing the information and might be required to
generate the list in response to an interrogatory). Thus, Lucky Lawnmower, Inc.
should respond that it has no documents responsive to the request. *See Mir v. L-3
Commc'ns Integrated Sys., L.P.*, 319 F.R.D. 220, 227 (N.D. Tex. 2016) (holding that a
party generally may not be compelled to create a document but may be required
to sign an authorization for the release of records).

G. Cost of Responding

In general, the Rules contemplate that each party will bear its own costs of pro-
pounding and responding to discovery during the pendency of the litigation, although a small subset of these discovery expenses may be awarded to the successful
party at the conclusion of the case as costs under Rule 54. A party believing discovery
costs should be allocated differently on an interim basis can seek a protective order
under Rule 26(c), as discussed in the *Policing Discovery* chapter.

These principles apply with equal force to the process of gathering, producing,
inspecting, and copying the documents produced under Rule 34, as well as to the
drafting of the requests and the responses. Thus, the responding party generally
incurs the cost of gathering, reviewing, labeling, and organizing all of the responsive
documents. The requesting party generally bears the cost of inspecting or copying
the documents.

H. Electronically Stored Information

Although discovery of Electronically Stored Information (ESI)—or *e-discovery*—is
fundamentally just the Rule 34 production request process applied to one form of

information (that stored electronically rather than on paper), the volume of ESI and the technological aspects of e-discovery raise a host of issues that sets ESI apart as a particularly thorny aspect of discovery. One estimate suggests that 281 billion emails were sent every day in 2018—that's 195 million emails per minute! Email Statistics Report, 2018–22, The Radicati Group, Inc. Thus, in most disputes, the volume of ESI will dwarf the volume of information captured on paper documents, often making ESI the focus of the production phase of discovery.

Moreover, people often view electronic communications as less formal and permanent than printed paper documents (even though, under most platforms, electronic communications are *more* permanent than a printed page, often captured on backup systems, lurking in deleted-items folders, etc.). People will say outrageous things in a text message or social media post that, on calm reflection, they wouldn't dream of writing in a formal memorandum. Yet those electronic communications can be just as devastating as exhibits in the courtroom. Indeed, in some very high-profile, high-dollar litigations involving technology companies (such as Microsoft, Apple, and Samsung), whose employees should understand electronic media better than most, many of the most damaging and critical documents were ESI. Thus, understanding ESI is a critical skill for litigators. *See* Zachary Wang, *Ethics and Electronic Discovery: New Medium, Same Problems,* 75 Def. Couns. J. 328, 329 (2008) (suggesting that failure to master the intricacies of ESI may violate Model Rule 1.1's requirement that a lawyer provide "competent representation").

1. ESI Is Fully Discoverable from Many Sources

As a starting point, there is no debate that ESI is fully discoverable just like a paper document. Rule 34(a)(1)(A) allows discovery of "electronically stored information . . . stored in any medium from which information can be obtained either directly or, if necessary, after translation by the responding party into a reasonably usable form." This language is deliberately vague, in recognition that the drafters cannot keep up with the pace of change of technology. Thus, for example, information exchanged on Snapchat or Slack would be discoverable even though those forms of communication did not exist when this language was drafted in 2006.

This broad swath of discoverable ESI encompasses data stored in many sources, on many platforms. To illustrate the proliferation of ESI and the repositories that must be searched for responsive information, consider a letter that is material to a dispute in litigation. If the letter was printed and stored in a file cabinet, it would certainly be discoverable, and its production would be relatively straightforward. Of course, that same letter stored on a computer would similarly be discoverable. But earlier drafts of the letter also stored on the computer would also be discoverable— such drafts are much more likely to be retained electronically than paper versions were, and some programs automatically create and retain versions of documents, particularly if multiple people collaborate on them. If the collaborators made redlined changes, those too would likely be captured by the computer and would be discoverable—perhaps along with information about who made each change and when each change occurred.

The search would not end there, however. If drafts of the document were shared among the collaborators by email, versions of the letter might be found in the inboxes or sent-mail folders of the collaborators even if not saved as versions by any of the collaborators. The emails might also contain relevant communications about the letter. Even if the collaborators had deleted all the emails (from their inboxes, sent-mail folders, and even from their deleted items folders) copies of those emails—and email attachments—might exist on backup systems for the collaborators' computers or on backups of the collaborators' smart phones.

Because of the way ESI multiplies and persists, it is not uncommon to have gigabytes, or even terabytes, of data that are potentially responsive and discoverable. With paper documents, the primary means of screening such potentially discoverable documents is to assign paralegals, associates, or contract attorneys to review the documents for privilege, work product, and responsiveness—a human would eyeball each document and make these assessments. That approach is simply unfeasible for a terabyte of data; both the cost and the delay would be enormous. However, the problems created by the volume of ESI are somewhat offset by the technology tools that have been developed to assist with the discovery process for ESI.

2. ESI Tools

In large or complex cases, and increasingly even in smaller and less complex cases, the discovery of ESI is aided by litigation support professionals using various technologies. These professionals may be employed by companies that provide litigation support services to lawyers or may be directly employed by a law firm. They may be lawyers, but often are not, and in either event are trained both in the processes used for e-discovery and in the technology tools that facilitate those processes. The lawyers handling the litigation will work closely with these e-discovery technicians to design and implement an e-discovery approach.

In terms of those tools, there are a variety on the market, and they are constantly evolving. Initially, most of the searching was accomplished using simple word searches or Boolean searches (searches that can look for words appearing in the same sentence or paragraph or occurring near each other). So, for example, to find documents potentially subject to the attorney-client privilege, the lawyers would craft a word search using the names of all known attorneys who might have been involved and words like "attorney," "legal," "privilege," etc. Paralegals or lawyers would then examine the results of the search, make privilege and work product determinations, and log shielded documents as appropriate.

The ESI tools have advanced far beyond such basic searches, however. Technology Assisted Review (TAR, sometimes called computer-assisted review or predictive coding) uses algorithms—essentially artificial intelligence—to find documents that word searches would miss. A typical TAR system might start with the legal team providing some examples of responsive and non-responsive documents—a set the system calls "seed" documents. The program analyzes the characteristics of the responsive and non-responsive documents and builds algorithms for sorting documents into each category. The legal team selects another group of documents and the program runs again, this time identifying the documents it selects as responsive by relying on the results of the first sort. The legal team then examines the accuracy of the results of this analysis and the algorithm "learns" from any corrections. This process is repeated (sometimes in batches, sometimes on a document-by-document continual basis) until the program produces results that satisfy some statistical measure of accuracy. TAR can often find documents that human review or simple word searches would miss, and courts generally view TAR as an appropriate method for discharging the responding party's duty to search for responsive documents. *See Rio Tinto PLC v. Vale S.A.*, 306 F.R.D. 125, 127 (S.D.N.Y. 2015) (it "is now black letter law that where the producing party wants to utilize TAR for document review, courts will permit it").

These same tools can assist the parties in other aspects of preparing their cases, beyond just responding to document requests. TAR can help parties look for and identify helpful documents in their own collections. Additionally, TAR can help the requesting party to comb through the mountain of ESI it receives to hunt for the "smoking guns" or needles-in-the-haystack of data.

3. Form of ESI Production

An issue closely connected to the use of TAR and related technologies is the form or format in which the ESI is produced. The form in which a document is created is typically referred to as "native format." For example, if a party uses Microsoft Excel to create a spreadsheet and then saves the spreadsheet to a computer, file server, or other storage device, the file would be an Excel spreadsheet in its native format. That same file, however, could be stored in many different electronic formats—as a pdf, jpeg, or tiff file, for example. The format can be important—many TAR programs or other technologies are designed to work optimally with one particular format. Accordingly, the Rules contain provisions related to the form for production.

Rule 34(b)(1)(C) allows the requesting party to specify the format for producing the ESI that is responsive to the requests. The responding party must then produce the ESI in the requested format or object to that format under Rule 34(b)(2)(D) (if, for example, the format in the request was cumbersome or expensive for the responding party, perhaps requiring conversion of the producing party's files into a different file type). Conversely, if the request is silent as to the form for production of ESI, Rule 34(b)(2)(E)(ii) authorizes the responding party to either produce the ESI in the form it is ordinarily maintained or to pick a different reasonably usable form—it may not pick an obscure or obsolete form. If the request is silent and the responding party picks a reasonably usable form, the requesting party has lost the right to demand the ESI in a different form more compatible with its technology—Rule 34(b)(2)(E)(iii) provides that a party only need produce ESI in one form. Accordingly, best practice is to specify the form in the production request that works best with the technology that the requesting party is planning to use.

4. Metadata

An issue associated with the form for production of ESI is whether metadata is captured and produced. Metadata (essentially, data about data) refers to the information that many computer programs store about the files that someone creates using the programs. Returning to our spreadsheet example, the "properties" box for a spreadsheet shows where the spreadsheet was stored, when it was created, who last modified it, when it was last modified, what those modifications were, and other information about the document. A printed version of the spreadsheet obviously does not capture this metadata. Likewise, the formats that are essentially images of the file (such as a pdf, jpeg, or tiff file) ordinarily do not capture the metadata. Conversely, the file in its native format, such as a .xlsx file, will include all the metadata. Additionally, it is possible to capture the metadata in a file that is associated with an image of the file, so long as measures are put in place at the time the image is created.

Metadata can be particularly important in cases where fraud or misconduct is suspected. Determining whether a document was last modified three years ago as part of the events that are being litigated, or six months ago once litigation had commenced, could be critical. Even in more mundane circumstances, however, metadata can be important—determining who worked on a document or refreshing recollections about the history of a document.

Similarly, again returning to our spreadsheet example, a simple image of a spreadsheet does not include the formulas, and cannot be manipulated (*e.g.*, sorted). Likewise, emails in native format can easily be sorted in a variety of manners—by sender, recipient, date, etc.—or organized into threads. Images of emails may not be so easily manipulated.[1]

---

1. Although it might be a violation of the rules of ethics and other laws to delete metadata that might be relevant to the litigation, there are many situations where litigators should strip metadata from documents they work on. For example, it is common for parties to exchange discovery requests in a word processing format so that the opposing party does not need to scan or key in the requests when preparing the response. Litigators should strip the metadata from such documents so as not to inadvertently supply information about the drafting of the document. Specifically, if a representative of the client made suggestions or comments to the document, you certainly would not want your opponent to have access to that information. The same concepts would apply to settlement agreements, briefs, etc.—make sure to strip the metadata from any document that is provided to someone whom you would not want to access the metadata.

Hypothetical

Q: Homeowner learns during discovery that Lucky Lawnmower, Inc. maintained a spreadsheet containing forecasts of future profits for sales of the Lucky 2000 lawnmower as affected by the addition of various safety features. This spreadsheet included considerations like the cost of designing the safety feature, the increased cost of the lawnmower with the safety feature included, and the likely cost of defending lawsuits in the absence of the safety feature. If Homeowner wants to obtain the maximum information contained in the spreadsheet, should Homeowner specify the format in the production request, and if so, what format should Homeowner choose?

A: In addition to simply containing number values, spreadsheets also contain formulas. Consider a column titled "net profit." The values in that column might be the result of a complex equation. In a paper printout of the spreadsheet, the only information that is revealed is the result of the calculation—the equation itself is not captured. Similarly, an ordinary pdf of the spreadsheet only contains the values, not the formulas. In the native format, however, one can view the formulas easily. Additionally, there are procedures to capture the formulas when creating images like pdfs. Accordingly, Homeowner should request the spreadsheet in native format or in another format that captures the formulas (and, if appropriate, should select the format in consultation with whomever will be assisting with the handling of the ESI in the litigation). If Homeowner does not specify the format, Lucky Lawnmower, Inc. may choose the format and might not choose a format that includes the formulas.

5. Preservation

Although the duty to preserve evidence related to a litigation extends broadly to all evidence, not just ESI, preservation issues—or issues related to the failure to preserve or "spoliation"—arise more frequently with ESI than with paper documents. The duty to preserve evidence arises when litigation has been commenced or is reasonably anticipated. *See Silvestri v. Gen. Motors Corp.*, 271 F.3d 583, 591 (4th Cir. 2001) ("The duty to preserve material evidence arises not only during litigation but also extends to that period before the litigation when a party reasonably should know that the evidence may be relevant to anticipated litigation."). Failure to preserve ESI in breach of this duty can result in sanctions under Rule 37(e), as discussed in the Policing Discovery chapter.

Preservation issues can arise in connection with ESI in a number of ways. At the most intentional level—with intent referring to the intent to delete, and not necessarily the intent to destroy evidence or affect the litigation—ESI can often be deleted with a couple of keystrokes on a computer. A party receiving an email that would be relevant to the litigation might delete it after reading it out of habit, without thinking about the duty to preserve it.

Some loss of evidence occurs without any intent or deliberate action, however. Many companies have email systems that automatically delete emails after a set period of time. Unless someone thinks to suspend that deletion cycle, it will continue to delete emails that should have been preserved. Likewise, every time a party modifies or saves a document, the metadata will change. And every time a party accesses a browser, the browser history changes. The loss of ESI under these scenarios is not malicious or even purposeful but may still violate the duty to preserve.

Litigators have a number of options designed to prevent or minimize the loss of ESI relevant to a litigation matter. For ESI held by the litigator's client, the litigator should arrange for a "litigation hold" letter to go out to all the likely record custodians informing them of the obligation to preserve relevant ESI. For ESI held by an opposing party, a range of options exists. At the minimal end of the scale, a litigator can send a letter to an opponent reminding it of the obligation to preserve ESI. A more involved option involves asking the court to enter a protective order requiring the parties to preserve ESI. Finally, under certain circumstances, a litigator can move for a protective order for the creation of mirror images of an opponent's servers or computers, so that all the information and metadata are preserved. If data has already been lost or destroyed, a litigator can also ask for forensic analysis of an opponent's computer systems.

FROM CLASSROOM TO PRACTICE

A. E-Discovery Planning

As the above discussion suggests, the e-discovery process proceeds much more smoothly and satisfactorily with advance planning and forethought. Some of this advance planning is forced on the parties externally. When the parties conduct their Rule 26(f) discovery planning conference and then either meet with the judge or submit their proposed discovery plan, e-discovery is a required topic. Many local rules and individual judge's standing chambers orders require the parties to discuss a variety of e-discovery issues as part of that process, and to bring any disagreements to the judge's attention.

In spite of this forced attention to e-discovery during the Rule 26(f) conference and in the parties' discovery plan, some lawyers treat these topics perfunctorily at the Rule 26(f) conference. It is not uncommon for lawyers to report to the court in their discovery plan that they do not foresee any unusual e-discovery issues. Then, when discovery commences in earnest, they realize that they disagree about issues like whether metadata should be preserved and produced or what information they will disclose to each other about their search methodologies. At that point, the only remedy if the parties cannot resolve their disagreement is a motion to compel or a motion for a protective order (at considerable expense and likely causing significant delay).

The process works much better if the parties carefully think through e-discovery issues *before* the discovery planning conference, so that they can engage with the opposing party meaningfully and resolve those issues that are readily resolved and identify the issues they cannot resolve. Such planning might involve engaging and meeting with an e-discovery consultant and the client's technical representatives before the planning conference to determine the preferred approaches to e-discovery and to identify likely problems. Using the above metadata example, the parties could exchange their positions regarding metadata, try to resolve them, and then present either a joint position or individual positions to the court as part of the Rule 26(f) report (leading to an earlier, quicker, and less expensive resolution).

Thus, the parties should come to the discovery conference as prepared as they can be to discuss issues like the technologies that the parties will use to gather responsive ESI, the record custodians whose files will be searched for responsive ESI, the form in which ESI will be produced, and whether metadata will be captured and produced. Such preparation does not guarantee that unanticipated e-discovery problems will not arise at a later stage of the litigation, but it does reduce that likelihood.

The likelihood of unanticipated e-discovery problems can be further reduced by using the provision of Rule 34 discussed above allowing early service of production requests, which was added to the Rules in 2015 specifically to alleviate some of the challenges that e-discovery presents. Ideally, if parties serve production requests before the Rule 26(f) conference, the responding parties will be able to identify potential e-discovery problem issues, such as old data no longer easily accessible or issues with the requested data format, that might not have been apparent to the requesting party and might not otherwise have arisen at the discovery conference. The parties can then tackle the problems at the discovery conference and either resolve the problems amicably or ask the court for assistance in resolving them.

Suppose, for example, Harry Homeowner planned to serve discovery seeking computer generated design documents for the Lucky 2000 lawnmower from the past twenty years. The documents from the past ten years are easily retrieved from the company's current file server, but older documents were generated using a legacy engineering program and are only maintained on external hard drives, from which retrieval is both costly and time-consuming. If Homeowner waits until after the parties conduct their Rule 26(f) conference to serve his discovery requests and the parties disagree about whether Lucky Lawnmower, Inc. should have to produce those older design documents and, if so, at whose cost, they will need to engage in motion practice to obtain a resolution. Alternatively, if Homeowner takes advantage of the early service provision, the parties could present the dispute to the court as part of their Rule 26(f) report or at the initial Rule 16 status conference, likely saving both time and money.

Hypotheticals: Mastering the Nuances

Pushing Up the Volume: In his lawnmower lawsuit, Homeowner serves on Lucky Lawnmower, Inc. a set of production requests that contains 35 separate requests. Lucky Lawnmower, Inc. objects to the set as exceeding the allowable number of production requests and therefore as being overly burdensome? Is Lucky Lawnmower, Inc.'s objection proper? Why or why not?

Trade Secrets: Homeowner serves on Lucky Lawnmower, Inc. a production request seeking design information about the safety features on the Lucky 2000. Lucky Lawnmower, Inc. has patents for some of the design features and views other features as "top secret" proprietary information. May Lucky Lawnmower, Inc. properly list these documents on its privilege log? What are its other options?

ESI: Homeowner serves on Lucky Lawnmower, Inc. a production request seeking all internal communications regarding the safety features on the Lucky 2000. The request does not provide any instructions about the manner of producing these communications, Must Lucky Lawnmower, Inc. organize the responsive documents, and, if so, what are its options? In what format(s) may it produce the responsive documents if some of them are stored electronically?

Objections: Homeowner serves on Lucky Lawnmower, Inc. a production request seeking documents from the prior 20 years related to any accidents involving the Lucky 1000 or the Lucky 2000. Lucky Lawnmower, Inc. believes that 20 years is too long a period for it to have to produce documents and believes that documents related to the Lucky 1000 are not relevant. Lucky Lawnmower, Inc.'s response states, "Lucky Lawnmower, Inc. objects to this production request. If Homeowner serves a less burdensome request, Lucky Lawnmower, Inc. will respond appropriately." Is Lucky Lawnmower, Inc.'s objection proper? If not, in what ways is it improper and how would you fix it?

PRACTICE SAMPLES

Sample 4-3: PRODUCTION REQUESTS

IN THE UNITED STATES DISTRICT COURT
DISTRICT OF WEST CAROLINA

Harry Homeowner,	)	
	)	
Plaintiff,	)	
	)	
v.	)	Civil Action No. 00-CV-98765
	)	
Lucky Lawnmower, Inc.,	)	
	)	
Defendant.	)	

Plaintiff's First Set of Production Requests
Directed to the Defendant

Harry Homeowner ("Homeowner") serves the following production requests on Lucky Lawnmower, Inc.

Instructions

1. Without limiting the definition of "document" stated below, documents covered by this Request include all documents in the possession, custody, and control of Lucky Lawnmower, Inc. and its agents, employees, or representatives regardless of their location, including all copies of such documents, the contents of which differ in any respect from the original.

2. All documents produced shall be segregated and identified according to the Requests to which they are primarily responsive, and if they are responsive to several Requests, shall be separately identified accordingly.

3. For each document responsive to any Request that is sought to be withheld for any reason, provide the following information: (i) the place, approximate time, and manner of recording or otherwise preparing the document; (ii) the name of the sender and the name and title of the recipient of the document, including all carbon copies or blind copies thereto; (iii) the name of each person who participated in the document's preparation; (iv) the name and position of each person to whom the document's contents have

been communicated by copy, exhibition, reading, or substantial summarization; and, (v) a statement of the basis on which the document is being withheld.

4. If documents have been destroyed, identify the person who decided to destroy them, the reason for the decision to destroy them, the person or parties who destroyed them, and the date (approximate if precise date is not known) of the destruction. Also, summarize and describe the contents of the destroyed document(s) as well as all persons who participated in the preparation of the document and addressees, recipients, or observers of the document.

5. All documents that respond, in whole or in part, to any part or clause of any paragraph of these requests shall be produced in their entirety, including all attachments and enclosures. Only one copy need be produced of documents that are responsive to more than one paragraph or are identical except for the person to whom it is addressed if you indicate the persons or group of persons to whom such documents were distributed. Documents that in their original condition were stapled, clipped, or otherwise fastened together shall be produced in such form.

6. All electronically stored documents, except for spreadsheets and databases, should be produced in searchable pdf format, with metadata captured and associated. Spreadsheets and databases should be produced in native format.

Definitions

1. "**And**" shall be understood to include and encompass "**or**" and vice versa.

2. "**Any**" shall be understood to include and encompass "**all**" and vice versa.

3. "**Each**" shall be understood to include and encompass "**every**" and vice versa.

4. The terms "**You**" and "**Your**" shall mean Lucky Lawnmower, Inc., as well as its parents, subsidiaries, affiliates, agents, employees, and/or representatives.

5. The term "**Complaint**" shall mean the pleading Homeowner filed to begin the lawsuit against Lucky Lawnmower, Inc. in the United States District Court for the District of West Carolina, and now docketed at No. 00-CV-98765.

6. The term "**Lawnmower**" shall mean the Lucky 2000 described in paragraph 14 of the Complaint.

7. The term **"Incident"** shall mean Homeowner's accident while using the Lawnmower, as alleged in paragraphs 15 through 19 of the Complaint.

8. The term **"Document"** shall mean all forms of written, printed, recorded, or otherwise preserved matter, including (but not limited to) all forms of graphic matter, photographic matter, sound reproductions, video reproductions, and electronically stored information. The term shall specifically encompass letters, correspondence, memoranda, notes, pamphlets, records, files, reports, forms, ledgers, medical records, studies, books, papers, diaries, calendars, charts, lists, receipts, invoices, purchase orders, checks, drawings, photographs, worksheets, sketches, graphs, data sheets, tapes, logs, tables, displays, and all other matter written, printed, recorded, transcribed, photographed, or otherwise set down or preserved in any form whatsoever, which is now or formerly was in Lucky Lawnmower, Inc.'s possession, custody, or control. Each copy of any Document that varies in any manner from any other copy of any Document shall be deemed to be a separate Document.

The term "Document" also expressly includes all electronic data stored on any Electronic Media. "Electronic data" means the original (or identical duplicate when the original is not available), and any non-identical copies (whether non-identical because of notes made on copies or attached comments, annotations, marks, transmission notations, or highlighting of any kind) of writings of every kind and description whether inscribed by mechanical, facsimile, electronic, magnetic, digital, or other means. "Electronic data" includes, by way of example only, computer programs (whether private, commercial, or work-in-progress), programming notes or instructions, activity listings of electronic mail receipts and/or transmittals, output resulting from the use of any software program, including word processing documents, spreadsheets, database files, charts, graphs, and outlines, electronic mail, and any and all miscellaneous files and/or file fragments, regardless of the media on which they reside and regardless of whether the electronic data exists in an active file, deleted file, or file fragment. "Electronic data" includes any and all items stored on computer memories, hard disks, floppy disks, CD-ROMs, removable media such as Zip disks, Jaz cartridges, Bernoulli Boxes and their equivalent, magnetic tapes of all types, microfiche, and any other vehicle used for digital data storage and/or transmittal. "Electronic data" also includes the file, folder tabs, and/or containers and labels appended to, or associated with, any physical storage device associated with each original and/or copy. "Electronic media" means any magnetic or other storage media device used to record electronic data. Electronic media devices may include, but are not limited to, computer memories, hard disks, floppy disks, CD-ROM, removable media such as Bernoulli Boxes and their equivalent, magnetic tapes of all types, microfiche, punched cards, and any other vehicle used for digital data storage and/or transmittal.

Production Requests

PLEASE PRODUCE THE FOLLOWING WITHIN 30 DAYS OF THE SERVICE OF THIS SET OF PRODUCTION REQUESTS:

1. All design documents, drawings, engineering documents or calculations, photographs, advertisements, or any other documents of any nature relating in any way to the Lucky 2000 lawnmower.

   RESPONSE:

2. All design documents, drawings, engineering documents or calculations, photographs, advertisements, or any other documents of any nature relating in any way to the Lucky 1000 lawnmower.

   RESPONSE:

3. All documents pertaining to any claims of injury allegedly suffered by any person while using the Lucky 2000 lawnmower.

   RESPONSE:

4. All instructions, warnings, labels, and other materials included with the purchase of the Lucky 2000 lawnmower.

   RESPONSE:

5. The results of any testing or analysis of the cause of any accidents allegedly occurring as a result of use of the Lucky 2000 lawnmower.

   RESPONSE:

6. A description of each safety measure on the Lucky 2000 designed or intended to prevent injury to users of the lawnmower should the blade strike a rock.

   RESPONSE:

7. All documents that support Your affirmative defense that Homeowner was contributorily negligent.

   RESPONSE:

Respectfully submitted,
Benjarvus, Green-Ellis, llc

By: ___/s/_____
Attorney for Plaintiff Harry Homeowner

[CERTIFICATE OF SERVICE]

Sample 4-4: ANSWERS TO PRODUCTION REQUESTS

IN THE UNITED STATES DISTRICT COURT
DISTRICT OF WEST CAROLINA

Harry Homeowner,	)	
	)	
Plaintiff,	)	
	)	
v.	)	Civil Action No. 00-CV-98765
	)	
Lucky Lawnmower, Inc.,	)	
	)	
Defendant.	)	

Response to Plaintiff's First Set of Production Requests

Lucky Lawnmower, Inc. serves the following response to the production requests (the "Requests") served by Harry Homeowner ("Homeowner").

General Objection

Lucky Lawnmower, Inc. objects to the Requests to the extent that they purport to impose obligations greater than those imposed by the Federal Rules of Civil Procedure. Lucky Lawnmower, Inc. will comply with the Federal Rules of Civil Procedure in responding to these Requests. Lucky Lawnmower, Inc. is not withholding any documents on the basis of this general objection.

Specific Responses

1. All design documents, drawings, engineering documents or calculations, photographs, advertisements, or any other documents of any nature relating in any way to the Lucky 2000 lawnmower.

RESPONSE: Lucky Lawnmower, Inc. objects to Request No. 1 as overly broad and burdensome in time, and will produce all nonprivileged responsive documents only from the past five years. Lucky Lawnmower, Inc. also objects to Request No. 1 as overly broad, burdensome, vague, and ambiguous in scope with respect to the phrase "any other documents of any nature relating in any way to the Lucky 2000 lawnmower," and will not produce any documents in response to this portion of the Request. Subject to, and without waiving, these objections, Lucky Lawnmower, Inc. will produce nonprivileged responsive documents.

2. All design documents, drawings, engineering documents or calculations, photographs, advertisements, or any other documents of any nature relating in any way to the Lucky 1000 lawnmower.

RESPONSE: Lucky Lawnmower, Inc. objects to Request No. 2 as not relevant to a claim or defense in this action.

3. All documents pertaining to any claims of injury allegedly suffered by any person while using the Lucky 2000 lawnmower.

RESPONSE: Lucky Lawnmower will produce all nonprivileged responsive documents.

4. All instructions, warnings, labels, and other materials included with the purchase of the Lucky 2000 lawnmower.

RESPONSE: Lucky Lawnmower, Inc. will produce all nonprivileged responsive documents.

5. The results of any testing or analysis of the cause of any accidents allegedly occurring as a result of use of the Lucky 2000 lawnmower.

RESPONSE: As it concerns the incident at issue in this lawsuit, Lucky Lawnmower, Inc. objects to Request No. 5 as seeking trial preparation materials, attorney-client privileged communications, and information shielded by this State's self-critical analysis privilege. As it concerns accidents other than the incident at issue in this lawsuit, Lucky Lawnmower, Inc. objects to Request No. 5 as overbroad in seeking information concerning accidents dissimilar to the incident at issue in this lawsuit and, therefore, not relevant to any claim or defense in this action. Lucky Lawnmower, Inc. is withholding documents related to accidents involving the Lucky 2000 lawnmower that are dissimilar to the incident at issue in this lawsuit.

6. A description of each safety measure on the Lucky 2000 designed or intended to prevent injury to users of the lawnmower should the blade strike a rock.

RESPONSE: Lucky Lawnmower, Inc. will produce all nonprivileged responsive documents following entry of a suitable protective order.

7. All documents that support Your affirmative defense that Homeowner was contributorily negligent.

RESPONSE: Lucky Lawnmower, Inc. objects to Request No. 7 as seeking trial preparation materials and attorney-client privileged communications.

Sincerely,
Kar, Phulconsul, & Steady, llc

By: ___/s/_____
Attorney for Plaintiffs

[VERIFICATION]

[CERTIFICATE OF SERVICE]

Sample 4-5: PRIVILEGE LOG

[For an example of a privilege log, see Sample 3-1.]

PART 4.
REQUESTS FOR ADMISSION—RULE 36

GETTING THE VIEW

Requests for Admission may feel like a re-opening of the pleading stage of a lawsuit. If it feels that way, it should. One party alleges a fact or a legal consequence. That party's adversary has a limited time to admit or deny that allegation (or explain why the adversary lacks the knowledge or information necessary to admit or deny it). A failure to timely respond risks an admission that may doom the adversary's claim or defense. *See* Fed. R. Civ. P. 8(a) & 8(b).

This sense of familiarity is more than accidental. By impelling an opposing party to admit or deny a matter, Rule 36 can produce admissions in much the same way as a complaint can. What makes Rule 36 unique is that it routinely occurs *after* the pleadings stage has closed and while the lawsuit is proceeding through discovery. By that point in the life of a civil lawsuit, the parties are likely to know much more than they did at the outset, when the case was first filed and answered. They may also, by then, have other or different facts and issues to explore, and may have already begun the process of preparing their side of the case and its evidence for the courtroom.

Therein lies the true power of Rule 36.

It re-opens a party-admission phase of the lawsuit, but does so at a time when the litigants' knowledge of the case, its facts, and its legal nuances is much more richly developed. It therefore provides an opportunity for more surgical, strategic admission-seeking than might have been available originally. It forces quick and non-evasive responses. It exposes any non-compliance to a potentially severe penalty. And, like all judicial admissions, it holds the promise of narrowing down the number of moving parts at trial by identifying certain facts and legal conclusions as un-contested (and, thus, no longer in need of being affirmatively proved by witnesses and exhibits).

Like the other tools of discovery, requests for admission are optional. No litigant needs to issue them to an opponent. But, because of the power and promise of Rule 36, most experienced litigators consider requests for admission as a potent role-player in their discovery arsenal.

HOW THIS DISCOVERY TOOL WORKS

Learning the Rule 36 mechanics is to learn its three core features: the types of admissions that can be sought, the burdens imposed on responders, and the uses of admissions in a legal proceeding. Each is discussed in turn.

A. The Types of Admissions That Can Be Sought

Rule 36(a) gives a party broad reach in posing requests for admission to an opponent. Four types of admissions can be sought from an adversary:

1. to admit a fact,
2. to admit the application of law to a fact,
3. to admit opinions about either, *and/or*
4. to admit the genuineness of a document.

As a discovery tool, remember that requests for admission may only seek information that is properly discoverable. *See* Fed. R. Civ. P. 26(b)(1) (information is discoverable if it is (a) relevant to a party's claim or defense, (b) nonprivileged, and (c) proportional to the needs of the case); Rule 26(b)(3)(A) (documents and tangible things may be protected from discovery if they are prepared by a party or its counsel in anticipation of litigation or trial). The reach of discoverability was discussed in the Scope of Discovery chapter earlier.

1. Admit a Fact

The first of these allowable types is easy to understand: a request to admit a fact. A patient suing her doctor for malpractice, for example, could ask her doctor to admit that he was actually not in the room during surgeries he was supposed to have performed (*e.g.,* "Admit that Dr. Gill was not present in the operating room at any time during Ms. Conaway's appendix surgery or her gastric bypass surgery.").

2. Admit a Document's Genuineness

The last of these allowable types is also easily understood: a request to admit the genuineness of a document. Because documents must not only be discoverable but also *admissible* in order to be used at trial, requests for admission can be helpfully used to establish several of the foundations necessary for admissibility under the rules of evidence. To use this type of request, the document at issue must accompany the request (or have been otherwise furnished or available to the opponent). In the same doctor malpractice example, for example, the attorney could use requests for admission to build the foundation for the admission of medical records (*e.g.,* "Admit that Exhibit 28 is a true and authentic copy of the original Operative Notes from Ms. Conaway's appendix surgery."). A further request could help build the foundation for a hearsay exception for those same documents (*e.g.,* "Admit that the original Operative Notes (of which Exhibit 28 is a copy) were made and kept by City Hospital in the regular, ordinary course of its business, were made at or near the time of Ms. Conaway's appendix surgery, and were made by a person with knowledge of that surgery.").

3. Admit the Application of Law to Fact, or Opinions

The two middle allowable types (a request to admit the application of law to fact or to admit opinions) seem very broad and vulnerable to serious mischief. For example, could an attorney demand that an opponent admit a legal principle, the elements of that legal principle, or that a party is liable or not liable under a legal principle? Because of the burdens imposed on parties in responding to requests for admission, this sort of strategy could prove expensive, disruptive, and unfairly burdensome.

THOMPSON

v.

BEASLEY

309 F.R.D. 236 (N.D. Miss. 2015)

BROWN, United States District Judge

[Plaintiff Thompson brought a federal civil rights action against Beasley, the Administrator of a county jail, alleging deprivation of due process and use of constitutionally excessive force. Beasley served Requests for Admission on Thompson's attorney.]

In his discovery requests, Beasley propounded twenty requests for admission, of which sixteen may be properly characterized as requests for admission of facts under Rule 36(a)(1). . . .

However, Beasley also propounded the following requests for admission that may be found to constitute legal conclusions falling outside the scope of Rule 36(a)(1):

1. Please admit that the Defendants are not liable and have no liability to Plaintiff for the incident which is the subject of this lawsuit.

2. Please admit that the sole proximate cause of Plaintiff's injuries or losses, if any, was his own negligent or intentional acts.

3. Please admit that Plaintiff was solely at fault for the incident which is the subject of this lawsuit.

4. Please admit that third parties were solely at fault for the incident which is the subject of this lawsuit.

While the rule allows a party to request an admission of "the application of law to fact," "[r]equests for purely legal conclusions . . . are generally not permitted." *Benson Tower Condo. Owners Ass'n v. Victaulic Co.*, 105 F.Supp.3d 1184 (D. Or. 2015) (collecting cases). Unfortunately "the distinction between the application of law to fact and a legal conclusion is not always easy to draw." *Id.*

* * *

Where courts have attempted to fashion a workable framework for distinguishing proper from improper requests for admission, they have rightfully focused on the plain text of the Rule, which permit a request to admit the *application of law to fact.* Under this approach, a court will look to the request itself to determine whether the requesting party has "connect[ed] the legal propositions contained in its admissions requests with the specific facts and circumstances of the case." . . . *See also Petrunich v. Sun Bldg. Sys., Inc.,* 2006 WL 2788208, at *5 (M.D. Pa. 2006) ("[T]he request that Defendants admit that Mr. Petrunich "was discriminated because of his age" is improper. Although this request refers to a party in the case, there is no factual basis to derive the legal conclusion that Defendants discriminated against Mr. Petrunich because of his age. In the absence of how Defendants discriminated against Mr. Petrunich, the request is too abstract to be an application of the law to the facts of the case."). Upon consideration, the Court concludes that the factual inquiry approach . . . is most consistent with the language and purpose of Rule 36. Accordingly, for a legally-related request to be deemed admitted in this case, it must connect the relevant legal proposition to specific facts and circumstances of the case.

Here, none of the legal propositions included in requests for admission 2–5 seek to establish a connection between the proposition and the specific facts and circumstances of the case. Accordingly, like the requests in *Petrunich*, Beasley's requests contain no factual basis to derive the proffered propositions and, therefore, such requests must be deemed improper legal conclusions . . . .

Q A

Hypothetical

Q: Consider our medical malpractice example above, where Ms. Conaway has sued her surgeon Dr. Gill for allegedly being absent from the operating room as her gastric bypass surgery occurred. Which of the following requests for admission would likely be found proper under the factual-connectedness test the court in *Thompson* followed?

1. Admit that Dr. Gill has committed medical malpractice.

2. Admit that, if Dr. Gill was absent from the operating room during Ms. Conaway's gastric bypass surgery, that absence would constitute medical negligence.

3. Admit that, if Dr. Gill had been absent from the operating room during Ms. Conaway's gastric bypass surgery, that absence would constitute a deviation from the standard of competent medical care unless Ms. Conaway had given her prior consent to the absence.

4. Admit that Dr. Gill should have his license to practice medicine revoked.

A: Framing requests for admission in a way that connects legal propositions to the facts and circumstances of the lawsuit helps protect against a successful objection. For this reason, Request Nos. 1 and 4 above are vulnerable; they do not marry the proposed legal conclusion to specific lawsuit circumstances. Request Nos. 2 and 3 make a more deliberate, tighter factual connection and, for that reason, are less vulnerable to objection.

4. Procedures for Requests

Requests for admission can only be issued to fellow parties in a lawsuit (thus, they cannot be used, for example, with nonparty witnesses or trial experts). Rule 36 requires that requests be "separately stated." This facilitates responses that are crisp and concise. Thus, compound requests, which would require a party to respond to multiple propositions embedded within a single request, are objectionable. Unlike interrogatories under Rule 33, there is no fixed national "cap" on the number of requests for admission that can be served. Courts may, however, in the exercise of their broad discretion in discovery, limit requests when used excessively. Finally, like all of the tools of discovery, requests for admission typically may not be issued to an opponent until after the Rule 26(f) planning conference has been completed (and, ordinarily, must be served such that they will come due before the deadline set by the court for the end of discovery). That planning conference was introduced earlier in the How Discovery Begins chapter.

B. The Burdens Imposed on Responders

A party served with requests for admission has 30 days to serve a response to those requests (unless the period is extended by the court or by written stipulation of the parties). This time window has a serious, built-in consequence that is unlike any other discovery tool. A failure to timely respond to a request for admission has the effect of *admitting* the issue. This "deemed" admission occurs automatically. Thus, in our doctor malpractice example, a failure to respond to a proper request (*e.g.*, "Admit that Dr. Gill was not present in the operating room at any time during Ms. Conaway's appendix surgery or her gastric bypass surgery") will mean that Dr. Gill is deemed to have *admitted* that he was not present at any time during those surgeries. Needless to say, this consequence can be devastating and case-ending.

Responses must be in writing, signed by the answering party or that party's attorney. Sometimes, admissions and denials can be done quite simply ("Admitted."; "Denied."). Provided such an answer is appropriate, there is no need for parties to embellish or explain their admissions or denials. But Rule 36 also requires that responses must "fairly respond to the substance of the matter," and that, when good faith requires a qualification, the responding party "must specify the part admitted and qualify or deny the rest." Fed. R. Civ. P. 36(a)(4).

Hypothetical

Q: In our medical malpractice example, suppose Dr. Gill sent Ms. Conaway this request for admission: "Admit that Dr. Gill conferred with Ms. Conaway in his private office on October 12 during which he discussed with Ms. Conaway her upcoming surgery and informed her of his customary practice of being absent from those portions of his surgeries during which his surgical fellow opens the patient's operative cavity and then closes the cavity at the conclusion of the operative procedure." Putting aside, for the moment, a possible objection to this request's compound nature, let's assume Ms. Conaway recalls this conference with Dr. Gill actually occurring. But, in her memory, it occurred on October 17 (not October 12), in his exam room (not his private office), and that Dr. Gill never mentioned any role any surgical fellow would play or that Dr. Gill might be absent at any point during the procedure. Can Ms. Conaway answer this request for admission simply with "Denied."?

A: No. A single-word answer ("Denied.") would be improper. Doing so would not "fairly respond to the substance of the matter" of the request and would neglect the several qualifications that good faith demands of Ms. Conaway. Instead, her answer would have to be more parsed: "Admitted that Dr. Gill conferred with Ms. Conaway. Denied that the conferral occurred on October 12 or in his private exam room. Denied also that the conferral included a discussion with Ms. Conaway about any customary practice during which Dr. Gill would be absent or that any surgical fellow would participate in the operative procedure."

Sometimes, a party cannot respond to a request for admission because that party simply does not know the answer to the question. Rule 36 permits a lack-of-knowledge response. But the Rule conditions such responses on a "reasonable inquiry." In other words, parties cannot evade a duty to admit or deny a request with an ostrich-like burial of their heads in the sand. Consider, for example, one intriguing use of this lack-of-knowledge response:

ASEA, INC.
v.
SOUTHERN PACIFIC TRANSPORTATION CO.

669 F.2d 1242 (9th Cir. 1981)

WALLACE, United States Circuit Judge

[Plaintiff Asea was a New York corporation that distributed electrical transformers. Asea contracted with Defendant Railroad to transport a transformer to a customer in California. Asea installed a recording device on the transformer to measure any impact it might suffer during the railroad journey. The transformer arrived in California in a damaged condition, and Asea's recorder revealed damaging impacts during the journey. Asea sued the Railroad for reimbursement for the loss. Asea served requests for admission on the Railroad, requesting admissions from the Railroad concerning the condition of the transformer at the time the Railroad first took custody of it, impacts during transit, location of the transformer during those impacts, the damage the transformer suffered, and the cost of the loss.]

[The Railroad responded to many of these Requests as follows:]

Answering party cannot admit or deny. Said party has made reasonable inquiry. Information known or readily obtainable to this date is not complete. Investigation continues.

* * *

[During discovery,] Asea became convinced that the railroads had known the actual cause of the impact on the transformer for many months, and therefore could have admitted or denied the requests for admissions. . . . [F]ive weeks prior to trial, Asea moved to have the requests ordered admitted. At the hearing on the motion, the railroads claimed that their responses were proper by authority of Rule 36(a) because they did not have any firsthand information. The district court . . . subsequently granted Asea's motion to order the matters admitted. . . .

The railroads contend their responses to the requests for admissions satisfied the requirements of Fed.R.Civ.P. 36(a). In the alternative, they argue that the sanction for failure of a party to make reasonable inquiry prior to answering a request for admission lies in an award of the expenses incurred in proving the fact at trial, pursuant to Fed.R.Civ.P. 37(c), and not in deeming the matter admitted. We have considered this issue carefully because it apparently is a question of first impression. . . .

The purpose of Rule 36(a) is to expedite trial by establishing certain material facts as true and thus narrowing the range of issues for trial. . . . [A] party may not refuse to admit or deny a request for admission based upon a lack of personal knowledge if the information relevant to the request is reasonably available to him. . . . The appropriate penalty for a party's failure to discharge that burden, however, is unclear.

Rule 36(a) provides that a matter may be deemed admitted if the answer "does not comply with the requirements of this rule." It is undisputed that failure to answer or object to a proper request for admission is itself an admission: the Rule itself so states. It is also clear that an evasive denial, one that does not "specifically deny the matter," or a response that does not set forth "in detail" the reasons why the answering party cannot truthfully admit or deny the matter, may be deemed an admission. . . . The railroads, however, argue that an answer complies with the requirements of Rule 36(a) if it states that the party has insufficient information to admit or deny the matter and that the party has made reasonable inquiry into all readily obtainable information.

* * *

We are not persuaded that an answer to a request for admission necessarily complies with Rule 36(a) merely because it includes a statement that the party has made reasonable inquiry and that the information necessary to admit or deny the matter is not readily obtainable by him. The discovery process is subject to the overriding limitation of good faith. Callous disregard of discovery responsibilities cannot be condoned. . . . The abuses of the current discovery rules are well documented. In our view, permitting a party to avoid admitting or denying a proper request for admission simply by tracking the language of Rule 36(a) would encourage additional abuse of the discovery process. Instead of making an evasive or meritless denial, which clearly would result in the matter being deemed admitted, a party could comply with the Rule merely by having his attorney submit the language of the Rule in response to the request. Since a district court may order that a matter is admitted only if an answer does not "comply" with the requirements of the Rule, it could be argued that the only sanction for a party's willful disregard of its obligation to make reasonable inquiry would be an award of the expenses of proving the matter at trial pursuant to Rule 37(c). Without disparaging the deterrent effect of such a sanction, we believe that restricting the district court's discretion in this manner would reduce a litigant's obligation to make "reasonable inquiry" into a mere semantic exercise, and thus severely undermine the policy embodied in Rule 36(a) of limiting the issues before trial.

We hold, therefore, that a response which fails to admit or deny a proper request for admission does not comply with the requirements of Rule 36(a) if the answering party has not, in fact, made "reasonable inquiry," or if information "readily obtainable" is sufficient to enable him to admit or deny the matter. A party requesting an admission may, if he feels these requirements have not been met, move to determine the sufficiency of the answer, to compel a proper response, or to have the matter ordered admitted. Although the district court should ordinarily first order an amended answer, and deem the matter admitted only if a sufficient answer is not timely filed, this determination, like most involved in the oversight of discovery, is left to the sound discretion of the district judge. . . . The general power of the district court to control the discovery process allows for the severe sanction of ordering a matter admitted when it has been demonstrated that a party has intentionally disregarded the obligations imposed by Rule 36(a).

Here, the district judge decided not to require an amended response. . . . But this was not the first discovery problem presented to the court. Far from it. A year of volatile and acrimonious fighting, during which many discovery disputes were placed before the judge as referee, had preceded it. Thus, we cannot say the district judge abused his wide discretion in not requiring amended responses. . . .

The *Asea* opinion illustrates more than just the prerequisites for a proper use of the lack-of-knowledge response option; it also highlights the penalties available to a court for a party's failure to comply with Rule 36. As noted earlier, the most daunting Rule 36 punishment is the one imposed on a party who fails to timely answer: a "deemed" admission. But the *Asea* decision confirms that his "deemed" admission punishment is also available to a party who supplies an insufficient answer, especially when that party knew more and was behaving in a deliberately evasive manner.

Thus, Rule 36 authorizes parties to respond to requests for admission in four different ways. Responding parties can:

1. object to the request (so long as the objection is well-founded),
2. admit the matter (fully or in part),
3. deny the matter (fully or in part), *and/or*
4. assert a lack of knowledge or information (fully or in part, but only if done properly).

A request is objectionable if the request seeks improper information or seeks proper information but does so improperly. The proper reach of discovery was discussed earlier in the Scope of Discovery chapter. By way of illustration, a request asking parties to admit the substance of an attorney-client privileged telephone call with their counsel would be objectionable. So, too, would be a request that is vague, ambiguous, or overbroad (*e.g.*, "Admit that, over the years, Dr. Gill is sometimes not always present in every operating room in some hospitals during certain procedures."). Objections may be asserted by a specific, textual objection ("Objection: this Request would invade the attorney-client privilege.") or by filing a motion for a protective order. *See* Fed. R. Civ. P. 26(c).

A few other features of Rule 36 practice are noteworthy.

First, the procedure for testing the adequacy of a party's response to a request for admission is by filing a motion. Such motions often come costly; the loser may be ordered to reimburse the winner for the winner's expenses and attorney's fees incurred in making or defending the motion. *See* Fed. R. Civ. P. 37(a)(5). Thus, a party (like the plaintiff in *Asea*) who files such a motion will likely either: (1) get its requested relief *and* a reimbursement of its motion costs; or (2) be denied its requested relief *and* be ordered to reimburse the opponent for the costs of defending the motion. So, the decision to file such motions is one to be made with care.

Second, if the court disagrees that the party's objection was well-founded, the court is obligated to order the objecting party to provide a substantive answer to the request.

Hypothetical

Q: Imagine that, in response to a request asking for his admission that he was absent from the operating room at times during Ms. Conaway's surgery, Dr. Gill had answered: "Denied." What if that denial, when made, was knowingly untrue? Wouldn't that be a clever discovery strategy?

A: It might be clever, but it also unethical and costly. As we will see in the Policing Discovery chapter later in this book, knowingly improper denials can be sanctioned. *See* Fed. R. Civ. P. 37(c)(2). If Ms. Conaway proves at trial that Dr. Gill was, in fact, absent at times during her surgery, she may be entitled to a reimbursement of all reasonable expenses (including attorney's fees) she incurred in having to make that proof. The court "must" grant her that reimbursement unless the request was objectionable or of no substantial importance, or Dr. Gill had some reasonable ground for believing his denial to be true. *Id.* So, if Ms. Conaway's attorney had to locate the surgical fellow who was present on the day of Ms. Conaway's surgery, fly her in from her home in Hawai'i, and pay for her room and board as she waited to testify that Dr. Gill did, indeed, leave the surgical room that day, those costs—along with Ms. Conaway's lawyer's time—will likely all be shifted to Dr. Gill.

C. The Uses of Admissions

Though powerful, the impact of Rule 36 is expressly circumscribed. Admissions obtained through this discovery tool are considered to be conclusively established. Thus, a party who admits (or is "deemed" as having admitted) a certain matter may not contradict it later at trial. Instead, the admission will bind the admitting party throughout the proceeding in a way that other discovery tools (like responses to interrogatories and deposition testimony) will not. But the admission stops there. Its effect is limited only to the proceeding in which it was given; an admission under Rule 36 may not be used as an admission "for any other purpose and cannot be used against the party in any other proceeding." *See* Fed. R. Civ. P. 36(b).

If a party who admits a matter later discovers that the matter should not have been admitted, the party can file a motion with the court to withdraw or amend its admission. *See* Rule 36(b). The court may, in its discretion, grant such a withdrawal or amendment if the presentation of the merits would be promoted and if the party who obtained the admission would not be prejudiced.[1]

---

1. The court's discretion to grant such relief is further constrained by Rule 16(e) if the admission is incorporated into a final pretrial order.

FROM CLASSROOM TO PRACTICE

A. Form

There is no officially prescribed form for requests for admission, and litigators tend to gravitate toward a styling that seems to be working for them in practice (or one they may have inherited from a mentor early on in their careers). Some litigators conclude each request with a space for the opponent to type in the answer (some litigators even include designed lines next to the words "Admitted" and "Denied", to try to funnel responding parties into austere and unlawyered answers). Most litigators also preface their requests with a series of "instructions" and "definitions" that they personally have added to, pruned, and refined over the years. Such "instructions" try to constrain the responding party in framing its answers and objections; "definitions" attempt to streamline the requests themselves by setting defined terms that appear repeatedly throughout the questioning (such as "Incident" to refer to the allegedly culpable event or "Product" to refer to an allegedly harm-causing instrument). Whether courts will actually respect an asking party's "instructions" and "definitions" is less certain.

B. The Ominous Danger of the "Forgotten" Discovery Tool

As potent a discovery tool as requests for admission are, it is surprising how often this tool is overlooked by practitioners (especially newer lawyers). In the bustle of a busy practice, with many clients and many cases on an attorney's agenda, with deadlines looming and trials approaching, the discovery tools that seem to receive the most attention are interrogatories, production requests, and depositions. Requests for admission often get forgotten. That disregard leaves an incredibly powerful litigation tool unused. What explains such neglect?

Perhaps, for many practitioners, it is because requests for admission feel both familiar and, ironically, foreign. Requests for admission feel familiar because of their similarity to pleadings; thus, less-experienced attorneys may be tempted to discount this tool because it feels like returning to already-trodden ground. Requests for admission feel foreign because of the special rules and unique dangers that accompany a use of Rule 36; thus, some attorneys may avoid the tool simply due to a lack of experience in safely using it. For other attorneys, ignoring requests for admission is just a casualty of a crowded professional schedule; since this tool may often work best late in a litigation's discovery period (after a good deal of knowledge about the dispute has been learned), requests for admission often fight a losing battle for time and attention as busy attorneys try, instead, to wrap up the discovery that is already scheduled and ready their cases for trial.

Whatever the explanation, nothing justifies ignoring Rule 36 Requests for Admission. The tool's power and punishment (for neglectful or insufficient responses) make it a critical consideration for every case's discovery phase. Requests for admission can narrow issues, eliminate witnesses and exhibits, streamline trials, and—when ignored or misplayed—devastate an opponent's claim or defense.

Which brings our discussion back to "deemed" admissions. No other discovery tool so imminently threatens a party's claim or defense than an ignored or overlooked request for admission. An unanswered request for admission becomes a "deemed" admission. Because such Rule 36 admissions are conclusive for the life of the litigation (absent leave of court to withdraw or amend them), the danger posed by requests for admissions is formidable. Wise practitioners should immediately and carefully calendar requests for admission when they arrive, being certain to note the day they come due and then planning diligently to ensure that they are responded to in a timely, appropriate manner.

Hypotheticals: Mastering the Nuances

The Mystery Denial: The patient in our doctor malpractice example, Ms. Conaway, serves a request for admission on the defendant Dr. Gill. The request asks, "Admit that, on the morning of Ms. Conaway's surgery, Dr. Gill was unable to perform Ms. Conaway's surgery because he was scheduled to participate in multiple surgeries at the same time." Dr. Gill responds to this request with a simple answer: "Denied." But what is Dr. Gill denying? Is he denying Ms. Conaway's accusation that the *reason* he failed to perform her surgery was because he was double-booked, or he is denying the *fact* that he was double-booked, or is he denying the *fact* that he was "scheduled" to be double-booked, or is his denial something else entirely? Because Rule 36 does not impose on Dr. Gill a duty to explain his responses, his one-word denial here may be entirely appropriate. But it doesn't much help Ms. Conaway and her lawyer. How can Ms. Conaway's lawyer obtain an explanation of this denial from Dr. Gill?

The Defeated Denial: Assume Ms. Conaway served another request for admission on Dr. Gill, which asks, "Admit that Dr. Gill made mistakes in surgical technique during Ms. Conaway's surgery due to fatigue he experienced because of several other surgeries he had performed on other patients earlier that same day." Dr. Gill's answer was equally simple: "Denied." Although not explained to Ms. Conaway, Dr. Gill's denial here was based on his firm conviction that he had committed no surgical mistakes during Ms. Conaway's procedure, that he was not fatigued during her operation, and that any post-surgical complications she experienced were due to other causes, unrelated to the surgery. But the jury disagreed. It found Dr. Gill liable for medical malpractice and awarded a sizable verdict in Ms. Conaway's favor. Ms. Conaway seeks to add to this award by filing a motion to have the court reimburse her for the costs of having to prove Dr. Gill negligent because, in her view, Dr. Gill should have admitted, not denied, that request. How should the court rule on that motion?

PRACTICE SAMPLES

Sample 4-6: REQUESTS FOR ADMISSION

IN THE UNITED STATES DISTRICT COURT
DISTRICT OF WEST CAROLINA

Clementine Conaway,	)	
	)	
Plaintiff,	)	
	)	
v.	)	Civil Action No. 00-CV-12345
	)	
Ernest W. Gill, M.D.,	)	
	)	
Defendant.	)	

Requests for Admission Directed to Defendant

Plaintiff Clementine Conaway requests that defendant Ernest W. Gill, M.D. admit, under oath, the following matters by serving a written response within thirty days of service.

Instructions

1. These Requests for Admission shall be considered continuing in nature and require supplementation if you obtain additional or different information after you serve your answers.

2. You are to answer these Requests on the basis of all information available to you, including all information obtained by or through other sources as well as all information in the possession of your attorneys, agents, employees, and other representatives.

3. If you are unable to fully answer any of these Requests, after exercising the diligence the law requires of you to acquire the information necessary to fully answer these Requests, answer the Requests to the fullest extent possible and explain your inability to answer the remainder.

4. If you object to any portion of any of these Requests on the basis that the information sought is encompassed by a privilege, the work-product protection, or other immunity, state:

   a. The basis for that objection with specificity; and

   b. Whether the objection is resulting in you actually withholding any information; and

   c. The factual foundation for your objection in sufficient detail so as to allow the court to pass on the merits of your objection.

Definitions

For the purposes of these Requests for Admission, the following definitions shall apply.

1. The term **"Ms. Conaway"** shall refer to the plaintiff in the Present Action, Clementine Conaway.

2. The terms **"you"**, **"your"**, **"yours"**, **"yourself"**, and **"yourselves"** shall mean to refer to Ms. Conaway, as defined above.

3. The term **"Dr. Gill"** shall refer to the defendant in the Present Action, Ernest W. Gill, M.D.

4. The term **"Complaint"** shall mean the pleading Plaintiff filed to begin the lawsuit against Earnest W. Gill, M.D. in the United States District Court for the District of West Carolina, and now docketed as Civil Action No. 00-CV-12345.

5. The term **"Document"** shall mean all forms of written, printed, recorded, or otherwise preserved matter, including (but not limited to) all forms of graphic matter, photographic matter, sound reproductions, video reproductions, and electronically stored information. The term shall specifically encompass letters, correspondence, memoranda, notes, e-mail, texts, social media posts, videotapes, sound or video recordings, faxes, telegrams, cables, pamphlets, records, files, reports, forms, ledgers, medical records, studies, books, papers, diaries, calendars, charts, lists, receipts, invoices, purchase orders, checks, drawings, photographs, worksheets, sketches, graphs, data sheets, tapes, logs, tables, displays, and all other matter written, printed, recorded, transcribed, photographed, or otherwise set down or preserved in any form whatsoever, which is now or formerly was in Plaintiff's possession, custody, or control. Each copy of any Document that varies in any manner from any other copy of any Document shall be deemed to be a separate Document.

Requests for Admission

1. Admit that Dr. Gill is licensed by the State of West Carolina as a medical doctor and surgeon.

   Admit: _____

   Deny: _____

   Response:

2. Admit that the term "attending surgeon" means a physician who will take primary responsibility for performing surgery on a patient.

   Admit: _____

   Deny: _____

   Response:

3. Admit that the applicable standard of care for medical practitioners dictates that attending surgeons be personally present and primarily involved in performing the surgery for which they are attending.

   Admit: _____

   Deny: _____

   Response:

4.   Admit that Ms. Conaway interviewed and considered three other surgeons for her appendix removal and gastric bypass before selecting Dr. Gill to perform those surgeries.

Admit: _____

Deny: _____

Response:

5.   Admit that Dr. Gill was hired by Ms. Conaway to be the attending surgeon on her two surgeries, namely the removal of her appendix and a gastric bypass.

Admit: _____

Deny: _____

Response:

6.   Admit that Dr. Gill agreed to participate as the attending surgeon for both the appendix surgery and gastric bypass surgery on Ms. Conaway.

Admit: _____

Deny: _____

Response:

7.   Admit that Ms. Conaway asked Dr. Gill to confirm for her that he would personally perform her appendix surgery and her gastric bypass surgery.

Admit: _____

Deny: _____

Response:

8.   Admit that Dr. Gill advised Ms. Conaway that he would personally perform her appendix surgery and her gastric bypass surgery.

Admit: _____

Deny: _____

Response:

9. Admit that Dr. Gill was not present in the operating room at any time during Ms. Conaway's appendix surgery or her gastric bypass surgery.

   Admit: _____

   Deny: _____

   Response:

10. Admit that the failure of a physician to be present in the operating room during a surgery for which he was serving as attending surgeon is a deviation from the standard of care required of licensed physicians and, thus, medically negligent.

    Admit: _____

    Deny: _____

    Response:

11. Admit that Dr. Gill was occasionally absent from the operating room during Ms. Conaway's appendix surgery and her gastric bypass surgery.

    Admit: _____

    Deny: _____

    Response:

12. Admit that a physician's absence, even temporarily, from the operating room during a surgery for which he was serving as attending surgeon is a deviation from the standard of care required of licensed physicians and, thus, medically negligent.

    Admit: _____

    Deny: _____

    Response:

13. Admit that, as a consequence of Dr. Gill's absence from the operating room during Ms. Conaway's appendix and gastric bypass surgeries, surgical errors were committed that Dr. Gill was not present to correct.

    Admit: _____

    Deny: _____

    Response:

14. Admit that, as a consequence of errors made during her surgery, Ms. Conaway now is in constant pain, is unable to walk without assistance, and has great difficulty concentrating and sleeping.

    Admit: _____

    Deny: _____

    Response:

15. Admit that Ms. Conaway's medical condition will not improve during her life.

    Admit: _____

    Deny: _____

    Response:

16. Admit that Ms. Conaway will be unable to work for the remainder of her life.

    Admit: _____

    Deny: _____

    Response:

17. Admit that the document attached as EXHIBIT "A" to these Requests for Admission is a true and authentic copy of the original Operative Notes from Ms. Conaway's appendix surgery.

    Admit: _____

    Deny: _____

    Response:

18. Admit that the original Operative Notes from Ms. Conaway's appendix surgery (of which EXHIBIT "A" is a copy) were made and kept by City Hospital in the regular, ordinary course of its business, were made at or near the time of Ms. Conaway's appendix surgery, and were made by a person with knowledge of that surgery.

    Admit: _____

    Deny: _____

    Response:

19. Admit that the document attached as EXHIBIT "B" to these Requests for Admission is a true and authentic copy of the original Operative Notes from Ms. Conaway's gastric bypass surgery.

    Admit: _____

    Deny: _____

    Response:

20. Admit that the original Operative Notes from Ms. Conaway's gastric bypass surgery (of which EXHIBIT "B" is a copy) were made and kept by City Hospital in the regular, ordinary course of its business, were made at or near the time of Ms. Conaway's appendix surgery, and were made by a person with knowledge of that surgery.

    Admit: _____

    Deny: _____

    Response:

Respectfully submitted,

BENJARVUS, GREEN-ELLIS, LLC

By: ____/s/_____
Attorney for Plaintiff
Clementine Conaway

[CERTIFICATE OF SERVICE]

Sample 4-7: RESPONSE TO REQUESTS FOR ADMISSION

IN THE UNITED STATES DISTRICT COURT
DISTRICT OF WEST CAROLINA

Clementine Conaway,	)	
	)	
Plaintiff,	)	
	)	
v.	)	Civil Action No. 00-CV-98765
	)	
Ernest W. Gill, M.D.,	)	
	)	
Defendant.	)	

Responses by Defendant to Plaintiff's Requests for Admission

In response to Plaintiff's Requests for Admission Directed to Defendant, Ernest W. Gill, M.D. answers as follows:

1. Admit that Dr. Gill is licensed by the State of West Carolina as a medical doctor and surgeon.

    Admit: _X_

    Deny: _____

2. Admit that the term "attending surgeon" means a physician who will take primary responsibility for performing surgery on a patient.

    Admit: _____

    Deny: _____

    Response: Admitted that the term "attending surgeon" means a physician who will take responsibility for a patient's surgery. Except as so admitted, denied.

3. Admit that the applicable standard of care for medical practitioners dictates that attending surgeons be personally present and primarily involved in performing the surgery for which they are attending.

    Admit: _____

    Deny: _X_

    Response:

4. Admit that Ms. Conaway interviewed and considered three other surgeons for her appendix removal and gastric bypass before selecting Dr. Gill to perform those surgeries.

    Admit: _____

    Deny: _____

    Response: After reasonable inquiry, the information known or reasonably obtainable by Dr. Gill is insufficient to enable him to admit or deny this statement.

5. Admit that Dr. Gill was hired by Ms. Conaway to be the attending surgeon on her two surgeries, namely the removal of her appendix and a gastric bypass.

    Admit: _____

    Deny: _____

    Response: Admitted that Dr. Gill was hired to serve as attending surgeon for the removal of Ms. Conaway's appendix and her gastric bypass. Except as so admitted, denied.

6. Admit that Dr. Gill agreed to participate as the attending surgeon for both the appendix surgery and gastric bypass surgery on Ms. Conaway.

    Admit: __X__

    Deny: _____

    Response:

7. Admit that Ms. Conaway asked Dr. Gill to confirm for her that he would personally perform her appendix surgery and her gastric bypass surgery.

    Admit: _____

    Deny: __X__

    Response:

8. Admit that Dr. Gill advised Ms. Conaway that he would personally perform her appendix surgery and her gastric bypass surgery.

    Admit: _____

    Deny: __X__

    Response:

9. Admit that Dr. Gill was not present in the operating room at any time during Ms. Conaway's appendix surgery or her gastric bypass surgery.

    Admit: _____

    Deny: __X__

    Response:

10. Admit that the failure of a physician to be present in the operating room during a surgery for which he was serving as attending surgeon is a deviation from the standard of care required of licensed physicians and, thus, medically negligent.

    Admit: _____

    Deny: __X__

    Response:

11. Admit that Dr. Gill was occasionally absent from the operating room during Ms. Conaway's appendix surgery and her gastric bypass surgery.

    Admit: __X__

    Deny: _____

    Response:

12. Admit that a physician's absence, even temporarily, from the operating room during a surgery for which he was serving as attending surgeon is a deviation from the standard of care required of licensed physicians and, thus, medically negligent.

    Admit: _____

    Deny: __X__

    Response:

13. Admit that, as a consequence of Dr. Gill's absence from the operating room during Ms. Conaway's appendix and gastric bypass surgeries, surgical errors were committed that Dr. Gill was not present to correct.

    Admit: _____

    Deny: __X__

    Response:

14. Admit that, as a consequence of errors made during her surgery, Ms. Conaway now is in constant pain, is unable to walk without assistance, and has great difficulty concentrating and sleeping.

    Admit: _____

    Deny: _____

    Response: Denied that errors were made during Ms. Conaway's surgeries. Except as so denied, and after reasonable inquiry, the information known to and readily obtainable by Dr. Gill is insufficient to enable him to further admit or deny this statement.

15. Admit that Ms. Conaway's medical condition will not improve during her life .

    Admit: _____

    Deny: _____

    Response: After reasonable inquiry, the information known to and readily obtainable by Dr. Gill is insufficient to enable him to further admit or deny this statement.

16. Admit that Ms. Conaway will be unable to work for the remainder of her life. .

    Admit: _____

    Deny: _____

    Response: After reasonable inquiry, the information known to and readily obtainable by Dr. Gill is insufficient to enable him to further admit or deny this statement.

17. Admit that the document attached as EXHIBIT "A" to these Requests for Admission is a true and authentic copy of the original Operative Notes from Ms. Conaway's appendix surgery.

    Admit: __X__

    Deny: _____

    Response:

18. Admit that the original Operative Notes from Ms. Conaway's appendix surgery (of which EXHIBIT "A" is a copy) were made and kept by City Hospital in the regular, ordinary course of its business, were made at or near the time of Ms. Conaway's appendix surgery, and were made by a person with knowledge of that surgery.

Admit: ___X___

Deny: _____

Response:

19. Admit that the document attached as EXHIBIT "B" to these Requests for Admission is a true and authentic copy of the original Operative Notes from Ms. Conaway's gastric bypass surgery.

Admit: ___X___

Deny: _____

Response:

20. Admit that the original Operative Notes from Ms. Conaway's gastric bypass surgery (of which EXHIBIT "B" is a copy) were made and kept by City Hospital in the regular, ordinary course of its business, where made at or near the time of Ms. Conaway's appendix surgery, and were made by a person with knowledge of that surgery.

Admit: ___X___

Deny: _____

Response:

Respectfully submitted,

KAR, PHULCONSUL, & STEADY, LLC

By: ____/s/_____
Attorney for Defendant
Ernest W. Gill, M.D.

Dated:

[CERTIFICATE OF SERVICE]

PART 5.
PHYSICAL AND MENTAL EXAMINATIONS—
RULE 35

GETTING THE VIEW

Rule 35 permits the physical or mental examination of a party if that party's physical or mental condition has been placed "in controversy." This is another of the Rules' discovery tools available to practitioners; parties are not *required* to seek an examination of their adversaries but may do so in a proper case when asking would serve their litigation strategy.

Consider, for example, a lawsuit filed by an automobile driver against a delivery van driver who had scraped negligently against her car. The plaintiff alleged a life-altering spinal injury and sought compensation from the delivery van driver for her past and future medical bills, for her lost wages and future earning capacity, for her loss of mobility and life's pleasures, and for past and future pain. Should the discovery process allow the defendant to attempt to verify the plaintiff's claim of physical injury? Or its extent and severity? Or how long it will persist, and whether (and when) it will resolve? Rule 35 provides the tool for pursuing just such a verification. The delivery van driver can seek and obtain a court order obligating the plaintiff to submit to a spinal examination by an appropriate physician of the van driver's choosing.

Today, examinations of an adversary's physical and mental condition are usually not controversial and occur frequently. Historically, the story was far different. Just before the turn of the 20th Century, the U.S. Supreme Court affirmed a trial judge's refusal to grant a physical examination of a woman who claimed that a railway's sleeping-car berth had fallen on her head, caused a concussion, ruptured brain and spinal membranes, and otherwise left her permanently injured. Explaining its refusal to permit an examination of the plaintiff, the Court wrote: "No right is held more sacred, or is more carefully guarded by the common law, than the right of every individual to the possession and control of his own person, free from all restraint or interference of others, unless by clear and unquestionable authority of law." *Union Pac. Ry. v. Botsford*, 141 U.S. 250, 251 (1891). While the plaintiff was free to display her wounds to the jury for her own advantage and to further her claim, the Court ruled that she was under no corollary obligation to allow the defendant to examine and confirm her injuries. "To compel any one, and especially a woman," wrote the Court, "to lay bare the body, or to submit it to the touch of a stranger . . . is an indignity, an assault, and a trespass," which was very rarely tolerated in English common law "and never, so far as we are aware, introduced into this country." *Id.* at 252.

But times change. By the time the Federal Rules of Civil Procedure took effect in 1938, such examinations were becoming more commonplace, though they remained on an uncertain footing. Rule 35 altered that tradition and installed a national rule for all federal courts expressly authorizing physical and mental exams under appropriate circumstances. It seems that the wisdom of the dissent in the Supreme Court's *Botsford* case had ultimately carried the day with the rule-drafters: "The end of litigation is justice. Knowledge of the truth is essential thereto. . . . It is said that there is sanctity of the person which may not be outraged. We believe that truth and justice are more sacred than any personal consideration . . . ." *Botsford*, 141 U.S. at 258–59 (Brewer, J., dissenting).

HOW THIS DISCOVERY TOOL WORKS

Rule 35 is distinctive among the discovery rules in several respects. One of the most significant distinctions involves the manner of seeking the discovery; a litigant is not entitled to a physical or mental examination of an adversary simply by requesting it (which is unlike a litigant's entitlement to, for example, interrogatory answers, the production of documents, or an entry upon land, each of which may be acquired merely upon the litigant's unilateral demand). Physical or mental exams, by contrast, require the litigant to obtain either: (1) a court order compelling the exam; or (2) consent of the party (by stipulation or otherwise) to submit to the exam. *See* Fed. R. Civ. P. 35(a).

A. Prerequisites

The standard for ordering a Rule 35 examination is fundamentally different from the standard for most other discovery devices. Whereas most discovery is governed by the relevance and proportionality test from Rule 26(b)(1), the trial court will not order a Rule 35 exam unless the physical or mental condition of the party to be examined is "in controversy," and then only upon a showing of "good cause." *See* Fed. R. Civ. P. 35(a). Frequently, the "in controversy"/ "good cause" requirements are obvious and not contested—for example, a plaintiff seeking damages for a physical injury has placed that physical condition in controversy.

What qualifies as "in controversy" and "good cause" can prove to be a nuanced inquiry when the parties to be examined have not put their own condition at issue. Consider the Supreme Court's decision in *Schlagenhauf v. Holder*, 379 U.S. 104 (1964). After a bus collided with a tractor-trailer, bus passengers sued the bus driver and the tractor-trailer company for personal injuries. The bus driver crossclaimed against the tractor-trailer company, and the tractor-trailer company alleged in its answer to the crossclaim that the bus driver was not physically or mentally fit to operate the bus. The tractor-trailer company moved for an order requiring the bus driver to submit to both mental and physical examinations by specialists in the fields of internal medicine, ophthalmology, neurology, and psychiatry. The bus driver opposed the motion.

SCHLAGENHAUF
v.
HOLDER

379 U.S. 104 (1964)

GOLDBERG, Associate Justice

The petition alleged that the mental and physical condition of Schlagenhauf [the bus driver] was 'in controversy' as it had been raised by Contract Carriers' answer to Greyhound's cross-claim. . . . [Contract Carriers' contended] that Schlagenhauf had seen red lights 10 to 15 seconds before the accident, that another witness had seen the rear lights of the trailer from a distance of three-quarters to one-half mile, and that Schlagenhauf had been involved in a prior accident. . . . [*Without convening a hearing, and solely on the basis of paper submissions, the trial court ordered Schlagenhauf to submit to nine separate types of examinations.*] * * *

Rule 35 on its face applies to all 'parties,' which under any normal reading would include a defendant. Petitioner contends, however, that the application of the Rule to a defendant would be an unconstitutional invasion of his privacy . . . . Discovery 'is not a one-way proposition. Issues cannot be resolved by a doctrine of favoring one class of litigants over another.' . . . We hold that Rule 35, as applied to either plaintiffs or defendants to an action, is free of constitutional difficulty and is within the scope of the Enabling Act. We therefore agree . . . that the District Court had power to apply Rule 35 to a party defendant in an appropriate case.

* * *

Rule 35 only requires that the person to be examined be a party to the 'action,' not that he be an opposing party vis-a-vis the movant. There is no doubt that Schlagenhauf was a 'party' to this 'action' by virtue of the original complaint. Therefore, Rule 35 permitted examination of him (a party defendant) upon petition of Contract Carriers and National Lead (codefendants), provided, of course, that the other requirements of the Rule were met. . . .

Petitioner next contends that his mental or physical condition was not 'in controversy' and 'good cause' was not shown for the examinations, both as required by the express terms of Rule 35. . . . [These requirements] are not met by mere conclusory allegations of the pleadings—nor by mere relevance to the case—but require an affirmative showing by the movant that each condition as to which the examination is sought is really and genuinely in controversy and that good cause exists for ordering each particular examination. Obviously, what may be good cause for one type of examination may not be so for another. The ability of the movant to obtain the desired information by other means is also relevant.

Rule 35, therefore, requires discriminating application by the trial judge, who must decide . . . whether the party requesting a mental or physical examination or examinations has adequately demonstrated the existence of the Rule's requirements of 'in controversy' and 'good cause,' which requirements . . . are necessarily related. This does not, of course, mean that the movant must prove his case on the merits in order to meet the requirements for a mental or physical examination. Nor does it mean that an evidentiary hearing is required in all cases. This may be necessary in some cases, but in other cases the showing could be made by affidavits or other usual methods short of a hearing. It does mean, though, that the movant must produce sufficient information, by whatever means, so that the district judge can fulfill his function mandated by the Rule.

Of course, there are situations where the pleadings alone are sufficient to meet these requirements. A plaintiff in a negligence action who asserts mental or physical injury . . . places that mental or physical injury clearly in controversy and provides the defendant with good cause for an examination to determine the existence and extent of such asserted injury. This is not only true as to a plaintiff, but applies equally to a defendant who asserts his mental or physical condition as a defense to a claim, such as, for example, where insanity is asserted as a defense to a divorce action.

Here, however, Schlagenhauf did not assert his mental or physical condition either in support of or in defense of a claim. His condition was sought to be placed in issue by other parties. Thus, under the principles discussed above, Rule 35 required that these parties make an affirmative showing that petitioner's mental or physical condition was in controversy and that there was good cause for the examinations requested. This, the record plainly shows, they failed to do. . . .

Nothing in the pleadings or affidavit would afford a basis for a belief that Schlagenhauf was suffering from a mental or neurological illness warranting wide-ranging psychiatric or neurological examinations. Nor is there anything stated justifying the broad internal medicine examination.

The only specific allegation made in support of the four examinations ordered was that the 'eyes and vision' of Schlagenhauf were impaired. . . . [W]e would be hesitant to set aside a visual examination if it had been the only one ordered. However, as the case must be remanded to the District Court because of the other examinations ordered, it would be appropriate for the District Judge to reconsider also this order in light of the guidelines set forth in this opinion.

The Federal Rules of Civil Procedure should be liberally construed, but they should not be expanded by disregarding plainly expressed limitations. The 'good cause' and 'in controversy' requirements of Rule 35 make it very apparent that sweeping examinations of a party who has not affirmatively put into issue his own mental or physical condition are not to be automatically ordered merely because the person has been involved in an accident . . . and a general charge of negligence is lodged. Mental and physical examinations are only to be ordered upon a discriminating application by the district judge of the limitations prescribed by the Rule. . . .

B. Examination Details

Satisfying the "in controversy" and "good cause" requirements are not the requesting party's only obligations. The requesting party must also set out in the motion the "time, place, manner, conditions, and scope of the examination, as well as the person or persons who will perform it." *See* Fed. R. Civ. P. 35(a)(2)(B). Requesting parties, thus, are usually able to choose the particular doctor who will conduct the examination. Can requesting parties make that choice by selecting the same doctor they often hire for such exams and who regularly seems to reach medical conclusions favorable to their side of the dispute? Consider the decision in *O'Sullivan v. Rivera*, 229 F.R.D. 184 (D.N.M. 2004), where the trial court ruled on the defendant's contested motion to examine a personal injury plaintiff.

O'SULLIVAN

v.

RIVERA

229 F.R.D. 184 (D.N.M. 2004)

BROWNING, United States District Judge

O'Sullivan has not established why Dr. Schultz [the defendant's chosen examiner] would be unable to impartially assist and enlighten the jury regarding O'Sullivan's alleged personal injuries. But even if Dr. Schultz were often called by defense lawyers or were conservative in his diagnoses and treatments, the Defendants would be entitled to obtain their own expert and secure an independent opinion about O'Sullivan's condition. The truth will more likely be obtained from the adversarial process than by taking the unexamined word of the plaintiff's expert.

When a court chooses an "impartial" expert, it often must select from a narrow group of experts, often from names submitted by the parties. Despite the court's best efforts to be fair and even-handed, the perception often is that the court has chosen a defense expert or a plaintiff expert, regardless whether the court intended to do so. Hence, rather than intruding into this case with a choice that might inadvertently tilt the playing field unfairly in favor of one side, the Court will let the parties' experts do their work and allow the jury to make the decision whom is most impartial and qualified. Accordingly, the Court should afford the Defendants the opportunity to rebut [plaintiff's doctor's] testimony with an expert of their choosing.

C. Additional Considerations

Even when an adversary's physical or mental condition is unquestionably "in controversy," courts will balance the requesting party's need for the examination against the various burdens on and risks to the examinee. With tests that are painful or invasive (such as drawing blood), a court might impose a greater burden on the requesting party to show "good cause." Similarly, in ruling on a contested request for a physical or mental examination, the courts may have to navigate the perilous issue of safety. Under what circumstances should the court permit an examination when that examination may, itself, result in further injury to the claimant? Consider the court's decision in *Pena v. Troup*, 163 F.R.D. 352 (D. Colo. 1995), where the court confronted a claim filed on behalf of a neurologically injured patient who alleged that, years earlier, during her birth, the presiding doctor had committed malpractice.

The defendant doctor sought an MRI of the patient's brain to assess whether her injury was a traumatic one (and, thus, possibly linked to medical malpractice at delivery) or a disease-related one (and, thus, likely unrelated to medical negligence). The complicating factor the judge encountered was the patient's neurological condition, which would necessitate the use of general anesthesia in order to properly perform the MRI.

PENA
v.
TROUP

163 F.R.D. 352 (D. Colo. 1995)

ABRAM, United States Magistrate Judge

"In determining what kinds of examinations to authorize, the court must balance the desire to insure the safety and freedom from pain of the party to be examined against the need for the facts in the interest of truth and justice."

. . .

Here, the Court must decide whether to order Plaintiffs to submit to a procedure which they deem to be unsafe. Although this is a question of first impression in this court, several other courts have addressed the issue. These courts have adopted the "burden-shifting" approach articulated in *Lefkowitz v. Nassau County Medical Center*, 462 N.Y.S.2d 903 (A.D. 1983). In *Lefkowitz*, plaintiff claimed that she became infertile because of defendant-physician's alleged negligence. Defendants requested that plaintiff submit to medical testing which was potentially dangerous. . . . In resolving this dilemma, the court adopted a burden-shifting approach, requiring plaintiff to show that the proposed test is *prima facie* potentially dangerous. . . . Once plaintiff satisfies this initial burden, the burden shifts to the party seeking the examination to demonstrate the need for the examination and its safety. . . . "Although the degree and type of proof necessary to show safety may vary from case to case, the seeking party generally is required to offer the affidavit of an expert or at least to cite from standard medical texts of which judicial notice could be taken." *Id.* Because defendants had not supplied such documentation to the court in *Lefkowitz*, the court held that defendants failed to meet their burden. . . .

Another case from New York also bears similarity to the instant case. *See Thomas v. John T. Mather Memorial Hosp.*, 556 N.Y.S.2d 720 (2 Dept.1990). In *Thomas*, defendants sought to compel the severely brain-damaged plaintiff to submit to an MRI or a Computed Axial Tomography ("CAT") scan while under sedation. Plaintiff sought a protective order on the ground that plaintiff's health would be endangered if he were compelled to submit to the scan while under sedation. Plaintiff's neurologist submitted an affidavit stating that "there is no medical reason or medical benefit for [the plaintiff] to undergo a C[A]T scan. Clearly anesthesia or sedation (including chloral hydrate) does represent a risk to [his] health." . . . In turn, defendants established that the risk to plaintiff was minimal and that plaintiff had submitted to CAT scans while sedated on previous occasions without consequence. . . . The court ordered plaintiff to submit to the scan and explained its decision as follows:

> Notwithstanding the plaintiff's assertions to the contrary, there is a need as well as a benefit to be derived from the CAT scan, since it may enhance the defendants' ability to prepare a defense. Indeed, the functional utility of such an exam and its validity as a discovery device is not in dispute. We note, moreover, that the plaintiff's expert offered no details as to the manner in which chloral hydrate would be harmful to the plaintiff nor did he address the fact that the plaintiff apparently tolerated several prior CAT scans without incident.

Other jurisdictions have employed analogous reasoning. . . .

The Court agrees with the jurisdictions which have adopted the *Lefkowitz* burden-shifting approach to decide cases such as this one. Under that standard, Plaintiffs must first demonstrate that it is *prima facie* potentially dangerous for Raquel to submit to the MRI under sedation or general anesthesia. Plaintiffs assert that the procedure poses substantial risk of harm to Raquel. Plaintiffs have furnished the Court with two affidavits. In the first affidavit, [an anesthesiologist] . . . opines:

> [I]t would be a breach of good medical practice to subject Raquel Pena to the risks of general anesthesia in order to perform an MRI as there is no sound basis to conclude such a study is necessary to the improvement of her underlying disease or overall general health. . . . [General anesthesia] carries inherent risks including death, brain damage, paralysis, spinal injury, respiratory problems, adverse drug reaction, injury to vocal cords, loss of vision, and varying degrees of physical pain. Those risk[s] are at least the same if not greater for Raquel Pena because of her cerebral palsy and the difficulties that condition could pose to the sedation itself in terms of intubation, positioning and monitoring. There is also the possibility of an adverse reaction between anesthetic agents and her anticonvulsant medications.

In the second affidavit, [Raquel's longstanding neurologist] . . . states that "the risks of general anesthesia are unacceptable for this patient." Based on these affidavits, Plaintiffs have demonstrated that general anesthesia is *prima facie* potentially dangerous for Raquel.

Because Plaintiffs have satisfied their burden, the burden shifts to Defendant to demonstrate the need for the MRI and its safety. Plaintiff argues that a CAT scan performed on Raquel in 1977, a few months after her birth, should be sufficient to meet Defendant's needs. However, due to the age of the film, the CAT scan is not available because it has been recycled by the hospital. Although a radiologist's report documenting the 1977 CAT scan exists, it makes no reference as to the timing or the cause of Raquel's injury. Moreover, even if the actual CAT scan were available, "it would not be helpful in this area because of the limitations of those scans and the images produced."

Defendant has submitted affidavits of two Board certified pediatric neurologists . . . and a Board certified anesthesiologist . . . . All three doctors concur that an MRI will provide vital information to the assessment of Raquel's injury. An MRI would enable doctors "to determine the extent of the intracranial pathology and whether the pathology is static or progressive and whether it is developmental or acquired. If the pathology is progressive or developmental, it is not due to birth related injury." Clearly, Defendant needs the MRI to aid in determining a critical issue in the case—causation.

Defendant has also met his burden of showing that the risks associated with the procedure are minimal to Raquel. [One of defendant's experts] opines that "an MRI is the medically accepted test of choice for imaging the central nervous system and is an extremely safe procedure. . . . While no medical procedure is 100% risk free, I believe Raquel can be sedated for the procedure with minimal risk." [A second expert] agrees: "An MRI can be performed safely under sedation or general anesthesia for patients such as Raquel Pena, especially if monitored by an anesthesiologist . . . . Sedation or general anesthesia for any patient (including Raquel Pena) involves some potential risk; however, in my professional opinion, the risk is low." . . . [S]everal medical articles support[ed that] opinion, including an article specifically addressing epileptic patients. This article found no significant change in epileptiform activity in patients who were subjected to a relatively new intravenous anesthetic called Propofol. . . . Finally, it is important to highlight that, in formulating his opinion, [one expert] noted that . . . Raquel had general anesthesia for a dental cleaning and restorations and had no complications from the anesthesia. "This history shows she can undergo anesthesia safely."

In light of the above evidence, Defendant has met his burden of showing the necessity for the MRI and the minimal risk associated with the procedure. Therefore, Plaintiffs should be compelled to submit Raquel to the MRI. *See Stinchcomb v. United States,* 132 F.R.D. 29, 31 (E.D.Pa.1990) ("It would not be fair to permit a plaintiff to rely on the very condition of which he complains to defeat a defendant's ability to prove that he did not cause that condition.").

Defendant agrees that the MRI can be performed in Texas—where Plaintiffs reside—by a radiologist and an anesthesiologist of Plaintiffs' choosing, that the mode of sedation or anesthesia be determined by the anesthesiologist, that Raquel's treating physician may supervise the MRI, and that Raquel's parents may be present during the procedure. Defendant also agrees to pay the costs incurred for the MRI.

IT IS ORDERED THAT Defendant's Motion for Independent Medical Examination is hereby granted consistent with this Opinion . . . .

D. Reports

Once the Rule 35 examination has been conducted, the person who is examined is entitled to a copy of the examiner's report. *See* Fed. R. Civ. P. 35(b). In this way, both sides – plaintiffs and defendants – are afforded access to the examiner's findings. But requesting this report comes with a consequence; if the person examined requests the report, the party who ordered the exam is then entitled to "like reports of all earlier or later examinations of the same condition." *See* Rule 35(b)(3). Any privilege the examined party might have had in those reports is deemed waived for this purpose. *See* Rule 35(b)(4). Such a waiver might not be especially consequential, however; the adversary might have had the right of access to those "like reports" in any event under other discovery rules.

FROM CLASSROOM TO PRACTICE

Often, in practice, Rule 35 requests for a physical or medical examination (sometimes also called an "IME" (Independent Medical Examination) by litigators) are performed by consent of the parties. Because the standards of "in controversy" and "good cause" are often easily assessed in most cases, parties frequently do not waste the money or time necessary to fight over these motions. But, on occasion, those fights do happen – when an examination request overreaches (into a type of exam or a manner of examination that the facts and circumstances do not warrant), when bona fide questions are raised about the fitness of the proposed examiner, when issues of examination safety arise, when the lawyer or other representative of the person to be examined insists on being present during the examination or on having the examination recorded, or when the examination is scheduled to occur at an inconvenient place or time. So, although physical and mental examinations are often routine and uncontroversial, exceptions exist.

QA

Hypothetical

Q: Suppose our automobile driver's attorney, in the lawsuit against the allegedly negligent delivery van driver, had pleaded in the complaint a demand for compensation for the automobile driver's physical ailments, lost wages, and inability to continue to pursue her chosen profession. Then, in a seemingly routine, almost throw-away manner, the attorney included "mental anguish" as an item of requested compensation. In doing so, the attorney may simply have copied-and-pasted standardized language used in other personal injury lawsuits. Is that passing reference to "mental anguish" enough to obligate the automobile driver to submit to a mental examination as well as a physical one?

A: Maybe. Although courts have differed, "the clear weight of authority on this issue shows that a simple claim of emotional distress does not *automatically* justify a Rule 35 order compelling an examination." *Nolan v. Int'l Bhd. of Teamsters Health & Welfare & Pension Funds, Local 705*, 199 F.R.D. 272, 275 (N.D. Ill. 2001). Courts often perform a more searching inquiry to ferret out whether "mental anguish" (or similar language) is merely a shorthand way of describing "humiliation, embarrassment, or any run-of-the-mill discomfort caused by unpleasant circumstances," in which case a mental examination may be refused. *Id.* at 275–76. Other courts may actually press the claimants for formal clarification: do the claimants propose to argue emotional injury and offer evidence to support that contention? If so, an examination will likely be ordered; if not, because claimants have placed themselves formally on the record on this issue, thereby relieving their opponent of the duty of preparing for and defending against that claim, an examination can confidently be denied. *See Nyfield v. Virgin Islands Tel. Corp.*, 2001 WL 378858, at *1–*3 (D.V.I. Apr. 17, 2001).

Perhaps the most perplexing challenge in physical or mental examinations is whether to seek one at all. Does such an examination serve the requesting party's litigation interests? While it is possible that the examination will reveal that an adversary's injuries do not exist at all or are not so serious as an adversary claims, the examination could also confirm precisely the opposite – that the injuries are, actually, present and that they are as serious as the claimant asserts (or, perhaps, moreso). Imagine the impact of that revelation. Opposing counsel's speech to the jury will highlight not just the claimant's injuries, but the validation of those injuries by the defendant's own physician ("Ladies and gentlemen of the jury, a few months ago, opposing counsel demanded that my client submit to an intrusive and embarrassing examination by a doctor she had never met before, whom she has never trusted with her medical care, and from whom she seeks no medical advice. Opposing counsel chose that doctor. And do you know what that doctor told opposing counsel? You guessed it. He agreed that my client was right all along. She is, as both sides now agree, seriously injured. You don't have to take my client's word for that. Take the word of opposing counsel's doctor instead!").

Hypotheticals: Mastering the Nuances

Rolling the IME Dice: Because a physical or mental exam can either help or hurt a party's litigating position, the decision to seek an exam involves a good bit of gambling. How does an attorney make a thoughtful, safe, prudent decision on whether to request or forego an examination?

Peeking Over the Doctor's Shoulder: There is no nationally uniform standard for who can attend and observe a physical or mental exam. Courts tend to decide that issue on a case-by-case basis. Should the attorney whose client is being examined try to attend the examination personally, or insist on having a physician of his or her choosing attend and watch? What strategies might influence those decisions?

PRACTICE SAMPLES

Sample 4-8: CONTESTED MOTION FOR EXAMINATION

IN THE UNITED STATES DISTRICT COURT
DISTRICT OF WEST CAROLINA

Jane Doe,	)	
	)	
Plaintiff,	)	
	)	
v.	)	Civil Action No. 00-CV-12345
	)	
Louisville Lawnmower, Inc. and	)	
Brooklyn Blade Co.,	)	
	)	
Defendants.	)	

Motion for Order Compelling Mental and Emotional Examination

Louisville Lawnmower, Inc. ("Louisville"), by and through its undersigned attorneys, Benjarvus Green-Ellis, LLC, files this Motion for Order Compelling Mental Examination of the plaintiff, Jane Doe ("Doe").

1. In this action, Doe asserts a claim for products liability arising out of an injury she allegedly incurred while using a lawnmower manufactured by Louisville to mow an overgrown hillside.

2. In her response to Louisville's interrogatories, Doe stated that, as a result of her physical injuries, Doe has suffered depression, anxiety, panic attacks, and post-traumatic stress disorder. Doe's interrogatory answers further state that Doe has received treatment from mental health professionals for these conditions.

3. Pursuant to Rule 35(a) of the Federal Rules of Civil Procedure, this Court may order a party whose mental condition is in controversy to submit to a mental examination by a suitably licensed or certified examiner upon a showing of good cause and on notice to all parties of the person to be examined. A motion to order such an examination under Rule 35(a) must

specify the time, place, manner, conditions, and scope of such an examination, as well as the person or persons who are to perform it. Fed. R. Civ. P. 35(a). This standard is met here.

4. Doe's complaint includes a claim for her mental and emotional injuries. Accordingly, she has placed her mental condition in controversy, and good cause thus exists to warrant the requested examination. *See, e.g., J.H. v. School Town of Munster,* 38 F. Supp. 3d 986, 988 (N.D. Ind. 2014) (allowing examination of the plaintiff's mental condition); *Flores-Febus v. MVM, Inc.,* 299 F.R.D. 338, 340 (D. P.R. 2014) (same).

5. Louisville attempted to arrange for Doe's mental examination by stipulation. Doe, however, has refused to grant her consent unless Doe's counsel be present during the examination.

6. Louisville has selected Dr. Strangelove to examine Doe. Dr. Strangelove opines that the presence of counsel for Doe during the examination would interfere with the examination. Dr. Strangelove's letter expressing this opinion is attached as Exhibit A.

7. For good cause shown, Louisville respectfully requests an order compelling Doe to submit to a psychological examination, during which Dr. Strangelove will administer psychological testing and ask interview questions concerning Doe's mental condition and mental health history, in order to assess the cause, nature, course, and potential diagnosis and prognosis of her cognitive and psychological condition in relationship to her alleged depression, anxiety, panic attacks, and post-traumatic stress disorder. Dr. Strangelove is a licensed psychologist who is board certified in forensic and clinical psychology. Dr. Strangelove's curriculum vitae is attached as Exhibit B.

8. Dr. Strangelove anticipates that the examination will require approximately three hours. Accordingly, Louisville moves that this Court's order specify that Doe's examination occur on October 31, 20___ starting at 9:00 a.m., to conclude no later than 1:00 p.m., at Dr. Strangelove's office, 1331 Fifth Avenue, Springfield, West Carolina.

9. Counsel are not routinely permitted to be present during Rule 35 examinations. *See, e.g., Ornelas v. S. Tire Mart, LLC,* 292 F.R.D. 388, 395–96 (S.D. Tex. 2013) (requiring special circumstances for counsel to be present). Here, Louisville has demonstrated that the requested examination would be compromised by the presence of Doe's counsel. Accordingly, Louisville respectfully requests that this Court's order limit attendance at the examination to Doe and Dr. Strangelove.

WHEREFORE, Louisville Lawnmower, Inc. respectfully requests that this Court issue the proposed order attached to this motion.

Respectfully submitted,

BENJARVUS, GREEN-ELLIS, LLC

By: _____/s/_____
Attorney for Defendant
Louisville Lawnmower, Inc.

DATED: September 10, 20____

IN THE UNITED STATES DISTRICT COURT
DISTRICT OF WEST CAROLINA

Jane Doe,	)	
	)	
Plaintiff,	)	
	)	
v.	)	Civil Action No. 00-CV-12345
	)	
Louisville Lawnmower, Inc. and	)	
Brooklyn Blade Co.,	)	
	)	
Defendants.	)	

Proposed Order for Mental Examination

AND NOW, this _____ day of September, 20____, having considered defendant's Motion for Order Compelling Mental and Emotional Examination, and plaintiff's response thereto, it is HEREBY ORDERED that the plaintiff, Jane Doe ("Doe"), will submit to an examination of her mental and emotional condition by Dr. Strangelove. During the examination, Dr. Strangelove will administer psychological testing and ask interview questions concerning Doe's mental condition and mental health history, in order to assess the cause, nature, course, and potential diagnosis and prognosis of her cognitive and psychological condition in relationship to her alleged depression, anxiety, panic attacks, and post-traumatic stress disorder. The examination will occur on October 31, 20___ starting at 9:00 a.m., to conclude no later than 1:00 p.m., at Dr. Strangelove's office, 1331 Fifth Avenue, Springfield, West Carolina. Attendance at the examination is limited to Doe and Dr. Strangelove.

BY THE COURT:

_____

J.

CERTIFICATE OF SERVICE

The undersigned hereby certifies that the foregoing document was filed electronically with the Clerk of Court, to be served by operation of the Court's electronic filing system to those attorneys of record registered with the Court's ECF system, this 10th day of September, 20___.

BENJARVUS, GREEN-ELLIS, LLC

By: ____/s/_____
Attorney for Defendant
Louisville Lawnmower, Inc.

Sample 4-9: STIPULATED ORDER FOR EXAMINATION

IN THE UNITED STATES DISTRICT COURT
DISTRICT OF WEST CAROLINA

Jane Doe,	)	
	)	
Plaintiff,	)	
	)	
v.	)	Civil Action No. 00-CV-12345
	)	
Louisville Lawnmower, Inc. and	)	
Brooklyn Blade Co.,	)	
	)	
Defendants.	)	

Stipulated Order for Mental Examination

AND NOW, this ___ day of September, 20___, pursuant to the parties' stipulation, it is HEREBY ORDERED that the plaintiff, Jane Doe ("Doe"), will submit to an examination of her mental condition by Dr. Strangelove. During the examination, Dr. Strangelove will administer psychological testing and ask interview questions concerning Doe's mental condition and mental health history, in order to assess the cause, nature, course, and potential diagnosis and prognosis of her cognitive and psychological condition in relationship to her alleged depression, anxiety, panic attacks, and post-traumatic stress disorder. The examination will occur on October 31, 20___ starting at 9:00 a.m., to conclude no later than 1:00 p.m., at Dr. Strangelove's office, 1331 Fifth Avenue, Springfield, West Carolina. Attendance at the examination is limited to Doe and Dr. Strangelove.

BY THE COURT:

_____

J.

CERTIFICATE OF SERVICE

The undersigned hereby certifies that the foregoing document was filed electronically with the Clerk of Court, to be served by operation of the Court's electronic filing system to those attorneys of record registered with the Court's ECF system, this 10th day of September, 20___.

BENJARVUS, GREEN-ELLIS, LLC

By: ____/s/_____
Attorney for Defendant
Louisville Lawnmower, Inc.

Sample 4-10: RULE 35 EXAMINATION REPORT

Samantha Strangelove, M.D.
1331 Fifth Avenue
Springfield, West Carolina 12123

November 15, 20___

Dear Attorney Benjarvus:

Per your request, I had the opportunity to evaluate Jane Doe in my office here at 1331 Fifth Avenue on October 31, 20___ beginning at 9:06 a.m. The examination concluded at 11:43 a.m.

I began my evaluation of Ms. Doe by informing her about the nature of this evaluation. She was informed that I was asked by you to take a history, perform a psychiatric examination, and review records for the purposes of rendering my opinion regarding her mental condition. She was informed that I cannot give any diagnostic or therapeutic advice, nor can I form a doctor/patient relationship with her. She was informed that I also cannot offer her any patient confidentiality. I received assurance from Ms. Doe that this was all understood, and Ms. Doe then consented to proceed with this examination.

Ms. Doe's spouse, Pat Doe, was present throughout the examination.

RECORD REVIEW

In preparation for and in conjunction with this examination, I had the opportunity to review copies of Ms. Doe's medical records as supplied to me by your law office. I am advised that those records were supplied to you by Ms. Doe's attorney and represent the totality of her medical records on the issue of her psychiatric condition. I understand that all of the records you delivered to me were photocopies of originals, and not the originals themselves. Because I have no plan to see Ms. Doe again, and because I have no facility for storing these records, I am returning the copies to you with this letter. I request that you retain these copies in your file so that, should the need arise, I may have access to and review them again. The records included in my review were the following:

[LISTING OF ALL RECORDS REVIEWED]

HISTORY OF INJURY

The history was provided to me by Ms. Doe.

Ms. Doe said she is a 43-year-old woman who worked as a manager for the ABC Accounting Firm located at 307 Main Street in town. On [DATE], she was using a lawnmower that, she reports, was manufactured by Louisville Lawnmower, Inc. to mow an overgrown hillside when the lawnmower malfunctioned causing the moving blade to disengage and launch unexpectedly into her right calf.

Ms. Doe reports that she was taken by an ambulance, summoned by her neighbor, to County Hospital , where she was admitted for emergency treatment. Dr. [NAME] performed a [PROCEDURE DESCRIBED].

Ms. Doe reported that her course of treatment was complicated by multiple infections while hospitalized. She was in the hospital for three weeks. She then was admitted two more times for infection related problems.

Ms. Doe said her case was further complicated by nerve damage which she believes was caused at the time of surgery. She reports that she has no complaint with Dr. [NAME], and is, to the contrary, quite satisfied with the surgery and medical treatment she received from him.

Ms. Doe reports that her calf is now "much improved," and that she has no recurring pain at all in her leg or lower extremities. Her main problem is that she has nerve damage in her leg, and this limits her mobility. She said that she trips a lot.

Ms. Doe recounts that months after her lawnmower incident she was also diagnosed with a rotator cuff problem. She is "guessing" it happened at the time of the fall. In any case, this was treated with therapy, and she has had a good result. She said she is doing "much better" and has no pain now in her shoulder.

Ms. Doe's medical condition is complicated by preexisting medical history of smoking (two packs per day), hypertension, esophageal reflux, low iron anemia, and sleep apnea. She has had a tonsillectomy, multiple uterine surgeries, and admissions for asthma and pneumonia.

Ms. Doe then advised that her injuries and her course of treatment and recovery has caused her to suffer from depression and anxiety. She reported that she episodically has panic attacks that cause her to "freeze" and impede her better judgment. She also stated she encounters frequent "flashbacks" to the hillside where the blade detached, leaving her disoriented and agitated. She believes this to be evidence of post-traumatic stress disorder.

Ms. Doe described for me two mental health professionals she has visited with to seek treatment for her depression, anxiety, and related mental conditions. She saw each of those professionals twice. Both professionals recommended a continued course of therapy, which Ms. Doe has not accepted. She feels the costs of each therapy session exceed its value and has discontinued treatment with both professionals.

PAST PSYCHIATRIC HISTORY

Ms. Doe reported that she suffered from no prior depression, anxiety, or emotional conditions before this incident. She denied having ever sought any psychiatric or emotional intervention from any professional prior to this incident.

PRESENTATION

Ms. Doe presents as a distressed, tearful patient, with apparent low energy and disinterest. On occasion, her answers to questions came only after prompting from her spouse. During our time together, her behavior was marked by fidgeting and nervousness and dramatic mood swings that seemed inconsistent with the tone or topic of the discussion at that moment.

CLINICAL EXAMINATION

I administered the following standardized emotional/psychological tests on Ms. Doe:

[TESTS NAMED AND DESCRIBED]

The results from each of those tests were as follows:

[RESULTS DESCRIBED]

IMPRESSIONS AND OPINIONS

Ms. Doe's manner of appearance, her behavior during our time together, and the results of the clinical testing I performed on her lead me to the following impressions and opinions, each of which I express within a reasonable degree of medical certainty. Needless to say, I reserve the right to amend these impressions if additional information provided warrants that. My opinions are as follows:

1. Ms. Doe experienced an emotionally traumatic event that led to physical injuries, many of which she contends have now resolved.

2. Ms. Doe appears credible, of average intelligence, oriented to time, place, and circumstance, with a concentration that was, at times, lucid and focused and at other times clouded and distant. She shows no evidence of incoherence or delusions, nor does she exhibit any signs suggestive of danger to herself or others as a result of her emotional status.

3. Ms. Doe is easily fatigued and has impaired motivation. Her approach to this examination showed a neutral attitude, and there were no indications of malingering.

4. I find no definitive reason to diagnose Ms. Doe as suffering from a major depressive disorder, although I acknowledge that condition cannot be conclusively ruled out at this time. I acknowledge that her lawnmower encounter seems to have been quite traumatic and could have precipitated a transient depressive episode. I found no definitive confirmation to lead me to that conclusion, however.

5. Ms. Doe seems unlikely to respond to psychotherapy, given her past and current insistence that such intervention is unproductive. Ms. Doe may respond to a course of psychopharmacological intervention, but that would require her to reconsider her reluctance to reengage with medical professionals.

Again, my impressions and opinions offered above are stated to a reasonable degree of medical certainty. I thank you for soliciting my opinion.

Sincerely,

Samantha Strangelove, M.D.

PART 6.

DEPOSITIONS—RULE 30
[ALSO RULES 27, 28, 31 & 32]

GETTING THE VIEW

Experienced litigators consider depositions to be among the most powerful (if not *the single most powerful*) tool in the discovery arsenal. Good reasons support that conclusion.

Depositions are usually live, in-person, question-and-answer sessions conducted under oath. The discovery-seeker poses oral questions to a sworn witness who replies with immediate oral responses. Depositions, then, are one of the very few discovery tools that occur in "real-time." Discovery is instantaneous. It is also fairly invulnerable to being "lawyered." Although the testifying witness may (and generally will) have an attorney present during the deposition, the ability of that attorney to frame, massage, or polish the witness's testimony is greatly limited. The witness must testify by answering the questions as they come—without much simultaneous aid or direction from his or her attorney. Of course, the witness and attorney may (and, in many contexts, will likely) have met before the deposition to prepare for the questioning, but neither the witness nor the attorney will usually know in advance the specific questions that will be asked. And, once the actual questioning begins, the role of the witness's attorney is even more sharply curtailed: beyond protecting the witness from unfair, improper, or belligerent questioning (and preserving certain objections for later), the witness's attorney sits as something of a spectator to a performance that then plays out live. In its passivity, the role of "defending" a witness at a deposition can be quite nerve-wracking for an attorney.

On the other hand, for the questioning attorney, the deposition setting offers a rich treasure-trove of opportunities. The substance, manner, and order of questions are all usually the questioner's prerogative. Because neither the witness nor the witness's attorney usually knows the questions in advance, and because the defending attorney's coaching ability during the deposition is sharply curtailed, the questioner is likely to obtain information that is especially genuine, candid, and forthcoming. Because the witness is sworn, the threat of perjury (should the witness lie while testifying under oath) serves only to ratchet up the likelihood of the witness's accuracy.

Consider, for example, a homeowner who sues a contractor for poorly installing a new roof that, during a heavy rain, leaked and destroyed the house's contents. The homeowner is likely to take the deposition of (or, "depose") the contractor about his work. During that deposition, the contractor might be asked, "When did you first install a new roof for a client?" The contractor might respond, "It's been a while now." The unique power of depositions is that it allows for *immediate follow-up as answers are given*. So, the homeowner's attorney might then ask, "How long is a while?" or, "Was it more than 10 years ago?" or, "What records do you keep showing when you first began installing roofs?"

The agility of instantaneous follow-up during depositions can also allow the questioner to probe areas that present themselves unexpectedly during the witness's testimony. For instance, the homeowner's attorney might ask, "Has any client ever reported you to the Better Business Bureau as a result of your roofing work?" If the contractor answered, "Not since the fire, no," the follow-up opportunities are legion: "What fire?"; "Why were you reported to the Better Business Bureau after that fire?"; "Did anyone accuse your roofing work of having contributed to the fire?"; "Describe that accusation"; "Was a criminal charge filed against you as a result?"; "Were you sued as a result?"; "Are you certain you weren't reported on any other occasion after the fire?"; "What records do you keep on roofing-client reports against you?"; "How many times were you reported before the fire?"; "To whom were you reported?"; "By whom were you reported?"; and "What were the specific roofing complaints your client(s) made against you?" All of these questions are possible because the deposition format allows the questioner to probe, in real-time, the witness's use of an unexpected four-word phrase ("Not since the fire").

Sometimes, follow-ups during depositions can be prompted by less obvious, more nuanced clues. A long, nervous pause by the witness. A stammering or defensive answer. An atypically evasive, jumbled, non-responsive answer. The witness's face flushing or draining of color. An agitated stolen glance by the witness to his or her attorney. Or even a curious non-answer ("Well, I . . . Oh, never mind. I thought you were asking me about a different fire.").

Sometimes, follow-ups can even come in the form of brand-new ideas or lines of questioning that spring to the questioner's mind for the first time as the deposition unfolds. While questioning the contractor, the attorney might unexpectedly recall a different roofing controversy involving a different neighborhood from a few years back and ask the contractor if he did any work at that site. Plainly, the opportunities are nearly boundless.

Thus, depositions are truly immersive experiences. Quite often, they produce valuable (and lawsuit-altering) moments that can be traced back to the very spontaneity and flexibility that are the defining characteristics of depositions. Consider our roofing contractor once again. Late in the deposition, the homeowner's attorney may ask the contractor why he didn't finish installing a certain portion of the homeowner's roof on one certain afternoon. The now-tired contractor unguardedly answered, "Because that whole day had been rough." The follow-up question: "What made the whole day rough?" The answer: "Me and the boys were out drinking the night before, and the next day was so brutally hot. It's amazing we could even see straight." Bingo. Game-changer. Lawsuit-altering moment.

Experienced litigators consider depositions to be powerful discovery tools because real-life tales similar to the fictional examples offered above are not unusual. They may not happen in every deposition or every lawsuit. But because of the "real-time," unforewarned, agile, spontaneous, perjury-sharpened nature of this discovery device, depositions have important features that no other discovery tool possesses.

Another early thought about depositions—they are not just one of the most valuable assets in an attorney's discovery tool bag, they are also the most fun. They require almost the same level of engagement, confrontation, strategy, and quick thinking as a trial, but happen far more often (and far less disruptively than a long trial would be to an attorney's life).

So, why are we learning about depositions now, at the very end of our discussion of the discovery tools? If depositions are so impactful, so case-altering, and so much fun, why didn't we discuss them earlier in this book? The answer is simple. As we'll learn below, a witness typically can be deposed only one time. If that deposition is taken early in the lawsuit, and then later there are important developments that emerge from interrogatory answers, production requests, party admissions, or physical or mental examinations, the opportunity to re-question that witness about all this new information is lost. For this reason, many attorneys often choose to hold off on taking depositions until other discovery tools have been used and have yielded their information. At that point, the attorney is optimally armed to conduct a fruitful deposition. But, then again, as we will also see below, cases vary; on occasion, circumstances might make an early deposition strategically wise. For many seasoned attorneys, that sequence exists, but it is the exception not the rule. Thus, because, more often than not, depositions follow after the use of other discovery tools, we have waited until now to introduce this important device.

HOW THIS DISCOVERY TOOL WORKS

The principal deposition rule is Rule 30 of the Federal Rules of Civil Procedure. Four companion rules—Rules 28, 29, 31, and 32—complement Rule 30 to complete the procedural package for this discovery tool. This package of Rules is best understood topically in six groups: when a deposition is permitted; the procedures for setting up a deposition; the logistics for conducting a deposition; special types of depositions; using deposition testimony; and sanctions for deposition misconduct. Each is now discussed in turn.

A. When a Deposition Is Permitted

A deposition can be taken of any party or non-party witness. *See* Fed. R. Civ. P. 30(a)(1). A deposition can also be taken of an entity (like a company, a partnership or association, or a government entity). *See* Fed. R. Civ. P. 30(b)(6) (these entity depositions are discussed below under "Special Types of Depositions"). Ordinarily, no court order is required to take a deposition. If the witness to be deposed is a party to the lawsuit, the procedures are simple. If the witness is not a party to the lawsuit (for example, a doctor who merely treated the plaintiff for injuries inflicted by the defendant or an accountant who merely prepared a corporate party's tax returns), the procedures are a bit more complex and a subpoena is needed.

Ordinarily, permission from a judge to conduct a deposition is not needed. But there are a few exceptions. A court order *is* required if the witness to be deposed is in prison. *See* Fed. R. Civ. P. 30(a)(2)(B). And either a court order or agreement of the parties is required to:

- Depose any witness more than once,
- depose any witness for longer than 7 hours or more than 1 day,
- depose more than 10 witnesses on any side of the lawsuit (*e.g.* plaintiffs taking more than 10 depositions, defendants taking more than 10 depositions, or third-party defendants taking more than 10 depositions),
- depose any witness before the parties have their Rule 26(f) discovery planning conference (except for exempted cases listed in Rule 26(a)(1) (B)), or
- depose any witness after the date fixed by the court's Rule 16(b)(3)(A) scheduling order for the completion of discovery.

See Rule 30(a)(2)(A).

B. Setting Up a Deposition

The judge is almost never present during a deposition. Instead, depositions are ordinarily coordinated and conducted by the parties themselves with only the witness, the attorneys, and a court reporter (perhaps a videographer, too) in attendance.

1. Authorized Officer

All depositions involve a witness's *sworn testimony*, and all depositions result in that testimony being preserved in some formal manner so that it can be used later in the lawsuit. Most often, depositions are preserved in the form of a written transcript that, verbatim, captures in print every question asked and every answer given. Sometimes, depositions are also preserved videographically, where the witness's testimony is visually and audibly recorded so that it can be played back at some later moment (usually, at trial). Someone has to perform this transcribing or recording task (the lawyers cannot do it because, obviously, they are not impartial and, in any event, will be preoccupied with the question-and-answer process itself). So, the questioning party will hire a court reporter (or "stenographer"), and maybe a videographer, to perform these transcribing/recording functions. It will also be the task of the court reporter to administer the oath and swear the witness, which will trigger the legal penalties for perjury. To be eligible to serve in this role, the court reporter must not be related to the parties or their attorneys, must not be financially interested in the outcome of the lawsuit, and must be authorized to administer legal oaths (either on special appointment by the court or by federal law or the law of the place where the deposition will take place). *See* Fed. R. Civ. P. 28.

2. Place of the Deposition

The Rules do not dictate where a deposition must be taken. Generally, the parties will agree in advance on the location (and if they can't, the court has the authority to set the location). Certain customary approaches have emerged by local practice or rule. Plaintiffs will usually be expected to come to the place where they filed their lawsuit and be deposed there. Defendants (who likely had no control over the selection of the forum) will typically be deposed where they work or live. Entities will usually be deposed at their headquarters. Non-parties will usually be deposed where they reside, work, or regularly transact business—although non-parties can be obligated to travel from those locations up to 100 miles to be deposed. *See* Fed. R. Civ. P. 45(c). Intractable disagreements over the place of a deposition are not welcomed warmly by the courts:

AVISTA MANAGEMENT, INC.

v.

WAUSAU UNDERWRITERS INS. CO.

2006 WL 1562246 (M.D. Fla. 2006)

PRESNELL, United States District Judge

[The parties in a lawsuit pending in Tampa, Florida could not agree among themselves on the place for a deposition, and the Judge was asked to intervene.]

Upon consideration of the Motion—the latest in a series of Gordian knots that the parties have been unable to untangle without enlisting the assistance of the federal courts—it is ORDERED: . . . at 4:00 P.M. on Friday, June 30, 2006, counsel shall convene at a neutral site agreeable to both parties. If counsel cannot agree on a neutral site, they shall meet on the front steps of [the federal courthouse in Tampa, Fla.]. Each lawyer shall be entitled to be accompanied by one paralegal who shall act as an attendant and witness. At that time and location, counsel shall engage in one (1) game of "rock, paper, scissors." The winner of this engagement shall be entitled to select the location for the . . . deposition to be held somewhere [in the greater Tampa area] . . . during the period July 11–12, 2006. If either party disputes the outcome of this engagement, an appeal may be filed and a hearing will be held at 8:30 A.M. on Friday, July 7, 2006 before the undersigned in Courtroom 3 [of the federal courthouse in Orlando, Fla., 84 miles and 1 ½ hours away]. . . .

3. "Notice" of the Deposition

The questioning attorney must give "reasonable notice" in writing to every other party of his or her intent to depose a witness. The proper amount of advance notice is not set by the Rules, but assessed under the particular circumstances (though a 10-day rule-of-thumb is often followed). The notice must contain: the name of the witness to be deposed (or a general description of the person, if the name is unknown); the date, time, and place of the deposition; the method to be used to preserve the witness's testimony; and any documents, things, electronically-stored information, or inspection-of-premises sought from the witness. *See* Fed. R. Civ. P. 30(b). If the witness is a party, this simple notice is sufficient (though party-witnesses must receive at least 30 days to make a production of documents, things, or electronically stored information or to permit an inspection of premises). If the witness is not a party, the notice must be supplemented by a subpoena served on the non-party witness who is to be deposed. *See* Fed. R. Civ. P. 45.

C. Conducting a Deposition

Depositions are often conducted in a conference room or meeting room, usually at one of the attorney's law offices. The process of conducting a deposition is well-defined one.

1. "Discovery Deps" Versus "Trial Deps"

Formerly, two different types of depositions were recognized by the law: "discovery deps" which were convened simply as a discovery tool; and "trial deps" (also known as "*de bene esse* deps") which were conducted with the intent of capturing testimony to be later presented at trial in lieu of that witness's "live" appearance. Today, this distinction is gone, at least in federal court. The procedures for conducting a deposition are now the same, whether the witness is being questioned principally for discovery or with the advance intent of using that preserved testimony at trial.

2. Preliminaries

Depositions begin with the court reporter making an on-the-record statement of his or her name and address; of the date, time, and place of the deposition; of the witness's name; and of the identity of all attendees. The court reporter then places the witness under oath. *See* Fed. R. Civ. P. 30(b)(5).

3. Questions and Answers

The questioning of the witness proceeds as it would at trial. The attorney who issued the notice of deposition begins, followed by other counsel, and ending with re-direct and re-cross questions. All deposition questioning must abide by the scope constraints imposed on all discovery devices (as discussed in the Scope of Discovery chapter). *See* Fed. R. Civ. P. 30(c)(1).

HALL
v.
CLIFTON PRECISION

150 F.R.D. 525 (E.D. Pa. 1993)

GAWTHROP, United States District Judge

[As a deposition began, the attorney defending a witness advised that witness that, should the witness desire to consult privately with him, all the witness need do was request it. Later, when the witness was shown a document during the questioning, the defending attorney requested a recess so that he could privately review the document with the witness. The attorney who convened the deposi-

tion objected to defending counsel's advice and subsequent recess, and then sought the court's intervention.]

The underlying purpose of a deposition is to find out what a witness saw, heard, or did—what the witness thinks. A deposition is meant to be a question-and-answer conversation between the deposing lawyer and the witness. There is no proper need for the witness's own lawyer to act as an intermediary, interpreting questions, deciding which questions the witness should answer,[FN.3] and helping the witness to formulate answers. The witness comes to the deposition to testify, not to indulge in a parody of Charlie McCarthy, with lawyers coaching or bending the witness's words to mold a legally convenient record. It is the witness—not the lawyer—who is the witness. As an advocate, the lawyer is free to frame those facts in a manner favorable to the client, and also to make favorable and creative arguments of law. But the lawyer is not entitled to be creative with the facts. Rather, a lawyer must accept the facts as they develop. Therefore, I hold that a lawyer and client do not have an absolute right to confer during the course of the client's deposition.

> [FN.3] I note that under Rule 32(d)(3)(A), objections to the competency, relevancy, or materiality of deposition testimony generally are preserved for trial. Therefore, counsel should not repeatedly interrupt the deposition to make these objections. Of course, the witness's counsel is free to object on the ground that a question asks for an answer which is protected by a privilege, and to make objections which would be waived if not raised immediately. *See* Fed. R. Civ. P. 32(d)(3)(B).

Concern has been expressed as to the client's right to counsel and to due process. A lawyer, of course, has the right, if not the duty, to prepare a client for a deposition. But once a deposition begins, the right to counsel is somewhat tempered by the underlying goal of our discovery rules: getting to the truth. Under Rule 30(c), depositions generally are to be conducted under the same testimonial rules as are trials. During a civil trial, a witness and his or her lawyer are not permitted to confer at their pleasure during the witness's testimony. Once a witness has been prepared and has taken the stand, that witness is on his or her own.

The same is true at a deposition. The fact that there is no judge in the room to prevent private conferences does not mean that such conferences should or may occur. The underlying reason for preventing private conferences is still present: they tend, at the very least, to give the appearance of obstructing the truth. * * *

These rules also apply during recesses. Once the deposition has begun, the preparation period is over and the deposing lawyer is entitled to pursue the chosen line of inquiry without interjection by the witness's counsel. Private conferences are barred during the deposition, and the fortuitous occurrence of a coffee break, lunch break, or evening recess is no reason to change the rules. Otherwise, the same problems would persist. A clever lawyer or witness who finds that a deposition is going in an undesired or unanticipated direction could simply insist on a short recess to discuss the unanticipated yet desired answers, thereby circumventing the prohibition on private conferences. Therefore, I hold that conferences between witness and lawyer are prohibited both during the deposition and during recesses.

The same reasoning applies to conferences about documents shown to the witness during the deposition. When the deposing attorney presents a document to a witness at a deposition, that attorney is entitled to have the witness, and the witness alone, answer questions about the document. The witness's lawyer should be given a copy of the document for his or her own inspection, but there is no valid reason why the lawyer and the witness should have to confer about the document before the witness answers questions about it. If the witness does not recall having seen the document before or does not understand the document, the witness may ask the deposing lawyer for some additional information, or the witness may simply testify to the lack of knowledge or understanding. But there need not be an off-the-record conference between witness and lawyer in order to ascertain whether the witness understands the document or a pending question about the document.

. . . Since the assertion of a privilege is a proper, and very important, objection during a deposition, it makes sense to allow the witness the opportunity to consult with counsel about whether to assert a privilege. Further, privileges are violated not only by the admission of privileged evidence at trial, but by the very disclosures themselves. Thus, it is important that the witness be fully informed of his or her rights before making a statement which might reveal privileged information. However, when such a conference occurs, the conferring attorney should place on the record the fact that the conference occurred, the subject of the conference, and the decision reached as to whether to assert a privilege.

Having discussed off-the-record witness-coaching, I now turn to a related concern: on-the-record witness-coaching through suggestive objections. . . . [T]he spirit of the prohibition against private conferences could be flouted by a lawyer's making of lengthy objections which contain information suggestive of an answer to a pending question. * * * [O]bjections and colloquy by lawyers tend to disrupt the question-and-answer rhythm of a deposition and obstruct the witness's testimony. Since most objections, such as those grounded on relevance or materiality, are preserved for trial, they need not be made.[FN.10] As for those few objections which would be waived if not made immediately, they should be stated pithily. *See* Fed. R. Civ. P. 32(d)(3).

> [FN.10] I also note that a favorite objection or interjection of lawyers is, "I don't understand the question; therefore the witness doesn't understand the question." This is not a proper objection. If the witness needs clarification, the witness may ask the deposing lawyer for clarification. A lawyer's purported lack of understanding is not a proper reason to interrupt a deposition. In addition, counsel are not permitted to state on the record their interpretations of questions, since those interpretations are irrelevant and often suggestive of a particularly desired answer.

* * *

Depositions are the factual battleground where the vast majority of litigation actually takes place. It may safely be said that Rule 30 has spawned a veritable cottage industry. The significance of depositions has grown geometrically over the years to the point where their pervasiveness now dwarfs both the time spent and the facts learned at the actual trial—assuming there is a trial, which there usually is not. The pretrial tail now wags the trial dog. Thus, it is particularly important that this discovery device not be abused. Counsel should never forget that even though the deposition may be taking place far from a real courtroom, with no black-robed overseer peering down upon them, as long as the deposition is conducted under the caption of this court and proceeding under the authority of the rules of this court, counsel are operating as officers of this court. They should comport themselves accordingly; should they be tempted to stray, they should remember that this judge is but a phone call away.

4. Objections

During the deposition, the attorneys (or the parties themselves if not represented by an attorney) can object to some portion of the proceeding. *See* Fed. R. Civ. P. 30(c)(2). Because the presiding judge will not be present at most depositions, there usually is no immediate ruling on a deposition objection. Instead, these objections are simply stated on the record and the deposition questioning then continues on. The stated objections are thereby memorialized for the written transcript, allowing the judge to consider, and later rule upon, any pertinent objections that have been made.

i. Objections to "Form"

A deposition question might be awkwardly phrased, confusing, or ambiguous. For example, in the lawsuit against the roofing contractor, the homeowner's attorney might have asked, "You told me that you had two meetings with the homeowner, one in June and one in July, and one meeting with the company that manufactured the roofing nails. During the meeting, what was said?" That deposition question is improperly worded. Do you see why, and what risk that impropriety poses? (It is a compound question: the questioner alerted the witness to three meetings and asked what occurred during one of them, without identifying which one. The witness, undirected in this way, might begin to describe one meeting's contents without, again, identifying to which meeting he is referring. The result is testimony about one meeting, with no clear indication whether that testimony relates to the June homeowner meeting, the July homeowner meeting, or the undated meeting with the manufacturer.) The roofing contractor's attorney can object to that sort of awkward question, but only if the objection is asserted immediately. If the attorney delays, the objection is deemed waived and the attorney's right to object later is lost. *See* Fed. R. Civ. P. 32(d)(3)(B). Why should such objections be lost through delay? It is because they can be corrected instantly, if the problem is called to the questioner's attention instantly. Leaving the objection unasserted, hanging mischievously in abeyance until later, is an unfair, inefficient strategy that the Rules foreclose.

ii. Objections to Substance

Alternatively, a deposition question could be substantively objectionable. The witness might (under the Federal Rules of Evidence, for example) be incompetent to answer the question posed, or the question might be legally irrelevant or immaterial. Consider if the homeowner's attorney asked the roofing contractor, "Your grandfather was a roofer; did clients ever complain about his roofing work?" Or, "I understand, in addition to your roofing business, you also operate a restaurant. Has any customer ever complained about your spaghetti and meatballs with red sauce?" Or, more distressingly, "After a long day working on a client's roof, how often do you stop for an extramarital fling on your way home?" Although many attorneys will state their objections to substantively objectionable questions, they are not required to do so (and some judges, like Judge Gawthrop in *Hall v. Clifton Precision*, even forbid it). Objections to the substance of a question are ordinarily not waived and can be asserted when the testimony is offered for admission at trial. *See* Fed. R. Civ. P. 32(d)(3)(A). Do you see why substantive objections are not waived in this way? Why are "substantive" objections treated differently than "form" objections? (Unlike "form" objections, calling these sorts of issues to the questioner's attention is unlikely to result in a cure—the questioner could well disagree with the objection, and a resolution from the judge will be required. Judges, however, do not sit in during most depositions, and interrupting a deposition every time a substantive objection is made to phone the judge for a ruling is disruptive, inefficient, and not welcomed by the court. Moreover, challenges to relevancy may best be assessed later, at the moment the testimony is being offered (whether to support a motion or at trial); only then, in context, is relevancy most reliably examined.) What other remedy does an attorney have to repel especially grave and intentionally objectionable questioning?

iii. The Manner of Making Objections

Because the witness is testifying (not the attorneys), courts disapprove of the strategy of using an objection or other commentary to argue with opposing counsel or to telegraph to the witness subtle advice on how to best answer a pending question. Rather, objections are considered improper unless they are stated "concisely" and in a "nonargumentative" and "nonsuggestive" way. *See* Fed. R. Civ. P. 30(c)(2). Sometimes that line is clear. Sometimes less so.

Hypothetical

Q: Prior to his deposition, the roofing contractor in our poorly installed roof hypothetical conferred with his attorney. His attorney reminded the contractor to be truthful, but that it is also fine to answer questions with "I don't know" if, in fact, the contractor truly does not know the answer to a posed question. The attorney reminded the contractor that good rarely comes from guessing at answers. State what you know, the attorney advised, but never guess. At his deposition, the roofing contractor is asked about the details of the contract he signed with the homeowner. "Do you remember reading through the contract before signing it?" asked the homeowner's lawyer. "I probably did," answers the contractor after a long, self-conscious pause. "What specifically do you remember about the terms of that contract?" was the next question. Here, the contractor answered, again after a pause: "Well, I imagine it probably contained the date we'd start working, maybe the address, and I'd think the scope of the work to be done would be in there, too." Next, the contractor was asked: "When was the precise date you contracted to start the work?" Here, the contractor paused again, then began, "Well, I'm not really all that certain, but it probably. . ." At this point, the contractor's exasperated attorney interjected, "Answer questions only if you know the answer! Don't guess!" Was that interjection proper?

A: For many years, attorneys, while defending a witness during a deposition, would use these sorts of interjections to subtly remind the witness not to guess or speculate during testimony. Defending attorneys would do so by sprinkling in comments here and there, like "answer only if you know" or "only if you recall" or "don't guess" at key moments. To many, those subtle interjections were seen as innocuous. But, today, that view is not shared by all courts. *See, e.g., In re Anonymous Member of S.C. Bar*, 552 S.E.2d 10, 17 (2001) (applying Judge Gawthrop's approach, explaining that "interjections during a deposition by the witness's attorney such as 'if you remember' and 'don't speculate' are improper because they suggest to the witness how to answer the question").

QA

Hypothetical

Q: During that same deposition, the attorney for the roofing contractor noticed numerous questions by the homeowner's attorney that were poorly worded, confusing, vague, compound, or otherwise objectionable. In other words, the questioning was flawed with many "form" objections. The roofing contractor attorney objected, as he is required to do, to these improperly worded questions and helpfully flagged for homeowner's counsel what his objection was: "Objection, that question was compound"; "Objection, that question was vague"; "Objection, that question misstates the witness's earlier testimony." Good objections?

A: You'd think so, but not all courts agree. By identifying *what specifically* he perceived to be wrong with the form of the question, the roofing contractor's attorney would seem to be doing exactly what the Rules require: objecting to form in a way that facilitates the immediate asking of an improved question. Alas, some courts consider an objection *containing* these sorts of added content to be indirectly suggestive to the testifying witness, and thus improper. *See Cincinnati Ins. Co. v. Serrano*, 2012 WL 28071, at *5 (D. Kan. Jan. 5, 2012) ("An objection that a question is 'vague' is usually, and in this instance was, a speaking objection[1] disguised as a form objection. It essentially expresses a concern that the witness may not understand the question. . . . [S]uch an objection to avoid a suggestive speaking objection should be limited to an objection 'to form,' unless opposing counsel requests further clarification of the objection."); *Druck Corp. v. Macro Fund (U.S.) Ltd.*, 2005 WL 1949519, at *4 (S.D.N.Y. Aug. 12, 2005) ("Any 'objection as to form' must say *only* those four words, unless the questioner asks the objector to state a reason."). Other courts not only disagree, but consider an objection *lacking* that added content to be *insufficient* notice to the questioner of the nature of the objection, and thus a waiver of the objection itself. *See Sec. Nat. Bank of Sioux City v. Abbott Labs.*, 299 F.R.D. 595, 604 (N.D. Iowa 2014) ("Unspecified 'form' objections are improper and will invite sanctions if lawyers choose to use them in the future."), *rev'd on other grounds*, 800 F.3d 936 (8th Cir. 2015); *Rakes v. Life Investors Ins. Co. of Am.*, 2008 WL 429060, at *5 (N.D. Iowa Feb. 14, 2008) ("[Some] contend that the objection should be limited to the words 'I object to the form of the question.' The Rule, however, is not so restrictive. . . . [T]he general practice in Iowa permits an objector to state in a few words the manner in which the question is defective as to form (e.g., compound, vague as to time,

---

1. A "speaking objection" is an objection "that contains more information (often in the form of argument) than needed by the judge to sustain or overrule it. Many judges prohibit lawyers from using speaking objections, and sometimes even from stating the grounds for objections, because of the potential for influencing the jury." BLACK'S LAW DICTIONARY 1241 (10th ed. 2014).

misstates the record, etc.). This process alerts the questioner to the alleged defect, and affords an opportunity to cure the objection."). So, what's the appropriate manner of objecting? Prudent practitioners should always check the local rules of court, chamber's rules, and local case law for clues. Failing any clear direction, the wisest practice is to state the perceived error in the question, but do so in the most concise way possible.

iv. Other Deposition Objections

The deposition process may prompt other objections, such as to the adequacy of the notice of deposition, to the qualification of the court reporter, or to the court reporter or videographer as they perform the tasks of preserving and delivering the deposition testimony. These sorts of objections must be made promptly after the contested conduct occurs or is discovered. *See* Fed. R. Civ. P. 32(d)(1)–(2), (4).

5. Instructions Not to Answer a Question

In earlier times, an attorney defending a witness at a deposition might have attempted to exert a heavy-fisted influence on the proceedings, to protect his or her witness or to minimize the damaging impact of bad testimony. One way of wielding such control was to turn to the witness and direct him or her not to answer a pending question. Today, instructions not to answer a question are permitted only in three, narrow circumstances—when necessary to: (1) preserve a privilege; (2) enforce a specific limitation that had been ordered by the judge; or (3) present a motion to the judge to terminate or limit further deposition questioning. *See* Fed. R. Civ. P. 30(c)(2). In the homeowner lawsuit against the roofing contractor, for example, the roofing contractor's attorney could appropriately instruct the contractor not to answer this question: "Before this deposition began, did you discuss with your attorney whether you should declare personal bankruptcy to protect yourself against the enormous liability you almost certainly have to my client?" Such a question would almost certainly be considered as invading the attorney-client privilege. But an instruction not to answer some different question on the basis of relevance, witness competence, or lack of first-hand knowledge would not be proper.

6. Post-Deposition Procedures

When the deposition formally ends, the court reporter will state on the record that all questioning has completed. If any exhibits were used during the questioning, the court reporter will attach those (or copies) to the finished transcript or video recording. The court reporter will retain all stenographic notes or recordings and will certify the original deposition transcript or recording as accurate and then deliver it to the attorney who noticed the deposition. All other parties in the case may purchase a copy from the reporter or videographer. The witness who testified may, upon request, review the finished transcript and notify the court reporter of any errors that witness believes were made in either form or substance by filling out an "errata sheet." *See* Fed. R. Civ. P. 30(b)(5)(C), (e), (f).

JACKSON
v.
TEAMSTERS LOCAL UNION 922

310 F.R.D. 179 (D. D.C. 2015)

BOASBERG, United States District Judge

"A deposition is not a take home examination." *Greenway v. Int'l Paper Co.*, 144 F.R.D. 322, 325 (W.D. La.1992). Plaintiffs are former employees of Giant Food, LLC, who were terminated from their positions . . . [and now] have filed suit against Giant and the two unions representing them, alleging that these three Defendants conspired to misrepresent the reasons for their firing and to induce them to sign disadvantageous severance agreements. In the course of lengthy and contentious discovery proceedings, a number of depositions were taken. After the conclusion of the depositions, six deponents submitted errata sheets revising significant and material portions of their testimony—in some cases, changing answers from "yes" to "no." . . . The explanations for these changes, enigmatically, were packaged in one-word descriptions, such as "clarification," "correction," or "mistake." Defendants now move to strike the errata sheets, arguing that Plaintiffs have violated Fed. R. Civ. P. 30(e) by improperly altering their deposition testimony after the fact.

II. Legal Standard

In seeking to determine the legal standard here, the central questions are straightforward: Under what circumstances may a deponent use an errata sheet to make material or contradictory changes to her deposition testimony?

. . .

The Court starts with the plain language of Rule 30(e)(1), which provides the mechanism by which a deponent may review a deposition transcript and make changes to that testimony: ". . . On request by the deponent or a party before the deposition is completed, the deponent must be allowed 30 days after being notified by the officer that the transcript or recording is available in which: (A) to review the transcript or recording; and (B) if there are changes *in form or substance*, to sign a statement listing the changes and the reasons for making them." Although the rule appears to clearly state the types of changes permitted in errata sheets—those "in form or substance"—it does not dictate how courts should treat such changes. * * *

The Court begins with an influential Second Circuit case. In *Podell v. Citicorp Diners Club, Inc.*, 112 F.3d 98 (2d Cir.1997), the plaintiff made an arguably "damaging" admission on a material matter in his deposition, and attempted to revise his testimony through contradictory errata sheets. . . . [The court] first offered an expansive view of Rule 30(e): " 'The language of the Rule places no limitations on the type of changes that may be made[,] . . . nor does the Rule require a judge to examine the sufficiency, reasonableness, or legitimacy of the reasons for the changes'—even if those reasons 'are unconvincing.'" It then explained: "At the same time, when a party amends his testimony under Rule 30(e), [t]he original answer to the deposition questions will remain part of the record and can be read at the trial. . . . Nothing in the language of Rule 30(e) requires or implies that the original answers are to be stricken when changes are made."

The court ultimately concluded that the district court was on "firm ground in holding that Podell was 'not entitled to have his altered answers take the place of the original ones,' and that his 'changed answers [became simply a] part of the record generated during discovery.'" In other words, Podell could not prevent the granting of summary judgment merely "by scratching out and recanting his original testimony" via errata sheets, and his doing so "[did] not weigh enough in the balance to create an issue of fact for a jury."

* * *

The Sixth, Seventh, Ninth, and Tenth Circuits, conversely, are more restrictive . . . [and hold that] errata sheets may typically be used for corrective, but not contradictory, changes—unless the contradictory change is a transcription error.

* * *

While these opinions thus employ a spectrum of approaches when considering errata sheets at summary judgment, this Court [will, in the absence of binding precedent, follow the view adopted by essentially every circuit] . . . . that material revisions should not be accepted absent convincing explanations.

* * *

The Court, consequently, will examine Plaintiffs' errata sheets *now* upon Defendants' Motion to Strike to determine whether and to what extent they will be permitted to stand. . . . The contents of the errata sheets, as alluded to previously, fall into three general buckets: (1) directly contradictory statements, (2) substantive and material additions, and (3) relatively minor clarifications. There are numerous examples of the first type. *See, e.g.,* . . . Exh. 3

(Errata Sheet of Donna Ward) at ECF p. 3 (changing "Correct" to "That is not correct") . . . .

There are even more examples of Plaintiffs' using the errata sheets to provide explanations and to expand on responses. *See, e.g.,* . . . Mathis Errata Sheet at ECF p. 3 (changing "silent" to "silent, but Giant did not disagree with statements made by Ferline").

Plaintiffs, finally, do submit some minor typographical or clerical revisions. *See, e.g.,* . . . Mathis Errata Sheet at ECF p. 3 (changing "401" to "401K"). These need no analysis since they are not challenged.

To justify their revisions, Plaintiffs rely, almost exclusively, on the following one-word explanations: "clarification," "correction," "completion," "mistake," "error," and "incomplete." These terse offerings do little but state the obvious; the Court presumes that Plaintiffs would not submit errata sheets but for *some type* of mistake or error. . . . What is missing is any thoughtful or clear articulation of the basis for what constitute significant alterations in sworn testimony.

* * *

The Court, consequently, will permit only those changes in this case that are typographical or clerical in nature.

D. Special Types of Depositions

The usual type of deposition is the deposition of a natural person conducted during the pendency of a civil lawsuit. But four other types of depositions are permitted for special needs.

1. Entity Depositions

Not every party is a natural person. Sometimes, a party or witness may be a business (*e.g.,* a manufacturing corporation, an accounting partnership, a dental limited liability company, etc.), or an association (*e.g.,* a fraternal society, a scout troop, community club, a nonprofit group, etc.), or a government agency (*e.g.,* a fire department, a turnpike commission, an airport authority, etc.). Even though these entities are not natural persons, they can still be deposed. These types of depositions are commonly known by the Rule that authorizes them: "a Rule 30(b)(6) deposition." It is a commonly used Rule, with special features.

i. Deposing—and Binding—an Entity

Although the law recognizes that organizations are legal entities separate from the people that comprise them, it is also true that organizations can only act through those people. The challenge, then, is obtaining deposition testimony that actually *binds* the organization in the same way that a natural person would be bound by his or her own, personal deposition testimony. By using Rule 30(b)(6), the questioner can compel an organization to nominate a person who will speak for the organization at a deposition. The testimony that nominee provides is then binding on the entity. *See Estate of Thompson v. Kawasaki Heavy Indus., Ltd.*, 291 F.R.D. 297, 303–04 (N.D. Iowa 2013) (surveying competing views, before ruling that testimony by a Rule 30(b)(6) designee witness is binding on the corporate party absent "some extraordinary explanation"). But "binding" in this sense is not absolute, just as it is not with the testimony of natural persons; although the entity is "stuck" with its designee witness's testimony (and can be impeached if contrary testimony is later offered), the Rule 30(b)(6) testimony does not rise to the level of a judicial admission—it, like any other testimony, "can be corrected, explained, and supplemented, and the entity is not 'irrevocably' bound to what the fairly prepared and candid designated deponent happens to remember during the testimony." *Snapp v. United Transp. Union*, 889 F.3d 1088, 1104 (9th Cir. 2018) (citation omitted). *Accord Vehicle Mkt. Research, Inc. v. Mitchell Int'l, Inc.*, 839 F.3d 1251, 1260–61 (10th Cir. 2016) ("We agree with our sister circuits that the testimony of a Rule 30(b)(6) witness is merely an evidentiary admission, rather than a judicial admission," and though it "is 'binding' in the sense that whatever its deponent says can be used against the organization," it "is not 'binding' in the sense that it precludes the deponent from correcting, explaining, or supplementing its statements") (citations omitted).

ii. Procedure for Rule 30(b)(6) Depositions

Unlike most other depositions, an entity witness is entitled to special, advance notice of the topics to be explored during the deposition. The notice of deposition for an entity must set out "with reasonable particularity the matters for examination." *See* Fed. R. Civ. P. 30(b)(6). Once it receives such a notice, the entity must select someone to testify on its behalf (who may be an officer, director, managing agent, or someone else). The entity may even select multiple persons for this task, prescribing the matters on which each different person will testify. *See id.* The selected spokesperson(s) need not have original knowledge of the matters for examination but may study in advance of the deposition to prepare. *See id.* In either event, at the deposition, when the selected witness testifies, he or she is testifying not as an individual witness but as the entity itself, and must present the collective knowledge of the entity, not just the witness's firsthand knowledge. [*Note*: An amendment to Rule 30(b)(6) is presently under consideration which would, if approved, require the deposing party and the deponent company's representatives to confer in good faith about the matters to be explored during the questioning and the identity of the spokeperson(s) who will testify on the entity's behalf.]

MEMORY INTEGRITY, LLC
v.
INTEL CORP.

308 F.R.D. 656 (D. Ore. 2015)

SIMON, United States District Judge

[T]he discovery device created by Rule 30(b)(6) was intended to assist both sides in the deposition process. Previously, officers or managing agents of a corporation who were deposed might use a technique known as "bandying," in which each witness in turn disclaims knowledge of facts that are known to other persons in the organization and thereby to the organization itself. This rule was intended to curb that practice. In addition, organizations at times were subjected to an unnecessarily large number of their officers and agents being deposed by a party who was uncertain of who in the organization has knowledge regarding some specific matter at issue. The . . . burden placed by this rule on a party required to produce a witness or witnesses "is not essentially different from that of answering interrogatories under Rule 33, and is in any case lighter than that of an examining party ignorant of who in the corporation has knowledge." Fed. R. Civ. P. 30, Advisory Committee Notes (1970 Amendments).

"In a Rule 30(b)(6) deposition, there is no distinction between the corporate representative and the corporation. The Rule 30(b)(6) designee does not give his personal opinion. Rather, he presents the corporation's 'position' on the topic. The designee testifies on behalf of the corporation and thus holds it accountable." *Sprint Commc'ns Co. L.P. v. Theglobe.com, Inc.*, 236 F.R.D. 524, 527 (D. Kan. 2006). Under this rule, "companies have a duty to make a conscientious, good-faith effort to designate knowledgeable persons for Rule 30(b)(6) depositions and to prepare them to fully and unevasively answer questions about the designated subject matter." *Id.*

For these reasons, the purpose underlying Rule 30(b)(6) would be "frustrated [if] a corporate party produces a witness who is unable . . . or unwilling to provide the necessary factual information on the entity's behalf." *Black Horse Lane Assoc., L.P. v. Dow Chem. Corp.*, 228 F.3d 275, 304 (3d Cir. 2000). Thus, the rule requires, if need be, that the responding party "must prepare deponents by having them review prior fact witness deposition testimony as well as documents and deposition exhibits." *United States v. Taylor*, 166 F.R.D. 356, 362 (M.D. N.C.1996). In short, corporate parties have an obligation to present witnesses who are capable of providing testimony on the noticed topics regardless of whether the information was in the witness's personal knowledge, provided that the information is reasonably available to the corporation.... [*See*] *Nutramax Labs., Inc. v. Twin Labs., Inc.,* 183 F.R.D. 458, 469 (D. Md.1998) ("The testimony of [Rule 30(b)(6)] witnesses also is not limited to matters within their personal knowledge, but extends to matters known or reasonably available to the party designating the witness.").

Because Rule 30(b)(6) places substantial responsibilities and burdens on the responding corporate party, the rule itself expressly requires that the party requesting the deposition "must describe with reasonable particularity the matters for examination." As one court has explained, "to allow the Rule to effectively function, the requesting party must take care to designate, *with painstaking specificity,* the particular subject areas that are intended to be questioned, and that are relevant to the issues in dispute." *Sprint,* 236 F.R.D. at 528. "Once notified as to the reasonably particularized areas of inquiry, the corporation then must not only produce such number of persons as will satisfy the request, but more importantly, prepare them so that they may give complete, knowledgeable, and binding answers on behalf of the corporation." *[Id.]*

iii. Non-Rule 30(b)(6) Entity Depositions

Rule 30(b)(6) permits the taking of the deposition of an entity itself. But that is not the only type of deposition that may be taken of entity participants. An attorney can choose, alternatively or additionally, to depose individual employees or representatives of the entity. Doing so is sometimes wise. Recall that the entity gets to choose who testifies for it during a Rule 30(b)(6) deposition. So, while the attorney taking a particular Rule 30(b)(6) deposition might be hoping the entity's president will be designated as the deponent (or its treasurer, chief information officer, senior product designer, director of marketing, etc.), that is certainly not guaranteed. If the attorney wants to learn what a specific individual affiliated with an entity knows, the only sure path to acquire that testimony is to request an ordinary (non-Rule 30(b)(6)) deposition of that person. For so-called "rank-and-file" employees, this process requires a subpoena. If the deponent is an officer, director, or other "control person" of the entity, a notice of deposition is sufficient (no subpoena is required). These procedures are discussed in greater detail in the Discovery of Nonparties chapter below.

2. Before-the-Lawsuit Depositions

Usually, depositions can only be taken after the lawsuit is filed. On occasion, however, depositions might need to be taken before the lawsuit is even begun. In the roofing contractor illustration, for example, the homeowner might have a terminally ill parent who was living in the house at the time the roof leak destroyed it. Because the homeowner's attorney is still investigating the claims, the complaint is not yet ready to be filed. But, in fear that the ill parent—a clear eyewitness—might be unavailable later, the homeowner's attorney could ask the court for permission to conduct a pre-filing deposition to preserve the parent's testimony. To do so, the attorney must supply the court and the anticipated adversaries with the subject matter of the future lawsuit, the interest of the questioner, the facts the questioner seeks to establish through the early deposition, why the deposition needs to be taken early, the names and addresses of all expected adverse parties, and the name, address, and expected testimony of the witness. *See* Fed. R. Civ. P. 27(a). The deposition can occur only if the court so orders.

3. After-the-Lawsuit Depositions

Depositions ordinarily cannot be taken after the lawsuit is over. If, however, an appeal may be (or has been) taken, there is the possibility that the judgment could be overturned on appeal and sent back to the lower court for further proceedings and trial. Consider the same homeowner's ill parent example above, but assume no pre-filing deposition was sought. If the homeowner's lawsuit was dismissed on the pleadings, the deposition stage of the case will have never arrived. Assume the homeowner appealed that dismissal. As the ill parent's condition worsens, the homeowner's attorney starts to fear that this testimony might become unavailable if the appeals court takes too long a time to consider whether to overturn the dismissal. In that circumstance, taking a deposition pending appeal works much like a before-the-lawsuit deposition. Court approval is needed, and the requesting attorney must show the name, address, and expected testimony of the witness and the reason for taking the deposition while the appeal is still unresolved. *See* Fed. R. Civ. P. 27(b).

4. Deposition by Written Questions

A final type of special deposition—infrequently used today given the advent of various inexpensive, remote, "real-time" communication tools—is deposition by written questions. This tool allows a party to depose a witness without being present to pose the questions. Instead, the deposing attorney writes out her intended questions for the witness, then shares those questions with all other attorneys in the case. The other attorneys prepare their own additional questions (which may then be supplemented with new re-direct and re-cross questions). The total bundle of questions is then delivered to a court reporter who will travel to and sit with the witness, verbally pose all the questions, transcribe all the witness's answers, and then formalize the completed transcript. *See* Fed. R. Civ. P. 31. Years ago, when communication was limited and travel was difficult and expensive, this tool offered a comparatively economical means for deposing distant witnesses. Today, with all sorts of simple, laptop-based, real-time communication platforms, this tool has largely disappeared from use.

E. Using Deposition Testimony

Deposition testimony is useful in at least two ways. First, it can unearth important new sources of discovery that can be explored with later interrogatories, production requests, depositions, or other discovery tools. Deposition testimony can, in this way, serve as an important "finding tool." Second, deposition testimony can actually create *evidence*— in the form of the preserved testimony itself. That evidence might be read to (or played-back for) the jury in place of the witness's "live" appearance at trial, or might be used to confront a "live" testifying witness who is answering questions at trial in a manner different from how that same witness testified during an earlier deposition. But before deposition testimony may be used as evidence, three prerequisites, set out in Rule 32(a) of the Federal Rules of Civil Procedure, must all first be met:

1. **Confrontation:** The party against whom the deposition testimony would be used must have been present or represented by an attorney at the deposition, or must have been given reasonable advance notice of the right to attend. (If insufficient notice was given and an appropriate objection was made, or if an early deposition was taken without court approval, the deposition testimony may be unusable.)

2. **Admissible:** The testimony would be admissible under the Federal Rules of Evidence if the witness were testifying "live" at the trial (so, for example, deposition testimony that is not relevant is inadmissible at trial, even though it was properly discoverable pretrial).

3. **Permitted Use:** The testimony fits within any of the following categories:

   a. *Impeachment:* The testimony is being used to contradict or impeach the deposition witness now testifying at trial; *or*

   b. *Other Uses:* If the testimony is not being used to contradict or impeach, it is admissible if:

      i. *Party:* The testimony is from a party or that party's agent or designee and is being used "for any purpose"; *or*

      ii. *Nonparty:* The testimony is from someone who is not a party, but only if that person is now unavailable because he or she is dead, ill or aged or infirm, imprisoned, or situated more than 100 miles from the courthouse or outside the country (and that absence was not "procured"); *or*

      iii. *Exceptional Circumstances:* The testimony is specially allowed by the court, on motion and notice and under "exceptional circumstances."

If one party uses only a part of a deposition, an opponent may insist that other parts be introduced when necessary to be fair. *See* Rule 32(a)(6). Significantly, that insistence forces the using party to modify its intended use of the deposition (ordinarily, parties must wait their turn to introduce evidence; this procedure allows the party whose turn has not yet come to force its adversary to offer more deposition testimony than it would otherwise prefer, to ensure that the factfinder appreciates the full context of the testimony).

F. Using Depositions of Treating Physicians

Doctors are frequent witnesses in civil lawsuits, sometimes because they are parties (*e.g.,* medical malpractice cases) but, more often, because they are critical eyewitnesses. Consider our roofing contractor hypothetical. If, included among the homeowners' claims are allegations that a collapse of the poorly installed roof caused a personal injury, a doctor's testimony will be essential to establishing at trial the severity of that injury, the prognosis for recovery, and the impact on the injured person's life. But if doctors were obligated to come to court to testify each time their patients had a lawsuit, their primary healthcare mission—caring for patients— could be dramatically interrupted. For this reason, some (but not all) courts permit the trial use of a treating doctor's deposition in lieu of "live" testimony, even if that doctor is otherwise "available" to attend trial in person. *See, e.g.,* Cal. Code Civ. Pro. § 2025.620(d) (allowing use of video deposition of treating/consulting doctors if they could be compelled to testify "live"); Ill. R. Civ. P. 212(b) (allowing use of deposition of physician or surgeon regardless of witness's availability to testify "live").

G. Sanctions for Deposition Misconduct

A federal court once admonished that "[a] suit at law is not a children's game, but a serious effort on the part of adult human beings to administer justice." *United States v. A.H. Fischer Lumber Co.*, 162 F.2d 872, 873 (4th Cir. 1947). Although made in a different context, this reminder is equally apt in the context of deposition discovery where the stakes are high, patience may be frayed, the attorneys are elbow-to-elbow with one another, and no judge is present to restrain emotions. The Rules endeavor to rein in deposition-related mischief in a number of ways:

- **Impeding, Delaying, or Frustrating:** Any person guilty of impeding, delaying, or frustrating the fair examination of a deposition witness (such as by speaking objections, improper instructions not to answer, etc.) may be ordered to pay the reasonable expenses and attorney's fees incurred by any party. *See* Fed. R. Civ. P. 30(d)(2). If that mischief interfered with the completion of a deposition, the court will also grant additional time for questioning. *See* Rule 30(d)(1).

- **Motion to Terminate or Limit:** When a deposition is being conducted in bad faith or in a way that is unreasonably annoying, embarrassing, or oppressive to a witness or a party, the court's intervention may be sought. By motion, a party may ask the court to limit the deposition or to terminate it entirely. (The objecting party can also insist that deposition questioning be suspended pending the court's ruling.) *See* Rule 30(d)(3). The party losing such a motion is at risk of having to pay the other side's motion costs, including attorney's fees. *See* Rule 30(d)(3)(C) & 37(a)(5).
- **Deposition No-Shows:** As described earlier, depositions are scheduled with a "notice of deposition" to all attorneys. If, in response to such a notice, an attorney appears for a properly scheduled deposition but the noticing party does not show up or the intended witness does not show up (because that witness was never properly subpoenaed), the appearing attorney can ask to be reimbursed for the expenses (and attorney's fees) of attending. *See* Rule 30(g).

FROM CLASSROOM TO PRACTICE

Lawyers learn the deposition mechanics fairly quickly. Though detailed, the requirements and procedures for depositions are easy to understand. The art of taking a deposition, by contrast, takes years of experience to master. Because of the many nuances, tactics, and strategies for taking a winning deposition, semester-long law school courses and multi-day continuing legal education seminars that focus just on deposition skills are becoming increasingly commonplace. For our purposes, a few key pointers are worth highlighting.

A. Taking a Good Deposition

Every litigator will develop his or her own unique style for taking a deposition, and that style may morph depending on the circumstances of each deposition. But most every successful deposition will have these attributes:

- **Timing:** Depositions may be taken quite early in the life of a civil case. Nothing forbids that. And sometimes, good strategy favors that timing. But, as discussed at the outset of this chapter, early depositions come with a drawback. They likely precede the benefit of information gathered through the later use of other discovery tools (like, for example, answers to interrogatories, produced documents, produced electronically stored information, and other materials). And because most witnesses can only be deposed once, this risks a lot of unexplored knowledge from those same witnesses that will hauntingly await the day of trial. For this reason, seasoned litigators often balance carefully the strategy of taking an early deposition (to lock in facts before too much thought and case preparation has occurred) against the benefit of waiting until a far fuller discovery record is in hand (to allow for more robust, informed questioning).

- **Strong Preparation:** Good deposition questioning is rarely stream-of-consciousness. Lawyers need to prepare well, with very clear objectives in mind. Those objectives can be numerous, including:

  ○ *"Pure" Discovery:* where the questioner is seeking to learn information from the witness that the questioner does not know beforehand (*e.g.*, "Who taught you how to install roofs?");

  ○ *"Document-ID" Discovery:* where the questioner attempts to authenticate a document or learn what the witness knows about it (*e.g.*, "Can you confirm that Exhibit 6 is an exact copy of the warranty you showed the homeowners at the time they hired you?"; "What does paragraph 12 in the warranty mean to you?");

    - Note: the documents a questioner intends to show a deposition witness should be prepared in advance, with a copy available to serve as the "original" (to be marked by the court reporter), other copies for distribution to other attending counsel, and a copy for use by the questioning attorney herself. One best-practice is to ensure that all such documents are pre-marked before the deposition, ideally using a uniform numbering scheme that all parties have agreed to in advance (thus, every subsequent use of a certain document in every subsequent deposition will always use the same identifying exhibit number).

  ○ *"Concession" Discovery:* where the questioner endeavors to obtain a concession or admission from the witness that will be helpful at trial (e.g., "You never told the homeowner this was your first roofing installation, did you?");

  ○ *"Knowledge-Exhaustion" Discovery:* where the questioner tried to box-in the witness so as to foreclose the possibility of later surprises at trial (e.g., "Other than the two notes we've just reviewed, did you make any other written notation, of any type, concerning your conversation with the homeowner?");

  ○ *"Preservation" Discovery:* where the questioner seeks answers from the witness in a manner intended to be used at trial in place of that witness's "live" appearance (such as when the witness is beyond the court's subpoena power, ill, or otherwise likely to be unavailable).

- **But Not Rigid Preparation:** Preparation should always assist, not impede, the deposition process. Too many pre-worded questions, inflexible topic organization, or rote checklists hinder the process. Many seasoned litigators prefer a to build for themselves a broad, flexible sketch of their intended topic areas to be covered in a deposition, leaving the phrasing and sequencing of individual questions to extemporaneity. This way, the well-prepared questioner has decided on *what* he or she intends to accomplish during the deposition, but his or her preparation notes remain agile enough to allow the questioner to easily take detours, as circumstances may advise, without ever losing the overall map of the deposition's objectives.

- **Careful Listening:** New lawyers often worry about appearing foolish or inexperienced, so they take a curious pride in asking a good question—without, afterwards, paying close attention to the answer their good question elicited. This ignores the whole purpose of taking the deposition in the first place. Because depositions allow for "on-the-go" follow-up, the questioner needs to be attentively listening as the witness answers the questions posed.

- **"Audibles" During the Deposition:** With attentive listening, the questioner will optimize his or her follow-up opportunities—to pursue fuller answers, to clarify ambiguities in answers, or to pursue entirely new lines of inquiry prompted by the witness's responses.

- **Adjusting a Question After Asking It:** Although eloquence in asking questions is a good thing, a jumbled, awkwardly phrased, or ambiguous question often creeps into a deposition. Experienced lawyers show no pride-of-authorship in such instances. They turn to the court reporter, confidently announce: "Strike that question," and begin again. Since this modification cleans up a potentially troublesome question, it sets the stage for a better, more responsive answer from the witness. Deposing lawyers should always bear the finish-line in mind: creating a clean, clear, easily understood question-and-answer exchange that could be shown, as evidence, to a factfinder.

- **Hearing the Bad Stuff:** Talented litigators differ on whether a questioner should ever deliberately invite a deposition witness to testify on a topic or event that is hurtful to the questioner's case or defense. Some litigators think "no": there is no certainty that the other side will learn about, or use, unfavorable information from a witness, and having the witness testify on those facts only preserves them (which makes the adversary's job easier). Other litigators think "yes": good preparation means not being surprised at trial, which requires knowing all the nasty, unhelpful, case-hurting facts well in advance of trial, when there is still time for the attorney to calmly develop strategies for dealing with (and, hopefully, neutralizing) those bad facts. We think the second view is the far better one.

- **Dealing with Objections from Other Attorneys:** New litigators are often taught to ignore all objections during a deposition and, instead, to plow trenchantly forward, blind to the content of opposing counsel's objections. It is sound advice to not get flummoxed by an adversary's objections or to let them interfere with the flow of the attorney's questioning. But ignoring objections entirely may be equally unwise. Objections to the form of a poorly phrased question are preserved only if asserted in time for the questioner to adjust the question. If such objections have merit, and if the questioner ignores them and stands on a poor question, both the question and the witness's answer are vulnerable to being stricken by the court. If the questioner is pursuing "pure" discovery, it may not matter whether the testimony is later deemed admissible (in such a case, the questioning will have still served its purpose—it likely opened the door to new avenues of information). If, however, the questioner might want to seek to introduce the testimony at trial, the sounder approach is to listen to the objections, weigh them with care, and decide—on an objection-by-objection basis—whether to rephrase a question in response.

- **Take a Final Break Before Stopping:** It is always good form to announce a short break in the deposition when the questioner feels he or she is finished with the questioning. Taking a few minutes to carefully review the deposition plan offers the questioner the ability to catch a breath and double-check to ensure everything that should get covered, actually got covered. Remember: absent a court order or agreement from all other attorneys, no witness can be deposed a second time.

B. Defending a Deposition Well

- **The "Potted-Plant" Syndrome:** Attorneys who defend a witness during a deposition often complain they become "potted plants," with only a modest ability to impact the questioning of a witness (mindful of the mandate of only concise, nonargumentative, and nonsuggestive objections, very rare instructions not to answer a pending question, and little opportunity to confer with the witness once the deposition is underway). For this reason, defending a deposition can be more challenging and nerve-wracking than taking one. With no control over the process and just milliseconds to decide whether to interpose an objection, the defending attorney must stay laser-focused for up to seven hours—a daunting task.

- **Defense "Style Points":** Ego being what it is, new attorneys often tend to try to flaunt their skills, cleverness, or chutzpah while defending a witness's deposition. More often than not, that's a poor choice. Objecting just to remind everyone you are still in the room can be counterproductive. Sometimes a leading, compound, or vague question will not merit an objection (for example, if it occurs in some innocuous moment during the deposition, such as where the witness's educational or employment background is being rotely elicited). Nor should defending counsel assume the responsibility for ensuring that the deposition is unfolding smoothly and cleanly so that the resulting transcript is clear. Interjections by defending counsel help alert the questioner to clumsy, muddled, or ambiguous moments in the deposition and, so alerted, the questioner is likely to endeavor to fix the problems and improve the transcript. That repair may not be helpful to the interests of the defending counsel's client. Accordingly, defending counsel should intervene only when necessary to abate a questioning risk that threatens to hurt the client.

- **Preparing the Witness:** The most effective "defense" of a witness's deposition comes well before the deposition ever starts. Attorneys should meet with their own witnesses in advance of the deposition to explain how the process works and to review anticipated questioning topics. Although it is ethically improper to "coach" a witness's testimony, the defending attorney can helpfully focus the witness's attention on likely areas of interrogation, build the witness's confidence by roleplaying and simulating the deposition experience, and guide the witness against losing concentration, volunteering information that hadn't been asked, or guessing at facts not known to him or her. Preparing a witness well for a deposition takes time, thought, and patience.

- **Protecting Witnesses from Abuse:** Most litigators behave appropriately during a deposition. But when they don't, the attorney defending the witness is there for protection. As discussed above, questioning attorneys are forbidden from proceeding in bad faith and from unreasonably annoying, embarrassing, or oppressing a witness. If this sort of misbehavior occurs, the defending attorney can object on the record and, if appropriate, recess the deposition to bring the conduct to the attention of the court.

- **Questioning Your Own Witness:** Deposition questioning follows the same procedure used at trial. The attorney who summoned the witness to testify begins, then tenders the witness over to other counsel for their questioning. Should you take the bait? Should defending counsel ever accept that invitation and interrogate their own witness? The default rule that most experienced attorneys follow is "almost never." Because this witness is yours (and obviously so, since you are defending her or him), it's very likely that you will be able to call that same witness to testify at trial under your own terms and in a manner that best suits your trial strategy. Consequently, experienced attorneys will generally refrain from questioning their own witnesses during depositions unless: (a) the witness makes a troublesome mistake or ambiguous statement that needs to be immediately cleared up; or (b) the witness might not be available for trial (because of, for example, age, infirmity, a distant home, or other physical unavailability).

Hypotheticals: Mastering the Nuances

More Time for a Deposition: Assume that one of the roofing contractor's employees is a craftsman from Italy who speaks English with great difficulty. That craftsman may have very important knowledge about the dispute, and the homeowner's attorney is worried that the language barrier and the 7-hour-per-deposition time limit imposed by the Rules will prevent a full and complete deposition of this potentially key witness. How can the attorney's concerns be addressed?

The Know-Nothing Rule 30(b)(6) Witness: The company "Lotsa-Tar, Inc." manufactured the tar used during the homeowner's roof replacement. The homeowner intends to depose that corporation concerning the manufacturing process for the tar, its ingredients, and the proper method for its application. Unfortunately, the witness the corporation sent to the deposition did not know the answers to most of these questions. This inadequacy could be the fault of the homeowner's attorney or Lotsa-Tar, Inc. Why might it be the fault of the homeowner's attorney? How could that attorney avoid this problem? Why, alternatively, might the fault lie with Lotsa-Tar, Inc.? How can the homeowner's attorney respond?

The "Black Hole" of Objections: During the deposition of the roofing contractor, the questioner found herself constantly tongue-tied and inarticulate. Time after time, she would ask confusing and compound questions. A few examples follow: "Mr. Contractor, you've been in this business for 15 years, or nearly 15 years, or at least more than 10 years, well, just about 10 years. It's in that range, right?"; "Mr. Contractor, when you spoke to my homeowner, and you did speak to my homeowner, right?, you always, or at least usually, or at least most of the time, spoken with him by phone or over the phone, isn't that right?" The contractor's lawyer objected appropriately to the ambiguous form of these questions and did so timely and properly. But with no judge present, what is the purpose of objecting? How are objections addressed? When? And what criteria will be used to consider what ought to be done with the witness's answers?

PRACTICE SAMPLES
Sample 4-11: NOTICE OF DEPOSITION

IN THE UNITED STATES DISTRICT COURT
DISTRICT OF WEST CAROLINA

Harold H. Homeowner,)

    Plaintiff,)

      v.)   Civil Action No. 00-CV-98765

Carmine X. Risso)
and Risso Roofing, LLC,)

    Defendants.)

Notice of Deposition of Frances Turner

KINDLY TAKE NOTICE that, in accordance with Rule 30 of the Federal Rules of Civil Procedure, plaintiff Harold H. Homeowner will take the deposition of Frances Turner by oral examination. The deposition will occur at the Law Offices of Tabatha Smith, Esq., 123 Spruce Street in Harbortown, West Carolina 29999, and commence at 9:30 a.m. on Tuesday, October 10, 20___.

The deposition will be taken before an officer authorized to administer oaths, and the testimony will be preserved both stenographically and by video recording.

TAKE FURTHER NOTICE that, in accordance with Rules 30 and 34 of the Federal Rules of Civil Procedure, the deponent is to produce at the time of the taking of the deposition all documents, electronically stored information, and things identified on Exhibit "A" attached to this Notice.

You are invited to attend and participate.

_____

Tabatha Smith, Esq.
Law Offices of Tabatha Smith, Esq.
123 Spruce Street
Harbortown, West Carolina 29999

Dated: 9/3/20____

EXHIBIT "A"

To Notice of Deposition of Frances Turner

For purposes of this Exhibit "A", the following terms and definitions shall apply:

A. The term **"HHH"** shall mean the plaintiff Harold H. Homeowner.

B. The term **"HHH Home"** shall mean the home owned by Harold H. Homeowner at 3601 Hawk Fly Drive in Harbortown, West Carolina, 29999.

C. The term **"New Roof"** shall mean the roof that defendants installed on the HHH Home.

D. The term **"communications"** shall mean letters, emails, texts, social media transmissions, phone messages, and every other contact of any kind.

PRODUCTION REQUESTS:

The deponent is directed to bring with him to the deposition for inspection and copying all documents, electronically stored information, and things concerning, discussing, mentioning, or otherwise relating in any way to:

1. The installation of the New Roof.

2. Any and all supplies used during the installation of the New Roof.

3. Any and all communications with, to, from, or about HHH, the HHH Home, or the New Roof.

[CERTIFICATE OF SERVICE]

Sample 4-12: NOTICE OF DEPOSITION UNDER RULE 30(b)(6)

IN THE UNITED STATES DISTRICT COURT
DISTRICT OF WEST CAROLINA

Harold H. Homeowner,	)	
	)	
Plaintiff,	)	
	)	
v.	)	Civil Action No. 00-CV-98765
	)	
Carmine X. Risso	)	
and Risso Roofing, LLC,	)	
	)	
Defendants.	)	

Notice of Rule 30(b)(6) Deposition of Lotsa-Tar, Inc.

KINDLY TAKE NOTICE that, in accordance with Rule 30(b)(6) of the Federal Rules of Civil Procedure, plaintiff Harold H. Homeowner will take the deposition, by oral examination, of Lotsa-Tar, Inc. The deposition will occur at the Law Offices of Tabatha Smith, Esq., 123 Spruce Street in Harbortown, West Carolina 29999, and commence at 9:30 a.m. on Thursday, October 12, 20____.

Lotsa-Tar, Inc. is hereby advised of your duty to designate one or more of your officers, directors, employees, agents, or other representatives who consent to testify on behalf of Lotsa-Tar, Inc. with regard to those subject matters identified on the attached Exhibit "A". Plaintiff requests that Lotsa-Tar, Inc. provide written notice to Plaintiff at least five (5) business days before the date of the deposition of the name(s) and position(s) of those individuals Lotsa-Tar, Inc. has designated to testify on its behalf and as to which subject matter(s) each designated witness will be responsible.

The deposition will be taken before an officer authorized to administer oaths, and the testimony will be preserved both stenographically and by video recording.

You are invited to attend and participate.

_____
Tabatha Smith, Esq.
Law Offices of Tabatha Smith, Esq.
123 Spruce Street
Harbortown, West Carolina 29999

Dated: 9/3/20____

EXHIBIT "A"

Subject Matters for Examination

In accordance with Rule 30(b)(6) of the Federal Rules of Civil Procedure, Plaintiff has described below the subject matters for this examination:

1. The history and details of Lotsa-Tar, Inc.'s contractual relationships with Risso Roofing, LLC.

2. The type of tar products that are recommended for a private home located at 3601 Hawk Fly Drive in Harbortown, West Carolina 29999, and the reasons for that recommendation.

3. The proper method for installing tar products on a private home located at 3601 Hawk Fly Drive in Harbortown, West Carolina 29999.

4. Instructions, training, and guidance provided by Lotas-Tar, Inc. to Risso Roofing, LLC concerning its tar products and the proper method for installing them.

5. All communications to and from Risso Roofing, LLC regarding Lotsa-Tar, Inc.'s tar products and their installation at any location, including but not limited to a private home located at 3601 Hawk Fly Drive in Harbortown, West Carolina 29999.

[CERTIFICATE OF SERVICE]

[SUBPOENA]

Sample 4-13: **TRANSCRIPT OF DEPOSITION**

```
1              IN THE UNITED STATES DISTRICT COURT

2              FOR THE DISTRICT OF WEST CAROLINA

3

4    HAROLD H. HOMEOWNER            )

5         Plaintiff,               )    CIV. ACTION NO.

6            v.                    )

7    CARMINE X. RISSO and          )    NO. 00-CV-56789

8    RISSO ROOFING, LLC,           )

9         Defendants.              )

10
```

11 **DEPOSITION of FRANCES TURNER**, a witness called on

12 behalf of the Plaintiff, taken pursuant to the

13 applicable provisions of the Federal Rules of Civil

14 Procedure, before Barry Boch, a Notary Public in and

15 for the State of West Carolina, at the Law Offices of

16 Tabatha Smith, Esq., 123 Spruce Street, Harbortown,

17 West Carolina 29999, on Tuesday, October 10, 20___,

18 commencing at 9:30 a.m.

19   BARRY K. BOCH

20   374 Rotary Bend Drive, Harbortown,

21   West Carolina 29991

22   (917) 427-8826

23

1   **APPEARANCES:**

2   TABATHA SMITH, ESQ.

3   Law Offices of Tabatha Smith, Esq.

4   123 Spruce Street

5   Harbortown, West Carolina 29999

6   (917) 427-9004

7   Attorney for Plaintiff

8

9   SPENCER J. U. CLAYTON, ESQUIRE

10   Howe & Clayton, LLP

11   100 Forest Parkway

12   Anderson, West Carolina 29993

13   (902) 555-9793

14   Attorney for Defendants

15

16   **STIPULATIONS**

17   It is hereby stipulated and agreed by and between

18   counsel for the respective parties that the witness

19   shall read and sign the deposition transcript under

20   penalty of perjury within 30 days of its receipt, but

21   that notarization of same is waived.

22

23

1   **FRANCES TURNER,**

2 a witness called for examination by counsel for the

3 Plaintiff being first duly sworn, was examined and

4 testified as follows:

5 BY ATTORNEY SMITH:

6 Q. Good morning, Mr. Turner.

7 A. Hi.

8 Q. By whom are you employed?

9 A. Rossy Roofing.

10 Q. How long have you been employed there?

11 A. About 17 months. Give or take.

12 Q. What do you do for Risso Roofing?

13 A. Amen installer.

14 Q. What training do you have as a roof installer?

15 A. My Dad and older brother installed roofs. Learned

16 the trade from them.

17 Q. Why aren't you still working with them?

18 A. Family, you know. It's a love-hate relationship.

19 More hate than love on a hot roof. Figured I could

20 ply my trade with less drama.

21 Q. What role, if any, did you have on the roofing job

22 at the home of Harold Homeowner?

23 A. I was there only for the first day.

24 Q. Why only the first day?

25 A. Risso pulled me off that job after the first day.

- 3 -

1   He had gotten a big contract to install a new roof

2   for a strip mall on the other side of town, and told

3   most of his guys to head over there for that job.

4   Q. So, what work had you done on Harold Homeowner's

5   roof?

6   A. Not much. We were still pulling off the old roof

7   when the boss reassigned me to the stip mall.

8   Q. Who was left to work on Harold Homeowner's roof?

9   A. The bee team.

10 Q. What do you mean, the bee team?

11 A. Well, there's the "a" team—the workers who are

12 really good, know their trade well, do fine work. All

13 of those guys were pulled to do the strip mall. The

14 leftover guys worked on the smaller jobs, like Harold

15 Homeowner's roof.

16 Q. Do you know the guys who worked that roof?

17 BY ATTORNEY CLAYTON: Objection; vague.

18 BY ATTORNEY SMITH: Let me re-phrase that. Do you

19 know the guys who were left to work on Harold

20 Homeowner's roof?

21 A. [WITNESS NODS.]

22 Q. I'm sorry, sir. You have to answer verbally.

23 A. Yeah. Yes. I know the guys.

24 Q. Why do you call them the "b" team?

25 A. Cause they were just okay. I mean, they weren't

1 bad dudes or anything. Just we were better. Us, the

2 better guys—more experienced—we were at the strip mall.

3 Q. In what ways were you better than the "b" team?

4 A. Seriously? Those guys weren't the smartest.

5 They needed a lot of direction. They'd leave stuff

6 lying around. Tools and stuff. They'd leave nails

7 in the driveway. They'd be on the roof on the phone

8 and do a lame job of securing the roofing tiles.

9 They'd put half-dried tar on.

10 BY ATTORNEY CLAYTON: Okay. Enough of this. I

11 object. Your questions to this witness are so poor,

12 so open-ended, that you've now confused him. You are

13 deliberately trying to trick him into saying things

14 that will cause him to lose his job, get sued himself,

15 or worse. This is outrageous, and I object to what

16 you are doing to this poor man.

17 A. Wait, I'm going to lose my job?

18 BY ATTORNEY SMITH: Mr. Turner, please don't get

19 distracted. Your job here today is to listen carefully

20 to my questions and answer them. Okay? Now, in what

21 other ways were the folks working on Harold Homeowner's

22 roof the bee team?

23 A. I didn't say they were all the "b" team. Come

24 to think of it, I can't really be sure who was on

25 that roof.

- 5 -

1   Q. Well, you just listed several ways ...

2   A. I wasn't thinking it through right. I don't know

3   for sure who was on that roof. So I can't help you.

4   Q. Sir, you just testified about workers leaving tools

5   around, leaving nails on driveways, talking on cell

6   phones and not making sure the roof tiles are installed

7   ...

8   A. No, no. This roof, I don't know. Some guys are

9   like that, in other companies. Not here. Risso's guys

10   are amazing. No one like that works for Risso.

11   Q. But you just said ...

12   A. I wasn't thinking. I don't remember who was on that

13   roof. I was only there one day myself, then went to the

14   strip mall. Can't recall. Can't help you.

15   Q. I have no further questions at this time.

16   BY ATTORNEY CLAYTON: Just one question. Mr. Turner, is

17   it your testimony that you don't recall the identities of

18   the employees working on Harold Homeowner's roof?

19   A. That's right. I don't.

20   Q. So, not recalling who those workers were, you can't

21   testify as to whether those workers were careful or not?

22   A. That's right. I don't remember them, not at all.

23   Q. No further questions.

24

25   WHEREUPON THE DEPOSITION WAS ADJOURNED

Sample 4-14: ERRATA SHEET FOR DEPOSITION TRANSCRIPT

ERRATA SHEET FOR THE TRANSCRIPT OF FRANCES TURNER

CASE NAME: HAROLD H. HOMEOWNER V. CARMINE X. RISSO
                  AND RISSO ROOFING, LLC

CASE NUMBER: CIVIL ACTION NO. 00-56789

DATE OF DEP'N: OCTOBER 10, 2021

DEPONENT: FRANCIS TURNER

CORRECTIONS BY THE DEPONENT:

Page	Line	Change From:	Change To:	Reason:
3	9	Rossy	Rossi	Mis-spelling
3	13	Amen	I am an	Transcription error
3	16	from them	from them and my uncle George	Incomplete answer
4	7	stip	strip	Mis-spelling
4	10	bee	"b"	Transcription error
5	22	bee	"b"	Transcription error

F Turner   _10/29/20_
Signature of Deponent   Date of Review & Signing

V

Discovery of Experts
Rules 26(a)(2) and 26(b)(4)

GETTING THE VIEW

Most non-lawyers have some notion of expert witnesses. They are sometimes viewed as "hired guns" to whom big companies pay hefty consulting fees to provide scientific testimony supporting their positions. Although that view is undoubtedly accurate in some cases, experts serve an important function in the civil litigation process and are a necessary component of many cases.

Consider, for example, Pauline, a child who has died from leukemia. Her father and mother, Peter and Penny Parents, moved to a home near a plywood factory six months before Pauline was diagnosed, and they sue Dagwood Plywood, claiming toxic emissions from Dagwood Plywood's manufacturing processes caused Pauline's leukemia. Should the Parents be able to have their claim against Dagwood Plywood submitted to the jury solely on the ground that their child's diagnosis occurred soon after their move into a house near Dagwood Plywood, asking the jury to conclude that the time proximity between these two events alone proves a causal connection? Or must the Parents be required to submit competent expert testimony explaining how and why Pauline's six-month exposure to Dagwood Plywood's emissions caused her leukemia?

We all might agree that the Parents' case is more powerful with an expert's corroboration, but is it really necessary? It is. In some situations, the decision as to whether to use an expert witness is strategic, involving a balancing of a variety of considerations, including: the cost of hiring the expert in light of the amount in controversy in the case, the complexity of the issues, the benefits of presenting the expert's opinions, and whether the opposing party has hired an expert of its own (and relatedly whether hiring an expert will force the opposing party to hire its own expert, resulting in a "battle of the experts"). In other situations, like the medical causation issue in Pauline's case, the courts have held that not only is expert testimony a good idea, it is *required*. *See Chapman v. Procter & Gamble Distributing, LLC*, 766 F.3d 1296, 1316 (11th Cir. 2014) (affirming summary judgment because the plaintiff did not submit qualified medical causation expert testimony). Otherwise, the jury is simply being invited to speculate based on coincidence and sympathy.

But we've gotten ahead of ourselves. The natural first question is, what is the difference between expert testimony and "regular," non-expert testimony? Is it simply that the expert has greater knowledge or "expertise" or a longer list of credentials and degrees?

That's a component, of course, but only a small part of the story. The fundamental difference between expert witnesses and non-expert witnesses is that expert witnesses are allowed to provide their *opinions* about a case even though they may not have had any involvement in the events surrounding the dispute. Witnesses who are not testifying as experts, often called "fact witnesses" or "percipient witnesses," are generally limited to testifying as to their *perceptions*—things they saw, heard, smelled, felt, tasted, thought, etc. Those sorts of non-expert fact witnesses may generally only offer opinions if those opinions are: based on their perceptions; helpful to the jury or judge; and not based on scientific, technical, or specialized knowledge. *See* Fed. R. Evid. 701.

Expert witnesses are different. Expert witness testimony consists primarily of opinions, and often those opinions are formed without any first-hand, percipient observations. In other words, expert witnesses are permitted to offer their opinions on events they may never have actually witnessed, first-hand, themselves. An accident reconstruction expert witness is a good example. That person will often be called into service long after the accident occurred. His or her expert opinions will be based not on having seen the accident occur, but on having studied the location, the wreckage, and the resulting injuries, and then, through sometimes elaborate computer modeling or mathematical calculations based on velocity and other physical forces, re-imagining how the accident most likely unfolded.

Importantly, opinion testimony from experts can have significant sway over the jury. Why? Consider who the attorneys in Pauline's case might hire. Their expert might be a licensed physician, educated at a prestigious Ivy League medical school, who has been practicing clinical medicine for many years. This expert might have developed a nationally renowned reputation in identifying and treating environmentally contracted cancers, perhaps even focusing on childhood illnesses, and may have written a veritable library of books and journal articles on that subject. When called to testify, this expert will turn and face the jury, and in a kindly, professorial manner explain the causes of environmentally contracted childhood cancers and the facts presented in Pauline's situation that persuaded the expert to conclude that Dagwood Plywood's emissions were the probable cause of Pauline's illness and, ultimately, her death. Wow. And that whole, impressive discussion would be made all the more memorable by a ruling from the judge, before the testimony even started, that formally declared, in the hearing of the jurors, that this witness is a judicially recognized expert for the purposes of the trial. How is the jury likely to receive this expert's testimony?

Because of the very real likelihood that the testimony of experts, like in this example, will carry significant weight in the eyes of the jury, the Federal Rules of Evidence task the trial judge with acting as a "gatekeeper" to ensure that only proper expert testimony is presented to the jury. This gatekeeping function has two major components. First, the court must ensure that the witness is qualified to serve as an expert. The witness's expertise may come from a variety of sources: knowledge, skill, experience, training, or education. *See* Fed. R. Evid. 702. Second, the court must ensure that the expert uses reliable scientific *methodologies*, not "junk science," and has the requisite "fit" to be helpful to the jury in its deliberations. *See* Fed. R. Evid. 702.

The United State Supreme Court introduced the current framework for assessing the reliability of expert opinions in its landmark opinion in *Daubert v. Merrell Dow Pharmaceuticals, Inc.,* 509 U.S. 579 (1993), and challenges to expert opinions are commonly referred to as "*Daubert* challenges." In *Daubert,* the Court rejected the old "*Frye* test," which had conditioned an expert's acceptability on the use of a scientific technique that was "generally accepted" as reliable in the scientific community (a standard that is still used by some state courts). *Id.* at 584. Instead of "general acceptance" as the gatekeeping standard, the *Daubert* analysis focuses on whether the expert used proper, rigorous scientific methodologies in forming the opinions. "Many considerations will bear on the inquiry, including whether the theory or technique in question can be (and has been) tested, whether it has been subjected to peer review and publication, its known or potential error rate and the existence and maintenance of standards controlling its operation, and whether it has attracted widespread acceptance within a relevant scientific community. The inquiry is a flexible one, and its focus must be solely on principles and methodology, not on the conclusions that they generate." *Id.* at 580.

Note that the *Daubert* analysis turns on the *nature of the testimony*, not the *qualifications of the witness.* In our leukemia example, if the Parents offered the Ivy League physician described above to testify as an expert on leukemia causation, the court would quite likely find her qualified as an expert in that field. If, however, she proposed to testify about the leukemia causation on the basis of voices she heard late at night when she looked in the mirror after consulting bewitched candles, as opposed to on the basis of scientific studies about leukemia, the court would exclude her testimony as not based on reliable scientific methodologies even though she was highly qualified. The following case excerpt illustrates the *Daubert* analysis.

RINK
v.
CHEMINOVA, INC.

400 F.3d 1286 (11th Cir. 2005)

BIRCH, United States Circuit Judge

[The plaintiffs sought to maintain a class action against Cheminova, Inc. for illnesses allegedly caused by pesticide spraying for fruit flies in Florida. The plaintiffs' experts opined that the pesticide had been exposed to high temperatures, causing them to become particularly toxic to humans. Cheminova brought a Daubert *challenge to the plaintiffs' experts, contending that their temperature assumptions were not based on rigorous scientific methodologies. The district court excluded the plaintiffs' experts as unreliable, and the plaintiffs appealed.]*

The admission of expert evidence is governed by Federal Rule of Evidence 702(d) as explained by *Daubert* and its progeny. Under Rule 702 and *Daubert*, district courts must act as "gatekeepers" which admit expert testimony only if it is both reliable and relevant. *See [Daubert v. Merrell Dow Pharmaceuticals, Inc.*, 509 U.S. 579, 589 (1993)]. District courts are charged with this gatekeeping function "to ensure that speculative, unreliable expert testimony does not reach the jury" under the mantle of reliability that accompanies the appellation "expert testimony." [*McCorvey v. Baxter Healthcare Corp.*, 298 F.3d 1253, 1256 (11th Cir. 2002).]

To fulfil their obligation under *Daubert*, district courts must engage in a rigorous inquiry to determine whether: "(1) the expert is qualified to testify competently regarding the matters he intends to address; (2) the methodology by which the expert reaches his conclusions is sufficiently reliable as determined by the sort of inquiry mandated in *Daubert*; and (3) the testimony assists the trier of fact, through the application of scientific, technical, or specialized expertise, to understand the evidence or to determine a fact in issue." *City of Tuscaloosa v. Harcros Chems., Inc.*, 158 F.3d 548, 562 (11th Cir. 1998) (footnote omitted). The party offering the expert has the burden of satisfying each of these three elements by a preponderance of the evidence. *See Allison v. McGhan Med. Corp.*, 184 F.3d 1300, 1306 (11th Cir. 1999).

In ascertaining reliability under the second *Daubert* prong, we have identified several factors which can be considered: (1) whether the expert's methodology can be tested; (2) whether the expert's scientific technique has been subjected to peer review and publication; (3) whether the method has a known rate of error; (4) whether the technique is generally accepted by the scientific community. [*Quiet Tech. DC-8, Inc. v. Hurel-Dubois UK Ltd.*, 326

F.3d 1333, 1341 (11th Cir. 2003).] This list of factors, however, "do[es] not exhaust the universe of considerations that may bear on ... reliability." *Id.; see also Kumho Tire Co.*, 526 U.S. at 150 ("*Daubert* makes clear that the factors it mentions do not constitute a 'definitive checklist or test.'") (citation omitted); *Daubert*, 509 U.S. at 594 (noting that the Rule 702 inquiry is "a flexible one"). District courts "have substantial discretion in deciding how to test an expert's reliability ...." *United States v. Majors*, 196 F.3d 1206, 1215 (11th Cir. 1999) (internal citation omitted).

The putative class representatives argue that Matson's exclusion was improper for two reasons. First, they argue that the district court improperly based its determination on Matson's general personal credibility, thereby assuming the role of the trier of fact. A thorough review of the record reveals that this objection is unfounded; the district court's exclusion of Matson was grounded in its criticism of his method, not his credibility. For example, the district court faulted Matson for his facile transposition of temperature data from one site to another. Under Matson's method, temperature data from the Texas storage site could be applied to the Georgia and Florida sites because storage conditions were supposedly similar and the sites were all in the same basic latitudinal range.

Transposition of data based on such conjecture and rough approximation lacks the "intellectual rigor" required by *Daubert. Kumho Tire Co.*, 526 U.S. at 152. Additionally, the district court critiqued Matson's conclusion that eighteen degrees should be added to the upper limit of the plausible temperature to which the [pesticide] was exposed. Whether it was based on evidence that some of the barrels at the Texas site were melting or evidence of radiant energy from the sun or an autocatalytic effect, the district court found, and we agree, that Matson's addition of eighteen degrees required the kind of scientifically unsupported "leap of faith" which is condemned by *Daubert. See Rider v. Sandoz Pharms. Corp.*, 295 F.3d 1194, 1202 (11th Cir. 2002). Apart from these particularized criticisms, the district court found Matson's methods of data transposition and temperature extrapolation failed under the reliability factors we mentioned in *Quiet Technology* because the methods were not tested, subjected to peer review, or generally accepted in the scientific community. Finally, the district court criticized Matson's method of continuing to use data in subsequent reports which was previously found to be unreliable. The record thus reflects that the district court properly rejected Matson on the basis of his flawed methodology.

Daubert challenges are typically made by filing a "motion *in limine*," a motion in advance of trial seeking to exclude certain evidence from being presented to the jury.

Although *Daubert* motions are not discovery motions, developing support for a *Daubert* challenge can be one of the most important goals of discovery in cases where the law requires expert testimony—in such instances, obtaining a court ruling excluding an opposing party's expert can be tantamount to winning the case. *See Chapman v. P&G Distrib., LLC,* 766 F.3d 1296, 1316–17 (11th Cir. 2014) (affirming summary judgment because, without experts excluded under *Daubert,* the plaintiffs could not satisfy the requirement that they prove medical causation by expert testimony). Sometimes an opposing party's expert report will be so poorly written as to support a *Daubert* motion on its face. More often, though, opposing experts are sufficiently experienced and skilled that, with the help of counsel, they are able to write a report that appears, on the surface, to be adequately grounded.

In these situations, the ammunition to mount a *Daubert* challenge must often be developed in discovery—usually during the expert's deposition. To be successful in gathering this ammunition, experienced attorneys will have detailed, targeted objectives for this expert discovery. They will have read all of the opposing expert's writings (and prior testimony from other cases, if that is available), case law involving challenges to similar experts, consulted with their own expert, and identified specific grounds for *Daubert* challenges that they hope to develop through discovery.

For example, the outcome of the *Rink* case above turned, in part, on the expert's "leap of faith" in making certain temperature assumptions. To set up this challenge, Cheminova likely probed the expert's basis for his temperature assumptions extensively during discovery, seeking data the expert relied on, evidence supporting the expert's assumptions, and any peer-reviewed articles supporting the expert's methodology. Cheminova may have also sought admissions regarding the lack of data, evidence, and peer-reviewed articles. In that fashion, Cheminova would have been able to bring a well-supported *Daubert* challenge regarding the temperature assumptions, knowing that the plaintiffs did not have a ready defense to the challenge.

Keep in mind, though, that not all testimony from a witness with expertise is expert testimony subject to the rules regarding expert discovery and this gatekeeping function. Suppose, for example, Pauline was cared for by a treating physician who the Parents later called to testify. That treating physician would be, in all likelihood, qualified to testify as an expert. However, a treating physician can sometimes testify as to her perceptions without regard to the expert rules. The reason is obvious— treating physicians will have a reservoir of knowledge that most testifying experts will lack: first-hand, percipient recollections of treating this patient. Thus, many courts would allow Pauline's treating physician to answer questions as a fact witness about whether she saw Pauline as a patient, what she observed while doing so, and what treatment she prescribed and administered. *See Goodman v. Staples The Office Superstore, LLC,* 644 F.3d 817, 824–26 (9th Cir. 2011) (discussing the various approaches courts take to this issue). But this exception only reaches so far. If Pauline's treating physician proposes to render opinions about the cause of Pauline's leukemia, then all the expert rules of procedure and evidence will apply. *See Higgins v. Koch Dev. Corp.*, 794 F.3d 697, 704 (7th Cir. 2015).

Hypothetical

Q: Suppose in our Dagwood Plywood lawsuit, Dagwood Plywood wants to offer testimony from Mike Manager, who was in charge of environmental matters for Dagwood Plywood. Manager has a master's degree in environmental engineering, numerous certifications, and over thirty years of experience in the industry. Must Dagwood Plywood designate Manager as an expert? Should it?

A: The answer depends on the type of testimony that Manager will offer. Manager would quite likely qualify as an expert based on his education and work experience. However, if Manager is simply going to testify about his first-hand knowledge about Dagwood Plywood's environmental practices, and isn't going to offer expert opinions, Dagwood Plywood can offer him as a fact witness. In this capacity, Manager would likely be permitted to testify about the pollution control measures used at the factory, the emissions released from the factory, and other technical, but factual, matters.

Many of the knottiest expert issues arise under the Federal Rules of Evidence and are thus outside the scope of this book. But discovery of those experts is not. As explained above, *Daubert* challenges typically turn on information developed during discovery. But even for experts who survive a *Daubert* challenge, discovery is critical—because the testimony of expert witnesses is likely to be highly influential in the jury's deliberations, preparing to confront that expert testimony will prove to be one of the most essential objectives of the discovery process. Trial lawyers need to accurately anticipate an expert's testimony and then develop a sound strategy for addressing it. None of that is possible without discovery of experts.

The Rules authorize only limited discovery related to expert witnesses. Much of the expert discovery occurs through one of the automatic disclosures, not by deploying one of the discovery tools, and many of the ongoing communications with experts are shielded from discovery altogether, as we will now learn.

HOW EXPERT DISCOVERY WORKS

A. Expert Disclosures—Rule 26(a)(2)

Mandatory (automatic) disclosures were introduced in the How Discovery Begins chapter. The middle of those three automatic disclosures pertains to expert witnesses. The general purpose of the disclosure is to place opposing parties on notice of the fact that the disclosing party intends to use an expert witness and of the nature of that witness's expert opinions. That way, the opposing parties are not surprised at trial by the appearance of an expert and have time to prepare to meet that testimony and, perhaps, look for their own counter-expert. The nature and extent of the expert disclosure, however, depends on the type of expert.

1. Categories of Experts

Rule 26(a)(2) divides the world of experts into three categories: (1) the typical expert hired to testify, (2) witnesses who haven't been hired but will render expert opinions, and (3) consulting experts who only operate behind the scenes. The first category—retained or specially employed expert—are what most people picture when they think about "hired gun" expert witnesses. We'll call them "retained experts." In our leukemia case involving Pauline, for example, the attorneys representing the parties would likely engage medical doctors, toxicologists, and/or epidemiologists to testify about the causation issues. These scientists would be paid for their time, and would fall into this first category of expert. Companies who are frequently embroiled in litigation sometimes hire employees whose duties include regularly testifying as expert witnesses, often to avoid paying experts on an hourly basis for their time. Such employees also fall into this first category of experts.

The second category of experts comprises those who will offer expert opinion testimony but who have not been retained or specially employed to testify. A treating physician is the classic example of such a witness. Recall the caveat discussed above: if the treating physician is going to offer opinions based on scientific knowledge, the physician may not present those opinions as a fact witness and instead must offer the opinion testimony as an expert witness. If the physician has not been retained and is not being paid by the party offering the testimony, the physician falls into this second category of experts.

The third and final category of experts comprises those who are not going to testify at all—often called "consulting experts." Such experts assist the legal team with understanding the technical issues in the case, and may help prepare the attorneys to cross-examine an opposing party's experts but are not expected to testify at trial. As the next section explains, Rule 26(a)(2) imposes different disclosure obligations for each category of expert witness.

2. Form and Content of Expert Disclosures

It is useful to think of Rule 26(a)(2) as a sliding scale, requiring an escalating degree of disclosure depending on the nature of the expert.

i. Retained Experts

Rule 26(a)(2) imposes the greatest disclosure requirements on the first category described above—retained experts. For retained experts, a party must disclose an expert report, signed by the expert, containing the following information:

- a complete statement of all opinions the expert will express and the basis and reasons for those opinions;
- the facts or data that the expert considered in forming the opinions;
- any exhibits the expert will use;
- the expert's qualifications, including a list of all of the expert's publications from the past ten years;
- a list of all cases in which the expert testified at trial or in deposition during the previous four years; and
- a statement of the compensation that the expert will receive for the testimony.

As one can see from this list, preparing a proper, complete expert report is a time-consuming and detail-oriented chore. It is a critical one, however, because (as explained below) failure to disclose a report meeting the requirements of Rule 26(a)(2) can result in exclusion of individual opinions or even exclusion of the expert altogether. Accordingly, attorneys should review reports prepared by their experts carefully to ensure that the reports meet all the requirements of Rule 26(a)(2).

Hypothetical

Q: During discovery in our Dagwood Plywood lawsuit, Dagwood Plywood learns that, while Pauline's expert *signed* the expert report, Pauline's lawyer actually *drafted* the report. Dagwood Plywood files a motion to strike the expert report, contending that it does not comply with Rule 26(a)(2). How will the court likely rule?

A: Rule 26(a)(2) only speaks to the signature of an expert report, it does not dictate who drafts the report. Courts have held that there is nothing improper about an attorney taking the laboring oar in drafting an expert report, so long as the opinions are those of the expert. *See Gruber ex rel. Gruber v. Sec'y of HHS*, 91 Fed. Cl. 773, 794 (2010) ("Under Federal Rule of Civil Procedure 26(a)(2)(B), counsel may conduct research or even prepare drafts of an expert's report, provided such work is based on the expert's prior substantive input."). Although the practice may comply with the rules, it does open avenues of cross-examination designed to suggest that the expert is really an advocate for the party, not a "pure" scientist providing unbiased guidance to the jury. Thus, the better practice is to have the expert prepare the first draft of the report. The attorney may then help edit the report to ensure that it complies with Rule 26(a)(2)'s disclosure requirements and to choose language with the right "spin." As discussed below, this back and forth between the expert and the attorney is generally shielded from discovery.

ii. Non-Retained Experts

For experts who have not been retained or specially employed, like treating physicians, the Rule 26(b)(2) disclosure is much more relaxed. The opposing party must be given notice of the nature of the expert's anticipated testimony, but this second category of experts is not burdened with the process of preparing a full-blown expert report. Instead, a party intending to call such an expert need only disclose:

- the subject matter on which the witness is expected to testify and
- a summary of the facts and opinions to which the witness is expected to testify.

This type of disclosure is typically prepared and signed by counsel (in consultation with the expert, of course), and resembles other discovery documents, with a case caption and all the other trimmings of typical court papers.

iii.   Consulting Experts

Finally, Rule 26(a)(2) ordinarily insulates the third category, consulting experts, from any disclosure. A party engaging a consulting expert does not even need to disclose the expert's identity, so that the consulting expert can provide full and accurate advice to the legal team without fear that any statements will come out in discovery and be used against the client.

3. Rebuttal Testimony

Because the use of experts is often discretionary and because information about each party's plans for expert testimony is typically not exchanged until the Rule 26(a)(2) disclosure, one party may sometimes disclose expert testimony that an opposing party did not anticipate. For example, suppose the Parents disclosed an environmental expert who rendered opinions about the nature of air emissions and liquid discharges into groundwater from Dagwood Plywood's plant. Dagwood Plywood might not have realized that the Parents intended to claim that Pauline was exposed through groundwater migration, and its environmental expert might not have formed any opinions regarding discharges into groundwater. Or perhaps Dagwood Plywood didn't engage an environmental expert on any issue. In such circumstances, the Rules allow Dagwood Plywood to arrange for and disclose "rebuttal testimony." *See* Rule 26(a)(2)(D)(ii). The courts have made it clear, however, that rebuttal testimony must truly be responding to the other party's expert—a party may not use this rebuttal authority to disclose opinions it should have disclosed in its original disclosure. *See Scott v. Chipotle Mexican Grill, Inc.,* 315 F.R.D. 33, 44 (S.D.N.Y. 2016) ("Rebuttal evidence is properly admissible when it will explain, repel, counteract or disprove the evidence of the adverse party.") (citations omitted).

4. Time and Sequence
for Disclosures

Rule 26(a)(2) sets a default time and sequence for expert disclosures. Parties must generally disclose expert testimony 90 days before the date set for trial, and rebuttal testimony 30 days later. However, courts often set different, case-tailored deadlines for expert disclosures in their Case Management Order. These court-ordered deadlines typically require expert disclosures shortly after the completion of fact discovery. The structure and sequence of the disclosures lies within the judge's discretion, taking into account the circumstances of the case and, sometimes, the parties' preferences. Sometimes, the court will order simultaneous disclosures, as provided in the default deadlines. Often, however, the court will require the plaintiff to make expert disclosures first, then require the defendant to make expert disclosures 30 or 60 days later, followed by rebuttal disclosures by the plaintiff.

5. Failure to Disclose/Inadequate Disclosure

The consequences for failing to make timely and complete expert disclosures are automatic and can be severe; Rule 37(c) requires the court to exclude any expert testimony not properly disclosed. This sanction is automatic and does not require a motion. In fact, often a party will have no way of knowing in advance that an opponent plans to present expert testimony that has not been disclosed—after all, it is the disclosure that puts parties on notice of the planned testimony. Thus, if an opponent attempts to introduce expert testimony at trial that was not properly disclosed, a party can simply object at that time.

Sometimes, though, a party will know that an opponent has failed to satisfy Rule 26(a)(2) well before trial. For example, if a party receives an expert report that fails to contain all of the required content, the party may file a motion right away seeking to exclude the expert testimony. Just like a successful *Daubert* challenge can result in summary judgment as discussed above, so too can a successful challenge based on failure to properly disclose the expert's opinions. The next case provides an example of the court's analysis of such a motion to exclude an expert's testimony based on the alleged failure of the expert disclosure to satisfy the requirements of Rule 26(a)(2).

U.S. ex rel. TENN. VALLEY AUTH.

v.

1.72 ACRES OF LAND IN TENN.

821 F.3d 742 (6th Cir. 2016)

SIMON, United States District Judge

[In a land condemnation proceeding to determine the value of the condemned property, the landowner disclosed an expert report for Ron Wilson. The Tennessee Valley Authority moved to exclude Wilson's testimony on the grounds that his report did not meet the requirements in Rule 26(a).]

Wilson's two-page report did not meet Rule 26(a)(2)(B)(i)'s requirement that an expert report be "a complete statement of all opinions the witness will express and the basis and reasons for them." Fed. R. Civ. P. 26(a)(2)(B)(i). Rule 37(c)(1) states that "[i]f a party fails to provide information or identify a witness as required by Rule 26(a) or (e), the party is not allowed to use that information or witness to supply evidence on a motion, at a hearing, or at a trial, unless the failure was substantially justified or is harmless." Fed. R. Civ. P. 37(c)(1).

The district court in this case specifically discussed Wilson's failure, in violation of Rule 26(a)(2)(B)(i), to give "a complete statement of all opinions the witness will express and the basis and reasons for them." Wilson provided no support for his opinion that the existence of above-ground power lines on the property would "materially and negatively impact the development" of a hotel, or that their very existence would "create both a visual and psychological barrier to guests thinking about staying at a hotel." Without more explanation of how Wilson came to this conclusion, his report does not satisfy the requirements of Rule 26(a).

As we have previously held, "Federal Rule of Civil Procedure 37(c)(1) requires absolute compliance with Rule 26(a), that is, it 'mandates that a trial court punish a party for discovery violations in connection with Rule 26 unless the violation was harmless or is substantially justified.' " *Roberts ex rel. Johnson v. Galen of Virginia, Inc.*, 325 F.3d 776, 782 (6th Cir. 2003) . . . . Additionally, the burden is on the potentially sanctioned party to show harmlessness. *Id.*

Because Wilson's expert report did not satisfy Rule 26(a) and Thomas did not meet his burden of showing that the error was justified or harmless, the district court did not abuse its discretion in excluding Wilson's report and testimony. Wilson's testimony was therefore inadmissible under Rule 37(c)(1) . . . .

A party may also file a motion to compel the opponent to disclose a proper report. The choice between these options is a strategic one (involving factors such as the likelihood of succeeding on the motion to exclude and the pros and cons of forcing the opponent to prepare a better report), and they are sometimes presented in the alternative—"please exclude my opponent's expert, or in the alternative require my opponent to disclose a proper report."

B. Expert Depositions

The disclosures just discussed are not the only discovery allowable from experts. Unless the court orders otherwise, the parties are also entitled to take an expert's deposition. For the typical retained expert, the deposition occurs following the disclosure of the expert's report. *See* Fed. R. Civ. P. 26(b)(4)(A). An expert deposition proceeds just like any other deposition, with one important distinction. In a nonexpert deposition, the party noticing the deposition is under no obligation to pay the deponent (other than the nominal witness fee and expenses that must be tendered along with a subpoena for a nonparty). In contrast, a party deposing an opponent's expert must pay the reasonable fees for the expert's attendance at the deposition (but not for the time preparing for the deposition). *See* Fed. R. Civ. P. 26(b)(4)(E).

C. Expert Trial Preparation Materials

In order to make communications between trial counsel and their experts freer and less cumbersome, the Rules provide that most such communications are shielded from discovery—testifying experts are essentially part of the trial team, and many of their communications are classified as protected trial preparation materials. For retained experts, draft reports are not discoverable. *See* Fed. R. Civ. P. 26(b)(4)(B). Thus, the attorney and the expert may exchange and mark up preliminary drafts of the proposed report without much fear that the drafts will be discovered and used against the expert. Likewise, the back-and-forth communications between lawyer and retained expert are not discoverable unless they:

- relate to the expert's compensation;
- identify facts or data that the attorney provided and that the expert considered in forming the opinions; or
- identify assumptions that the party's attorney provided and that the expert relied on in forming the opinions.

See Fed. R. Civ. P. 26(b)(4)(C).

Hypothetical

Q: Alice Attorney, counsel for Dagwood Plywood, hired Erica Epidemiologist to render opinions about whether exposure to formaldehyde causes leukemia in humans. Epidemiologist was a nationally renowned epidemiologist, but had very little experience testifying as an expert. Accordingly, Attorney and Epidemiologist communicated extensively by email about the litigation. Some of those emails discussed litigation strategy, some discussed possible avenues of cross-examining Parents' expert, and some provided Epidemiologist with data regarding concentrations of formaldehyde measured in the community where the Dagwood Plywood factory was located. Additionally, Attorney edited several drafts of Epidemiologist's report and sent those edited drafts to Epidemiologist by email. Parents filed a motion to compel Dagwood Plywood to produce all of these email communications and the edited drafts. Will the court likely grant Parents' motion?

A: The court will probably grant the motion in part and deny it in part. Rule 26(b)(4)(C) requires disclosure of communications which provide facts that the expert relied on in forming her opinions. It is likely here that Epidemiologist relied on the data regarding formaldehyde concentrations in forming her opinion about whether exposure at those concentrations can cause leukemia. The other communications and the draft reports are shielded from discovery by Rule 26(b)(4)(C). *See United States Commodity Futures Trading Comm'n v. Newell,* 301 F.R.D. 348 (N.D. Ill. 2014) (holding that draft expert reports and communications about topics other than those listed in Rule 26(b)(4)(C) are not discoverable).

These protections do not extend to our second category of experts—witnesses who were not retained or specially employed to testify but who will offer expert testimony at trial, such as treating physicians. Thus, such experts are relieved of the obligation to prepare an expert report but are considered by the Rules as less a part of the trial team, so their communications are not shielded as trial preparation materials.

As for our third category of experts, all communications with non-testifying experts consulted in anticipation of litigation are shielded from discovery except in "exceptional circumstances" where it is impracticable for an opposing party to obtain the facts or opinions held by the consulting expert by other means. *See* Fed. R. Civ. P. 26(b)(4)(D)(ii). Circumstances that might qualify as exceptional include situations where the object or condition at issue has been destroyed or changed and instances where there are no other available experts in the field or subject area at issue. Thus, for example, the court found exceptional circumstances warranting discovery of a consulting expert in a case involving a mudslide where the consulting expert had examined the mudslide immediately after it occurred and the scene had changed before the opposing party had an opportunity to have an expert examine the scene. *See Delcastor, Inc. v. Vail Assocs., Inc.,* 108 F.R.D. 405, 409 (D. Colo. 1985).

FROM CLASSROOM TO PRACTICE

A. Selecting Experts

Working with experts can be one of the most challenging and rewarding aspects of complex civil litigation. Choosing the right expert is a critical first step in the process. As with many aspects of litigation, selecting the right expert is a strategic decision based on a variety of considerations; there is no "one size fits all" approach.

For example, there may be highly qualified experts on a particular issue whose primary occupations are supporting litigation as testifying or consulting experts. There may also be highly qualified experts who primarily teach or practice in their discipline but may be willing to testify in the right circumstances. There are advantages and disadvantages of each type of expert. The litigation support specialist will typically have a much better understanding of the litigation process, may be more artful in drafting an expert report and in understanding how best to conduct herself at a deposition, and may be a skilled communicator on the witness stand. At the same time, the jury may perceive such witnesses as "professional experts for-hire" with compromised credibility—in other words, jurors may perceive that such witnesses have been paid to say whatever would be helpful to the party who retained them, as opposed to offering an unbiased scientific opinion. Conversely, a prominent specialist from a prestigious hospital may have immense credibility with the jury but be unaccustomed to drafting an expert report, resistant to the need to confer with trial counsel to prepare for her testimony, and inarticulate or aloof when explaining her opinions in a way that jurors can understand. A face-to-face meeting with expert candidates may help assess some of these factors.

Research also plays an important role in expert selection. Careful litigators will search online for any materials mentioning the person under consideration for engagement as an expert to determine whether that candidate has ever been found "not qualified" by any court to offer expert opinions or had opinions excluded under the court's gatekeeping duties. Litigators will also want to search for inconsistent opinions or other evidence an opponent might use to attack the proposed expert's credibility. Talking to other attorneys who have used or opposed the expert may yield further information about the expert candidate.

B. Initial Engagement

An important consideration when working with an expert is ensuring that the expert understands her role—to give honest testimony. From the selection process, through drafting the report and testifying at a deposition, to testifying at trial, the lawyer should explain to the expert that the private, strategizing discussions with the lawyers about phrasing and trial tactics are not intended to cause the expert to render an opinion she does not believe—which is both unethical and a poor strategy.

For these reasons, attorneys often initially engage an expert as a consulting expert. They can then have full, frank, open discussions with the expert and learn the expert's true opinions and concerns. If the attorney is comfortable using the expert to testify, then the attorney will convert the expert to a testifying expert at the time for expert disclosures. If not, the attorney will leave the expert in the consulting category and may look for another expert (or may look to settle the case!).

C. Expert Depositions

Expert depositions are often among the most pivotal moments in civil discovery, and usually also the most challenging. Because of the importance of expert testimony in a lawsuit (and the weight a jury is likely to assign to that testimony), attorneys must not only prepare their own experts well for their testimony but must also do a comprehensive job in mastering the strengths and weaknesses in their opponents' experts' testimony as well. Much hangs on the outcome of the depositions of experts, and it's not all just trial readiness. The transcripts of expert witnesses are often the fodder for numerous pretrial motions: motions to narrow the witness's testimony (or exclude it altogether) under the court's gatekeeping duties (as discussed above), motions in limine to alter the scope of the trial, and even motions for summary judgment to terminate the entire lawsuit before trial. The depositions of experts, then, often have critical—perhaps trial-dispositive—consequences. It's a quite stressful discovery task for attorneys, but also one that many attorneys consider the most engaging.

Attorneys preparing to take an expert's deposition need to become something of quasi-experts themselves in the subject areas involved in the experts' portions of the case, in order to effectively spar with the actual expert. Expert depositions can easily stray into areas where the attorney is not nearly as familiar with the technical topics as the expert. And the opposing expert will (almost certainly) be prepared by her counsel to expect questioning that is designed to question, weaken, undermine, or outright defeat the expert's opinions. So, the expert is on guard. Defensively, the expert may try to use as much technical jargon as possible during his or her deposition answers to befuddle the attorney, smooth over vulnerabilities in the expert's thinking or analysis, or distract the attorney from aspects of the conclusions where the expert feels uncertain. All in all, this is quite the chess match: an expert who possesses the technical knowledge but not the skills of the law against an attorney skillful at the law but lacking the full technical mastery of the expert.

Of course, in many circumstances, it is just not possible for an attorney to develop true expertise in every technical topic where the expert will testify. At the same time, thorough preparation can make an expert deposition successful. Because expert reports are disclosed before expert depositions, the report can serve as a roadmap for the deposition. The attorney taking the deposition will know in advance each opinion of the opposing expert and the information, materials, and logic the expert is using to support each opinion. Well-prepared attorneys will have met with their own experts to plan the deposition of the opposing expert, and it is not uncommon for a lawyer to bring an expert to a deposition to assist during the examination. The attorney should have carefully mastered all of the relevant literature, studies, and other information listed in the report as supporting the expert's opinions, and will have gathered and digested any studies or literature that are inconsistent with the expert's opinions. The attorney also should have reviewed case law involving challenges to similar experts to determine what types of challenges have been successful. It can be powerful to argue to the court that, "the court in x case disqualified the expert for these reasons, all of which apply equally to the expert in our case."

Despite intense preparation, most attorneys will occasionally find themselves on uncertain ground during expert depositions. Do not be afraid to admit not knowing something and to ask the expert to explain a term or a concept. In fact, many experts are naturally inclined to explain things. If you say to an expert, "I don't understand what you just said, would you please explain it," you may convert a reluctant witness giving single syllable responses into a "Chatty Cathy." If you hand an engineer a piece of graph paper and a pencil, you will have the expert making diagrams and writing down formulae in no time, and that piece of paper may contain important information that would have been difficult to elicit orally during the deposition.

Hypotheticals: Mastering the Nuances

Clearing the Air: In the leukemia lawsuit asserting negligence claims against Dagwood Plywood, the Parents disclose their experts first, and disclose four experts: an MD, a toxicologist, and an epidemiologist to testify about medical causation, and an environmental scientist to testify about the chemicals found in the environment surrounding Dagwood Plywood. The lawyer for Dagwood Plywood is contemplating including among her experts one who would testify about the environmental control measures that typical companies in the plywood industry use. What considerations should the lawyer evaluate in deciding whether to retain and disclose this expert?

Fudging the Numbers: While taking the deposition of Dagwood Plywood's epidemiologist, the Parents' lawyer asks the epidemiologist, "Who drafted the expert report?" The epidemiologist responds that Dagwood Plywood's lawyer prepared the first draft, and that the epidemiologist did some minor editing and then signed the report. What use can the Parents make of this information? Can the Parents have the expert excluded?

PRACTICE SAMPLES

Sample 5-1: EXPERT REPORT

A Report on Specific Causation
of Acute Lymphoblastic Leukemia in
Pauline Parents

In the Matter Of:
Parents v. Dagwood Plywood
Prepared for: Cal Dempsey, Esq.
Prepared by: Frank Johnson, M.D.

I am a Board-Certified Medical Toxicologist practicing in the state of West Carolina. I received my M.D. at the University of New Mexico School of Medicine in 1979, completed a Surgery Internship at the Springfield Medical Center, and an Occupational and Environmental Medicine Residency at the National Institute of Occupational Safety and Health (NIOSH) Educational Resource Center (ERC) at the University of West Carolina. I hold a Master of Science degree in toxicology from the University of West Carolina, and I have been a practicing physician in Springfield, West Carolina since 1980. I am also the president of EnviroTox, a company that I formed to conduct toxicology consulting work such as that which I have rendered in this case. My billing rate for my work on this case was $450 per hour.

Pauline Parents died from leukemia. I was asked whether I might form an opinion as to the most probable cause of Pauline's death, after reviewing the following documents:

1. Pauline Parents's medical records;

2. James Corbelli, Ph.D.'s report and opinions;

3. Dr. D. Matthew Jameson's affidavit;

4. The U.S. Center for Disease Control (CDC) report;

5. Information retrieved from internet research; and

6. Additional materials that have been provided to me.

Based upon my review of the foregoing, I have formed the following opinions:

First, it is my opinion that it is more probable than not that Pauline Parents was exposed to formaldehyde during the time when she and her family resided near the Dagwood Plywood factory. It is also most likely that Pauline had elevated concentrations of formaldehyde in the tissues of her body.

Second, it is my opinion that it is more probable than not that Pauline Parents's exposures to formaldehyde were not from natural sources, but came from Dagwood Plywood's air emissions. That opinion is supported by Dr. Jameson's studies.

Third, I also share the opinion of the U.S. Center for Disease Control and other esteemed scientific agencies and scientists that formaldehyde is a human carcinogen.

Fourth, it is my opinion that Pauline Parents was more likely than not genetically predisposed to leukemia, and that her exposure to formaldehyde from the Dagwood Plywood plant acted as a "carcinogenic promoter" that more likely than not shortened the time of Pauline Parents's cancer development. My opinion is that it is more probable than not that formaldehyde acts as a promoter of leukemia cell growth. My opinion does not exclude formaldehyde as a direct carcinogen or as an agent that, itself, could initiate carcinogenic transformation in susceptible tissues. That opinion is based upon my medical training and experience.

Fifth, Pauline Parents had genetic markers associated with leukemia based on facts contained in her medical records.

Sixth, is my opinion that, to a reasonable degree of medical probability, formaldehyde released into the air, and potentially into the groundwater, by Dagwood Plywood was a substantial causative factor producing the leukemia suffered by Pauline Parents, whether alone or in combination with other substances present in the community. That opinion is based on each of the foregoing sources of information.

I may supplement these opinions based on any additional information I review in conjunction with this engagement.

> A copy of my CV and a list of the cases in which I have testified are attached.

> /s/

> Frank Johnson, M.D.

Sample 5-2: EXPERT CURRICULUM VITAE (RESUME)

CURRICULUM VITAE

Name: Frank Johnson
Address: 7032 East Rosewood Street,
Springfield, West Carolina 55555
(555) 290-6066 (w)
(555) 395-6876 (c)
fjohnson@peds.wcarolina.hosp.edu

EDUCATION

1975 B.S.E.	Euphoria State University Euphoria, Kansas
1979 M.D.	University of West Carolina School of Medicine Springfield, West Carolina
1983–1984 MS	School of Toxicology University of West Carolina Springfield, West Carolina

POST DOCTORAL TRAINING

1979–1981	Surgery Internship Springfield Medical Center
1981–1983	Occupational and Environmental Medicine Residency National Institute of Occupational Safety and Health Educational Resource Center University of West Carolina

EMPLOYMENT

1980–Present	Emergency Room Doctor Springfield Medical Center, Springfield, West Carolina
2007–Present	President EnviroTox Springfield, West Carolina

COMMITTEES

1989–Present	American Board of Emergency Medicine
2000–2008	American Board of Preventive Medicine

CERTIFICATIONS

Board Certified by the American Academy of Emergent Care Physicians

Board Certified by the American Academy of Toxicology

ARTICLES

(1) Johnson, F.: Triage for multiple symptom elderly patients. AMERICAN JOURNAL OF EMERGENCY MEDICINE, 1987

(2) Johnson, F.: Covering costs for uninsured or underinsured patients. JOURNAL OF EMERGENCY MEDICINE, 1992

(3) Johnson, F.: Candor Compels Us to Acknowledge Doctors Generally Can't Trace Environmental Illness Causes Reliably. BRITISH JOURNAL OF RESPIRATORY MEDICINE, 1993

(4) Johnson, F.: Identifying acute poison exposure symptoms. JOURNAL OF EMERGENCY NURSING, 1994

(5) Johnson, F.: Diagnosis or treatment, the ER doctor's dilemma. EMERGENCY MEDICINE, 1999

(6) Johnson, F.: Causation under the medical and legal dialect. EMERGENCY MEDICINE, 2001

Sample 5-3: EXPERT INVOICE

EnviroTox
7023 East Rosewood Street, Springfield, West Carolina 55555

INVOICE NO.: 4259   Bill To: Cal Dempsey
Customer: Cal Dempsey

DESCRIPTION	HOURS/QTY	RATE	DATE	AMOUNT
Document Review/ Parents Medical Records	0.75	$450	9/13	337.50
Document Review/ Parents Medical Records	1.5	$450	9/17	675.00
Document Review/ Parents Medical Records	0.5	$450	9/20	225.00
Document Review/ Parents Medical Records	3	$450	9/25	1,350.00
Document Review/ Parents Medical Records	1	$450	9/26	450.00
Document Review/ Parents Medical Records	2.5	$450	9/27	1,125.00
Document Review/ Parents Medical Records	2.25	$450	9/28	1,012.50
Consultation Telephone Time	0.75	$450	9/30	337.50
Document Writing	1.25	$450	10/1	562.50
Document Review	3.5	$450	10/1	1,575.00
Document Preparation	0.5	$450	10/1	225.00
Consultation Telephone Time	1	$450	10/1	450.00

Total:	$8,325.00
Payments/Credits:	$5,000.00
Balance Due:	$3,325.00

Sample 5-4: **EXPERT DEPOSITION TESTIMONY**

1   By Counsel:

2   Q. Good morning, Dr. Johnson.

3   A. Good morning.

4   Q. As I think you know, my name is Steve Goodman,

5   and I represent Dagwood Plywood in this matter.

6   You're aware of that?

7   A. Yes.

8   Q. You've been deposed several times in the past?

9   A. Yes.

10   Q. So, you're generally familiar with the ground

11   rules for depositions?

12   A. Yes, that's correct.

13   Q. Counsel for the Parents has provided me with a

14   copy of your CV, which I am handing you and

15   marking as Exhibit 1. Would you please look this

16   over, confirm that it is in fact your CV, and let

17   me know if there is anything in your CV that is

18   not accurate?

19   A. This appears to be my CV and I believe everything

20   in it is accurate. Of course, there are lots of

21   things I've done and details about my career

22   that are not specifically listed here, but what

23   is here is accurate.

1   Q. Okay, I may come back to your background later,

2   but I'd like to jump right into your opinions.

3   I'm going to hand you what I'm going to mark as

4   Exhibit 2 and ask if you can identify Exhibit

5   2.

6   A. This is a statement or declaration of my

7   preliminary opinions dated October 1.

8   Q. That's your first expert report in this case?

9   A. In a manner of speaking.

10   Q. What do you mean, "in a manner of speaking"?

11   A. Well, I wouldn't necessarily call it an expert

12   report. I think what I stated was it was a

13   declaration of preliminary opinions, and that's,

14   I think, a more accurate representation.

15   Q. The title of Exhibit 2 contains the word report—

16   you did not consider this to be an expert report?

17   A. Well, in a manner of speaking, as I said before,

18   but I consider my amended report to be the

19   definitive expert report that I've prepared.

20   Q. Okay. We'll come back to your amended report,

21   but I'd like to start with your October 1

22   declaration of preliminary opinions—do you mind

23   if I call it a report, recognizing that you

24   prefer declaration of preliminary opinions?

1   A. That's fine.

2   Q. Thanks. Let's start with the fourth opinion in

3   your report. It states, "Fourth, it is my opinion

4   that Pauline Parents was more likely than not

5   genetically predisposed to leukemia, and that

6   her exposure to formaldehyde from the Dagwood

7   Plywood plant acted as a 'carcinogenic promoter'

8   that more likely than not shortened the time of

9   Pauline Parents's cancer development. My opinion

10   is that it is more probable than not that

11   formaldehyde acts as a promoter of leukemia

12   cell growth. My opinion does not exclude

13   formaldehyde as a direct carcinogen or as an

14   agent that, itself, could initiate carcinogenic

15   transformation in susceptible tissues. That

16   opinion is based upon my medical training and

17   experience." Did I read that accurately?

18   A. Yes.

19   Q. What genetic defects did Pauline have that made

20   her predisposed to leukemia?

21   A. Well, I can't tell you specifically, because,

22   first of all, there weren't any real genetic

23   tests done on Pauline or her mother, Penny. The

24   specific genetic loci for the development of

1   leukemia are varied, and there are many different

2   types of genetic abnormalities that have been

3   associated with the evolution of acute

4   lymphoblastic leukemias. So, for Pauline, I

5   could not tell you, with specificity, what may

6   have been the exact nature or location of the

7   genetic damage, if, in fact, it occurred in that

8   way. But, remember, my opinions are not limited

9   to the ability of formaldehyde to merely produce

10   initiation of cancer, acting as an initiator. I

11   think there's substantial evidence that

12   formaldehyde acts as a complete carcinogen, and

13   in that sense it's much more dangerous than most

14   carcinogens in that it has the ability not only

15   to initiate carcinogenesis, but also has a

16   strong propensity to promote carcinogenesis,

17   has a promoter effect.

18   Q. Okay. What evidence do you have in mind or are

19   you relying on, rather—strike that. What

20   evidence—what evidence are you relying on that

21   formaldehyde is a promoter?

22   A. Well, there's an experiment that was done—I

23   think it was Woo's experiment—that showed that

24   animals who had been treated—they're looking at

1   mammary cancers with molybdenum and formaldehyde

2   as factors. And the formaldehyde, in the presence

3   of—I think they looked at molybdenum, and I

4   think it was Woo's study, if I'm not correct—if

5   I'm not mistaken—showed substantial increase in

6   the rate of mammary tumor production, as, again,

7   an example of a promotion effect. There was

8   also—

9 Q. The Woo study—is that the one referenced in your

10   amended report?

11 A. Yes.

12 Q. It's your understanding that the Woo study used

13   formaldehyde and molybdenum?

14 A. Well, let me refer to my amended report to be

15   more precise about it. In my report on page 17,

16   I describe the study I referred to was actually

17   Wei, W-e-i, et al., 1985, and it involved

18   molybdenum and formaldehyde. In this study, the

19   authors showed, and they concluded, there was

20   an inhibitory effect of molybdenum on mammary

21   carcinogenesis, but there was a promoting effect

22   of formaldehyde on the tumor growth. These were

23   Sprague Dawley rats and some of the rats had

24   inhaled formaldehyde and for some of the rats

1   the authors had implanted molybdenum pellets,

2   and some rats got both treatments. And the rats

3   that just got the molybdenum had lower mammary

4   cancer rates than would be expected, but the

5   rats that got both treatments had an incidence

6   rate of cancer that was 79 percent after 125

7   days. And after 198 days, the formaldehyde-

8   treated rats had a cancer incidence of 95.7

9   percent. Nearly all of them had cancer. So, that

10   was evidence of the promotion effect of cancer

11   and formaldehyde.

12 Q. That study actually involved cigarette smoke,

13   not pure formaldehyde?

14 A. Yes, but cigarette smoke contains formaldehyde—

15   that's well documented.

16 Q. Did Wei mention formaldehyde specifically in the

17   article you have just described?

18 A. Not that I recall.

19 Q. And the Wei study measured rates of mammary

20   cancer, not leukemia?

21 A. I think that's correct, but keep in mind that

22   formaldehyde is a complete carcinogen.

23 Q. The Wei article does not state that formaldehyde

24   is a leukemia promoter?

1   A. I think that's correct.

2   Q. The Wei article does not say anything at all

3   about formaldehyde acting as a promoter of any

4   type of cancer, correct?

5   A. Yes, that's correct.

6   Q. Okay. Do you have any study in mind that suggests

7   or determines that formaldehyde is a promoter

8   with respect to leukemia?

9   A. With respect to leukemia, no.

10   Q. With respect to cancer of any sort?

11   A. I believe, in respect to rhabdomyosarcoma, there

12   was evidence of enhanced ability of formaldehyde

13   to produce rhabdomyosarcomas. The Kalinich

14   study I'm referring to.

15   Q. Okay. Is it your understanding that the Kalinich

16   study involved formaldehyde?

17   A. It was cigarette smoke, which contains

18   formaldehyde, that was used.

19   Q. Does the study mention formaldehyde specifically?

20   A. I'd have to look at the study. I can't recall

21   specifically.

22   Q. And was that study a study of formaldehyde as a

23   promoter?

24   A. They exposed the animals to a strain of virus

1   and then to high concentrations of cigarette

2   smoke, containing formaldehyde, and there was

3   the increased rate of rhabdomyosarcomas that

4   were produced.

5   Q. Wouldn't that suggest that that the combination

6   of the virus and the cigarette smoke was an

7   initiator rather than promoter?

8   A. It could be both. As I said before, I think that

9   formaldehyde has this ability to be a promoter

10   and a complete carcinogen, not just initiator,

11   but promoter.

12 Q. Did that study say anything about formaldehyde

13   being a promoter?

14 A. No, I don't believe it did.

15 Q. Are you aware of any study that says that

16   formaldehyde is a promoter?

17 A. I can't recall any at the moment.

18

19

20

21

22

23

24

VI

Discovery of Nonparties
Subpoenas; Informal Discovery
Rule 45

GETTING THE VIEW

The discovery devices discussed in the Discovery Tools chapter can be very effective for obtaining documents, admissions, and other information from an opposing party. Often, though, there are nonparties who have important information too, and they are not obligated to respond to production requests, interrogatories, requests for admission, or deposition notices.

Suppose, for example, Ellen Employee was badly injured while using a crimping machine at work. She sues the manufacturer, asserting a products liability claim for defective design of the machine. Employee's attorney would like to gather information from Wally Witness, a co-worker who was present when the accident occurred. Employee's attorney knows that Witness, a nonparty, is not obligated to respond to interrogatories or appear pursuant to a deposition notice. Does that mean that Employee's attorney cannot obtain information from Witness or other nonparties? No, there are two primary means for obtaining information from nonparties.

The first is by subpoena. Rule 45 authorizes lawyers to issue subpoenas to nonparties. A subpoena is one form of legal "process," similar in effect to a summons, which requires the recipient, if properly served, to participate in a lawsuit in some fashion. Whereas a summons requires a defendant to appear and defend a lawsuit, a subpoena requires the recipient to provide information to the parties, either in the form of discovery or trial testimony.

The discovery obtainable by subpoena is narrower than the discovery obtainable from parties, however. Discovery subpoenas are generally limited to requests for production of documents and depositions. Thus, a lawyer cannot obtain answers to requests for admission or answers to interrogatories from a nonparty. This limitation balances the need to obtain information from nonparties with the fact that nonparties typically have no stake in the outcome of the litigation, and accordingly should be shielded from the full burden of party discovery.

The second is by informal discovery. No rule of ethics or procedure prevents a lawyer representing a party in litigation from conducting informal interviews with nonparty witnesses or from asking nonparties if they have any memories, opinions, documents, or things relevant to the litigation. Informal discovery can be less expensive than discovery by subpoena, and can have some strategic advantages as well.

HOW SUBPOENAS WORK

A. Overview of Rule 45

Rule 45 is one of the longest rules in the Federal Rules of Civil Procedure, and it has a complex structure. It can be understood in two main groups of content: (1) Rules 45(a) and 45(b) contain the provisions authorizing the issuance and service of subpoenas; and (2) Rules 45(c), 45(d), and 45(e) contain protections for the subpoena recipient. In addition, Rule 45(f) contains procedures for transferring a motion related to a subpoena from the court where the action is pending to the court where performance is to occur, and Rule 45(g) clarifies that the court may use its contempt powers to enforce subpoenas.

B. Subpoena Procedures
1. Contents of a Subpoena

Like other court papers, a subpoena lists the court and caption of the action in which the subpoena is issued. It then describes the actions demanded of the recipient, much like a deposition notice or a production request. It can command production/inspection of documents or property, including ESI (sometimes called a *subpoena duces tecum*), the recipient's appearance to give testimony (sometimes called a *subpoena ad testificandum*), or both. It *must* include the language listed in Rules 45(c) and (d) designed to notify recipients of their rights and obligations. Blank subpoenas are generally available through court websites or through the clerk's office, and contain the requisite language and blank spaces for the other required contents.

Like discovery served on parties, subpoenas are limited to matters within the scope of discovery under Rule 26(b)(1)—nonprivileged matter relevant to any party's claim or defense and proportional to the needs of the case. *Sherrill v. Dio Transp., Inc.*, 317 F.R.D. 609, 612 (D.S.C. 2016).

2. Issuance of a Subpoena

A subpoena issues from the court where the action is pending (regardless of where the recipient is located or where performance will occur). It generally does not, however, require any court involvement, or even permission. Nor does it require action by the clerk's office or the U.S. Marshals. Rather, attorneys are authorized to issue subpoenas as they see fit. This is an awesome power—an attorney can simply issue a subpoena and, unless excused by the court, the recipient is bound by law to perform the tasks demanded in the subpoena and is vulnerable to sanctions for failure to comply (subject to the limitations discussed below).

3. Service of a Subpoena

Recall that, in order to provide proper notice to a defendant that a lawsuit has been commenced and to obligate the defendant to appear and defend against the plaintiff's claims, the plaintiff must serve both the complaint *and a summons* on the defendant, in accordance with Rule 4; service of the complaint alone, without a summons, does not "attach" the defendant and make the defendant bound by the outcome of the proceeding. That initial "original" service of process on the defendant is accomplished using the forms of service authorized by Rule 4 (such as personal service, abode service, etc.). Just like a defendant is not "attached" to a case and required to defend it until properly served with process, a nonparty is not obligated to take any action until properly served with process. A subpoena is the process for a nonparty.

Rule 45(b) states that a subpoena must be served by any nonparty who is at least 18 years old and must be "delivered" to the named person. Although the subpoena issues from the court where the action is pending, it may be served anywhere in the United States. *Gucci Am., Inc. v. Weixing Li*, 135 F. Supp. 3d 87, 96 n.1 (S.D.N.Y. 2015). The courts are divided as to whether that entails in-hand personal service or may be accomplished by delivery to the person's residence or workplace. *See, e.g., Ott v. City of Milwaukee*, 682 F.3d 552, 557 (7th Cir. 2012) (personal service not required); *Gowan v. Mid Century Ins. Co.*, 309 F.R.D. 503, 514 (D.S.D. 2015) (personal service required). If the subpoena requires attendance (such as at a deposition or hearing), the service must also include one day's attendance fee and mileage (the attendance fee is set by statute in 28 U.S.C. § 1821 and is, often, woefully inadequate to compensate a witness for the burdens imposed by a subpoena).

In addition to service on the person subject to the subpoena, a lawyer issuing a subpoena must also serve it on all the other parties to the litigation (but this service is regular service on counsel by regular mail (or commonly, by agreement of counsel, by email), not original service of process). If the subpoena is for deposition testimony, the lawyer issuing it also serves a deposition notice under Rule 30.

Importantly, if the subpoena includes a demand to produce documents, the issuing lawyer must serve it on all other parties *before* serving it on the recipient, so that they may make any objections, protect privileged matter, and obtain their own copies of any documents produced in response.

4. Nonparties Only

In general, a subpoena is not necessary to obtain documents or testimony from a party—Rules 34 and 30 authorize such discovery without the formalities and limitations of a subpoena. When the parties are individuals, determining a subpoena recipient's status as a party or nonparty is usually obvious—one need look no further than the caption of the complaint. When corporations or other entities are parties, however, determining whether an individual associated with the entity requires a subpoena can be more complex. The general rule is that officers, directors, and "managing agents" of a corporate party are also considered the party for purposes of discovery. Thus, one party can request (or, "notice") the deposition of the president of another party without the need for a subpoena. *In re Honda Am. Motor Co.,* 168 F.R.D. 535, 540 (D. Md. 1996).

Determining who qualifies under the vague phrase "managing agent" of a corporate party is not as straightforward as determining the corporation's officers and directors. For example, in our Lucky Lawnmowers, Inc. lawsuit from the Production Request section, suppose Homeowner wants to take the deposition of Eloise Engineer, the company's director of engineering. Is she a managing agent? *In E.I. DuPont de Nemours and Co. v. Kolon Indus., Inc.,* 268 F.R.D. 45, 48 (E.D. Va. 2010), the court described the law on this issue as "sketchy."

E.I. DUPONT DE NEMOURS & CO.
v.
KOLON INDUS., INC.

268 F.R.D. 45 (E.D. Va. 2010)

PAYNE, United States District Judge

[DuPont alleged that Kolon stole its secret processes and technologies for manufacturing Kevlar. DuPont sought to take the deposition of five employees or former employees of Kolon. It was having difficulty serving them with subpoenas,

so it sought to require Kolon to make them available pursuant to deposition notice based on their alleged statuses as managing agents.]

WHETHER THE PROPOSED DEPONENTS
QUALIFY AS MANAGING AGENTS

A. Applicable Law

The phrase "managing agent" appears in several places in the Federal Rules of Civil Procedure pertaining to discovery. However, the framework for determining whether a particular person qualifies as a managing agent is primarily a construction of decisional law concerned with ensuring that an organization is deposed through its proper representatives concerning the matters at issue in the litigation. The examining party may request that the organization select and produce a representative deponent who is an officer, a director, or a managing agent of the entity; alternatively, the examining party may select a particular officer, director, or managing agent for deposition and order the organization to produce the person. *In re Honda, Am. Motor Co.*, 168 F.R.D. 535, 540 (D. Md. 1996). In the latter scenario, the organization, upon notice of the deposition, must produce the specified individual. *Id.* If the specified person, however, is not an officer, director, or managing agent, then the examining party "must resort to Fed. R. Civ. P. 45 for subpoenas on non-party witnesses." *Id.*

As both parties recognize, "[t]he law concerning who may properly be designated as a managing agent is sketchy." *Id.* "Largely because of the vast variety of factual circumstances to which the concept must be applied, the standard . . . remains a functional one to be determined largely on a case-by-case basis." [*Founding Church of Scientology, Inc. v. Webster*, 802 F.2d 1448, 1452 (D.C. Cir. 1986).]

Honda . . . effectively synthesized the several factors that generally are considered in making a case-specific determination of a person's managing agent status: (1) the discretionary authority vested in the person by the corporation; (2) the employee's dependability in following the employer's directions; (3) whether the individual is more likely to identify with the corporation or the adverse party in the litigation; and (4) the degree of supervisory authority in areas pertinent to the litigation. [*Honda*, 168 F.R.D. at 540–41.] Of these factors, the third—the employee's identity of interests with his employer as opposed to the opposing party—is "paramount." *Id.* at 541. * * *

Ordinarily, managing agent status is determined as of the time of the deposition, not as of the time when the activities disputed in the litigation occurred. *Honda*, 168 F.R.D. at 540. Thus, "[t]he general rule is that former employees cannot be managing agents of a corporation." *Id.* at 541. However, like most rules, this one has exceptions. When a managing agent is fired "to avoid disclosure in pending or potential litigation," or when "the managing agent has been or might be reappointed to another position in the corporation," managing agent status that exists at the time of the events at issue does not magically disappear with the person's termination or reassignment. *Id.* The reason for these exceptions is obvious: without them, an organization could manipulate discovery and frustrate the purpose of the rule simply by moving its managers around whenever it wished to prevent them from being deposed.

B. Kolon's General Objections

DuPont posits that there are eight people who may be deposed as managing agents based on discovery provided to date. It, of course, is necessary to consider the circumstances relating to each proposed witness individually to decide the motion to compel depositions. However, there are two points which Kolon raises in opposition to the motion that can be considered generally: (1) the effect of the proposed witnesses' resistance to the directive given by Kolon that they appear for deposition under Rule 30(b)(6);[1] and (2) the consequence of the termination or reassignment of the witnesses whose depositions DuPont seeks to compel. Those issues will be addressed before assessing the circumstances relating to each putative managing agent witness.

1. The Resistance Offered to Deposition by the Putative Managing Agent Deponents

It is true, as Kolon observes, that a person's refusal to appear for a deposition, "even at the expense of sanctions for the entity defendants," may indicate that the person does not share an identity of interest with the corporation that employs him. * * * However, that precept does not help Kolon in this case for several reasons.

First, the facts indicate a substantial similarity of interest between Kolon and the persons in question. Kolon still employs most of them and pays their salaries. Kolon also pays for all but two of them to be represented by independent counsel, and, of those two, one of them has not been located. Although the fact of independent representation demonstrates that Kolon and the individuals do not have perfectly identical interests, Kolon is nonetheless spending money to keep these persons on the payroll, and to pay the fees of the top flight lawyers whom Kolon has retained to represent them. It is highly improbable that Kolon is spending such sums out of disinterested gener-

---

1. For an explanation of Rule 30(b)(6), enabling depositions of a representative of a company on specified topics, see the *Discovery Tools — Depositions* chapter above.

osity, or altruism. It is much more likely that this expense is being incurred to help these employees who, after all, were acting in Kolon's behalf, and apparently at its direction, when they took the actions about which they are to be deposed. These circumstances point to a similarity of interest, not to a conflict.

Second, contrary to Kolon's view, the question of identity of interest is not merely one of how strongly these employees identify with Kolon. This facet of the test focuses on the extent to which they identify with Kolon as opposed to DuPont. When one compares the record respecting the nexus between these employees and Kolon, the company that employs them and that provides money and services to them, with the relationship the employees have to DuPont, the company that accuses them of conniving to steal its trade secrets, it is rather clear that their interests identify closely with Kolon and not at all with DuPont. That the employees might claim a privilege in response to a particular question is of only marginal relevance in the identity of interest analysis.

Third, Kolon indicates that the reluctance to date of the deponents to testify is not due to adversity of interest between the persons and Kolon, but because of their fear that evidence will be used to incriminate them. . . . Whatever else this argument may bespeak, it rather clearly discloses an identity of interest between Kolon and the putative deponents: neither the proposed deponent-employees nor Kolon have any interest in being held accountable for misappropriation of DuPont's trade secrets and confidential information. Of course, the interest of DuPont is to hold Kolon accountable. Thus, the aspect of the identity of interest analysis that counts whether the deponent-employees are aligned with Kolon, rather than DuPont, is satisfied and augers in favor a finding that employees are managing agents. * * *

2. The Record Warrants an Exception to the General Rule that Managing Agency is Determined as of the Time of the Deposition

The Court rejects Kolon's contention that its removal of these persons from positions of managing agency necessarily negates their managing agent status as a matter of law. Mindful of the general rule that former employees are not managing agents, the Court finds ample evidence to demonstrate that an exception is warranted in this case, at least for the limited purpose of requiring them to appear at depositions. The timing and circumstances of Kolon's reassignment or termination of its employees render the true status of the proposed deponents highly suspect, and allow for a strong inference that Kolon is moving its employees around like chessmen, conveniently shielding them from DuPont's access. That is reinforced by Kolon's vacillation on the issue in this litigation.

Of course, deposition testimony could reveal that the putative deponent-employees are not managing agents. However, on this record, DuPont has demonstrated that the termination and reassignments of the proposed deponents are sufficiently suspect to warrant a deviation from the general rule that the deponent should be a managing agent at the time of the deposition. The circumstances surrounding the termination and reassignments will be explored at deposition, but, as the record now stands, it warrants a finding that the personnel actions appear to be contrivances to avoid the general rule.

C. Protections for the Recipient

Mindful of the need to protect nonparties from excessive burden, Rule 45(c) imposes limitations on how far a subpoena recipient must travel. Of course, every subpoena subjects the recipient to some burden, so Rule 45(c) only attempts to *minimize* that burden, not *eliminate* it altogether.

1. Place of Performance

One way in which Rule 45(c) limits the burden on the recipient is by restricting the distance the recipient may be required to travel when performing the actions commanded by the subpoena. To that end, a subpoena may only compel performance by a nonparty within 100 miles of where the nonparty resides, is employed, or regularly transacts business in person. For subpoenas commanding testimony, the deposition must occur within this distance limitation, and for subpoenas commanding production of documents, the production must occur within this distance limitation.

2. Undue Burden or Expense

In addition to the limitation on the location of the performance required by a subpoena, Rule 45 imposes an obligation on a party serving a subpoena to avoid imposing "undue" burden or expense on the recipient. Again, every subpoena imposes burden, so it is only "undue" burden—an undefined term subject to the court's very broad discretion—that the serving party must avoid. Rules 45(d) and (e) set forth language that must be included in every subpoena alerting subpoena recipients to their protection from undue burden and their other rights and duties.

Hypothetical

Q: In our Lucky Lawnmowers, Inc. case, Harry Homeowner serves a subpoena on Lawnmower Engineering, Inc., an engineering firm that Lucky Lawnmowers, Inc. engaged to assist in its lawnmower designs. In the subpoena, Harry Homeowner requests documents in 58 broad categories, including requests for all emails, draft and final design drawings, memoranda, and specifications related to the Lucky 2000 and the Lucky 1000 models from the past 25 years. Did Homeowner comply with Rule 45(d) in drafting and issuing this subpoena?

A: Although Homeowner would have an opportunity to explain the need for such a broad subpoena, a court might conclude that the time and breadth scope of this subpoena breached Homeowner's duty to avoid imposing undue burden on a nonparty. Homeowner likely could anticipate that gathering virtually every document generated over 25 years related to two different products would be quite onerous. *See In re: Modern Plastics Corp.*, 890 F.3d 244, 250–51 (6th Cir. 2018).

D. Challenges to and Enforcement of Subpoenas

One aspect of subpoena practice that differs substantially from other discovery practice is the manner of objecting to and seeking enforcement of subpoenas. While a party receiving excessive or improper discovery must often file a motion for an order protecting that party from the discovery (as discussed in the Policing Discovery chapter), a nonparty may simply send a letter objecting to a subpoena within 14 days of its service. Fed. R. Civ. P. 45(d). That letter objection then relieves the recipient nonparty of the obligation to perform the tasks commanded by the subpoena unless the party issuing the subpoena files a successful motion asking the court to compel the performance. This is another instance where the rules try to lessen the burden on nonparties because of their limited interest in the outcome of the litigation.

These contrasting procedures are illustrated by Homeowner's intended deposition of Engineer, the manager of engineering for Lucky Lawnmowers, Inc. If Engineer is considered a "managing agent," then Homeowner initiates the deposition simply by sending a deposition notice to Lucky Lawnmowers, Inc., naming Engineer as the witness. If Lucky Lawnmowers, Inc. believes that the location set for Engineer's deposition unreasonably requires Engineer to travel 200 miles, Lucky Lawnmowers, Inc. must (if meeting and conferring with Homeowner doesn't resolve the dispute) file a motion for an order relieving it of the obligation to have Engineer appear for the deposition. If Engineer fails to appear for the deposition, Lucky Lawnmowers, Inc. will be subject to sanctions even if it had already advised Homeowner that it objected to the deposition notice as imposing an unreasonable burden.

In contrast, if Engineer is not deemed a "managing agent," then Homeowner must issue a subpoena and serve it on Engineer (in addition to serving a deposition notice on Lucky Lawnmowers, Inc.). If the subpoena requires Engineer to travel 200 miles, all she need do is send a letter objecting to the deposition. She is then relieved of the obligation to appear for the deposition unless Homeowner files a motion to compel that persuades the court to order Engineer to comply with the subpoena.

The ability to write a simple letter objection is limited to the subpoena recipient, however. A party believing that the discovery sought from a nonparty by subpoena is improper must file a "motion to quash" the subpoena or a motion for a protective order prohibiting or limiting the discovery under the subpoena.

E. Performance of Subpoenas

Performance of the tasks in a subpoena proceeds much like the equivalent discovery tasks. If the subpoena is for a deposition, the deposition proceeds like any other deposition except that, typically, the attorneys for the parties do not represent the witness, and thus generally may not instruct the witness not to answer questions. *Cf.* Rule 30(c)(2). Sometimes, the nonparty recipient will retain his or her own counsel and bring them to the deposition; in such a case, the witness's counsel may instruct the witness not to answer a question in accordance with the limitations in Rule 30. See the discussion of deposition conduct in the Discovery Tools—Deposition chapter.

If the subpoena requires production of documents, the rules for document production in Rule 34 generally apply. Accordingly, the subpoena will reach documents in the recipient's possession, custody, or control that are responsive and within the scope of discovery as prescribed in Rule 26(b)(1) and described in more detail in the Discovery Tools—Requests for *Production* chapter.

FROM CLASSROOM TO PRACTICE

Although a notice of deposition technically does not obligate a rank-and-file employee of a corporate party to appear for a deposition, the lawyer representing the corporation will often agree to produce the employee voluntarily, without the need for a subpoena. Accordingly, as a matter of both convenience and professional courtesy, most experienced litigators will discuss the matter with opposing counsel before serving a subpoena on an employee, and most experienced litigators will agree to produce the employee voluntarily without a subpoena.

Conversely, sometimes a subpoena can be helpful to a nonparty. In our Lucky Lawnmowers, Inc. lawsuit, for example, suppose that Harry Homeowner has a neighbor who works at Lucky Lawnmowers, Inc. They chatted, and Homeowner tells his lawyer that the neighbor has information that will help in the lawsuit, but is worried that he will lose his job if he appears to be cooperating with Homeowner. Homeowner's lawyer could issue a subpoena to the neighbor so that the neighbor has "cover" with Lucky Lawnmowers, Inc.—the neighbor would then be perceived as testifying under threat of contempt of court, not voluntarily.

In addition to issuing a subpoena to provide "cover" if helpful to the nonparty witness, lawyers will sometimes take other measures to ease the burden on a nonparty. A lawyer wanting to prevent a nonparty witness from becoming hostile: might contact the witness in advance to discuss service of the subpoena in a manner that does not embarrass the witness (such as avoiding service at the witness's workplace); might offer to schedule a deposition at a time, on a day, or in a manner to minimize the disruption for the witness; and might even offer to compensate the witness to attend a meeting to prepare for the deposition (but not for the witness's time at the deposition, because that would give the appearance of paying the witness for his or her testimony).

HOW INFORMAL DISCOVERY WORKS

A subpoena carries the full force of the court—including contempt powers—and is an invaluable tool when a nonparty possesses important information but will not provide it voluntarily. At the same time, the subpoena procedures contain significant limitations, require notice to opposing parties, and provide the recipient with a host of protections. When a nonparty is cooperative (making a subpoena unnecessary), informal discovery can have significant advantages.

There is no defined set of informal discovery tools—the only real limitation is the imagination of the party seeking the informal discovery (subject, of course, to legal and ethical constraints—an attorney cannot, for example, break into a building to examine documents "informally" or violate federal or State wiretap laws). One of the most common forms of informal discovery is Internet searches. A treasure trove of information may be available about a corporate party's formation, organization, financial condition, advertising, litigation history, etc., just by snooping around on the computer.

Likewise, important, and sometimes highly impactful, information about a party may exist on the various social media platforms. Sometimes a party's social media content includes specific comments about the litigation that may be embarrassing to the party or even call into question the validity of the party's position. Even when the social media content does not specifically discuss the litigation, it may call into question the party's integrity or honesty.

Private investigators are another form of informal discovery. Investigators can, of course, take photographs of a plaintiff doing the limbo in a public dance hall (potentially case-devastating evidence if that plaintiff is suing to recover for a back injury she claims to be debilitating), but can also undertake more mundane background gathering assignments, such as photographing the scene of an incident, identifying and interviewing witnesses, or locating property held by an opposing party. Private investigators thus can be helpful resources, but at the same time, experienced attorneys are thoughtful about using private investigators. When a big corporation hires a private investigator to "dig up dirt" about an individual plaintiff, the optics can be unfavorable. Like most litigation decisions, an attorney should hire a private investigator only after careful balancing of all of the circumstances.

One of the simplest and most effective forms of informal discovery is direct contact with nonparty witnesses. A lawyer is generally free to meet with and interview a nonparty and to ask him or her for relevant information, documents, and ESI. The beauty of such informal interviews and document gathering is that it occurs without participation by (or even awareness by) opposing parties, unlike discovery conducted pursuant to a subpoena. With an informal interview, if the witness's testimony proves to be unhelpful (or downright harmful), that fact does not automatically come to the attention of opposing parties (in contrast to deposition testimony).

Q A

Hypothetical

Q: Harry Homeowner believes his next-door neighbor can provide helpful testimony and has some helpful photographs. What are Homeowner's options regarding obtaining this evidence, and what are the advantages and disadvantages of each approach?

A: Homeowner could issue a subpoena to the neighbor to appear at a deposition and to bring to the deposition any photographs related to the accident. Remember, though, that the rules require service of a subpoena on all other counsel of record. Accordingly, Homeowner would have to serve a copy of the subpoena on Lucky Lawnmowers, Inc.'s counsel, who could participate in the deposition and obtain copies of the photographs. That might be fine if the neighbor's testimony and photographs are helpful to Homeowner, but suppose they are not? By using the subpoena process, a lawyer ensures that the opposing party will obtain all the same information. Alternatively, instead of using the formal subpoena process, Homeowner could arrange for the neighbor to meet informally with Homeowner's lawyer. The lawyer can ask almost any question she chooses without objection or interference from an opposing lawyer. If the testimony is harmful to Homeowner's case or the photographs are disadvantageous, Homeowner could decide not to list the neighbor as a witness, and might not need to reveal the neighbor's identity as someone with knowledge about the incident unless Lucky Lawnmowers, Inc. serves discovery that compels disclosure of the neighbor's identity. Alternatively, if the neighbor's testimony and photographs are helpful, Homeowner can take affirmative steps to list the neighbor as a witness and to list the photographs as exhibits.

Be mindful, though, of the rules of ethics regarding ex parte contacts with an opposing party. When the opposing party is an individual, the rules are straightforward—if that individual is represented by counsel, then lawyers for other parties may not communicate with the individual without the presence or permission of the individual's counsel. *See* Model Rules of Prof'l Conduct R. 4.2. When the opposing party is an organization like a corporation, however, the ethics rules are more nuanced, and sometimes vary from state to state. Generally, officers, directors, and "control" personnel or managing agents are deemed to be the equivalent of the party for purposes of evaluating who may be interviewed ex parte. Likewise, most states consider former, and even present, low-level employees to be distinct from the party, and thus fair game for an informal interview. *See, e.g., U.S. EEOC v. Placer ARC,* 147 F. Supp. 3d 1053, 1065 (E.D. Cal. 2015). In general, it is a good practice to conduct jurisdiction-specific research to determine the ethical propriety of ex parte contact with particular categories of employees of a party.

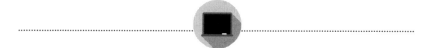

FROM CLASSROOM TO PRACTICE

One potential pitfall of informal discovery is a potential contest over the admissibility of testimony or documents obtained informally. The rules of evidence do not allow the lawyer conducting the interview to recount the witness's story before the jury, nor offer the witness's written statement or affidavit into evidence. One way to address admissibility issues is to call the witness to testify live at trial, both to testify as to his or her observations and actions and to authenticate any documents. Taking a written statement during informal discovery can provide a helpful safeguard in the event that the witness later changes his or her testimony at trial—while not admissible to prove the truth of the statement, the statement may be useful for impeachment.

Another solution is to follow the informal interview with a formal deposition if the circumstances warrant this extra step. The informal interview allows the lawyer to evaluate the strategic advantages of using the witness at trial and to make an informed decision about the value of preserving that testimony via a deposition. The informal interview may also shape the lawyer's approach to the deposition, helping to sharpen the focus of the scope of the direct examination to only those topics revealed as helpful during the informal interview.

Nonparty witnesses, however, are not under any obligation to participate in an informal interview, and lawyers should be careful not to pressure a witness into giving an informal interview. Indeed, many lawyers give a "civil Miranda" disclosure to nonparty witnesses, advising them that they are not under any obligation to speak with the lawyer and that they are entitled to obtain their own lawyer if they choose.

Hypotheticals: Mastering the Nuances

Digging up Dirt: At an informal interview of Homeowner's neighbor, Lucky Lawnmowers, Inc. wants to ask the neighbor questions about a rumor the lawyer heard that Homeowner was having an extra-marital affair. Is that information within the scope of discovery? What happens if the information is outside the scope of discovery—is it objectionable?

What to Do with the Dirt: At the informal interview of Homeowner's neighbor, Lucky Lawnmowers, Inc. learns that Homeowner told the neighbor that Homeowner was planning to exaggerate the severity of his pain in order to enhance his damages. What, if anything, should Lucky Lawnmowers, Inc. do to preserve the neighbor's information?

Remote Dirt: Homeowner wants to take the deposition of a former employee of Lucky Lawnmowers, Inc. The former employee now lives in the neighboring state, about 200 miles from the court where the lawsuit is pending. Can Homeowner serve a subpoena on the former employee? If so, how and where would Homeowner serve the subpoena? Where may the subpoena compel the former employee to appear and testify? If the subpoena orders the former employee to appear at a conference room near the courthouse, what should the former employee do?

PRACTICE SAMPLES

Sample 6-1: SUBPOENA

IN THE UNITED STATES DISTRICT COURT
DISTRICT OF WEST CAROLINA

Harry Homeowner,	)	
	)	
Plaintiff,	)	
	)	
v.	)	Civil Action No. 00-CV-98765
	)	
Lucky Lawnmowers, Inc.,	)	
	)	
Defendant.	)	

SUBPOENA TO TESTIFY AT A DEPOSITION
IN A CIVIL ACTION [2]

To: Eloise Engineer

Testimony: **YOU ARE COMMANDED** to appear at the time, date, and place set forth below to testify at a deposition to be taken in this civil action. If you are an organization, you must designate one or more officers, directors, or managing agents, or designate other persons who consent to testify on your behalf about the following matters, or those set forth in an attachment:

Place:555 Main Street, Springfield, West Carolina

Date and Time: 2/29/20____, 9:00 a.m.

The deposition will be recorded by this method: Video recording and stenographic

Production: You, or your representatives, must also bring with you to the deposition the following documents, electronically stored information, or objects, and must permit inspection, copying, testing, or sampling of the material:

---

2. This form is based on Form AO 88 (Rev. 02/14) Subpoena to Appear and Testify at a Hearing or Trial in a Civil Action, which may be obtained on the website of the Administrative Office of the United States Courts.

The following provisions of Fed. R. Civ. P. 45 are attached—Rule 45(c), relating to the place of compliance; Rule 45(d), relating to your protection as a person subject to a subpoena; and Rule 45(e) and (g), relating to your duty to respond to this subpoena and the potential consequences of not doing so.

Date: 1/10/20____

CLERK OF COURT

_____   OR   s/   _____
Signature of Clerk or Deputy Clerk   *Attorney's signature*

The name, address, e-mail address, and telephone number of the attorney representing *Harry Homeowner*, who issues or requests this subpoena, are: Benjarvus Green-Ellis, LLC

Notice to the person who issues or requests this subpoena

If this subpoena commands the production of documents, electronically stored information, or tangible things before trial, a notice and a copy of the subpoena must be served on each party in this case before it is served on the person to whom it is directed. Fed. R. Civ. P. 45(a)(4).

PROOF OF SERVICE

**(This section should not be filed with the court
unless required by Fed. R. Civ. P. 45.)**

I received this subpoena for *(name of individual and title, if any)* on *(date)*.

I served the subpoena by delivering a copy to the named individual as follows:

_____

_____

on *(date)* _____ ; or

I returned the subpoena unexecuted because: _____

_____

Unless the subpoena was issued on behalf of the United States, or one of its officers or agents, I have also tendered to the witness the fees for one day's attendance, and the mileage allowed by law, in the amount of $.

My fees are $ _____ for travel and $ _____ for services, for a total of $ _____ .

I declare under penalty of perjury that this information is true.

Date: _____

_____
Server's signature

_____
Printed name and title

_____
Server's address

AO 88A (Rev. 02/14) Subpoena to Testify at a Deposition in a Civil Action (Page 3)

Federal Rule of Civil Procedure 45 (c), (d), (e), and (g) (Effective 12/1/13)

(c) Place of Compliance.

(1) *For a Trial, Hearing, or Deposition.* A subpoena may command a person to attend a trial, hearing, or deposition only as follows:

(A) within 100 miles of where the person resides, is employed, or regularly transacts business in person; or

(B) within the state where the person resides, is employed, or regularly transacts business in person, if the person

(i) is a party or a party's officer; or

(ii) is commanded to attend a trial and would not incur substantial expense.

(2) *For Other Discovery.* A subpoena may command:

(A) production of documents, electronically stored information, or tangible things at a place within 100 miles of where the person resides, is employed, or regularly transacts business in person; and

(B) inspection of premises at the premises to be inspected.

(d) Protecting a Person Subject to a Subpoena; Enforcement.

(1) *Avoiding Undue Burden or Expense; Sanctions.* A party or attorney responsible for issuing and serving a subpoena must take reasonable steps to avoid imposing undue burden or expense on a person subject to the subpoena. The court for the district where

compliance is required must enforce this duty and impose an appropriate sanction—which may include lost earnings and reasonable attorney's fees—on a party or attorney who fails to comply.

(2) *Command to Produce Materials or Permit Inspection.*

(A) *Appearance Not Required.* A person commanded to produce documents, electronically stored information, or tangible things, or to permit the inspection of premises, need not appear in person at the place of production or inspection unless also commanded to appear for a deposition, hearing, or trial.

(B) *Objections.* A person commanded to produce documents or tangible things or to permit inspection may serve on the party or attorney designated in the subpoena a written objection to inspecting, copying, testing, or sampling any or all of the materials or to inspecting the premises—or to producing electronically stored information in the form or forms requested. The objection must be served before the earlier of the time specified for compliance or 14 days after the subpoena is served. If an objection is made, the following rules apply:

(i) At any time, on notice to the commanded person, the serving party may move the court for the district where compliance is required for an order compelling production or inspection.

(ii) These acts may be required only as directed in the order, and the order must protect a person who is neither a party nor a party's officer from significant expense resulting from compliance.

(3) *Quashing or Modifying a Subpoena.*

(A) *When Required.* On timely motion, the court for the district where compliance is required must quash or modify a subpoena that:

(i) fails to allow a reasonable time to comply;

(ii) requires a person to comply beyond the geographical limits specified in Rule 45(c);

(iii) requires disclosure of privileged or other protected matter, if no exception or waiver applies; or

(iv) subjects a person to undue burden.

(B) *When Permitted.* To protect a person subject to or affected by a subpoena, the court for the district where compliance is required may, on motion, quash or modify the subpoena if it requires:

(i) disclosing a trade secret or other confidential research, development, or commercial information; or

(ii) disclosing an unretained expert's opinion or information that does not describe specific occurrences in dispute and results from the expert's study that was not requested by a party.

(C) *Specifying Conditions as an Alternative.* In the circumstances described in Rule 45(d)(3)(B), the court may, instead of quashing or modifying a subpoena, order appearance or production under specified conditions if the serving party:

(i) shows a substantial need for the testimony or material that cannot be otherwise met without undue hardship; and

(ii) ensures that the subpoenaed person will be reasonably compensated.

(e) **Duties in Responding to a Subpoena.**

(1) *Producing Documents or Electronically Stored Information.* These procedures apply to producing documents or electronically stored information:

(A) *Documents.* A person responding to a subpoena to produce documents must produce them as they are kept in the ordinary course of business or must organize and label them to correspond to the categories in the demand.

(B) *Form for Producing Electronically Stored Information Not Specified.* If a subpoena does not specify a form for producing electronically stored information, the person responding must produce it in a form or forms in which it is ordinarily maintained or in a reasonably usable form or forms.

(C) *Electronically Stored Information Produced in Only One Form.* The person responding need not produce the same electronically stored information in more than one form.

(D) *Inaccessible Electronically Stored Information.* The person responding need not provide discovery of electronically stored information from sources that the person identifies as not reasonably accessible because of undue burden or cost. On motion to compel discovery or for a protective order, the person responding must show that the information is not reasonably accessible because of undue burden or cost. If that showing is made, the court may nonetheless order discovery from such sources if the requesting party shows good cause, considering the limitations of Rule 26(b)(2)(C). The court may specify conditions for the discovery.

(2) Claiming Privilege or Protection.

(A) *Information Withheld.* A person withholding subpoenaed information under a claim that it is privileged or subject to protection as trial-preparation material must:

(i) expressly make the claim; and

(ii) describe the nature of the withheld documents, communications, or tangible things in a manner that, without revealing information itself privileged or protected, will enable the parties to assess the claim.

(B) *Information Produced.* If information produced in response to a subpoena is subject to a claim of privilege or of protection as trial-preparation material, the person making the claim may notify any party that received the information of the claim and the basis for it. After being notified, a party must promptly return, sequester, or destroy the specified information and any copies it has; must not use or disclose the information until the claim is resolved; must take reasonable steps to retrieve the information if the party disclosed it before being notified; and may promptly present the information under seal to the court for the district where compliance is required for a determination of the claim. The person who produced the information must preserve the information until the claim is resolved.

(g) Contempt.

The court for the district where compliance is required—and also, after a motion is transferred, the issuing court—may hold in contempt a person who, having been served, fails without adequate excuse to obey the subpoena or an order related to it.

VII

Supplementing Discovery Responses

Rule 26(e)

GETTING THE VIEW

Discovery requests are supposed to be answered correctly and completely the first time. That is every responding party's obligation. *See* Fed. R. Civ. P. 26(g). But, on occasion, it doesn't work out that way. Sometimes, information that ought to have been shared gets overlooked by the litigants, notwithstanding their earnestness and good intentions. More frequently, litigants come to learn new information or new details, or locate new documents or electronically stored information, *after* a discovery request is already answered. Should there be a duty on the part of a responding party to "update" discovery responses, either to correct a mistaken omission of information or to convey newly learned information?

For many years, the answer to this updating dilemma was unclear. Some courts obliquely suggested that responding parties "should" update their earlier discovery responses, without imposing much by way of consequence if they failed or refused to do so. Some courts would enforce an asking party's instruction in its discovery requests to an opponent that those discovery requests were to be considered "continuing," and thus in need of updating as information changed. Other courts took the opposite approach and refused to enforce such an instruction or duty. Still other courts took a more demanding view and inferred—as a matter of law—a duty to update, whether or not the asking party had requested it.

283

Today, the answer is no longer unclear. Information supplied to an adversary in response to a discovery obligation *must* be supplemented if the earlier response is either incomplete or incorrect. *See* Fed. R. Civ. P. 26(e)(1)(A).

HOW THIS SUPPLEMENTATION DUTY WORKS

A. What Triggers the Duty to Supplement

An answering party has a duty to supplement an earlier discovery response when it "learns" that its earlier response is, "in some material respect," either "incomplete" or "incorrect." *See* Fed. R. Civ. P. 26(e)(1)(A). In addition, an answering party has a duty to supplement if ordered to do so specially by the court. *See* Rule 26(e)(1)(B). To be clear, this duty of supplementation does not excuse a party's original obligation to respond properly and fully the first time (and a failure to respond properly the first time is sanctionable, as discussed in the Policing Discovery chapter below). Rather, the duty to supplement is triggered where a party commits an oversight now in need of correction or learns new information that now renders its original answers incomplete. In both circumstances, the answering party must update its earlier (now incorrect or incomplete) discovery responses with fresh, supplemented answers.

Three qualifications are noteworthy. First, this supplementation duty applies only when (and then timely after) the answering party "learns" that its prior responses are incomplete or incorrect. One court has sharpened this inquiry by noting that the supplementation obligation "arises when the disclosing party reasonably should know that its prior discovery responses are incomplete, *e.g.* because the party has now obtained information it did not previously have." *Jama v. City & Cty. of Denver*, 304 F.R.D. 289, 299–300 (D. Colo. 2014).

Second, the supplementation duty applies only when the original response is incomplete or incorrect "in some material respect," a circumstance one court has interpreted to mean "an objectively reasonable likelihood that the additional or corrective information could substantially affect or alter the opposing party's discovery plan or trial preparation." *Sender v. Mann*, 225 F.R.D. 645, 653–54 (D. Colo. 2004). Caution, here, is wise. Because of the inherent imprecision in conducting such a context-dependent inquiry, and mindful of the risk of sanctions should the court disagree with a non-disclosure decision, liberally interpreting this duty of supplementation will often be the more prudent course.

Third, this supplementation duty only applies where the "additional or corrective information has not otherwise been made known to the other parties during the discovery process or in writing." *See* Fed. R. Civ. P. 26(e)(1)(A). Consequently, if the opponent has already obtained the new information in discovery or in writing, there may be no need to supply the information again through a Rule 26(e) supplement.

JAMA
v.
CITY AND COUNTY OF DENVER

304 F.R.D. 289 (D. Colo. 2014)

KRIEGER, Chief United States District Judge

[Plaintiffs filed a federal civil rights action against Denver, Colorado alleging a law enforcement policy, practice, and custom of making improper arrests. During discovery, the plaintiffs requested that Denver conduct a search of its database to identify mistaken identity arrests and detention. The results of that search produced 237 cases that the plaintiffs believed involved potential identification issues involving others (non-plaintiffs). The plaintiffs later made a fourth supplemental disclosure identifying from those cases "108 (presumably) new witnesses, each of whom was alleged to have 'facts relating to arrest based on mistaken identity, including communications to and from law enforcement officers, court proceedings, circumstances of arrest, and length of detention.'" Denver moved to strike the disclosure as untimely and prejudicial.]

Rule 26(a) required the Plaintiffs to make initial disclosures of: (i) the name (and address and telephone number, if known) of "each individual likely to have discoverable information . . . that [the Plaintiffs] may use to support [their] claims," along with a statement of the subjects of that information; and (ii) a copy of all documents in the Plaintiffs' possession that the Plaintiffs may use to support their claims. The mandatory disclosures serve several purposes, including eliminating surprise, promoting settlement, and giving the opposing party information about the identification and locations of persons with knowledge so as to assist that party in contacting the individual and determining which witnesses should be deposed.

Rule 26(e)(1)(A) requires that the Plaintiffs supplement their Rule 26(a) disclosures "in a timely manner" upon learning that their initial disclosures were incomplete, if "the additional or corrective information has not otherwise been made known to the other parties during the discovery process."

1. *Whether supplemental disclosures were necessary*

It appears to be undisputed that the Plaintiffs did not disclose the identities of most of the 108 individuals in the Fourth Supplemental Disclosures in either their initial Rule 26(a) disclosures or in any of the three prior supplemental disclosures. They submit alternatively that: (i) they were not obligated to identify such individuals to Denver because Denver already knew about them; or (ii) they "re-disclosed" the identities of such individuals to Denver in correspondence that requested Denver to make particular document productions. Neither argument is availing.

* * * Rule 26(a)(1)(A) requires each party to identify those persons who have information that the party "may use" in support of its claims. A Rule 26 disclosure requires more than just the name of the person with such information; it also requires disclosure of the address and telephone number of the person and the information that such person has. The clear purpose of such disclosure is to permit the party receiving the disclosure to be able to understand what information the person has and to consider contacting the person in order to ascertain the significance of the individual's knowledge or to depose the individual. . . . [Although the Plaintiffs, in discovery, had requested that Denver] identify individuals who may have been victims of mistaken arrest, such identification did not tell Denver who the Plaintiffs thought might have useful information, what information that was or how to contact such person. The most that can be said about the Plaintiff's request is that it advised Denver that Plaintiffs thought that *some* of these persons *might* have information that *might* prove useful. That is not sufficient disclosure under Rule 26(a).

* * * By reviewing its own records, Denver could identify persons who were arrested based on a mistaken identity . . . . But because the purpose of the disclosure under Rule 26(a) was to inform Denver of which individuals *the Plaintiffs* believed had pertinent information, what the information was and how to contact the individual, Denver's identification of individuals in response to discovery requests did not relieve Plaintiffs of the obligation of disclosing the individuals who they thought had useful information.

The Plaintiffs also contend that they *did* disclose (in the Plaintiffs' parlance, "re-disclose") the individuals to Denver in correspondence relating to further requests for production. . . . The Plaintiffs contend that, upon receiving Denver's production of the search results, they "re-disclosed" 83 of the 100 individuals to Denver in the course of "a multitude of discovery-conferral letters," thus satisfying their obligations under Rule 26(a) and (e). . . .

This Court has reviewed those letters, and finds nothing therein that could be said to constitute the kind of designation constituted by Rule 26(a)(1)(A). . . .

* * * [T]he Plaintiffs' references to various individuals in its correspondence with Denver reflects the *starting* point of the Plaintiffs' inquiry into

whether an individual should eventually be disclosed, not the point at which the Plaintiffs have completed their inquiry and are prepared to make a disclosure subject to the Rule 26(g) certification. . . . If, as the Plaintiffs suggest, the correspondence can be deemed to be substitute disclosure, the Plaintiffs are necessarily contending that *Denver* should somehow be obligated to determine which of the 237 individuals mentioned in the . . . letter would be among the 100 that the Plaintiffs ultimately decided to use in support of their claims. Such an argument does nothing to advance the notice-giving principles underlying Rule 26(a), (e), and (g). . . .

Finally, the Plaintiffs argue that, pursuant to Rule 26(e), supplemental disclosure of the individuals was unnecessary because those individuals had been "made known" to Denver "during the discovery process" under Fed. R. Civ. P. 26(e)(1)(A)—*i.e.* in the Plaintiffs' correspondence requesting additional document production for the individuals. In this context, it is important to consider the precise language of Rule 26(e): it directs that a party must supplement a disclosure when "some material respect [of] the disclosure is incomplete" unless *"the additional . . . information"* necessary to make the disclosure complete has been previously disclosed. . . .

When one considers the purposes of Rule 26(a) disclosures—eliminating surprise, providing the opposing party with an ability to contact persons the disclosing party may use—it is clear that the information the Plaintiffs were required to disclose was *which particular* mistaken identity arrestees, culled from the pool of those revealed in Denver's search results, had information that the Plaintiffs intended to use. In this sense, the fact that the Plaintiffs had mentioned the names of the 100 individuals on the Fourth Supplemental Disclosures in prior discovery requests is not sufficient to satisfy Rule 26(e), because such requests also referred to more than a hundred other individuals that the Plaintiffs did not consider worthy of disclosure.

* * *

2. *Timeliness*

Rule 26(e) requires that any supplemental disclosures be made "timely." The obligation to supplement arises when the disclosing party reasonably should know that its prior discovery responses are incomplete, *e.g.* because the party has now obtained information it did not previously have. . . . Thus, the timeliness question is driven largely by the question of when the Plaintiffs came into possession of the documents that would lead them to identify the particular individuals they would make use of in proving their claims.

The record reflects that Denver completed a significant portion of the production requested by the Plaintiffs in February 2010, and that it had conclusively completed that production by no later than the beginning of July 2010.

Thus, the Plaintiffs' Fourth Supplemental Disclosures, made in November 2011, came some 16 months after Denver had produced all of the relevant records, nearly two years after Denver had produced a substantial amount of the total material requested.

The Plaintiffs do not offer any particular explanation as to why, in the exercise of due diligence, it required anywhere from approximately a year and a half to two years to digest the materials provided by Denver, settle on the particular arrestees that the Plaintiffs intended to use as witnesses, and to disclose those witnesses. The Plaintiffs' correspondence indicates that, although the Plaintiffs requested (and Denver produced) several thousand pages of documents, the Plaintiffs were keenly aware of basic details of most of the mistaken identity arrests, the documents that had been produced with regard to each, and the documents remaining outstanding with regard to each. . . . Thus, the Court finds that the Plaintiffs have not identified circumstances that would warrant the lengthy delay between completion of the production and the filing of the Fourth Supplemental Disclosures, and thus, the Court finds that the Plaintiffs' supplementation of its disclosures under Rule 26(e) was not timely.

C. Sanction

Having thus concluded that the Plaintiffs' Fourth Supplemental Disclosures violated Rule 26(a) and (e), the question turns to the appropriate sanction to be imposed.

The Court must choose a sanction that is both just and related to the particular issue that was implicated by the discovery violation. . . . The parties agree that *Woodworker's Supply, Inc. v. Principal Mut. Life Ins. Co.*, 170 F.3d 985, 993 (10th Cir. 1999), establishes the factors that the Court should consider in imposing a sanction: (i) the prejudice or surprise to the party entitled to receive the disclosures; (ii) the ability of that party to cure such prejudice; (iii) the extent to which allowing the undisclosed evidence would disrupt the trial; and (iv) the disclosing party's bad faith or willfulness. The Court will examine each factor in turn.

1. Prejudice to Denver

The untimeliness of the Plaintiffs' Fourth Supplemental Disclosure poses several forms of prejudice to Denver. First, and most tangibly, it resulted in the nullification of Denver's [earlier-filed] summary judgment motion [which the court denied, without prejudice,] . . . largely because the issues surrounding the admissibility of the material in the Plaintiffs' untimely disclosures bear significantly on Denver's motion. At a minimum, then, much of the time and attorney's fees already incurred by Denver in preparing and filing this motion were wasted as a result of the Plaintiffs' untimely production which, if allowed to stand, would significantly reshape the nature and contents of Denver's motion.

Similarly, the Plaintiffs' untimely production poses prejudice to Denver in the form of additional and undue delay in the resolution of this already-aged matter. If the Plaintiffs had made a timely supplemental disclosure—*i.e.* in or about July 2010, shortly after Denver's production had been completed—Denver's summary judgment motion could have been filed more than a year earlier, and if necessary, the matter could be one year closer to resolution via trial. Indeed, it can be said that all further proceedings in this case are prejudicial to Denver .... Thus, the Court finds that Denver is also prejudiced by both past and future delay in this action that is attributable to the Plaintiffs" untimely disclosures.

Denver also argues that, should the disclosures be permitted to stand, it would request an opportunity to reopen discovery to determine what information t[he] disclosed witnesses might have. Assuming, without necessarily finding, that re-opening discovery would be an appropriate remedy, the delay and expense associated with such additional discovery proceedings also represents a form of prejudice that Denver has suffered.

2. *Denver's ability to cure*

To the extent Denver's prejudice is purely monetary and quantifiable—*e.g.* attorney's fees expended in making the summary judgment motion, fees actually expended conducting any re-opened discovery—it is arguable that this prejudice could be completely cured simply by awarding Denver those attorney's fees against the Plaintiffs.

But as to the more intangible types of prejudice—undue delay of the action and the unquantifiable expenses associated therewith—a potential cure is more elusive. No award of this Court can directly compensate Denver for the delay in the resolution of the case.

3. *Trial disruption*

This factor is effectively addressed by the discussion above. Although there is no trial date set in this case, and presumably, any curative sanction would produce its effect before any trial commences, there has been, and will continue to be, significant disruption and delay to the prompt and expedient resolution of this matter as a direct result of the Plaintiffs' untimeliness.

4. *Plaintiffs' bad faith or willfulness*

The record is particularly unclear as to what activities the Plaintiffs' litigation team engaged in between the bulk of Denver's document production in February 2010 and the filing of the Fourth Supplemental Disclosures in November 2011. As recited in the chronology above, the Plaintiffs state that [their primary lawyer on these issues] . . . was permitted to withdraw in August 2010, and the Plaintiffs' lead counsel had gone on "sabbatical" from June–August 2011. Assuming—certainly without necessarily finding—these the withdrawal of the lawyer with primary responsibilities over the documents at issue here dissipates some degree of the Plaintiffs' culpability for the delay, the fact remains that from August 2010 to June 2011, a period of nearly a year, the Plaintiffs' current legal team was aware that their colleague with primary familiarity with the documents at issue here had withdrawn and that they themselves were now obligated to review and assess Denver's production and to make whatever supplemental disclosures were occasioned thereby. It is unclear how counsel spent this period, with the exception of lead counsel's "sabbatical." Although the Court does not begrudge anyone a vacation, it cannot excuse an attorney's decision to neglect unfinished and overdue work to the detriment of an opposing party.

Simply put, the Court does not find anything in the record to suggest that the Plaintiffs' counsel acted in affirmative bad faith—*e.g.* with a malicious or obstructive intent—but the Court does find that the record supports a conclusion that Plaintiffs' counsel were, at the very least, neglectful of their obligations to Denver and to the judicial process.

5. Balancing the factors and selecting a sanction

Taken as a whole, the Court finds that the *Woodworker's* factors militate in favor of a significant sanction. The Plaintiffs' untimely disclosures have worked considerable tangible and intangible prejudice to both Denver and to the Court's ability to efficiently resolve this case. Although perhaps only negligent, rather than willful, the fact remains that the Plaintiffs themselves are entirely culpable for that prejudice.

This Court finds that a sanction that disregards any *new* material in the Fourth Supplemental Disclosures is appropriate in these circumstances. Although such a sanction does not compensate Denver for the delays attendant to consideration of the Plaintiffs' Objections, it effectively restores Denver to the position it was in at the time it filed its summary judgment motion. Such a sanction is also commensurate with the degree of diligence with which the Plaintiffs themselves pursued the litigation; in other words, the Plaintiffs' disregard of their obligation to supplement their disclosures is reflected by the Court disregarding those neglected disclosures. At the same time, because the sanction only applies to materials and witnesses that were disclosed for the *first* time in the Fourth Supplemental Disclosures, the Plaintiffs enjoy the right to use any previously disclosed evidence.

B. What Must Be Supplemented

When triggered, the duty to supplement applies to a party's initial disclosures (under Rule 26(a); a party's interrogatory answers (under Rule 33), a party's responses to requests for production (under Rule 34), and a party's answers to requests for admission (under Rule 36). *See* Fed. R. Civ. P. 26(e)(1)(A). The duty also applies to any expert who must supply a written report to the opposing side and to any information given by that expert during his or her deposition. *See* Rule 26(e)(2).

Thus, by its terms, there is no general Rule 26(e)-based duty to supplement a physical or mental examination (under Rule 35) or any deposition testimony *other* than one given by an expert who is obligated to supply a written report. (The court may, in an appropriate circumstance, impose additional supplementation duties on the parties. *See* Rule26(e)(1)(B).)

C. When Must It Be Supplemented

A party's duty to supplement either its initial disclosures or its responses to interrogatories, production requests, or admission requests must be performed in "a timely manner." *See* Fed. R. Civ. P. 26(e)(1)(A). Although the Rule gives no further, fixed guidance on timing, courts have expected parties to discharge their supplementation duties "at appropriate intervals during the discovery period." *See AVX Corp. v. Cabot Corp.*, 252 F.R.D. 70, 77 (D. Mass. 2008). Such supplementation has the salutary benefit of allowing the recipient to follow up with additional discovery—during the discovery period—should it be thought necessary. The time by which an expert must supplement his or her written report (and deposition testimony, if deposed) is a bit more certain: that supplementation must occur by the time the party's pretrial disclosures come due. *See* Rule 26(e)(2).

Hypothetical

Q: Under Rule 26(e), therefore, the *duty* to supplement exists and that duty must be honored in *a timely manner*. But what must a receiving party do to *trigger* those supplementations? Must a party's attorney routinely send a "request for supplementation" to those who have answered earlier discovery requests? *Should* a party do so?

A: The Rule imposes no such obligation. *See AVX Corp. v. Cabot Corp.*, 252 F.R.D. 70, 77 (D. Mass. 2008) ("the duty to supplement is a continuing duty and a 'party may not free itself of the burden to fully comply' by placing 'a heretofore unrecognized duty of repeated requests for information on its adversary.'") (citation omitted). Thus, whether or not an adversary nudges an answering party about making a supplement, the legal *obligation* to supplement prior discovery answers will arise if the prerequisites of Rule 26(e) have occurred. Nonetheless, many attorneys have adopted an informal practice of "nudging" supplements by occasionally reminding their adversaries of this supplementation obligation, especially when it is believed that fresh, unexchanged information may have come to those adversaries' knowledge.

D. Consequences of a Failure to Supplement

Although sanctions for misbehavior in discovery is addressed comprehensively in the Policing Discovery chapter below, special repercussions follow a failure to supplement. The typical—and seemingly automatic—consequence for a failure to supplement is that the delinquent parties may not themselves use the undisclosed information in their own motion practice, hearings, or at trial (unless the judge deems the failure to supplement "substantially justified" or harmless). *See* Fed. R. Civ. P. 37(c)(1). But courts enjoy flexibility in setting an appropriate punishment. In addition to (or instead of) an evidentiary preclusion, a court may order the delinquent party to reimburse the adversary for expenses and fees caused by the failure to supplement, may inform the jury of the failure to supplement, or may impose other appropriate sanctions. *See* Rule 37(c)(1)(A)–(1)(C).

FROM CLASSROOM TO PRACTICE

The duty to supplement is an important discovery obligation that, in the frenzy and bustle of a crowded litigation practice, can be overlooked. Litigators often calendar for themselves a discovery review, at which they will double-check their own prior discovery answers to confirm that the information they have supplied is still complete and correct.

That diligence should also be reciprocated. To ensure that an adversary is equally careful and conscientious, litigators may, as discussed above, nudge their adversaries to action by serving them with a "request for supplementation." As we've learned, such a request should be unnecessary, but litigators will often prefer to have the supplemented information rather than a discovery fight before the court. Nudging an adversary into action often gets the job done. It may also make a judge more inclined to impose sanctions should the adversary fail to supplement notwithstanding not only the Rule 26(e) obligation but also a reminder sent by the other side.

Hypotheticals: Mastering the Nuances

The Lack of Follow Up: Shopper brings a false imprisonment lawsuit against Grocery Store, alleging that the store's security guard wrongfully detained her on suspicion of shoplifting. In Grocery Store's Rule 26(a)(1) initial disclosures served at the beginning of the lawsuit, Grocery Store identified, by name, three persons known to be eyewitnesses to Shopper's attempted thefts. Next to each person's name, Grocery Store wrote: "address and telephone number unknown at this time; investigation continuing." Grocery Store never served a supplement to these initial disclosures. On the second day of trial, Grocery Store announced its intent to call the three witnesses to testify after the lunch recess. Shopper's attorney immediately objected, informing the judge of the missing supplementation. Grocery Store responded by highlighting that Shopper's attorney never followed up or pressed Grocery Store for an update, nor was a motion ever filed with the court demanding a supplement. Should Grocery Store be permitted to offer the three witnesses' testimony at trial?

The Deposition Unveiling: Buyer purchased a car from Auto Maker, only to later discover that the car's front hood would sometimes pop loose. One day, while driving down a busy highway, Buyer's car hood popped loose and then opened fully, startling Buyer and obscuring his vision in a way that caused a bad crash. Buyer filed a claim against Auto Maker for product liability. Early in discovery, Buyer served Auto Maker with interrogatories requesting details on any other hood-popping incidents with this model of car. Auto Maker responded that it knew of none. During the deposition of Auto Maker's senior vice president, Buyer's attorney asked the witness whether she was aware of any hood-popping incidents. The witness answered that she was, that the company knew of three such incidents. The witness then explained the details of those three incidents in her testimony. Now aware that its prior interrogatory answer was incorrect, does Auto Maker need to have its attorney serve on Buyer's counsel a supplement containing that information?

PRACTICE SAMPLES

Sample 7-1: REQUEST FOR SUPPLEMENTATION

IN THE UNITED STATES DISTRICT COURT
DISTRICT OF WEST CAROLINA

Pat and Vickie Traggler, *individually and on behalf of* *the decedent Max Traggler,*))))	
Plaintiffs,)	
v.)	Civil Action No. 00-CV-98765
USafe Swim Co.,))	
Defendant.)	

Defendant's Request for Supplementation

Defendant USafe Swim Co. ("USafe") requests that plaintiffs Pat and Vickie Traggler, individually and on behalf of decedent Max Traggler, supplement all disclosures and discovery responses to supply any further information necessary to make those disclosures and discovery responses complete and correct, as required by Rule 26(e) of the Federal Rules of Civil Procedure. Specifically, USafe requests from the Plaintiffs supplementations to:

1. Plaintiffs' Rule 26(a) Initial Disclosures, as served on or about August 6, 20____.

2. Plaintiffs' Answers to Defendant's First Set of Interrogatories, as served on or about October 3, 20____.

3. Plaintiffs' Answers to Defendant's Second Set of Interrogatories, as served on or about January 19, 20____.

4. Plaintiffs' Answers to Defendant's Third Set of Interrogatories, as served on or about March 8, 20____.

5. Plaintiffs' Answers to Defendant's First Set of Requests for Production, as served on or about October 3, 20____.

6. Plaintiffs' Answers to Defendant's First Set of Requests for Admission, as served on or about February 1, 20____.

Respectfully submitted,

BENJARVUS, GREEN-ELLIS, LLC

By: _____/s/_____
Attorney for Defendant USafe Swim Co.

DATED: April 14, 20____

[CERTIFICATE OF SERVICE]

Sample 7-2: SUPPLEMENTATION OF INTERROGATORIES

IN THE UNITED STATES DISTRICT COURT
DISTRICT OF WEST CAROLINA

Pat and Vickie Traggler,	)	
individually and on behalf of	)	
the decedent Max Traggler,	)	
	)	
Plaintiffs,	)	
	)	
v.	)	Civil Action No. 00-CV-98765
	)	
USafe Swim Co.,	)	
	)	
Defendant.	)	

Plaintiffs' Supplemental Answers to
Defendant's First Set of Interrogatories Directed to Plaintiffs

Plaintiffs Pat and Vickie Traggler (the "Tragglers"), individually and on behalf of Max Traggler, a minor, hereby supplement their original answer to

Defendant USafe Swim Co.'s First Set of Interrogatories Directed to Plaintiffs, which Plaintiffs served on March 11, 20____, as follows:

1. The Tragglers supplement their original answer to Interrogatory No. 1 as follows: Max Traggler lived briefly at his grandparents' home—207 Maple Drive, Harbortown, West Carolina 29999—while his parents' home was undergoing an extensive renovation.

2. The Tragglers supplement their original answer to Interrogatory No. 2 as follows: See additional copies of medical records, attached.

3. The Tragglers' answers to Interrogatory Nos. 3–12 need no further supplementation at this time.

Sincerely,

KAR, PHULCONSUL, & STEADY, LLC

By: ____/s/____
Attorney for Plaintiffs

Dated: May 4, 20____

[VERIFICATION]
[CERTIFICATE OF SERVICE]

VIII

Policing Discovery

All the chapters of this book, until now, have introduced the tools and procedures of civil discovery and how they are supposed to work. It all amounts to a powerful toolbox for exchanging important information helpful in preparing for, and trying, a civil lawsuit.

When the discovery process operates as it should, proper and well-tailored requests for information are met with timely, appropriate, and substantive responses. Once concluded, the discovery process will have allowed both parties to appreciate the strengths and vulnerabilities of one another's positions, will have enabled the parties to prepare competently for trial, and will have positioned the case toward a possible negotiated resolution as the litigants become able to place a well-informed value on the lawsuit. In sum, the discovery process will have bought the Rule 1 "touchstones" of federal civil procedure a good bit closer: the "just, speedy, and inexpensive" determination of the parties' dispute.

But what if the discovery process does not work as it should? What if the parties do not cooperate with one another? What if they make unreasonable, extravagant information demands calculated to cause more pain than light? What if, without good reason, they refuse to respond to discovery requests, respond incompletely or deceptively, or otherwise frustrate the information exchange process? Conversely, what if there is a good reason for the resistance? What if discovery is sought or resisted on thoughtful grounds that the adversary, with equally thoughtful logic, disputes? What then?

This chapter is about how the parties and the courts are empowered to keep the discovery process on track and the information-exchange machinery humming. A simple fact scenario will help guide us through this array of policing procedures and tools.

Consider a business dispute among members of a large family, all in the sandwich restaurant business. While the founding grandparents (the matriarch and patriarch of the family) were alive, the business flourished. The family had opened ten separate restaurants throughout the region, and profits were flowing. But, after a time, things turned. The grandparents passed away, the economy suffered a downturn, and the family began to split badly. Some family members pressed for an aggressive investment of time and money to dramatically expand the number of restaurants as a way of increasing cash flow. Other family members advocated for a conservative retreat, proposing to open no new restaurants, close less-profitable ones, and consolidate the enterprise as a way of shielding the business until the economy rebounded. Tempers flared, animosities exploded, and soon the family members found themselves in court, angrily fighting each other for the right to control the destiny of the family business.

This chapter will rely on these battling restaurateurs—the aggressive clan versus the conservative clan—to illustrate how civil discovery is policed.

HOW THESE DISCOVERY DEVICES WORK

A powerful array of tools and procedures exists to help manage and police discovery problems. We will explore them now in turn.

A. Problems at the Outset—Discovery Planning

In the How Discovery Begins chapter, we learned that the parties are required to meet with one another at the outset of their lawsuit to talk through preliminary issues and to collaborate on preparing a joint discovery plan to be submitted in writing to the court. The hope is that this conferral will begin a collaborative working relationship among the parties, smoke out anticipated trouble areas, and propose a mutually agreeable framework for the coming discovery process.

The battling restaurateurs want no part of any such cooperative process. They are each bound and determined to accommodate nothing. The conservative clan's attorney proposes a date and location for the conference, which the aggressive clan immediately opposes. Instead, they propose an alternate date and location they know to be impossibly inconvenient to the conservative clan. A tentative discovery plan is drafted and circulated by the aggressive clan's attorney, which the conservative clan instantly attacks as unfair and devious. Nothing gets done. The parties don't meet; no joint discovery plan is ever submitted.

Here, the court is given great latitude. The court may sanction any party or attorney who fails to participate in good faith in preparing and submitting a discovery plan. The court may require the offender to pay any reasonable expenses, including attorney's fees, incurred as a consequence of that failure. Before doing so, the court must, of course, afford both parties an opportunity to be heard. *See* Fed. R. Civ. P. 37(f).

B. Problems with Mandatory Disclosures

The three types of mandatory disclosures—initial disclosures, expert disclosures, and pretrial disclosures—are designed to be exchanged automatically. Unless they are excused or modified by the Rules, by court order, or by party stipulation, they are obligatory.

Here, again, the battling restaurateurs are fighting each other mercilessly. The aggressive clan serves no initial disclosures at all (and why bother . . . that would only be helpful to the other side). The conservative clan, worried about the mandatory nature of initial disclosures, serves a set, but their disclosure is woefully incomplete. They list just two family members as witnesses and only a small handful of business documents as exhibits. Throughout the litigation, that meager list is never supplemented.

1. Sanctions

Failing to meet a mandatory disclosure requirement is a dangerous, potentially calamitous, strategy. A party who fails to provide information in its disclosures may not later use that information to support a motion, at a hearing, or at the trial itself, unless the court finds that the omission was "substantially justified" or was, under the circumstances, harmless. *See* Fed. R. Civ. P. 37(c)(1). Absent those two curing exceptions, a party who leaves a witness off its disclosure list or who fails to identify an exhibit in its disclosure list may not use that witness or exhibit later on in the lawsuit. *See id.* The debilitating ramifications of that preclusion are plain—without witnesses or evidence, a party will be hard-pressed to prove its claims or defenses.

In addition to this preclusion effect, the court may also order the failing party to pay the reasonable expenses, including attorney's fees, that its adversary suffered as a consequence of the nondisclosure and may, as yet a further sanction, even alert the jury to the failing party's behavior. *See* Rule 37(c)(1)(A)–(1)(B). Telling the jury about a discovery non-disclosure may seem an odd sanction, but it is considered by many trial attorneys to be a deeply troubling development (and, thus, an effective deterrent against non-disclosures). Why? Consider the case below.

LICHTENSTEIN
v.
UNIVERSITY OF PITTSBURGH MEDICAL CENTER

2013 WL 6577401 (W.D. Pa. 2013), *aff'd*, 598 F. Appx. 109 (3d Cir. 2015)

CONTI, Chief United States District Judge

[Jamie Lichtenstein sued her former employers for wrongful discharge. Her supervisor was deposed during discovery, testifying that Lichtenstein was given oral warnings about her tardiness at work which were, later, memorialized in written notations in Lichtenstein's employee file. But no such writings were ever identified during mandatory disclosures, or later produced during subsequent discovery.]

[As a sanction,] the court gave the following instruction to the jury:

In this case, you have heard testimony from Deborah Lidey, the supervisor . . . who terminated the Plaintiff, regarding the claimed existence of written documentation of verbal warnings that were issued to the Plaintiff. Under the applicable Court Rules, this information was required to be provided to the Plaintiff in advance of trial, and defendants did not provide that written documentation.

* * * The imposition of the sanction set forth in Rule 37(c)(1)(B) was supported by the evidence presented to the court . . . . * * * Along with cross-examination of Lidey, during closing argument, counsel for plaintiff was free to argue that Lidey lacked credibility as a witness because although she testified that plaintiff received verbal warnings and there was a written record of those warnings, defendants failed to produce that evidence to plaintiff or the jury. This is an argument that plaintiff could not have made to the jury had [defendants] produced the evidence to plaintiff.

But, even here, the array of available sanctions is sweeping. Under appropriate circumstances, and following an opportunity for the parties to be heard, the court may impose still other sanctions, instead or in addition. The Rules set out a number of options for the court to consider:

1. ***Established for the Case:*** directing that the issue or factual substance that is the subject of the discovery matter at issue be deemed as established—in the manner the prevailing party claims—for the remaining

duration of the lawsuit (for example, in the *Lichtenstein* case above, deeming it "established" that no written record of verbal warnings was ever made)

2. **Prohibition:** forbidding the failing party from supporting (or opposing) a claim or defense, or from introducing certain matters in evidence (for example, forbidding Ms. Lichtenstein's employer from offering evidence of any such written record of verbal warnings)

3. **Striking the Pleadings:** in whole or in part (for example, striking all or some pertinent portion of the answer filed by Ms. Lichtenstein's employer)

4. **Staying the Proceedings:** until the failure is remedied (for example, barring all further discovery or other trial preparation activities until the mystery written record of verbal warnings is delivered to Ms. Lichtenstein)

5. **Dismissal:** in whole or in part (for example, of any counterclaim that Ms. Lichtenstein's employer may have included in its answer)

6. **Default** (for example, terminating the lawsuit by entering a final judgment in Ms. Lichtenstein's favor)

7. **Contempt of Court** (for example, imposing on Ms. Lichtenstein's employer a per-day fine until the mystery written record of verbal warnings is produced)

See Fed. R. Civ. P. 37(c)(1)(C) (incorporating Rule 37(b)(2)(A)). As we will see, other Rules invoke this same sanctioning array when authorizing courts to discipline other sorts of discovery mischief (and, to avoid repeating this same list on each of those occasions, those later discussions will refer the reader back to the listing here, with the reference "Rule 37(b) Sanctioning Array"). As the breadth of this sanctioning authority makes clear, the power of the trial court to rein in misbehavior during mandatory disclosures is enormous.

This array of sanctions is not limited to just failures to make initial disclosures; it applies equally to all mandatory disclosures required by the Rules.

2. Motions to Compel

There is, importantly, another noteworthy tool remaining in the arsenal for policing discovery. A party enduring an opponent's failure to make a proper disclosure will still be lacking the information that the mandatory disclosures were intended to supply. Sanctions may be appropriate and helpful, but they may not be enough. Consider again our "battling restaurateurs" example. Among the required initial disclosures is the right to inspect any insurance policy that might be available to satisfy any possible judgment the lawsuit produces. The aggressive clan has made no initial disclosures at all, and the conservative clan thus has no idea whether the aggressive clan has, for their side of the family business, purchased such an insurance policy. That could be critically important information for the conservative clan to learn. If the aggressive clan has no such insurance policy in place, the conservative clan's whole litigation strategy might change. Continuing to litigate, in the absence of insurance coverage, may mean that any money damages the conservative clan could win in the lawsuit would come only from the restaurant business income. In effect, without insurance, the conservative clan might essentially be funding their own damages or might be left with an uncollectable judgment. In such a case, it may not make much sense for the conservative clan to litigate.

To cure this lack of information, the conservative clan could file a *motion to compel* with the court. The objective of a motion to compel is to *obtain* discovery that has been sought but not provided. It is a request for a court order. Before doing so, the Rules require the moving party to certify it has conferred in good faith with the other side (or has attempted, unsuccessfully, to do so) in an effort to obtain the missing discovery—in this case, the disclosure—without involving the court. *See* Fed. R. Civ. P. 37(a)(1). The motion would request the court to issue an order directing the delinquent party to make the required disclosures and may also include a request for court-ordered sanctions. *See* Rule 37(a)(3)(A).

The very prospect of the filing of a motion to compel serves as yet another pressure-point to rein in unjustified delinquency. If the court grants the motion (or if the delinquent party is nudged into action only after the motion is filed), the court "must" require the delinquent party to pay the movant's reasonable expenses incurred in making the motion, including attorney's fees. *See* Rule 37(a)(5)(A). The court will do so only after affording the parties an opportunity to be heard. *See id.* If, however, the required pre-filing good faith conferral did not occur, or if the non-disclosure was "substantially justified," or if both parties prevail in part (*e.g.,* the motion is granted in part and denied in part), or if other circumstances convince the court that an award of expenses would be unjust, the court will forebear and no expenses/fees award will be ordered (or, if ordered, the award will be apportioned accordingly). *See* Rule 37(a)(5)(A)(i)–(A)(iii) & (a)(5)(C). What constitutes "substantially justified"? Is a party's own, subjective conviction that it should not be required to make the requested disclosures enough to avoid an expenses order? Consider the case below.

PARSI

v.

DAIOLESLAM

778 F.3d 116 (D.C. Cir. 2015)

WILKINS, United States Circuit Judge

[The nonprofit advocacy group NIAC sued Daioleslam, a blogger, for making allegedly defamatory posts on a website. In discovery, to establish his defense to the allegations of defamation, Daioleslam sought certain digital calendar entries and emails that NIAC had not disclosed or produced during discovery. NIAC argued that an award of expenses was not appropriate because its non-disclosure had not been made in subjective bad faith.]

A party is "substantially justified" in opposing discovery or disobeying an order "if there is a 'genuine dispute,' or 'if reasonable people could differ as to the appropriateness of the contested action.'" *Pierce v. Underwood*, 487 U.S. 552, 565 (1988) (internal citations and brackets omitted); *see, e.g., Maddow v. Procter & Gamble Co.*, 107 F.3d 846, 853 (11th Cir. 1997) (party was substantially justified in opposing motion to compel production where it believed case law supported its position).[FN12] The substantial justification requirement serves to prevent sanctions that " 'chill' legitimate efforts at discovery."

> [FN12] The 1970 Amendment Advisory Committee Notes to Rule 37 explain the rationale behind this exemption from mandatory sanctions: "On many occasions, to be sure, the dispute over discovery between the parties is genuine, though ultimately resolved one way or the other by the court. In such cases, the losing party is substantially justified in carrying the matter to court. But the rules should deter the abuse implicit in carrying or forcing a discovery dispute to court when no genuine dispute exists. And the potential or actual imposition of expenses is virtually the sole formal sanction in the rules to deter a party from pressing to a court hearing frivolous . . . objections to discovery."

Reasonable people cannot differ about whether a party is entitled to withhold relevant documents without articulating any claim of privilege. NIAC's calendar entries were relevant to proving Daioleslam's defense, in that they might reveal meetings with officials that suggested the truth of his allegedly defamatory statements. *See* FED. R. CIV. P. 26(b)(1) ("Parties may obtain discovery regarding any nonprivileged matter that is relevant to any party's claim or defense. . . ."). [NIAC argues] that the District Court's ultimate conclusion that they had not deleted emails in bad faith demonstrates the reasonableness of their position, but this Court cannot ground its review in hindsight. . . .

[For these and other discovery missteps, the trial court awarded nearly $200,000 in monetary sanctions, a ruling the court of appeals here affirmed in large part.]

A motion to compel that is denied also can carry deterring financial consequences. If the court finds a party's motion to compel to be unmeritorious, the court may issue a protective order to safeguard the victor against the requested (but refused) disclosure and, also, "must" require the defeated movant to pay the non-movant's reasonable expenses incurred in opposing the motion, including attorney's fees. *See* Rule 37(a)(5)(B). Following an approach similar to the one it would follow had the motion been successful, the court will award expenses only after affording the parties an opportunity to be heard and will refuse to make any award if the motion is found to have been "substantially justified" or if circumstances otherwise make an award unjust. *See id.* Consequently, filing a motion to compel on a lark, merely to be aggressive or harassing, or without a formidable basis, poses serious financial risks to the movant; thus, the structure of the Rules seeks to deter baseless motions.

A closing word about monetary sanctions—the Rules, as we have seen and as we'll see again below, occasionally use the word "must" to describe a court's duty to award monetary sanctions. That feels, then, like such sanctions are always obligatory, not discretionary. In practice, however, monetary sanctions seem to be the exception, not the norm. Although the Rules often use the word "must," the court's duty is still conditioned on a finding of violation and the absence of substantial justification. Herein lies the discretion that many courts assume. Courts often sidestep mandatory monetary sanctions where the discovery failure is not repeated or egregious.

C. Problems with Responses to Interrogatories and Production Requests

Unless a court order or party stipulation provides otherwise, a litigant must respond to interrogatories and production requests within 30 days of service. *See* Fed. R. Civ. P. 33(b)(2); Rule 34(b)(2)(A). A party who serves interrogatories or production requests, yet receives no timely response, may file a motion with the court for sanctions, provided the party has first conferred (or attempted to confer) in good faith with the delinquent party to attempt to resolve the delay. *See* Rule 37(d)(1)(A)(ii) & (d)(1)(B). Depending on the circumstances, the court may impose almost any of the array of sanctions described earlier (excluding the sanction of contempt). *See* Rule 37(d)(3) (incorporating most of Rule 37(b)(2)(A)). *See generally* Rule 37(b) Sanctioning Array (listed in the Problems with Mandatory Disclosures discussion, Part B.1., above). In addition to or instead of those possible sanctions, the court "must" require the delinquent party to pay the movant's reasonable expenses caused as a consequence of non-response, including attorney's fees, unless the lack of a response was "substantially justified" or other circumstances make an expenses award unjust. *See* Rule 37(d)(3).

Again, from the requesting party's perspective, sanctions alone are usually not sufficient. That party likely still wants substantive responses to what it had sought— namely, actual answers to its interrogatories and production of the documents, tangible things, and electronically stored information it requested. To obtain that sort of order from the court, the requesting party also will have to follow the motion to compel procedures, discussed in detail above.

But a complete failure to respond is not the only (or even the most frequent) problem with interrogatories and production requests. Far more often, the opponent *will* serve a response to interrogatories and production requests, and the problem will lie with the adequacy of those responses. For example, the response may contain objections that the requesting party believes to be unfounded, or offer only a partial or unclear response, or perhaps include only a well-lawyered dodge away from a substantive answer. These sorts of *inadequate* responses can also be addressed to the court for resolution using the motion to compel procedures discussed above. *See* Rule 37(a)(3)(B)((iii)–(a)(3)(B)(iv). In this regard, one final observation is important—the Rules pronounce that any "evasive or incomplete" response to interrogatories or production requests "must be treated" as the equivalent of a failure to respond at all, with all of the ensuing sanctions again available for the admonishing court to consider using. *See* Rule 37(a)(4).

D. Special Problems with Production Requests: Electronically Stored Information

In years past, requests for production were vexing. Often, the challenge was the staggering number of boxes filled to their brims with correspondence, memoranda, file notes, articles, bylaws, board minutes, ledgers, charts, logs, statements, certificates, invoices, reports, studies, agreements, contracts, calendars, and a myriad of other types of papers. The challenge, back then, was the numbing chore of thumbing through page after page after page of this physical mountain of material looking for information useful for the litigation.

Those were the good old days. Today, requests for production are exponentially more vexing for a new reason: the breathtaking explosion in the volume of information stored not on paper but electronically. How should the discovery process deal with information that sprawls into the terabytes or exabytes of data? The sheer volumes are nearly incomprehensible. Yet, that is the task that confronts many civil litigants. The process of developing sensible systems to manage this undertaking continues to be refined, but two norms have already been codified into the discovery

Rules. The production of electronically stored information was discussed in detail in the Discovery Tools—Requests for Production chapter earlier. Now, we turn to a few unique challenges with that type of discovery that are treated with special rules.

Hypothetical

Q: Suppose the conservative clan in our family restaurateur battles believes that the aggressive clan was secretly keeping multiple sets of financial records; an "official" one that they showed the conservative clan, but also a covert, separate one that showed the substantially higher revenues their stores were actually earning. To explore this possibility, the conservative clan sent a request for production of electronically stored information to the aggressive clan, demanding digital copies of all credit charges, checks received and processed, and records of cash accepted at every one of their store locations in every city since the family business began. Assume the aggressive clan starts to gather this information but quickly discovers that the requested data will amount to many terabytes of information, all of which is intermixed with other, unrelated data, and will take months (or even years) to gather and cull. Does the aggressive clan have to undertake this awesome assignment?

A: The Rules create a procedure for this sort of circumstance. Parties are preliminarily excused from having to produce electronically stored information from sources that they identify to be "not reasonably accessible because of undue burden or cost." *See* Fed. R. Civ. P. 26(b)(2)(B). The requesting party, then, may file a motion to compel with the court, insisting on the production. *See id.* (If it were considered strategically wise to do so, the resisting party could preempt such a filing by making a filing of its own, seeking the court to enter a protective order to bar the production. *See id.*) In either case, the resisting party must bear the burden of showing that the information sought is truly "not reasonably accessible because of undue burden or cost." *See id.* If the resisting party carries that burden, the court may disallow the requested discovery in its entirety, or may set conditions on its production (such as shifting a portion of the cost of gathering and producing the information onto the requesting party), or may even order the requested production notwithstanding its burden and cost, upon a showing by the requesting party of good cause. *See id.*

Hypothetical

Q: Now suppose that the aggressive clan in our restaurant fight serves a request for production of electronically stored information on the conservative clan, asking for all emails, documents, and other data files that relate to the degree of effort the conservative clan made to market and grow the business's customer base. The conservative clan located many such files, and dutifully produced them. But it also discovered that several other, highly relevant computer files had been "corrupted" and were now no longer retrievable. The requesting party (the aggressive clan) filed a motion for sanctions, contending that the conservative clan was guilty of spoliation of key evidence. Were they guilty of spoliation?

A: The loss of electronically stored information long bedeviled the courts, with some judges imposing a draconian standard of what constituted sanctionable spoliation and other judges following a more flexible, lenient approach. National disuniformity on the issue abounded. After the issue had confounded the courts for several years, the Rules were at last amended to create a nationally consistent approach to this question, now codified in Fed. R. Civ. P. 37(e):

- No sanctions for spoliation may be considered unless there was a duty to preserve it (a duty discussed in greater detail in the Discovery Tools—Requests for Production chapter above).

- Assuming such a duty existed, no sanctions for spoliation may be imposed if the lost data can be recovered or duplicated.

- If the data loss occurred *despite* reasonable efforts made to preserve it (for example, if the loss occurred because of some random public utility failure that unexpectedly incinerated the neighborhood power grid), again, no sanctions for spoliation may be imposed even though the data cannot be recovered or duplicated.

- However, if the data loss occurred *because* a party failed to take reasonable efforts to preserve it *and* if the other party is prejudiced as a result of the loss of the information, the court will order measures appropriate to cure that prejudice suffered by the requesting party.

  - (Note—the measures imposed by the court must not be punitive; instead, they must be limited to effecting a cure, and no more, and may not include the severe sanctions listed in the next bullet entry below.)

- Finally, if the data loss occurred because the responding party *acted with the intent to deprive* the requesting party of the information's use during the lawsuit, then the court may impose aggressive sanctions: (a) it may presume the lost data would have been unfavorable to the responding party, (b) it may instruct the jury that it may (or must) presume the same, or (c) it may dismiss the lawsuit or enter a judgment by default.

So, now, following this amendment to Rule 37(e), the analysis of whether to sanction the conservative clan for their "corrupted" data files is far clearer. First, was there a duty on the part of the conservative clan to preserve those now-"corrupted" files? That will likely depend on when the corruption occurred and whether, at that time, litigation between the conservative clan and aggressive clan on marketing behavior was imminent. For purposes of argument, let's assume a duty of preservation existed. Second, can the "corrupted" files be recovered by the intervention of skilled information technology experts? If it can, no sanctions are permitted. If it can't, the analysis continues. Third, did the "corruption" to the data files occur notwithstanding the conservative clan's reasonable efforts to maintain the safety of those files? If the files were stored on the business's central computer with adequate controls to protect the integrity of that information (as one might assume, if this were the business's primary means for data retention), no sanctions are permitted. But if the conservative clan recklessly downloaded unsecure files onto their computer, failed to maintain responsible anti-virus and anti-malware programs, and otherwise treated their data files indifferently, the analysis continues. Fourth, does the loss of access to the "corrupted" files prejudice the aggressive clan? If it doesn't, no sanctions are permitted. If it does, remediating measures may be appropriate, but only to the degree necessary to cure that prejudice. If, however, the loss of access to the "corrupted" files was caused by the conservative clan's deliberate uploading of a computer-damaging software, made with the intent to ensure that deprivation, then the full measure of sanctions described in Rule 37(e) will be permitted.

E. Problems with Responses to Requests for Admission

Requests for admission always merit an attorney's special attention. Recall that this discovery device contains its own, built-in litigation grenade, ready to explode in the lap of the careless litigant. The Rules require that a party respond to requests for admission within 30 days of being served. Failure to do so (absent a court order or party stipulation) can be devastating—all such unanswered requests are considered, by operation of the Rule, to have been admitted. *See* Fed. R. Civ. P. 36(a)(3). Such automatic admissions can be withdrawn if the court so orders, but only if doing so will promote the presentation of the lawsuit's merits and not prejudice the opponent's presentation or defense. *See* Rule 36(b). Unintentional admissions can be truly devastating—both to the case and to an attorney's career.

Attorneys sometimes try to sidestep this admission risk by timely responding, albeit with only an objection or some oblique answer. In such a case, the requesting party may file a motion with the court to "determine the sufficiency" of the response. If the response was an objection, the court will order that an answer be served if the court finds the objection improper. *See* Rule 36(a)(6). If the response was substantive but insufficient, the court may order either that the matter requested be considered admitted for the purposes of the litigation or that the responding party substitute an amended answer for the insufficient one. *See id.*

Another foolhardy tactic is to timely respond to a request for admission by denying it, irrespective of the truth of the matter requested. This tactic carries its own penalty. If a party is later able to prove as true what the responding party improperly denied, the court must order the denying party to reimburse the proving party for the reasonable expenses, including attorney's fees, it incurred in making that proof. *See* Rule 37(c)(2). Of course, no such reimbursement order will be entered: if the request, when made, was objectionable; if the admission requested "was of no substantial importance"; if the denying party had reasonable grounds for believing as it did; or if other good reasons exist for the denial. *See id.*

Hypothetical

Q: Anticipating their use of key documents at trial, the conservative clan in our family restaurateur battle might have served requests for admission on their opponents which, among other things, asked for an admission that certain of those key documents were authentic for purposes of their admissibility at trial. Just to be belligerent, the aggressive clan denied each and every document authenticity request. Assume they had no genuine, factual basis for doing so. Will that misbehavior excuse the conservative clan of the chore of proving those documents authentic at trial?

A: No. The conservative clan will now have to summon document custodian witnesses to appear at trial and testify as to each document's authenticity. But because they lacked any responsible ground for opposing authenticity, the aggressive clan will likely be ordered to reimburse the expenses (including counsel fees) incurred in making those trial-day authenticity proofs (unless the documents at issue were "of no substantial importance" in the lawsuit). *See* Fed. R. Civ. P. 37(c)(2).

F. Problems with Depositions

As we learned in the Discovery Tools—Depositions chapter earlier, oral depositions are considered by many trial attorneys to be the most agile, effective, and productive of the various discretionary discovery tools. But here, unlike almost every other discovery procedure, the attorneys (and, sometimes, their parties) are actually eyeball-to-eyeball with one another. They are, most often, sitting physically across a conference table from each other, and with that proximity, the risk for mischief soars as the examples below illustrate.

Hypothetical

Q: The conservative clan's attorney may have decided to take the oral deposition of one of the parties, say, the senior member of the aggressive clan. The conservative clan issues and properly serves a notice of deposition on the person to be deposed. That witness, however, fails to appear at the appointed time to testify. What option does the conservative clan have to remedy this non-appearance?

A: The Rules permit the conservative clan to file a motion for sanctions for this non-appearance. See Fed. R. Civ. P. 37(d)(1)(A)(i) & (d)(1)(B). The court may grant the conservative clan's motion, choosing, once again, from among most of the array of sanctions described earlier. See Rule 37(d)(3) (incorporating Rule 37(b)(2)(A), but excluding the sanction of contempt). See generally Rule 37(b) Sanctioning Array (listed in the Problems with Mandatory Disclosures discussion, Part B.1., above). Whether instead of or in addition to those possible sanctions, the court "must" require the delinquent party to pay the movant's reasonable expenses caused as a consequence of non-response, including attorney's fees, unless the lack of a response was "substantially justified" or other circumstances make an expenses award unjust. See Rule 37(d)(3).

Hypothetical

Q: Now, let's assume the aggressive clan's senior member does, in fact, show up to be deposed, but, during her deposition, she refuses to answer the attorney's questions or does so only in an evasive or incomplete manner. What options, then?

A: In that instance, the questioning attorney may file a motion to compel, abiding by the procedures detailed above. *See* Fed. R. Civ. P. 37(a)(3)(B)(i) & (a)(4). The questioning attorney even has the option of adjourning the current deposition in order to file that motion, or instead may complete the questioning and then file the motion later. *See* Rule 37(a)(3)(C).

Hypothetical

Q: Maybe it is not the witness who misbehaves during the deposition, but her defending attorney. Perhaps that attorney objects to the questioning in a manner that is improperly verbose, argumentative, or suggestive of some preferred answer. Or maybe the attorney improperly instructs the witness not to answer a question. What, then?

A: In each of those instances, the deposition may be suspended in order to allow the questioning attorney to file a motion with the court to remedy the defending attorney's misbehavior (or may, if the attorney so chooses, complete the deposition and seek sanctions afterwards). *See* Fed. R. Civ. P. 30(c)(2). Conversely, if the *questioning* attorney misbehaves—by, for example, conducting the deposition in bad faith or in a way to unreasonably annoy, embarrass, or oppress the witness—the defending counsel can likewise suspend the deposition in order to file a motion. *See* Rule 30(d)(3)(A). The court is empowered to terminate or limit the scope of a deposition, *see* Rule 30(d)(3)(B), or to issue appropriate sanctions (including reasonable expenses and attorney's fees) against anyone who impedes, delays, or frustrates an oral deposition, *see* Rule 30(d)(2).

G. Problems with Physical/Mental Exams

Examinations of a party's body or mind can only occur upon motion and court order (or agreement of the parties). *See* Fed. R. Civ. P. 35(a). If a court issues such an order and the party fails to appear for examination, the court may impose nearly any of the array of sanctions described earlier. *See* Rule 37(b)(2)(B) (incorporating Rule 37(b)(2)(A), but excluding the sanction of contempt). *See generally* Rule 37(b)(2) (B) (incorporating Rule 37(b)(2)(A)). The court, however, will forebear from imposing any such sanctions if the non-complying party shows it was unable to produce the examinee. *See id.*

H. Problems with Disobedience to a Court's Discovery Orders

The motion to compel procedures were introduced and explained above. Motions to compel are filed to invite the court to issue an order directing that another party make some past-due disclosure or respond to some unanswered (or inadequately answered) discovery request. If the court grants the requested motion, the stakes rise. A court order is then at issue, and continued intransigence constitutes a disobedience of the judge. With only a few exceptions, discussed above, the familiar array of sanctions become once again available to the court in reining in this disobedience. *See* Fed. R. Civ. P. 37(b)(2)(A). *See generally* Rule 37(b) Sanctioning Array (listed in the Problems with Mandatory Disclosures discussion, Part B.1., above). A party seeking a remedy for disobedience of a court's discovery order need not first convene a meet-and-confer session with the adversary.

FROM CLASSROOM TO PRACTICE

Discovery fights do not occur in every lawsuit. Nasty discovery fights are rarer still. But they happen. The authors of this book practiced complex civil litigation in federal court for many years, and our own personal experiences and those of our colleagues encountering strategically uncooperative, and downright nasty, misbehavior in discovery cannot be counted on just one hand (or even both hands and more than a few toes). So, preparing for uncooperative behavior in discovery and aggressive discovery fights merits some discussion.

  If civil lawsuits are fairly analogized to "battles" in business suits, then discovery is the part that most closely resembles hand-to-hand combat. It is not an overstatement to say that few battles are as pitched and ferocious as discovery fights can sometimes prove to be. The stakes are high, the clients' animosities can filter through to the attorneys, and the fighting occurs at close range. The contests are also easily polarized. Requests in discovery that seem excessive are sometimes characterized as vicious attempts to ratchet up the litigation nastiness and pain to a point that will compel a capitulation. Efforts to resist discovery requests are sometimes characterized as evil attempts to hide smoking guns that would otherwise reveal the black-hearted motivations of the possessor. It's hard to be civil with those sorts of perspectives.

So, judges are left to sort through this melee. In theory, the Rules supply judges with the impressive arsenal of tools outlined above to police discovery. In practice, judges are often exhausted and exasperated by these fights. On occasion, they might attempt to defuse the conflict in the hope that a clearer perspective might win the day.

ZENITH RADIO CORP.
v.
MATSUSHITA ELEC. INDUS. COMPANY

478 F. Supp. 889 (E.D. Pa. 1979),
vacated sub nom. on other grounds, 631 F.2d 1069 (3d Cir. 1980)

BECKER, United States District Judge

[Plaintiff radio and television companies filed antitrust lawsuits charging certain Japanese companies with conspiring to "take over the American consumer electronic products industry." Attorneys described the lawsuits as "so massive as to make them unique in the annals of United States antitrust and trade regulation litigation." Faced with a monumental discovery management task, the presiding judge issued a creative order designed to mitigate discovery burdens on everyone.]

"Time Out" Rule

A. Statement of Rule

For no good cause shown` each side will be entitled to three (3) time outs between now and the date of trial. A time out is defined as a one week period in which no discovery can be served, all deadlines are postponed and counsel can generally goof off.

1. The procedure for calling a time out will be as follows:

Both plaintiffs and defendants will designate one individual as the official time out persons (hereinafter referred to as the "Designated Whistler"). The designated whistler will be issued a whistle from the case liaison logistics committee which will be strung around his, her or its neck. When a time out is desired, the designated whistler will go to the offices of opposing lead counsel . . . and blow the whistle three (3) times. Thereafter there will be a one (1) week time out.

2. As stated above, each side is entitled to three time outs. However during the period of the two month warning (See Part B below) each side will be entitled to only one time out, providing that side still has remaining at least one time out.

3. Time outs must not be called on two consecutive one week periods. That is there must be an intervening week between time out periods. This rule is designed to prevent counsel from spending more than one week of their time with their family, friends, partners and associates.

4. As stated above, each side will be entitled to only three time outs. Any attempt by any side to exceed this three time out limit will be regarded by the Court as a serious infraction of the rules (hereinafter "illegal use of whistle"). The sanction for illegal use of whistle will be that such counsel attempting to exceed the three time outs will have his, her or its desk moved five yards (in the event of a non-flagrant violation) or fifteen yards (in the event of a flagrant infraction) further from the jury box at trial.

B. Two Month Warning

As stated above, there will be a two month warning. Such a two month warning will be called by the Court two months prior to trial. At this point, there will be a three day stoppage of the clock in which all counsel will be required to get their personal affairs in order. Personal affairs will include such items as Last Will and Testament, final instructions to spouse and family, arrangements for publication of memoirs and other less important details. During the two month warning, the clock will run continuously except for time outs described in Part A above.

> * No good cause shown is defined as family events, such as anniversaries, birthdays, sporting events involving siblings, laziness, genuine ennui (pronounced NUE); drunkenness, firm events, such as annual dinner dance or outing; and anything else which helps attorneys to keep their sanity during the course of these proceedings.

More often, judges just settle in and try to hammer through to a resolution. But, prevailing over that effort is a frustration with the frequency, tone, incivility, and, occasionally, incorrigibility of these fights. Consider this candid opinion of one who has long labored in the fields of discovery fights:

NETWORK COMPUTING SERVICES CORP.
v.
CISCO SYSTEMS, INC.

223 F.R.D. 392 (D.S.C. 2004)

ANDERSON, Chief United States District Judge

Before addressing the question of whether sanctionable conduct has occurred and, if so, what sanction is appropriate, the court will briefly recount its experience with discovery disputes in recent years. Unlike a majority of District Judges who routinely relegate discovery disputes to Magistrate Judges, this court has always heard and decided its own discovery matters. After seventeen years on the bench, the undersigned has concluded that, despite the best efforts of Congress, the Advisory Committee on Civil Rules and other similar bodies, litigation expenses continue to rise, often due to ever-increasing discovery demands and ensuing discovery disputes. As Judge Patrick Higginbotham has observed, "The discovery beast has yet to be tamed."

Additionally, refereeing contentious discovery disputes is, in my view, perhaps the most unwelcome aspect of a trial judge's work. For example, United States District Judge Wayne Alley once vented his displeasure with discovery battles in the following order:

> . . . If the recitals in the briefs from both sides are accepted at face value, neither side has conducted discovery according to the letter and spirit of the Oklahoma County Bar Association Lawyer's Creed. This is an aspirational creed not subject to enforcement by this Court, but violative conduct does call for judicial disapprobation at least. If there is a hell to which disputatious, uncivil, vituperative lawyers go, let it be one in which the damned are eternally locked in discovery disputes with other lawyers of equally repugnant attributes. *Krueger v. Pelican Prod. Corp.*, No. 87–2385–A (W.D. Okla. Feb. 24, 1989).

Resolving contentious discovery disputes is especially difficult in those cases (and there are many) where both sides have behaved badly. Judges often find themselves in a position similar to NFL referees, who have to peel the

316 PRACTICING CIVIL DISCOVERY

players off of each other in an effort to find the player in the middle who started the melee. The answer is not always clear and the decision of what sanction, if any, to impose is especially difficult where there is a degree of fault on both sides.

Also, numerical inflation appears to be setting in. In past years, discovery battles typically involved "thousands of documents." Recently, however, one attorney suggested to me at a discovery hearing that, including the request for electronic mail communications, a production request was "likely to exceed one million pages." Further, the parties often overreach in their discovery requests[FN.5] and stonewall interrogatories from their opponents.[FN.6] Hardball discovery, which is still a problem in some cases,[FN.7] is costly to our system and consumes an inordinate amount of judicial resources.

> [FN.5] As one court colorfully observed: Even if one is entitled to embark on a fishing expedition, one must at least use "rod and reel, or even a reasonably sized net [; not] drain the pond and collect the fish from the bottom." *In re IBM Peripheral EDP Devices Antitrust Litig.,* 77 F.R.D. 39, 42 (N.D. Cal. 1977).

> [FN.6] I have presided over one discovery dispute where the defendant's attorney objected to an interrogatory, which essentially sought the names of witnesses, on the grounds that it was burdensome and oppressive, while at the same time propounding an identically-worded question in his own interrogatories.

> [FN.7] I hasten to add that not all civil disputes involve extensive discovery requests or hardball discovery tactics. In many cases, litigants and their attorneys behave professionally throughout the litigation.

In addition, this court's own firsthand observation of discovery expenditures in civil litigation yields the inescapable conclusion that litigants expend enormous amounts of money on discovery in cases that do not even make it to trial. A recent case on this court's docket is illustrative. [That case] involved two female employees who had sued their corporation for sexual harassment in state court. The claimed harassment involved one corporate officer who allegedly groped and inappropriately touched the two employees in the privacy of his office, with no third party witnesses. The claims asserted in the cases were all state law claims for assault and battery, intentional infliction of emotional distress, and the like. There were no complicated Title VII claims or other unique issues in either of the cases—the cases presented a pure swearing contest involving no more than three potential eyewitnesses (the two victims and the defendant). The cases eventually settled prior to trial. The controversy made its way to this court's docket in a declaratory judgment action brought by the insurance companies who refused to provide a defense. In that case, which only involved state law claims, the defense team spent a staggering $1.5 million to engage in discovery prior to settling the cases.

In light of the preceding, this court has reluctantly concluded that changes to the rules of civil procedure and other well-intentioned reforms will have only a marginal impact in those cases where abusive and hardball discovery practices occur. It is the undersigned's sincere belief that contentious and expensive discovery battles will continue to present challenges to the judicial system, and that these challenges should be answered by trial judges, who occupy the best vantage point from which to resolve these controversies.

Ergo, some advice is prudent in this delicate arena. A tepid welcome (at best) awaits any party to a discovery dispute. Judges do not bound from their beds each morning in the gleeful hope that some new discovery fight will be sitting atop their desks in chambers. But appreciating this reality is useful and, if navigated skillfully, an advantage.

First, overreaching is rarely rewarded when discovery turns into a fight. The well-tailored, measured discovery request is far better positioned than one that asks for an unwieldy, virtually unlimited amount or type of information. Similarly, resisting a discovery request as posed, but offering some type of credibly balanced middle-ground, is likely to strike an exasperated judge as sensible and responsible. Victory in a discovery dispute often turns on simple reasonableness. The more reasonable a request or a resistance, the more likely it is to prevail.

Second, being right on the law and facts matters. The procedures for conducting discovery are mature ones; most have been around for more than three-quarters of a century. They should be well-known and carefully read. The scope of allowable discovery depends on the individual claims and defenses, to be sure, but here, too, robust precedent often exists to inform the way—at least by example. A sound command of the discovery tools, of the breath of permitted discovery as interpreted in the controlling jurisdiction, and of how the requests pair (or do not pair) with the case's claims and defenses is critical.

Third, the wise attorney approaches every discovery dispute meet-and-confer opportunity not only in good faith, but with a thoughtfully considered strategy. Achieving a compromise may sometimes be unrealistic but proposing one that is then brusquely rejected creates a helpful record. Always think of the meet-and-confer process as having two objections: first, as an opportunity to actually resolve disputes; and, second, as building for the court a record of reasonable behavior in the event no resolution is reached. Memorialize oral discussions with a written confirmation, and draft that confirmation as though it might be an exhibit demonstrating how reasonably you have behaved; again, reasonableness often wins.

Fourth, clarity of argument counts. An angry, stumbling, blunderbuss argument will usually come across as strident and unyielding, not the model of reasonableness the discovery advocate should be aspiring to convey. Conversely, a calm, organized, and articulate presentation, crisply setting out a measured position anchored in precedent or scholarship, is likely to inspire confidence in the advocate and favor for the position.

Fifth, the equitable maxim of "unclean hands"[1] applies, at least indirectly, to discovery fights. A history of discovery missteps darkens the prospects of any litigant. So, too, does discovery fight recidivism. Judges who are repeatedly called upon to umpire shrill discovery battles are likely to arrive annoyed, impatient, and intolerant. When the time comes for you to file a discovery motion (and that time will most certainly come), you don't want to arrive marred with bad history or a poor reputation for discovery cooperation. Ideally, you should enter any discovery fray free from current or prior blame (or, at least, as the victor in any controversy that came before).

Discovery fights will occur, and most civil litigants will have their full share of them. Positioning those fights well, especially given the courts' displeasure in refereeing them, can make all the difference.

Hypotheticals: Mastering the Nuances

Pure-Hearted Omissions: Deliberately failing to include a witness or an exhibit on an initial disclosure or pretrial disclosure, or failing to disclose a testifying expert witness and supply an expert report, will preclude the nondisclosing party from using those witnesses or exhibits as motion support, at a hearing, or at trial. What if the omission was unintentional? Or, what if the omission occurred because the witness or exhibit had not yet been discovered? Can a party who fails to disclose a witness or exhibit as required by the mandatory disclosure rules fix that omission?

---

1. *See generally Precision Instrument Mfg. Co. v. Auto. Maint. Mach. Co.*, 324 U.S. 806, 814–15 (1945) (explaining "the equitable maxim that 'he who comes into equity must come with clean hands'" as "far more than a mere banality. It is a self-imposed ordinance that closes the doors of a court of equity to one tainted with inequitableness or bad faith relative to the matter in which he seeks relief, however improper may have been the behavior of the defendant. That doctrine is rooted in the historical concept of court of equity as a vehicle for affirmatively enforcing the requirements of conscience and good faith. This presupposes a refusal on its part to be 'the abetter of iniquity.' Thus while 'equity does not demand that its suitors shall have led blameless lives,' as to other matters, it does require that they shall have acted fairly and without fraud or deceit as to the controversy in issue.") (citations omitted).

Half-Hearted Omissions: Failing to disclose or to respond to a discovery request is a basis for sanctions. But what if the party provides a disclosure or a response, but crafts it in a way that is deliberately obscuring or misleading? For example, what if the battling restaurateurs supplied a set of initial disclosures that contained this disclosure of the witnesses having discoverable information that may be used to support its claims or defenses: "All our employees." Or, what if the battling restaurateurs answered an interrogatory that asked for total profits earned annually by each their restaurants, but provided only this response: "A lot." In both cases, a response was, technically, given. Is there a remedy for these sorts of disclosures and discovery responses?

PRACTICE SAMPLES

Sample 8-1: MOTION TO COMPEL

IN THE UNITED STATES DISTRICT COURT
DISTRICT OF WEST CAROLINA

Daphne Genoa, Robert Genoa,	)	
Alex Hinton, Maggie Hinton,	)	
Connie Genoa, Mitchell Genoa,	)	
Horace Genoa, and Mandy Berry,	)	
	)	
Plaintiffs,	)	
	)	
v.	)	Civil Action No. 00-CV-98765
	)	
Stephanie Woodard, Albert Woodard,	)	
Pat Pitts, Yvonne Pitts,	)	
Bert Genoa, Max Genoa, and	)	
Veronica Genoa,	)	
	)	
Defendants.	)	

<u>Motion to Compel Substantive Responses</u>
<u>to Interrogatories and Production Requests</u>
<u>and for Sanctions</u>

Plaintiffs Daphne Genoa, Robert Genoa, Alex Hinton, Maggie Hinton, Connie Genoa, Mitchell Genoa, Horace Genoa, and Mandy Berry (collectively, "Genoa Family") filed this lawsuit against defendants Stephanie Woodard, Albert Woodard, Pat Pitts, Yvonne Pitts, Bert Genoa, Max Genoa, and Veronica Genoa (collectively, "Woodard Family") to resolve disputed questions of operational control over a shared asset, a ten-store sandwich business. In accordance with Rules 37(a)(3)(B)(iii) and 37(a)(3)(B)(iv) of the Federal Rules of Civil Procedure, the Genoa Family respectfully requests that this Court order the Woodard Family to supply substantive responses to outstanding interrogatories and production requests, and further, that this Court impose monetary sanctions against the Woodard Family in accordance with Rules 37(b)(2), 37(a)(4)–(a)(5), and 37(d)(3) in an amount appropriate to reimburse the Genoa Family for the reasonable expenses, including attorney's fees, incurred in making this motion, and for other expenses incurred in the delay. In support of this Motion, the Genoa Family states as follows:

Motion to Compel Interrogatory Answers

1. On July 1, 20___, the Genoa Family properly served counsel for the Woodard Family with Plaintiffs' First Set of Interrogatories Directed to All Defendants, with contained five interrogatories.

2. In accordance with Rules 6(d) and 33(b)(2) of the Federal Rules of Civil Procedure, answers and objections were due 30 days following service (with three additional days to accommodate for service by mail), or Monday, August 5, 20___.

3. The Woodard Family served their responses belatedly, on Friday, August 17, 20___. The responses were not just late, but evasive and incomplete:

    a. To Interrogatory No. 1, which asked for a description of each Defendant's job and responsibility in the sandwich shop business, the response given was: "All defendants work there, and work hard."

    b. To Interrogatory No. 2, which asked for the hours worked at the sandwich shop business by each Defendant during each week in 20___ and 20___, the response given was: "See answer to Interrogatory No. 1."

    c. For Interrogatory No. 3, which asked for a description of each Defendant's personal responsibility for accounting, bookkeeping, and other financial tasks for the sandwich shop business, the response given was: "See answer to Interrogatory No. 1."

    d. For Interrogatory No. 4, which asked whether each Defendant maintained any job or occupation for compensation during 20___ and 20___ other than the sandwich shop business, the response given was: "Objection, this request seeks information that is not discoverable."

e. For Interrogatory No. 5, which asked whether each Defendant had vacationed away physically from the sandwich shop business during 20___ and 20___ and, if so, for the time spans of those absences, the response given was: "Objection, this request seeks information that is not discoverable."

4. Each of the first three responses was improper. Interrogatory Nos. 1, 2, and 3 sought specific, factual information concerning each Defendant's workplace job and responsibility, hours worked, and financial obligations. The responses provided no substantive responses to any of these three interrogatories and, thus, are facially deficient. *See* Fed. R. Civ. P. 37(a)(3)(C) (confirming that "an evasive or incomplete . . . answer or response must be treated as a failure to . . . answer, or respond").

5. The last two responses purported to assert objections on the basis of relevance. First, any such objections are considered waived because they were not asserted within the 30-day period established by Rule 33(b)(2). *See Davis v. Fendler*, 650 F.2d 1154, 1160 (9th Cir. 1981) ("Generally, in the absence of an extension of time or good cause, the failure to object to interrogatories within the time fixed by Rule 33, FRCivP, constitutes a waiver of any objection."). Second, the information sought is abundantly relevant for purposes of federal civil discovery. As the U.S. Supreme Court has confirmed, information sought in discovery is properly relevant if it "bears on, or . . . reasonably could lead to other matter that could bear on" a claim or defense in this lawsuit. *Oppenheimer Fund, Inc. v. Sanders*, 437 U.S. 340, 351 (1978). Because the information sought in Interrogatory Nos. 4 and 5 relates to the Defendants' personal availability for (or absence from) work at the physical sandwich shop locations, the requested discovery readily satisfies this standard.

6. On August 31, 20___, the undersigned counsel emailed counsel for the Woodard Family, advising of the deficiency in these interrogatory answers and requesting an immediate supplementation. Counsel for the Woodard Family responded by email that same day, advising: "Our responses stand as written; we will serve no supplementation."

Motion to Compel Production Request Responses

7. On July 1, 20___, the Genoa Family also properly served counsel for the Woodard Family with Plaintiffs' First Set of Requests for Production of Documents, Tangible Things, and Electronically Stored Information.

8. The Production Requests sought the right to inspect six categories of information, namely: (a) the financial and banking records of each sandwich shop operated by the Defendants; (b) the advertising and marketing files for each such shop; (c) the payroll records for each such shop; (d) the time sheets for each employee at each such shop; (e) all files, correspondence, and emails concerning the hours and personnel coverage at each such shop; and (f) all financial forecasts and projections for each such sandwich shop for 20___, 20___, and 20___.

9. Responses to these Production Requests were due, in accordance with Rules 6(d) and 34(b)(2)(a) of the Federal Rules of Civil Procedure, 30 days following service (with three additional days to accommodate for service by mail), or Monday, August 5, 20___.

10. On August 31, 2020, the undersigned counsel emailed counsel for the Woodard Family, advising of the past-due status of the production requests, and asking for an immediate service of responses. Counsel for the Woodard Family responded by email that same day, advising: "We have no intention, now or in the future, of responding to your offensive production requests."

11. The Woodard Family's counsel's informal, conclusory declaration that the Production Requests were "offensive" is woefully improper. First, no objections could be properly lodged to these Production Requests; the time for objecting had long since lapsed. *See In re U.S.*, 864 F.2d 1153, 1156 (5th Cir. 1989) ("We readily agree with the district court that as a general rule, when a party fails to object timely to interrogatories, production requests, or other discovery efforts, objections thereto are waived."). Second, even had counsel's email not been weeks late, the "offensive" contention would not qualify as a proper objection. *See* Rule 34(b)(2)(B) (objections to production requests must "state with specificity the grounds for objecting to the request, including the reasons"). Plainly, the Woodard Family's counsel failed to do so.

12. As of September 6, 20___, the Woodard Family has still served no responses of any kind to the Production Requests.

Motion for Sanctions

13. As the certification accompanying this Motion verifies, the undersigned counsel has attempted in good faith to obtain the delinquent discovery from the Woodard Family by contacting counsel. As the representations in Paragraphs 6 and 10 recite, the attempt was unsuccessful in obtaining substantive responses to Plaintiffs' interrogatories and document requests.

14. In accordance with Rule 37(a)(5)(A), the party prevailing on a motion to compel is entitled to receive, following an opportunity for the parties to be heard, a reimbursement for its reasonable expenses incurred in obtaining the relief it requested unless the nonresponses were substantially justified. Here, no such claim of justification has even been offered.

15. In accordance with Rule 37(a)(4), an evasive or incomplete discovery response constitutes a failure to respond. Failures to respond, in turn, permit the court to enter an appropriate further sanction. Here, the Genoa Family seek, as a sanction, the payment of reasonable expenses, including attorney's fees, caused by the Woodard Family's failure to properly respond. The Genoa Family request a conference with the Court during which those additional expenses and fees might be itemized and examined.

WHEREFORE, Plaintiffs Genoa Family respectfully request that their motion to compel and motion for sanctions be granted.

Respectfully submitted,

BEAUFORD, ANDERSON, & BILTMORE, LLC
By: ____/s/_____
Attorney for Plaintiffs Genoa Family

Dated: September 5, 20____

[CERTIFICATE OF SERVICE]

BENJARVUS, GREEN-ELLIS, LLC

By: ____/s/_____
Attorney for Defendant
Louisville Lawnmower, Inc.

**CERTIFICATE OF GOOD FAITH ATTEMPTS TO RESOLVE
DISCOVERY DISPUTE**

Counsel for Plaintiffs Genoa Family hereby certifies to the Court that a good faith attempt to resolve the present discovery dispute was attempted, as follows:

• On August 31, 20____, undersigned counsel sent, by email directed to counsel for Defendants Woodard Family, a written request that substantive responses be served immediately to the inadequately answered Plaintiffs' First Set of Interrogatories Directed to all Defendants and to the as-yet unanswered Plaintiffs' First Set of Requests for Production of Documents, Tangible Things, and Electronically Stored Information.

• On that same day, August 31, 20____, counsel for Defendants Woodard Family responded by email, stating as follows:

    ○ To the request for a supplementation to the Woodard Family's responses to the interrogatories: "Our responses stand as written; we will serve no supplementation."

    ○ To the request for responses to the production requests: "We have no intention, now or in the future, of responding to your offensive production requests."

                    Respectfully submitted,

                    BEAUFORD, ANDERSON, & BILTMORE, LLC
                    By: ____/s/_____
                    Attorney for Plaintiffs Genoa Family
                    Dated:

Dated: September 5, 20____

IX

Discovery Planning and Strategy

GETTING THE VIEW

Understanding the *mechanics* of discovery—the scope of discovery, the limitations and protections on discoverability, and the nuts and bolts of the various discovery techniques—are necessary prerequisites to being successful in the discovery phase of civil litigation. But they are not the only prerequisites. While it is impossible to be effective in discovery without a thorough understanding of the discovery mechanics, appreciating the *strategy* of discovery can make the difference between a bland, idle, superficial use of this enormous discovery power and sharply focused, efficient, and productive discovery that will contribute to a favorable litigation outcome. There are two key mindsets that are instrumental to *strategic discovery*.

A. Be Thoughtful and Case-Specific

The first is to approach discovery thoughtfully and idiosyncratically. In other words, skilled litigators think about the approach to discovery that best fits the specific case they are working on, rather than rotely following the patterns they typically use. For example, an attorney might have a favorite set of sample interrogatories she uses in personal injury cases. That's a fine start, but just a start. The careful attorney will take that favored sample and tailor the questions to explore the peculiar circumstances of each given case. Likewise, in most cases, attorneys tend to serve at least one round of written discovery (at a minimum, production requests) before taking any depositions. This sequence offers an important advantage to the requesting attorney—it will allow that attorney to use the documents produced in response to that production request while preparing for and conducting those depositions. It's an approach that is likely prudent in most cases. Sometimes, however, it may be more advantageous to reverse that approach, to take the opponents' depositions as soon as possible, to pin down their stories early in the case and prevent them from conforming or reconciling their testimony with the documents.

Similarly, many depositions start typically with a fairly standard recital of the procedures and conventions for the deposition. The lawyer taking the deposition explains the process, the need for verbal responses, the difficulties for the court reporter if the lawyer and witness talk over each other, protocols for taking breaks, etc. After these routine announcements, most depositions then proceed to background information about the witness's educational and work history. This early sequence can lead to a cleaner transcript and can allow the witness to relax and, ideally, may promote less guarded and more forthcoming testimony. Sometimes, however, deferring those preliminaries, or even skipping them altogether, and instead launching right into the heart of the matter with tough questions may be more effective, catching the witness off guard. There are countless other illustrations, but the point is the same. Discovery should never be a lock-step march along the same procedural path followed in every case. Discovery is power, and it needs to be adjusted and tailored for each case to optimize its value.

B. Work Backwards from Your Endpoint

The second essential mindset for strategic discovery is to think about the process with the endpoint in mind, working backwards from that final goal. The objective of the discovery process is not simply to gather all of the documents and information, then to plan a legal strategy reactively. Rather, the objective is to develop a legal strategy, then to use discovery to implement that strategy. Of course, that strategy is not static—information gleaned during discovery may cause shifts in the legal strategy and in trial themes. The point, though, is that discovery ought to be aimed, targeted. It is not the chore of a museum curator, collecting information for the mere joy of collecting it. Rather, discovery ought to be viewed as an opportunity to gather support for *your* legal positions and to understand the evidence your opponent will use to oppose your legal positions.

This distinction may seem academic in the abstract, so consider an example.

Paul Painter was injured while using a Level Home Ladder, manufactured by Level Ladders, and sued Level Ladders for product liability in federal court. One approach to discovery for Painter might be to gather all the information that might be relevant to Painter's claim. Painter might serve discovery asking for every document Level Ladders has relating in any way to the ladders it manufactures, as well as for background information about the corporate structure and hierarchy of the company. Such broad and all-encompassing discovery typically generates *less* information and *fewer* documents than narrower, but focused and targeted, discovery. For example, a production request asking for every document relating to the case is far more likely to draw objections than it is to result in a comprehensive production of the relevant documents. Moreover, by serving broad discovery requests, Painter's counsel has given the adversary—Level Ladders's counsel—discretion as to how to construe the requests and what information to provide or withhold. Painter may miss important documents if he conducts discovery in this generic fashion, and most experienced attorneys are more nuanced in their approach to discovery.

With an intermediate level of planning and a somewhat more thoughtful and targeted approach, Painter could serve discovery asking for all the documents related to the design of the Level Home Ladder. Painter could serve interrogatories asking about other accidents or claims related to the Level Home Ladder. Painter could take the deposition of a representative of Level Ladders, and explore these topics in more detail. Painter could then hire an expert when the time approached for expert disclosures and share the documents, interrogatory answers, and deposition testimony gathered during discovery with the expert so that the expert could try to identify design defects in the ladder.

Suppose, however, that after the expert reviewed all the information that Painter had obtained during discovery, the expert told Painter that she believed it likely that the Level Home Ladder should have a locking mechanism comparable to the locking mechanism on the company's professional-grade ladder, the Level Pro Ladder. Unfortunately, she advised Painter, in order to offer her expert opinion—"to a reasonable degree of scientific certainty" as required by caselaw—she would need to examine the design documents for the Level Pro Ladder. Additionally, she would need some additional pieces of information that would have been easy to obtain during the depositions but is not readily obtainable otherwise. But it's now too late! Discovery is over and Painter cannot obtain the expert testimony he needs to proceed with his case.

A better approach is to start from the end and work backwards. That end might be trial or it might be summary judgment (or both, or potentially some other endpoint, depending on the circumstances). By thinking about the evidence you will need at trial to win your case *before you take your discovery*, you can avoid the sinking feeling of realizing in the days leading up to trial that you have neglected one or more key elements of your case. If Painter had realized on day one that he would need an expert and had engaged the expert right away, he could have consulted with the expert about what information the expert needed Painter to gather during discovery.

Likewise, it is important to conduct the appropriate legal research before starting discovery. Find out what evidence or circumstances led to success for a similarly situated party, and try to develop that same evidence or the same circumstances in your case. Then, you can argue to the judge that your case mirrors another case and presents virtually identical circumstances, thereby encouraging the judge to issue a similar ruling favoring your client. If you wait until after discovery to fully explore the case law, you are essentially leaving your fate up to chance, hoping that the facts you develop will happen to match a favorable case.

One approach to successful discovery planning is to begin work on a discovery plan/proof outline right at the outset of the case. Developing a discovery strategy and a plan to implement that strategy *before* you start discovery is the best way to minimize the "doh!" moments after discovery is completed, when you realize that you missed an important topic or have no way of getting a key piece of evidence into the record. As an added advantage, it leads to more defensible discovery. All discovery implicates proportionality—a careful balancing of the likely benefits of the discovery to the requesting party and the burdens to the responding party, with the judge being the final arbiter of where the proper balance lies. If you serve broad, open-ended discovery, the burden to respond is likely to be high and you are likely to have a difficult time explaining to the judge why your need for the information justifies that burden. "Judge, this case is very important, so I simply need every document in existence," is unlikely to resonate with a judge. Having a clear, well-developed strategy, implemented through focused, targeted discovery, both minimizes the likelihood of challenges and increases the likelihood that you can successfully defend your discovery in the event your opponent chooses to bring a challenge.

HOW DISCOVERY PLANNING AND STRATEGY WORKS

A common tool for preparing for trial is a "proof outline." In a proof outline, a lawyer lists each fact she hopes to establish at trial. Then, for each fact, the lawyer lists the evidence she will introduce to prove that fact. This evidence might be in the form of live witness testimony, documents, deposition testimony, discovery responses, or admissions in the pleadings. The outline then might list the evidentiary foundation for each piece of evidence. Thus, a proof outline helps organize all the evidence that a party must introduce at trial.

But a proof outline is not just useful as a trial preparation tool. It can also become a roadmap for discovery if it is created before discovery commences by adding the contemplated sources of the evidence. For example, if the party intended to prove a certain fact using live testimony, the witness giving the testimony might be the party, an opposing party, or a nonparty witness. If the party will supply the testimony, the party's lawyer does not need to conduct any discovery—the lawyer can interview the client informally to prepare for the testimony. If the testimony must come from an opponent or nonparty witness, the lawyer might choose to develop the required testimony through a deposition. Similarly, required documents can be obtained cooperatively from the client, through a production request from an opponent, or by subpoena from a nonparty witness. The evidentiary foundation for such documents might be developed through a request for admission as to the document's authenticity or through deposition testimony. And so on. In this fashion, a party's proof outline can also be expanded to serve as the party's *discovery plan*.[1]

The combined discovery plan/proof outline is not limited to the listed elements of the claims or defenses the party seeks to prove at trial. Litigation is sometimes described as storytelling, with the objective of painting a picture that causes the jury or judge to want your side to win. This "storytelling" mindset applies at every stage of litigation, not just in your closing argument to the jury. A motion to dismiss or a motion for summary judgment should tell a story of why it is fair for the court to resolve part or all of the case in your favor at that point in the procedure, without the need for a trial. Even a discovery motion should tell a story, although it might be a very different story from your overall case themes. Persuasive advocacy typically involves instilling in the decision-maker a strong emotional or equitable feeling that you *should* win, and stories do that better than dry, clinical, pedantic expositions about the law.

Accordingly, your discovery plan/proof outline should include the evidence you will use for storytelling purposes as well. Thus, Painter might want to guide the jury to perceive Level Ladders as a distant and disinterested wealthy corporation easily able to afford a judgment that would be meaningful to Painter but not to the company. Those facts are not strictly relevant to a claim or defense but might be part of Painter's strategy and therefore should be on the discovery plan/proof outline. Conversely, Level Ladders will want to personalize the company for the jury and may want Painter to seem like a less sympathetic plaintiff. Developing facts to support these equities—building your story—needs to start during discovery; waiting until your trial preparations will often be too late.

In addition to the evidence supporting your own client's positions, a proof outline should also address the evidence to counter your opponent's positions. Thus, if Level Ladders asserted contributory negligence as a defense in its answer, Painter's discovery plan/proof outline should address the evidence Painter hopes to offer to counter that defense as well as the evidence required to establish Painter's product liability claim.

---

1. In this chapter, the term "discovery plan" refers to one party's strategic roadmap for developing evidence and admissions during discovery, not to the joint discovery plan that the parties submit to the court pursuant to Rule 26(g), as discussed earlier in the How Discovery Begins chapter.

Finally, a discovery plan/proof outline cannot be a static document, drafted early in the case and then marked off as a completed task and set aside. As new evidence is developed, anticipated or otherwise, and as the legal theories evolve, the discovery plan/proof outline should be revised and updated.

FROM CLASSROOM TO PRACTICE

Discovery is often characterized as, hands-down, the single most boring, monotonous, technical, unimportant, and noncreative stage in civil litigation. As this book has demonstrated, nothing could be further from the truth.

Approach discovery with that awareness in mind. Discovery is where winning occurs (or, more precisely, where the fruits of victory are plucked). Discovery is not the short-straw, hold-your-nose task given to the rawest, most inexperienced new attorney in the shop because it is the least important aspect of the process. To the contrary, considering its enormous power, the autonomy of the attorneys entitled to use it, and the scope of creativity it permits, discovery should be one of the most carefully planned stages in civil litigation.

For a variety of reasons, though, including the time-consuming nature of discovery and the higher billing rates for more experienced lawyers, discovery tasks often trickle down to the newest attorneys on the litigation team. Given your newfound appreciation of the critical nature of discovery, your knowledge of discovery mechanics and strategy, and your awareness of the awesome power of the discovery tools, you may recognize the opportunity that a discovery assignment presents to affect the outcome of a case and to demonstrate value to an assigning attorney.

But attorneys' schedules are often overloaded, and with all the other obligations competing for the busy attorney's attention, it is sometimes tempting to relegate discovery planning to a low-priority task. After all, an attorney may have been through the discovery process dozens or hundreds of times and may feel sufficiently experienced to believe he or she already knows the types of things needed to be developed in discovery. It is not unheard of to see a lawyer come to an important deposition with a blank notepad, confident in his ability to "think on his feet," so confident in his abilities that he thinks he doesn't need notes. Don't view such lawyers with admiration, as so experienced and skilled as to have transcended the need for notes. Instead, view those lawyers as likely to miss important lines of questioning or to forget to follow up on an offhand remark in the middle of an answer. Thorough preparation is not a sign of inexperience; it is a sign of diligence and vigorous representation.

Likewise, it may be tempting to look online or in a firm's document repository for a set of discovery from a similar case and cut-and-paste your caption onto that model. While it is both efficient and smart to start with a good sample document, and while it may be tempting to simply adopt a set of discovery drafted by a lawyer likely more experienced than you are, successful litigators resist that temptation. Everything you do in discovery should be deliberate, thoughtful, and tailored for your specific case.

Moreover, conduct this deliberation, research, and planning comprehensively at the beginning of the case—piecemeal planning is likely to lead to oversights and mistakes. Although discovery planning costs some money to the client at the beginning, over the course of a case, good planning *saves* money for the client and makes the discovery process far more productive.

Hypotheticals: Mastering the Nuances

Planning for a Motion: In a case where the plaintiff is claiming that her exposure to chemical emissions from a chemical processing plant near her home caused her illness, the plant hopes to win the case by excluding all of the plaintiff's causation experts (see the Discovery of Experts chapter for an explanation of this process). If you represent the plant, how would you go about planning your discovery to maximize your chances of succeeding in excluding the plaintiff's experts?

Begin at the Beginning?: In the case described above, the attorney for the plant is taking the deposition of the plaintiff's lead causation expert. The attorney does not start the deposition with the typical instructions about the rules for the deposition and does not ask the expert any questions about her educational background or work history. Instead, the attorney's first questions probe a study that the expert didn't mention in her report, and that runs counter to the expert's positions. Why might the attorney have omitted the instructions? Why might the attorney have skipped questions about the expert's background?

PRACTICE SAMPLES

Sample 9-1: DISCOVERY PLAN/PROOF OUTLINE

Painter's Discovery Plan/Proof Outline

[Note: this is an example of a portion of a discovery plan/proof outline address-ing only the elements of Painter's design defect strict products liability claim against Level Ladders. Assume that the applicable state law lists the three ele-ments shown below for this claim.]

I. **Strict Liability**

   A. The product contained an "unreasonably dangerous" defect that in-jured a user or consumer of the product;

   Facts:

   1. The ladder used a defective rivet at one of the joints which failed to keep the ladder locked while in use.

     Evidence: the broken ladder; design drawings of the ladder; evi-dence of other failures of the rivet; expert testimony as to the defective design; metallurgic analysis of the rivet—report and testimony from laboratory employee or through the expert?

     Evidentiary issues: the ladder requires authentication—FRE 901 (testimony from Painter); Level Ladder's documents should be admis-sible as business records—FRE 803(6); expert testimony—FRE 702; metallurgic analysis—expert may rely on regardless of admissibility—FRE 703, otherwise, call laboratory scientist to testify and authenticate the report (qualify as an expert?)

     Discovery: requests for admission as to authenticity of docu-ments; document requests for documents related to other failures; Rule 30(b)(6) deposition topics re same; prepare FRCP 26(a)(2) expert disclosures

   2. Painter both purchased and was using the ladder when it collapsed and injured him.

     Evidence: testimony from Painter; credit card receipt for his pur-chase of the ladder; medical records; testimony from his treating phy-sician(?)

Evidentiary issues: testimony from Painter is ordinary fact testimony—supplement FRCP 26(a)(1) disclosure if necessary; credit card receipt is a business record—FRE 803(6); medical records—FRE 803(4); expert testimony—FRE 702; metallurgic analysis—expert may rely on regardless of admissibility—FRE 703; treating physician testimony (research to determine if need to qualify as an expert, supplement FRCP 26(a)(1) disclosure if necessary)

Discovery: requests for admission as to authenticity of credit card receipt, medical records, and ladder—supplement FRCP 26(a)(1) disclosure if necessary; prepare FRCP 26(a)(2) expert disclosures if needed

B. The defect caused an injury while the product was being used in a way that it was intended to be used or in a way that was foreseeable to the manufacturer;

Facts:

1. Painter was using the ladder to reach a high area in the intended manner and was not standing on either of the top two rungs of the ladder.

Evidence: testimony from Painter; advertising by Level Ladders; instructions for the Level Home Ladder; discovery responses (?); testimony from a representative of Level Ladders; expert testimony (if Level Ladders does not admit Painter's use was intended)

Evidentiary issues: testimony from Painter is ordinary fact testimony—supplement FRCP 26(a)(1) disclosure if necessary; Level Ladder's documents should be admissible as business records—FRE 803(6); discovery responses are party admissions—FRE 801(e); Level Ladders' representative's testimony is admissible under Rule 32 and FRE 801(e); expert testimony—FRE 702

Discovery: document requests for advertising and instructions; requests for admission as to authenticity; requests for admission and interrogatories as to intended uses; Rule 30(b)(6) deposition topics re same; prepare FRCP 26(a)(2) expert disclosures

C. The product hadn't been substantially changed from the condition it was in when it left the manufacturer's control;

Facts:

1. Painter had not modified the ladder since he purchased it.

Evidence: the broken ladder; testimony from Painter; admissions from Level Ladders; deposition testimony from a representative of

Level Ladders; expert testimony (if Level Ladders does not admit that Painter had not modified the ladder)

Evidentiary issues: the ladder requires authentication—FRE 901 (testimony from Painter); testimony from Painter is ordinary fact testimony—supplement FRCP 26(a)(1) disclosure if necessary; discovery responses are party admissions—FRE 801(e); Level Ladders' representative's testimony is admissible under Rule 32 and FRE 801(e); expert testimony—FRE 702

Discovery: requests for admission and interrogatories as to lack of modification; Rule 30(b)(6) deposition topics re same; prepare FRCP 26(a)(2) expert disclosures

X

Appealing Discovery Rulings

GETTING THE VIEW

It is not uncommon for the parties to disagree during discovery. When they do, the parties are generally dutybound to meet and confer in an attempt to resolve those disputes, privately, before involving the judge. Nevertheless, sometimes those efforts at negotiation fail and the court's involvement is necessary. As you learned in the Policing Discovery chapter, in such a case, the parties will present their respective views to the trial judge, either orally or in the form of a written motion, and the court will rule by issuing an order.

But what if the court's order reaches a wrong decision?

The ramifications of an incorrect court order (or, more precisely, an order a party believes to be incorrect) can be far-reaching. Discovery orders do not usually resolve the ultimate question of admissibility of witness testimony and evidence. Instead, discovery orders resolve a far more basic, foundational question: can the other side even get to *see* or *hear* the evidence at all? Think about that. If a court order rules that certain documents are not discoverable or that a certain witness cannot be deposed, the impact is—quite literally—obliterating. The undiscovered information remains not just undeveloped but, often, entirely unknown. What would those documents have shown? What would that witness have disclosed? The requesting party is unlikely to ever know.

The opposite is equally unsettling. If, for example, a court order rules that certain documents are discoverable, notwithstanding a claim of privilege, or that every computer in a large company must be searched exhaustively for months for discoverable information, the impact can be monumental. The requesting parties could get to see and read something private, personal, confidential, or otherwise shielded from prying eyes that they ought never to have seen or read. And, once that information is seen and read, the impact of its lost protection is irremediable—the receiving party cannot "un-know" it and is unlikely to forebear from using it. In a worse case, that information might end up being posted—anonymously—on the Internet for all the world to see. Likewise, a sprawling, enterprise-wide search of a company's computers could disrupt the entity's operations for weeks or months, force unproductive deployment of personnel that derails the company's business, and impose breathtaking financial costs. Again, once endured, there is usually no way to undo those disruptions, personnel interruptions, and costs.

There is, then, quite a premium on ensuring that discovery orders are decided correctly. The advocacy of the parties endeavors to do that in the first instance, to ensure that the trial judge appreciates the parties' competing views, understands the issues at stake, and focuses on the controlling legal principles that must be applied in ruling. But, still, the trial judge could make an error. If she does, what are the opportunities for the disgruntled party to obtain effective review of that order on appeal?

HOW THIS DISCOVERY CONCEPT WORKS

This book is devoted to trial-level discovery practice, so the mechanics and complexities of appellate procedure are fairly well beyond the book's scope. But, even while focusing just on trial-level discovery practice, a few brief observations about appealing discovery rulings are necessary.

First, civil litigants ordinarily cannot appeal anytime a judge rules against them. Instead, litigants usually have to wait until the court has entered its "final decision" or "final order" in their lawsuit before they can appeal. *See* 28 U.S.C. § 1291. As the Supreme Court has explained it, a final decision or order "is one which ends the litigation on the merits and leaves nothing for the [trial] court to do but execute the judgment." *Catlin v. United States*, 324 U.S. 229, 233 (1945). This means that, most of the time, rulings by the trial judge on discovery disputes (and, for that matter, rulings on nearly every other pre-judgment dispute) will remain binding and in effect until the lawsuit is over and a final judgment has been entered. Then, and, most likely, only then, may a disgruntled litigant appeal one or more of the trial judge's rulings to the appeals court. *See John's Insulation, Inc. v. L. Addison & Assocs.*, 156 F.3d 101, 105 (1st Cir. 1998) (noting that an appeal from a lawsuit's final judgment "encompasses not only that judgment, but also all earlier interlocutory orders that merge in the judgment"). Consequently, a trial judge's "incorrect" discovery ruling is almost certain to continue to govern the lawsuit until the case is concluded.

Second, there are just a few exceptions to this "final decision" or "final order" rule. For example, a party can sometimes take an immediate appeal from an interim order that the trial judge believes involves some "controlling question of law" as to which a "substantial ground for difference of opinion" exists, if permitting that immediate appeal might "materially advance the ultimate termination of the litigation." *See* 28 U.S.C. § 1292(b). But, as one court wrote, those sorts of exceptional appeals are "hen's-teeth rare." *See Camacho v. Puerto Rico Ports Auth.*, 369 F.3d 570, 573 (1st Cir. 2004). And another court noted that, given the broad authority vested in trial judges to supervise and manage discovery, it may well be impossible for any discovery ruling to ever involve the "controlling question of law" needed to fit within this exception. *See White v. Nix*, 43 F.3d 374, 377 (8th Cir. 1994). If that weren't enough of an uphill climb, consider this: this path to an immediate appeal requires a court order permitting it from *both* the trial judge (who, almost certainly, thinks his or her ruling is not in error) and the court of appeals. *See* 28 U.S.C. § 1292(b).

Another exception permits appeals from certain "collateral orders" that conclusively resolve an important issue that is "completely separate from the merits of the action" and is otherwise "effectively unreviewable" on a later appeal. *See Coopers & Lybrand v. Livesay*, 437 U.S. 463, 468 (1978). Yet, this exception, too, is unlikely to apply to a trial court's discovery rulings. *See Firestone Tire & Rubber Co. v. Risjord*, 449 U.S. 368, 377 (1981) ("we have generally denied review of pretrial discovery orders"). The Supreme Court reaffirmed the narrowness of this exception when it held that even a serious dispute over whether the attorney-client privilege shields a particular document from discovery is not enough to allow an immediate appeal of the trial judge's ruling that it ordered the disclosure. *See Mohawk Indus. v. Carpenter*, 558 U.S. 100 (2009).

Third, the only truly reliable path to an immediate, pretrial appeal of a trial judge's discovery ruling is attorney disobedience. The attorney could defy the trial judge's discovery ruling, be declared in contempt of court, and then immediately appeal the contempt order by arguing that the trial judge's underlying discovery ruling (the one the attorney disobeyed) was incorrect. *See Mohawk Indus.*, 558 U.S. at 111–12; *Firestone Tire & Rubber Co.*, 449 U.S. at 377. (You'll remember, from the *Scope of Discovery* chapter, that Attorney Fortenbaugh took this very approach in the landmark *Hickman v. Taylor* case.) That path is, of course, crowded with risk. The attorney's reputation and ethical standing will hang in the balance, and that exposure is deeply unsettling when one considers the enormous latitude the law grants trial judges in resolving discovery disputes. *See, e.g., Gov't of Ghana v. ProEnergy Servs., LLC*, 677 F.3d 340, 344 (8th Cir. 2012) (noting that appellate review of discovery rulings is "both narrow and deferential" and that an appeals court will not overturn a discovery ruling " 'absent a gross abuse of discretion resulting in fundamental unfairness in the trial of the case' ") (citations omitted).

So, is there a path to have a trial judge's discovery rulings reviewed on appeal? Yes. But that review is almost certain to occur only after the lawsuit is over and concluded, and the intrusiveness of that review is limited by the respect the appeals court will show to the trial judge's sweeping discretion in managing discovery. All this prompts some very practical realizations.

FROM CLASSROOM TO PRACTICE

Appeals are unlikely to offer much in the way of meaningful relief from incorrect discovery rulings by a trial judge, at least not in most instances.

First, as noted above, the ruling will ordinarily be cloaked with the trial judge's broad discretion which, alone, greatly reduces the chance for a reversal. *See Bennett v. Hartford Ins. Co. of Midwest*, 890 F.3d 597, 603 (5th Cir. 2018) ("Considering the broad discretion given to trial courts on discovery issues, it is 'unusual [for an appellate court] to find abuse of discretion in these matters,'" meaning that reversals will occur only in an "unusual and exceptional case.") (citations omitted). *See also Transcon. Gas Pipe Line Co., LLC v. Land Lot 1049*, 910 F.3d 1130, 1156 (11th Cir. 2018) ("discovery rulings will not be overturned unless it is shown that they resulted in 'substantial harm to the appellant's case'").

Second, the harmless error principle will apply to any discovery ruling. *See* Fed. R. Civ. P. 61 ("the court must disregard all errors and defects that do not affect any party's substantial rights"). *See also Tagupa v. Bd. of Directors*, 633 F.2d 1309, 1312 (9th Cir. 1980) ("The harmless error doctrine applies to discovery orders."). Consequently, a lawsuit's final judgment will be disturbed to remedy an incorrect discovery ruling only if the appeals court finds that the error might have affected the ultimate outcome of the case.

Third, to appeal, there usually needs to be a final judgment, and most civil cases do not end with a final judgment. Most are settled or terminated by dismissal. *See* Patricia L. Refo, *Open Statement—The Vanishing Trial*, 30 Litig. 2 (Winter 2004) ("In 1962, 11.5 percent of federal civil cases were disposed of by trial. By 2002, that figure had plummeted to 1.8 percent."). Thus, the opportunities for appealing a discovery ruling are rare.

Accordingly, appellate relief from incorrect discovery orders is usually more a theoretical prospect than a modern, practical reality. Obtaining an appellate reversal is not impossible, but certainly unlikely. Far more likely, victory in civil discovery will occur, if at all, before the trial judge. Mindful of that reality, learning how the discovery procedures work and how to use them properly and strategically is an indispensable skill for every civil trial lawyer.

That, after all, is why this book was written.

Index of Primary Authorities

*[Sources listed in **BOLD** are excerpts]*

28 U.S.C. § 1291 336

28 U.S.C. § 1292(b) 337

28 U.S.C. § 1782 11

28 U.S.C. § 1821 263

Supreme Court Committee Appointment Order, 295 U.S. 774 (1934) 9

AMCO Inc. Co. v. Inspired Techs., Inc., 648 F.3d 875 (8th Cir. 2011) 103

Anderson v. United States, 417 U.S. 211 (1974) 56

ArcelorMittal Indiana Harbor LLC v. Amex Nooter, LLC,
    2016 WL 614144 (N.D. Ind. Feb. 16, 2016). 57

ArcelorMittal Indiana Harbor LLC v. AMEX Nooter, LLC,
    320 F.R.D. 455 (N.D. Ind. 2017) **26**

***ASEA, Inc. v. So. Pacific Transp. Co.,* 669 F.2d 1242 (9th Cir. 1981). 148**

Ashland Elec. Prod., Inc. v. Bombardier Transp. Holdings) USA, Inc.,
    2005 WL 8174460 (D.N.H. Oct. 21, 2005) 104

Auburn Sales, Inc. v. Cypros Trading & Shipping, Inc.,
    2016 WL 3418554 (E.D. Mich. June 22, 2016) 123

Avista Mgmt., Inc. v. Wausau Underwriters Ins. Co.,
    2006 WL 1562246 (M.D. Fla. 2006) **193**

AVX Corp. v. Cabot Corp., 252 F.R.D. 70 (D. Mass. 2008) 291

Barnes v. D.C., 270 F.R.D. 21 (D.D.C. 2010) 93

Bear Republic Brewing Co. v. Central City Brewing Co.,
    275 F.R.D. 43 (D. Mass. 2011). 72

Bell Atl. Corp. v. Twombly, 550 U.S. 544 (2007). 10, 13

Bennett v. Hartford Ins. Co. of Midwest, 890 F.3d 597 (5th Cir. 2018) 338

Bottoms v. Liberty Life Assur. Co. of Bos., 2011 WL 6181423
    (D. Colo. Dec. 13, 2011) 104

Boyington v. Percheron Field Servs., Ltd., 2016 WL 6068813
    (W.D. Pa. Oct. 14, 2016) **59**

Brown Shoe Co. v. United States, 370 U.S. 294 (1962) 32

Camacho v. Puerto Rico Ports Auth., 369 F.3d 570 (1st Cir. 2004) 337

Catlin v. United States, 324 U.S. 229 (1945) 336

Chapman v. Procter & Gamble Distrib'g, LLC, 766 F.3d 1296
    (11th Cir. 2014). 230, 234

Cincinnati Ins. Co. v. Serrano, 2012 WL 28071 (D. Kan. Jan. 5, 2012). 200

Coleman v. Starbucks, 2015 WL 2449585 (M.D. Fla. May 22, 2015) 104

Coopers & Lybrand v. Livesay, 437 U.S. 463 (1978). 337

***Curtis v. Metro. Life Ins. Co.*,**
    2016 WL 687164 (N.D. Tex. Feb. 19, 2016). 58

Dang v. Cross, 2002 WL 432197 (C.D. Cal. Mar. 18, 2002) 104

Daubert v. Merrell Dow Pharms., Inc., 509 U.S. 579 (1993). 231

Delcastor, Inc. v. Vail Assocs., Inc., 108 F.R.D. 405 (D. Colo. 1985). 243

Diversified Prod. Corp. v. Sports Ctr. Co., 42 F.R.D. 3 (D. Md. 1967) 104

Druck Corp. v. Macro Fund (U.S.) Ltd., 2005 WL 1949519
    (S.D.N.Y. Aug. 12, 2005) 200

***E.I. DuPont de Nemours & Co. v. Kolon Indus., Inc.*,**
    268 F.R.D. 45 (E.D. Va. 2010) 264

Erfindergemeinschaft UroPep GbR v. Eli Lilly & Co., 315 F.R.D. 191
    (E.D. Tex. 2016) 94

Estate of Thompson v. Kawasaki Heavy Indus., Ltd., 291 F.R.D. 297
    (N.D. Iowa 2013) 205

Firestone Tire & Rubber Co. v. Risjord, 449 U.S. 368 (1981). 337

Gomas v. City of New York, 2009 WL 962701 (E.D.N.Y. Apr. 8, 2009). 36

Goodman v. Staples The Office Superstore, LLC, 644 F.3d 817
    (9th Cir. 2011). 234

Gov't of Ghana v. ProEnergy Servs., LLC, 677 F.3d 340 (8th Cir. 2012) 337

Gowan v. Mid Century Ins. Co., 309 F.R.D. 503 (D.S.D. 2015) 263

Gruber ex rel. Gruber v. Sec'y of HHS, 91 Fed. Cl. 773 (2010) 238

Gucci Am., Inc. v. Weixing Li, 135 F. Supp. 3d 87 (S.D.N.Y. 2015) 263

Hall v. Clifton Precision, 150 F.R.D. 525 (E.D. Pa. 1993). **194**

Heraeus Kulzer, GmbH v. Biomet, Inc., 633 F.3d 591 (7th Cir. 2011) 11

Hickman v. Taylor, 329 U.S. 495 (1947) **64**

Higgins v. Koch Dev. Corp., 794 F.3d 697 (7th Cir. 2015). 235

Hobley v. Chicago Police Commander Burge,
   225 F.R.D. 221 (N.D. Ill. 2004) 78

In re Anonymous Member of S.C. Bar, 552 S.E.2d 10 (2001). 199

In re Auction Houses Antitrust Litig., 196 F.R.D. 444
   (S.D.N.Y. 2000) 95

In re Honda Am. Motor Co., 168 F.R.D. 535 (D. Md. 1996). 264

In re Professionals Direct Ins. Co., 578 F.3d 432 (6th Cir. 2009) 70

In re Rail Freight Fuel Surcharge Antitrust Litig., 281 F.R.D. 1
   (D.D.C. 2011) 93

In re: Modern Plastics Corp., 890 F.3d 244 (6th Cir. 2018). 269

Inline Packaging, LLC v. Graphic Packaging Int'l, Inc.,
   2016 WL 7042117 (D. Minn. 2016) **51**

Intel Corp. v. Advanced Micro Devices, Inc., 542 U.S. 241 (2004) 11

Jackson v. Teamsters Local Union 922, 310 F.R.D. 179
   (D.D.C. 2015) **202**

Jama v. City & Cty. of Denver, 304 F.R.D. 289
   (D. Colo. 2014) **284**

John's Insulation, Inc. v. L. Addison & Assocs., 156 F.3d 101
   (1st Cir. 1998) 336

Lichtenstein v. Univ. of Pittsburgh Med. Ctr., 2013 WL 6577401
   (W.D. Pa. 2013), *aff'd*, 598 F. Appx. 109 (3d Cir. 2015) **300**

Lynn v. Monarch Recovery Mgmt., Inc., 285 F.R.D. 350
   (D. Md. 2012) **98**

Memory Integrity, LLC v. Intel Corp., 308 F.R.D. 656 (D. Ore. 2015) **206**

Mir v. L-3 Commc'ns Integrated Sys., L.P., 319 F.R.D. 220
   (N.D. Tex. 2016) 126

Mohawk Indus. v. Carpenter, 558 U.S. 100 (2009). 337

Network Computing Servs. Corp. v. Cisco Sys., Inc.,
   223 F.R.D. 392 (D.S.C. 2004) **315**
Nolan v. Int'l Bhd. of Teamsters Health & Welfare & Pension Funds,
   Local 705, 199 F.R.D. 272 (N.D. Ill. 2001). 177
Nudd v. Burrows, 91 U.S. 426 (1875). 8
Nyfield v. Virgin Islands Tel. Corp., 2001 WL 378858
   (D.V.I. Apr. 17, 2001). 177

O'Sullivan v. Rivera, 229 F.R.D. 184 (D.N.M. 2004). **172**
Oppenheimer Fund, Inc. v. Sanders, 437 U.S. 340 (1978) 51
Ott v. City of Milwaukee, 682 F.3d 552 (7th Cir. 2012). 263

Parshall v. Menard, Inc., 2017 WL 980501 (E.D. Mo. Mar. 14, 2017). 56
Parsi v. Daioleslam, 778 F.3d 116 (D.C. Cir. 2015). **303**
Pena v. Troup, 163 F.R.D. 352 (D. Colo. 1995) **173**
Phillips v. C.R. Bard, Inc., 290 F.R.D. 615 (D. Nev. 2013). .63
Precision Instrument Mfg. Co. v. Auto. Maint. Mach. Co.,
   324 U.S. 806 (1945). 318

Rakes v. Life Investors Ins. Co. of Am., 2008 WL 429060
   (N.D. Iowa Feb. 14, 2008) 200
Rink v. Cheminova, Inc., 400 F.3d 1286 (11th Cir. 2005). **232**
Rio Tinto PLC v. Vale S.A., 306 F.R.D. 125 (S.D.N.Y. 2015) 129

Schlagenhauf v. Holder, 379 U.S. 104 (1964) **169**
Scott v. Chipotle Mexican Grill, Inc., 315 F.R.D. 33 (S.D.N.Y. 2016) 239
SEC v. Yorkville Advisors, LLC, 300 F.R.D. 152 (S.D.N.Y. 2014) 75
Sec. Nat. Bank of Sioux City v. Abbott Labs., 299 F.R.D. 595
   (N.D. Iowa 2014), *rev'd on other grounds*, 800 F.3d 936
   (8th Cir. 2015). 200
Segar v. Holder, 277 F.R.D. 9 (D.D.C. 2011). 75
Sell v. Country Life Ins. Co., 189 F. Supp. 3d 925 (D. Ariz. 2015) 123
Sender v. Mann, 225 F.R.D. 645 (D. Colo. 2004). 284
Sherrill v. Dio Transp., Inc., 317 F.R.D. 609 (D.S.C. 2016) 263
Silvestri v. Gen. Motors Corp., 271 F.3d 583 (4th Cir. 2001). 131
Small v. Amgen, Inc., 2016 WL 7228863 (M.D. Fla. Sept. 28, 2016). 59
Snapp v. United Transp. Union, 889 F.3d 1088 (9th Cir. 2018) 205

Societe Nationale Industrielle Aerospatiale v.
U.S. Dist. Court for S. Dist. of Iowa, 482 U.S. 522 (1987)..................12

St. Jude Medical S.C., Inc. v. Janssen-Counotte,
305 F.R.D. 630 (D. Or. 2015).......................................**119**

Sunshine Heifers, LLC v. Moohaven Dairy, LLC,
13 F. Supp. 3d 770 (E.D. Mich. 2014).................................103

Tagupa v. Bd. of Directors, 633 F.2d 1309 (9th Cir. 1980)...................338

Thai Le v. Diligence, Inc., 312 F.R.D. 245 (D. Mass. 2015) 71

Thompson v. Beasley, 309 F.R.D. 236 (N.D. Miss. 2015) **144**

Transcon. Gas Pipe Line Co., LLC v. Land Lot 1049,
910 F.3d 1130 (11th Cir. 2018) 338

U.S. EEOC v. Placer ARC, 147 F. Supp. 3d 1053 (E.D. Cal. 2015).............274

U.S. ex rel. Tenn. Valley Auth. v. 1.72 Acres of Land in Tenn.,
821 F.3d 742 (6th Cir. 2016) **240**

Union Pac. Ry. v. Botsford, 141 U.S. 250 (1891).........................167, 168

United Oil Co. v. Parts Assocs., 227 F.R.D. 404 (D. Md. 2005)...................51

United States Commodity Futures Trading Comm'n v. Newell,
301 F.R.D. 348 (N.D. Ill. 2014) 243

United States ex rel. Landis v. Tailwind Sports Corp.,
317 F.R.D. 592 (D.D.C. 2016) **95**

United States v. A.H. Fischer Lumber Co., 162 F.2d 872 (4th Cir. 1947).........210

Upjohn Co. v. United States, 449 U.S. 383 (1981)............................63

Vehicle Mkt. Research, Inc. v. Mitchell Int'l, Inc.,
839 F.3d 1251 (10th Cir. 2016) 205

Wesley Corp. v. Zoom T.V. Prods., LLC,
2018 WL 372700 (E.D. Mich. Jan. 11, 2018).........................**100**

West Penn Power Co. v. NLRB, 394 F.3d 233 (4th Cir. 2005)...................51

White v. Nix, 43 F.3d 374 (8th Cir. 1994) 337

Zenith Radio Corp. v. Matsushita Elec. Indus. Co.,
478 F. Supp. 889 (E.D. Pa. 1979), *vacated sub nom.*
***on other grounds*, 631 F.2d 1069 (3d Cir. 1980)** **313**

Index of Secondary Authorities

Barda, Ela & Rouhette, Thomas, *The French Blocking Statute and Cross-Border Discovery*, 84 Def. Coun. J. 1 (2017) 12

Black's Law Dictionary (10th ed. 2014) 200

Bonner, Robert J., Evidence in Athenian Courts (1905) 6

Childs, William G., *When the Bell Can't Be Unrung: Document Leaks and Protective Orders in Mass Tort Litigation*, 27 Rev. Litig. 565 (2008) 80

Cover, Robert M., *For James Wm. Moore: Some Reflections on a Reading of the Rules*, 84 Yale L.J. 718 (1975) 77

Discovery, 1997 A.B.A. Sec. Litig. 23 14

Easterbrook, Frank H., *Discovery as Abuse*, 69 B.U. L. Rev. 635 (1989) 13

Fortenberry, Joseph E., *A Note on the Purpose of Roman Discovery*, 9 J. Legal Hist. 214 (1988) 7

Friedman, Joel Wm. & Collins, Michael G., The Law of Civil Procedure: Cases and Materials (3d ed. 2010) 12

Frost, Christopher C., Note, *The Sound and the Fury or the Sound of Silence?: Evaluating the Pre-Amendment Predictions and Post-Amendment Effects of the Discovery Scope-Narrowing Language in the 2000 Amendments to Federal Rule of Civil Procedure 26(b)(1)*, 37 Ga. L. Rev. 1039 (2003) 51

GLASER, WILLIAM A., PRETRIAL DISCOVERY AND THE ADVERSARY
   SYSTEM (1968) 9

Harvard Law Review Ass'n, *Developments in the Law—Discovery*,
   74 HARV. L. REV. 940 (1961). 7

Karl, David J., *Islamic Law in Saudi Arabia: What Foreign Attorneys
   Should Know*, 25 GEO. WASH. J. INT'L L. & ECON. 131 (1991) 11

Marr, Bernard, *How Much Data Do We Create Every Day?
   The Mind-Blowing Stats Everyone Should Read*, FORBES (May 21, 2018)
   (available at https://www.forbes.com/sites/bernardmarr/ 2018/05/21
   /how-muchdata-do-we-create-every-day-the-mind-blowing-stats
   -everyone-should-read/#7d66e41460ba) 13

Millar, Robert Wyness, *The Mechanism of Fact-Discovery: A Study in
   Comparative Civil Procedure*, 32 ILL. L. REV. 261 (1937–38). 7

Mochizuki, Toshiro M., *Baby Step or Giant Leap? Parties' Expanded
   Access to Documentary Evidence Under the New Japanese Code of
   Civil Procedure*, 40 HARV. INT'L L.J. 285 (1999) 11

MODEL RULES OF PROF'L CONDUCT R. 4.2. 273

Refo, Patricia L., *Open Statement—The Vanishing Trial*,
   30 LITIG. 2 (Winter 2004). 338

RICE, PAUL R., ATTORNEY-CLIENT PRIVILEGE IN
   THE UNITED STATES (2018–2019). 61, 63, 73

SCHEINDLIN, SHIRA A., CAPRA, DANIEL J., & THE SEDONA
   CONFERENCE, ELECTRONIC DISCOVERY AND DIGITAL EVIDENCE:
   CASES AND MATERIALS (2009) 14

STORY, JOSEPH, COMMENTARIES ON EQUITY JURISPRUDENCE
   § 1484 (3d Eng. ed. 1920) 8

Subrin, Stephen N., *David Dudley Field and the Field Code:
   A Historical Analysis of an Earlier Procedural Vision*,
   6 LAW & HIST. REV. 311 (1988) 8

Subrin, Stephen N., *Discovery in Global Perspective: Are We Nuts?*,
   52 DEPAUL L. REV. 299 (2002) 11

Subrin, Stephen N., *Fishing Expeditions Allowed: The Historical
   Background of the 1938 Federal Discovery Rules*, 39 B.C. L. REV.
   691 (1998) 7, 8, 9, 10

Sunderland, Edson N., *Improving the Administration of Civil Justice,*
    in 167 ANNALS OF THE AMERICAN ACADEMY OF POLITICAL &
    SOCIAL SCIENCE 75–76 (1933) 9

Wang, Zachary, *Ethics and Electronic Discovery: New Medium,*
    Same Problems, 75 Def. Couns. J. 328 (2008)........................127
WRIGHT, CHARLES ALAN, THE LAW OF FEDERAL COURTS
    (4th ed. 1983) 9–10